Preface

Welcome to Abaco! Great Abaco Island and its cays form one of the largest bodies of semi-protected waters in the Bahamian/Caribbean area. The Sea of Abaco is a perfect cruising ground for small boats—harbours or sheltered areas are usually close by and it is almost always possible to anchor in shallow water. Miles of secluded beaches can be found, and many settlements or towns are just a few miles apart offering excellent marinas, restaurants and other services. The people of Abaco are friendly and helpful; they are gracious hosts who will do their best to make your visit a pleasant one. Enjoy the beautiful waters, beaches, and people of Abaco, but please remember to respect the privacy of Abaconians as well as the fragile physical environment in order to save both for future generations.

Abaco continues to rise and overcome the challenges over the last two years from the pandemic following the blow from one of the most powerful hurricanes in history. More businesses continue to open, expand and regrow everyday. Marsh Harbour, the buisiness hub of Abaco, again provides for every need and rapidly more and more of the wants of residents and visitors. With two large grocery stores, construction and parts suppliers, and the building and reopening of shopping centre's there are many resources. The out islands also again offer restaurants, shopping, and many rentals and services. The people of Abaco continue to be welcoming hosts to vistors enjoying the islands.

This book covers Abaco generally from north to south. Besides the Table of Contents, the directory chart on the inside front cover provides a quick reference for finding desired information. We have continued to perform hydrographic surveys in Abaco. We continue to check routes and entrances and have provided updated charts. In September of 2021 Dont Rock continued to be somewhat deeper than before the storm. The smaller recent changes are shown on the updated charts. There is some debris in the water in some areas – mainly close to shoreline near structure damage. However, much has been removed and efforts are continuing. Many charts and Marina maps have been updated. Extra caution is still advised close to shore and in harbours. We have continued to mark wrecks and debris, also note that submerged pilings at the time of publication are shown on charts in Marsh Harbour and White Sound (Elbow Cay). Also, while the prudent mariner always is on the lookout for debris this still deserves extra attention in Abaco. Observations, suggestions and information continue to be much appreciated.

This is the 33rd annual edition of this guide. Our system of waypoints optimizes the advantages of using GPS for navigation, making cruising the Abaco islands and cays easier and more enjoyable. Thousands of boats have used our waypoint system successfully. It makes transit of areas safer and more secure, especially when visibility is limited by rain or a course directly toward the sun. All should remember that GPS is a navigationail aid—it is not a substitute for watching where you are going with a sharp eye. If you are uncertain of where your are, stop the boat and clarify before continuing. Use of our system certainly does not preclude expoloration and gunkholing—two of the joys and rewards of cruising in Abaco.

Important Note Regarding Charts

Despite the fact that we have been diligent and used the latest available technology to make our charts accurate, our survey was not uniform—some areas received more attention than others. Therefore, the accuracy of the charts varies somewhat. This, combined with shifting sand bars, and possible errors made in transcribing the data, make it necessary for us to remind all users that the prudent navigator will never rely solely on only one source of information. The author and publisher disclaim all liability for any errors or omissions. The author and publisher disclaim all warranties, expressed or implied, as to the quality, merchantability or fitness of this book and its charts for any particular purpose. There is no substitute for a sharp lookout on any boat to avoid possible hazards and dangers. All depths are given in feet at Mean Lower Low Water (MLLW).

Because Mean Lower Low Water is the average of lower low tides, all should be aware that the water will be more shallow on spring low tides (full moon and new moon) than the charts indicate. Tide times and heights calculated by the United States National Ocean Survey can be found in the tide tables on pages 169- 172. All course headings are given in magnetic, but true north is up on all charts. The charts and waypoints are all based on WGS84 map datum, and users should be certain their receivers are set accordingly. The termination of selective availability by the United States government and the advent of WAAS (Wide Area Augmentation System) has made GPS more accurate and more reliable, but all navigators should remember to trust their eyes and not over-rely on any single source of information or aide to navigation.

Double Breasted Cays Photo by Lisa Dodge September 2021

Table of Contents

Charts listed generally north to south

Abaco Chart Directory, inside front cover

Preface / Note Re: Charts, 1
Abaco Hurricanes, 4-5
General Visitor Information, 4- 14
Cell Phones and Internet, 12

Approaches to Abaco, 16

Grand Bahama Section, 20- 24
Indian Cay Channel and West End, 22
Dover Snd., Waterway, Bell Chn., 24

Walker's Cay to Carters Cays, 26
Walker's Cay, 28
Grand Cays, 30
Double Breasted Cays, 32
Strangers Cay, 34
Carters Cays, 36

Carters Cays to Moraine Cay, 38
Fish Cays (North), 40
Hawksbill Cays and Fox Town, 41
Moraine Cay, 42

Moraine Cay to Spanish Cay, 43
Allans-Pensacola Cay, 44
Spanish Cay, 46

Spanish Cay to Green Turtle Cay, 48
Cooperstown and Powell Cay, 49
Manjack and Crab Cays, 50
Green Turtle Cay, 52

Green Turtle to Marsh Harbour, 56
Marsh Harbour to Little Harbour, 57

Whale Cay Channel, 60

Sand Banks and Dont Rock, 62
Treasure Cay, 64
Great Guana Cay, 66
Man-O-War Cay, 74- 75
Hub of Abaco, 80
Marsh Harbour, 82
Boat Harbour, 92
Elbow Cay and Hope Town, 96- 97
White Sound, 106

Lubber's Bank, Channel, Tilloo Cut, 112
Tavern Cay to Lynyard Cay, 116
Snake Cay, 117
Tilloo Pond to North Bar Channel, 118
Little Harbour, 119- 120

Lynyard Cay to Hole-in-the-Wall, 122
Little Harbour to Cherokee Sound, 124
Schooner Bay, 126
Sandy Point, 128

North Eleuthera, 130
Bimini, 132

Snorkeling/SCUBA Guide, 135- 143

Deep Draft in Abaco, 144

The Most Common Marine Mammals of Abaco, 146
Fishing in Abaco, 153
Abaco Road Map, 158

Brief History of Abaco, 162

Medical Tips for Tropical Waters, 165
Business Directories, 168
Tide Tables, 169- 171
Indexes - Place Names, Advertisers, 173
Ferry and Shipping Map, 174

Thunderstorm SE of Treasure Cay, Sept. 2021 Photo by Lisa Dodge

Royal Poinciana

Copyright © White Sound Press, a division of White Sound International Limited, 2022. All rights reserved. No portion of this work may be reproduced by any means without the specific, written consent of White Sound Press. Violations of copyright will be vigorously pursued. ISBN 9780932265623

Additional copies of this cruising guide may be ordered from White Sound Press, 379 Wild Orange Drive, New Smyrna Beach, Florida 32168 USA. Phone: 386 423-7880 Fax: 386 423-7557. All our publications may be ordered on the web at www.wspress.com. E-Mail: orders@wspress.com.

Front Cover: Double Breasted Cays, Photo by Lisa Dodge September 2021

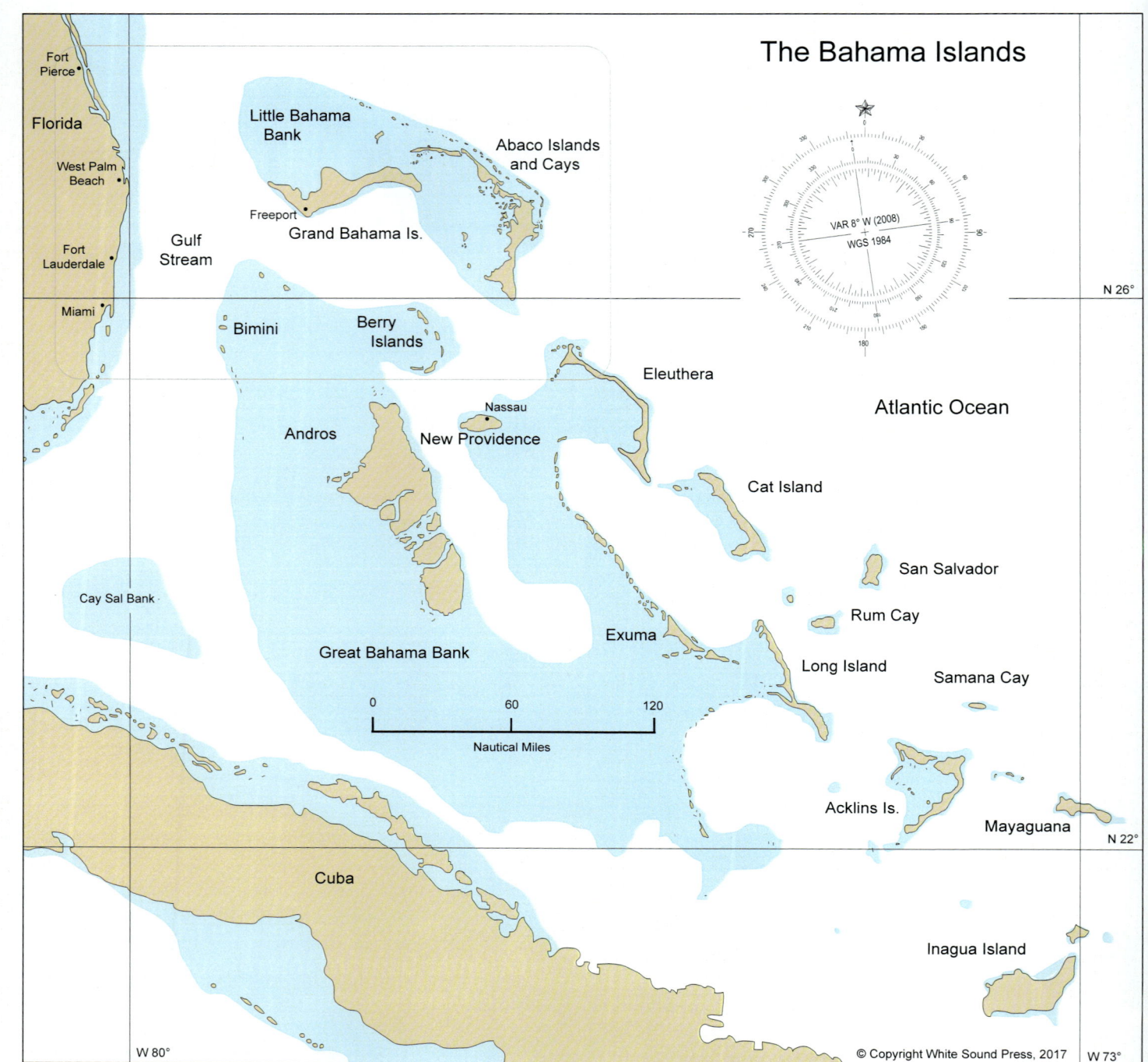

ABACO AND THE BAHAMAS

The Bahama Islands are located east and southeast of South Florida and stretch about 550 miles toward Cuba and Hispaniola. They consist of 29 islands, 661 cays and 2387 rocks, according to an official count made for Governor Rawson W. Rawson's report in 1864. We do not know if anyone has tried to count since then. Most of the Bahamian islands are located on banks—very unique geologic structures which rise thousands of feet from the deep ocean floor and have only 10-40 feet of water over their flat tops. They are huge underwater plateaus with higher areas which protrude above the ocean's surface to form the islands. The principal banks are Little Bahama Bank in the northwest Bahamas, and Great Bahama Bank in the central Bahamas.

The population of the islands is almost 400,000 (2017). Over 70% of the people live in Nassau, the capital, located on New Providence Island. Freeport, located on Grand Bahama Island, is the second largest city in the country and Marsh Harbour, Abaco, is the third largest. Most Bahamians are of West African descent; the 15% of the population which is white descend from emigrants from Bermuda during the 1600s, and British Loyalists who left the United States shortly after independence, many of whom settled in Abaco. Beginning during the late twentieth century and extending to the present, a significant number of Haitians have migrated to The Bahamas. The islands were a British colony until 1973; since then they have been an independent member of the British Commonwealth with a parliamentary democratic system of government. Abaco is located at the northern end of the island chain. According to Gov. Rawson, Abaco includes 2 islands, 82 cays and 208 rocks. The population was about 17,000 in 2010.

NAVIGATION IN ABACO

The Global Positioning System (GPS) is clearly the most significant improvement in navigation made during the twentieth century. It is truly amazing that a handheld electronic device costing $100-$200 can tell you where you are, where you wish to go, and how long it will take you to get there. No boat should go to the Bahamas without a GPS receiver. The advent of differential GPS and the end of selective availability (the intentional de-grading of the signal by the United States Department of Defense) in May 2000 has made GPS more accurate for all users. The Wide Area Augmentation System (WAAS) receivers, which became available in 2001 at very reasonable prices, regularly provide accuracy within 10-20', and new GPS receivers which will utilize the Glasnost (Russian) and Galileo (European) satellite constellations as well as the US GPS system will provide even greater accuracy and reliability.

This cruising guide maximizes the advantages of GPS and the benefits it can provide. We offer a system of waypoints rather than random waypoints outside each harbour. We have refined the system over the years; we hope you find it practical and enjoyable. Except where noted, the continuous course lines connecting the waypoints are at least 6' deep at Mean Low Water (MLW) and free of obstructions (please note that **discontinuous course lines are for small boats** and generally carry only about 3' MLW). See pages 169- 171 for tide tables for Abaco during 2022 (and page 172 for a tide table for Dec., 2021).

While GPS is a wonderful navigational aide, the prudent mariner will not over-rely on it or any other single aide to navigation. Eyeball navigation and the use of the magnetic compass can confirm the information provided by GPS and vice versa. Cruisers visiting the Bahamas will quickly learn to know the approximate depth of the water on the basis of water color—which ranges from dark blue for deep ocean water, to medium blues, teals and greens in 10-25' over sand, to pale blues and greens in shallow water over sand (4'-10') and white in 1'-3'. Coral heads are brown, as are rocky bars—both should be avoided. It is important to learn how to determine water depth based on colour because there is no better navigational device than your eyes, but some persons have greater color sensitivity than others and read the depth better than others. No one can do it going into the sun, in the middle of a rain squall, or at dusk, or at night. All mariners should try to maximize the advantages of all available aides to navigation.

Nightime navigation presents special challenges not only because it is not possible to visually read the water depth but also because many navigation lights are unreliable. The five knot rule is prudent—if you are going no more than five knots and hit even a solid object such as a rock, you will most likely live to tell the story.

To best utilize our GPS system set your GPS datum to WGS 1984, utilize routes rather than "go to," pay close attention to cross track error by utilizing the appropriate screen (or "page") on your receiver, be aware that older non-WAAS receivers are not as accurate as newer units, and use your eyes and your compass to confirm or question what your GPS tells you. If you are unsure of where you are, stop and figure it out before proceeding.

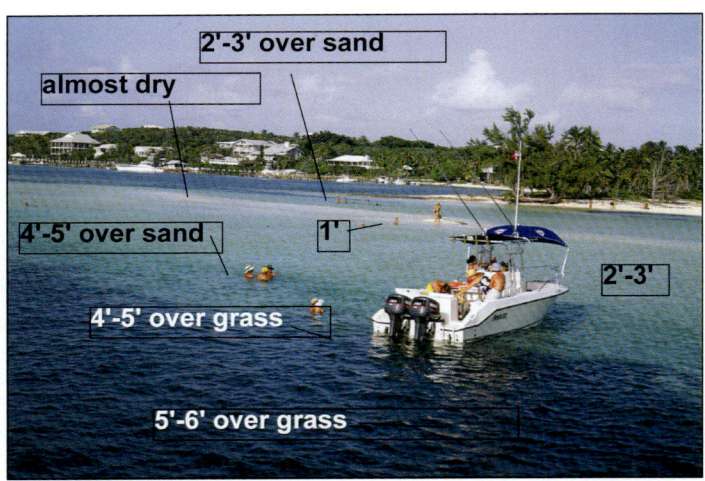

The depth of the water can be determined by colour. This generally requires good sunlight. Photo taken at Tahiti Beach, Elbow Cay, summer 2001.

Complex sand banks can be built by strong tidal current flows through openings between cays (called cuts or passages in Abaco and often "inlets" in the US) along the edge of the bank. These areas are usually volatile because storms combined with strong current flows can move tons of sand in just a few hours. Two dinghies explore this bar at the northwest end of Double Breasted Cays. Photo by Steve Dodge, 3 June 2013

Support the Bahamas Air-Sea Rescue Association.

You are not required to take an active part in BASRA.

Send $40.00 for one year's membership dues to:

BASRA ABACO, Hope Town, Abaco, Bahamas

The Sea of Abaco is long and narrow—protected from the west and southwest by Great and Little Abaco Islands, and from the Atlantic Ocean on the east and northeast by a string of cays over 100 miles long and a barrier reef outside of those. The result is a comfortable and relaxed cruising area for small and large boats with snug harbours, isolated anchorages, and beautiful beaches. There is nothing comparable in the Bahamas or the entire Caribbean. This photo, taken from the south looking north, shows Tilloo Cay, Lubbers Quarters, Elbow Cay with Hope town near the north end, Man-O-War Cay as well as Matt Lowe's Cay and part of Sugar Loaf Cay. Photo by Steve Dodge, 2008.

WEATHER & WEATHER REPORTS

Abaco is within the trade wind belt, so most of its weather is the result of the prevailing easterly winds. In the winter they tend to be easterly or northeasterly, and in the summer easterly or southeasterly. Winter winds are usually a few knots stronger than the summer winds, which average 5-10 knots.

This easterly pattern is disturbed in the winter by outbreaks of cool continental air from the United States. These cold fronts are preceded by wind from the southwest. When the front passes, the wind shifts to the west or northwest and often blows hard (20-25 knots is common). Most cool fronts are dry, and the temperature dips to about 58 degrees. The wind eventually clocks to the northeast after the frontal passage; this process sometimes takes a couple of hours—more often a couple of days.

In the summer the usual 5-10 knot southeast breeze is sometimes disturbed by afternoon thunderstorms which build over the land mass of Great Abaco Island during the day. These storms sometimes meander against the prevailing southeast breeze and move from Abaco out to the cays. They have plenty of lightning and thunder, and lots of water, but the high winds are usually short-lived. The summer weather pattern may also be disturbed by a low pressure trough in the prevailing easterlies. These bring higher winds, overcast skies, and showers. If the winds in a trough (sometimes also called a wave) begin circular movement and reach 33 knots, the trough becomes a tropical storm. If the winds reach 64 knots, it becomes a hurricane. Hurricane season throughout the tropics extends from 1 June to 1 December.

There are a number of excellent weather forecasts available in the Abacos. The cruiser's net on channel 68 at 0815 features an excellent weather report and prediction based on data collected from several sources. Gulf Stream crossing predictions are also provided. Silbert Mills of Radio Abaco (FM 93.5) gives a complete report at 0700, 0800 and again as part of the evening news at 1800. In addition, Bahamian AM radio weather reports can be heard on ZNS Nassau (1540 kHz) at 0735 and 0755 (summary) and ZNS Freeport (810 kHz). The NOAA Wx forecasts can sometimes be heard on VHF Wx channels 1, 2, or 3 if a good antenna is available. These are continuous and give Florida coastal reports and prognoses. Also, some cruisers regularly share their information and knowledge regarding the weather; listen on VHF 16 for announcements regarding the working channel which will be used.

Weather information is available almost 24 hours a day for those with short wave radios. The Waterway Radio and Cruising Club gives a report each day at 0745 on 7.268 MHz. This includes the Bahamas, SW North Atlantic, the Florida coast, and the Gulf of Mexico. All are welcome to listen, and hams with general class licenses or higher may join in if they have their Bahamas reciprocal licenses. For more frequent reports listen to NMN, WLO, or WOM; schedules are as follows:

Time (UTC)*	NMN - Coast Guard, Portsmouth, Virginia				
	4426	6501	8764	13089	17314
0400, 0530, 1000	x	x	x		
1130, 1600	x	x	x		
1730			x	x	x
2200, 2330		x	x	x	
	WLO - Mobile, Alabama				
Eastern Time	4369	8806	13152	17362	22804
0100, 0700, 1300, and 1900	x	x	x	x	x

*UTC is Coordinated Universal Time. Eastern Standard Time is 5 hours behind UTC and Eastern Daylight Time is 4 hours behind UTC.

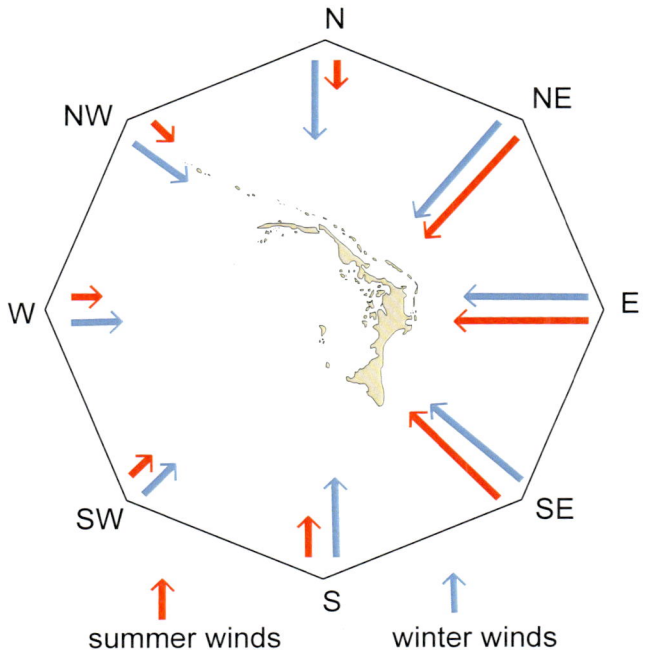

Approximate frequency of wind direction in Abaco in summer and winter shown by arrow length

summer winds   winter winds

A large portion of The Bahamas on 23 April 2009. A cool front had moved through the northern and central Bahamas and clear dry air provides an excellent view of the banks and islands. The cloud cover in the southeastern portion of the photo is forward of the front. Photo courtesy of National Aeronautics and Space Administration.

WEATHER SITES ON THE WEB AND CROSSING THE GULF STREAM
by Harry Weldon

When planning a crossing of the Gulf Stream in a small boat, wind speed and direction are probably the most important factors in deciding when to cross. I look for 10-15 or less and no northerly component in the wind. The Web can be an excellent source of information; the following are a few of the sites I use for gathering information useful in planning a crossing: http://www.barometerbob.com Provides detailed weather reports on the Cruiser's Net each morning (VHF68, 8:15 am), and posts the reports and predictions on this web site. Also includes specific reports for crossing the Gulf Stream, and for boats going south or north from Abaco. http://www.wpc.ncep.noaa.gov/medr/medr.shtml (Weather Prediction Center) This is a good site for a broad overview of weather patterns showing fronts and spacing of isobars. What you really want to find is a nice fat high-pressure dome sitting right on top of the Northern Bahamas and Florida with isobars spaced wide apart. This is fairly common in the summer months. With all of the prediction models, I look for consistency in the prediction as it moves from the three or four day to the 24-hour prediction. This doesn't happen all that often but when it does you can sometimes find a window in an otherwise lousy bit of weather. http://www.aviationweather.gov/windtemp/plot I look at this site several times a day even when I'm not crossing. Here you will find current surface wind conditions and predictions to about 48 hours out. The 0 to 12-hour forecast are updated every three hours, the rest are updated twice a day at 0 and 1200 UTC. http://www.ndbc.noaa.gov/station_page.php?station=lkwf1 Reports conditions at Lake Worth, Florida. http://www.ndbc.noaa.gov/station_page.php?station=SPGF1 Reports conditions at Settlement Point, Grand Bahama. c The NOAA text forecast. While not always the most reliable, this is a good check of the others. http://tropicalatlantic.com/radars/live/bahamas/ for Bahamas radar.' windfinder.com provides wind forcasts and also shows predictions for several locations in Abaco.

For an easy way to view some of these and several other weather sites, visit www.rockybay.com/weather. Check out Florida Goes 16, Capeweather, and Pivotal Weather just to name a few.

On all of the weather sites, be sure to look at the date/time stamp and reload often. Safe crossing.

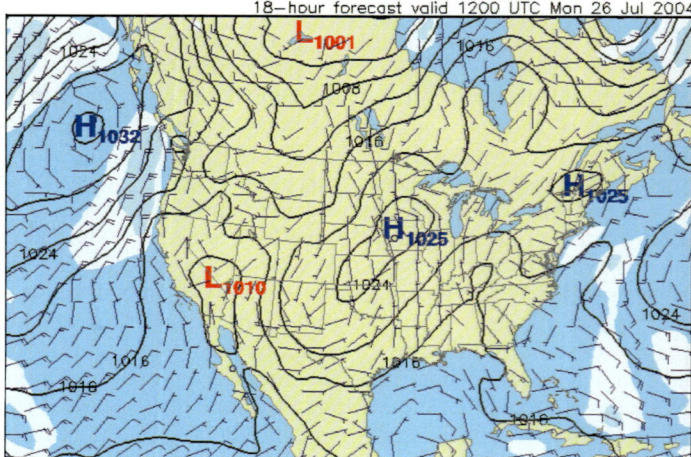

Selected portions of the home page at www.barometerbob.com for 19 August 2018 show the comprehensive weather information which is posted on this page on a daily basis. There are links to webcams at White Sound and Hope Town on Elbow Cay. A text version of the forecast, which is broadcast on the Cruiser's Net at 0815 each morning, is posted on the site each morning. Also, the Cruiser's Net is recorded each morning and is available on the Internet (after about 9:30 am) at www.abacoinet.com. Click on Audio Services and then Cruiser's Net.

Screen shot of Florida and the northern Bahamas from the GOES (Geostational Operational Environmental Satellite) on 19 August 2018 at 11:22 AM. The satellite transmits time lapse visual photos of the eastern United States and northern Caribbean. Cloud movement over Abaco can be seen and studied in real time..Go to:
http://rammb-slider.cira.colostate.edu/?sat=goes-16&sec=conus&x=6122&y=5268&z=3&im=12&ts=1&st=0&et=0&speed=130&motion=loop&map=1&lat=0&p%5B0%5D=16&opacity%5B0%5D=1&hidden%5B0%5D=0&pause=0&slider=-1&hide_controls=0&mouse_draw=0&s=rammb-slider

RADAR AND SATELLITE WEATHER
by Jeff Dodge

The availability of up to date weather information has made boating safer. The widespread availability of internet access has made checking weather while planning your trip possible, even while in the islands. For most, this will be adequate.

For those who want real time weather information on board there are two principal options—on board radar and XM weather (WXWorx). On board radar has historically been extremely expensive, but new add-on digital radar which connect to a gps chart plotter display have become quite reasonable. Garmin offers GMR 18 and GMR 18HD 18" radomes for $1000 and $1200 retail prices respectively. The least expensive currently available head unit is the GPSMap 741xs with a SRP of $1300.

XM weather broadcasts radar images from National Weather Service radar systems via satellite to surface receivers as a commercial service. An advantage is that the user gets the "big picture" available from the Weather Service's high powered doppler radar systems. The disadvantages are that the local picture for the vessel's location will be in smaller scale, and there are subscriber fees for the service. Garmin offers the GXM 51 XM weather receiver for $600. It will interface with a wide array of garmin's GPSMap products, including the $400 Gpsmap 421. WXWorx makes a hardware receiver which will connect to a computer by usb, serial, or ethernet for $830.00. Software is not included. The Least expensive bundle with software, antenna and receiver with usb interface lists for $1,182. Subscriptions for XM Weather range from $10 - $50 / mo depending upon the service level desired.

The new doppler radar at Marsh Harbour airport is operational and is used by the Meteorological Office (usually called the Met Office) in Nassau for their weather reports. It will be part of a system of similar installations in Nassau, Long Island and Mayaguana. When all four are fully integrated the data will be available online. Earliest possible date for this is July 2019 but, of course full integration of the four radars may take more time.

Enjoy The Bahamas Tax-Free Advantage.
No Income Taxes. No Capital Gains Taxes. No Inheritance Taxes.

NASSAU, THE BAHAMAS | +1.242.322.2305 | INFO@SIRBAHAMAS.COM | SIRBAHAMAS.COM

OBSERVATIONS RE: PASSAGES BETWEEN THE SEA OF ABACO AND THE ATLANTIC OCEAN

All passages between the Sea of Abaco and the Atlantic Ocean are at times impassable due to breaking seas. This condition is locally known as a "rage sea." These are not always the result of high winds; they may also be caused by ocean swells generated by far-away Atlantic storms. Some passages may be better than others in certain wind conditions. For example, Jane and Newell Garfield once reported that North Bar Channel, which is used by the mailboat and generally considered to be one of the best and safest passages, was not passable during several days. A rage sea was the result of a strong northeaster. But the passage at Little Harbour, just four miles to the south, was viable because of some protection provided by a protruding reef. The best passage on any particular day depends on wind direction and strength, on the orientation of the passage, and on tidal current—it is almost always much better to transit the passages on a rising tide with current flowing from the Atlantic Ocean to the Sea of Abaco. One should note that Little Harbour, North Bar Channel, and Tilloo Cut generally face east, whereas all passages north of Tilloo Cut generally face northeast.

Also, everyone should be aware that there is another way of getting from Eleuthera or Exuma or Nassau into Abaco Sound. Tom and Sue Dickes were holed up at Eleuthera waiting to get to Abaco with a strong northeaster which they knew would make entering the Sea of Abaco treacherous. Instead of waiting, they sailed around the west side of Abaco, around Little Abaco Island, and around Crab Cay. It added some miles, but the sailing was good and they avoided negotiating a breaking or near breaking inlet. They arrived at Green Turtle Cay while some boats were still waiting for a break in the weather to leave Spanish Wells.

Tilloo Cut on a typical summer day, and Tilloo Cut on 17 September 2003. The rage seas were caused by the passage of hurricane Isabel a couple of hundred miles offshore. Reports on conditions in the passages between the Atlantic Ocean and the Sea of Abaco are given on the Cruisers Net (0815/VHF 68) each morning.

photo by Justin Noice

ANCHORING, ANCHOR LIGHTS, AND POWER CABLES

The Bahamas functions under International Rules of the Road (rather than the U. S. Inland Rules), and under these rules there is no such thing as a "designated anchorage." All boats are therefore required by law to show a 32-point anchor light visible for 2 miles from sundown to sunup. However, even the most casual observer will soon notice that there are many boats moored or anchored on a long-term storage basis in many of Abaco's harbours which show no anchor light, so it has become common practice to anchor in harbours without showing a light. It is very important that this practice, which is still illegal, not be extended to areas outside harbours. No one should conclude that because there is an anchor in a certain place on a chart, that the spot is a designated anchorage. Remember, there are no designated anchorages in the Bahamas. All boats anchoring outside of harbours must show an anchor light. To do otherwise is to foolishly risk damage and injury to one's own boat and crew, to endanger the property and lives of others, and to break the law.

Also, when anchoring outside of harbours try to avoid the most direct access routes to those harbours as well as the high voltage electrical cables both of which are marked on our charts.

If you should accidentally snag a power line with your anchor, you will probably not be able to raise the anchor, and therefore you will not be certain of what you have snagged. But if it is in or near the power cable area, assume you have snagged a cable, and do not try to free it. The power cables carry 13,200 volts. Attempts to raise the anchor may well result in a disastrous electrical shock or in severing the power cable which supplies electricity to hundreds of people, or in both. The best thing to do is to buoy the rode, leave it there, and call Bahamas Power and Light at 367-2740. They will arrange for the return of your anchor to you.

Sometimes one anchor is enough, and sometimes it is best to use two. One is almost always adequate for daytime anchoring, or for anchoring in protected areas in settled weather. If the passage of a cool front is expected before morning, it is usually best to set a second anchor off to the west or northwest about 90° from the first (the wind often blows SW before a frontal passage). When anchoring in an area of strong tidal flows, the boat will lie to the current rather than the wind, and the current will reverse direction 180° about every six hours. This reversal could result in pulling the anchor out backwards, and it may not reset easily. In this situation a Bahamian Moor is desirable. Two anchors are set—one "upstream" and one "downstream"—with the boat inbetween. Both anchors are secured at the bow, allowing the boat to swing to current and wind.

LEGAL ENTRY - CUSTOMS AND IMMIGRATION
by Jon Dodge

Currently each person enteering the Bahamas is required to obatain a Health Visa, site: https://travel.gov.bs/ In addition, there is a new option (early 2021) for an online boat clearance submission, site: https://www.bahamascustoms.gov.bs/visitor-info/marine-vessel-declarations-cruising-permits/ This has been designed to ease the paperwork and payment process opon arrival. All boats entering the Bahamas are required to clear customs and immigration as soon as it is practical by going to a Port of Entry. If the first landfall is not a Port of Entry, going ashore is not allowed, and the vessel should proceed to a Port of Entry. The yellow quarantine flag (a yellow rectangle) should be flown to indicate that the boat has not yet cleared. Convenient Ports of Entry for boats traveling from the United States to Abaco include: West End and Port Lucaya on Grand Bahama, Bimini, Nassau, and Grand Cays, Spanish Cay, Green Turtle Cay, Treasure Cay and Marsh Harbour in Abaco. Clearance must be first priority—before re-fueling, lunch or shopping. Only the captain is allowed to leave the boat until the paperwork is completed. Required documents include the boat's registration certificate and passports for all United States citizens on board. Citizens of other countries may need to apply for a visa in advance of entry and should check with an appropriate Bahamian embassy before departure for the Bahamas. Import permits are required for pets; they are available for $11.20 from the Director of Agriculture, Gladstone and Mannings Roads, Nassau, Bahamas. (Phone is (242) 397-7450) Firearms must be accompanied by a valid permit, and must be kept under lock and key while in the Bahamas. The fee schedule is now a flat $150 (cash only) for a three-month cruising permit, fishing permit and departure taxes (paid in advance) for up to three persons for boats up to 34 feet. Add $29. per person if there are more than 3 persons on the boat (for departure tax). The fee for boats 34' - 100' is $300. Check online for longer stays and larger vessels. After clearing, foreign boats should fly the Bahamian courtesy flag (ensign) from the starboard spreader or nearest equivalent. For the return trip to the US check https://www.cbp.gov/travel/pleasure-boats-private-flyers for current requirements and information.

FISHING AND DIVING REGULATIONS
by Jon Dodge

1. Foreign vessels must obtain a sportfishing permit. These are now provided when foreign vessels clear into The Bahamas and the cost is included in the flat fee. Foreign fishermen may fish from a Bahamian rental boat without a permit; the boat rather than a fisherman receives the permit. Each vessel shall have no more than six (6) rods/reels in use at one time unless the operator is in possession of a permit authorizing the use of more rods/reels.
2. Use of any spear or net (other than landing net) must be endorsed in writing on a fishing permit. Spear guns of any type are illegal in the Bahamas. Pole spears and Hawaiian slings used while free diving are legal, but only with the proper permit. It is illegal to spear within 200 yards of any shore. No underwater air supply may be used while spearing fish.
3. All parks and preserves are restricted areas (outlined with red on charts). No spearing, fishing or shelling of any kind is permitted within the boundaries of these parks and preserves.
4. New Flats Fishing regulations were effective 9 January 2017:
Special Flats license: Daily, weekly or yearly. The condensed version of the new regulation is that only Bahamian registered vessels with a Bahamian certified fishing guide and licensed anglers may engage in flats fishing. It appears the exception is a licensed angler by themselves on a Bahamian or permitted sportfishing boat or licensed anglers wading who did not access the flats by boat. (If two people are on a boat there must be a Bahamian guide.)Fines for violations from $250 - $5000 and/or up to 3 months imprisonment. Details and license applications at: https://www.bahamas.gov.bs/wps/portal/public/marine/DOMR/

Boat Bag Limits and Closed Seasons:
Billfish Must be released (some exceptions for tournaments)
Migratory Fish (King, Dolphin, Tuna, Wahoo)- Boat limit- 18
Demersal fish (Groupers, Snappers, etc.)- Boat limit- 20 fish or 60 lbs.; no Grouper or Rockfish under 3 lbs.; three month closed season for Nassau Grouper 1 Dec-28/29 Feb.
Crawfish- Boat limit- 10; at least 3.25" carapace or 5.5" tail; no females with eggs (red berries under tail) may be taken; Season closed 1 April - 31 July.
Conch- Boat limit- 6; adults only (well-formed flared lip).
Turtle, Live coral, Sea Fans, Starfish, Sharks - prohibited

Note: All cruisers should be aware that the Government of The Bahamas is very serious about enforcing its fishing and diving regulations, and that stiff penalties may be imposed for simple possession of out-of-season, undersized, or prohibited items, even if they were purchased from Bahamian fishermen. Visitors may legally purchase fish from Bahamians, but should have documented receipts and invoices to clarify the origin of any fish above their bag limit. Closed season for grouper may be adjusted as more is learned about the Grouper's reproductive cycle.

VHF RADIO TIPS AND COURTESY

Channel 16 is a calling channel only; switch to a working channel after establishing contact. Wait for a quiet space before trying to establish contact. Channel 68 is now also used as a calling channel in Abaco for cruisers, with channel 16 reserved for making contact with local marinas and restaurants, and for emergencies. Do not give the USA call—it is time consuming and unnecessary. Simply give the call name of the party you wish to contact, repeat it, then give your call name. Example: Falusi, Falusi, Sand Dollar. Wait a second after pressing the microphone button before speaking so your first word(s) will not be cut off; give the electrons a chance. Some VHF radios require that the "SELECT" button be pressed before the radio can be switched to another channel.

Do not use the following channels for non-emergency conversations; they are reserved for the following specified purposes:
06- local taxis
16- Emergencies/local businesses/calling channel
22A- BASRA (Bahamas Air Sea Rescue) / Coast Guard
65- Dolphin research
66- Port operations
68- Cruising boat calling channel
70- Digital selective calling
71- Fishing tournaments (February - July)
72- Hope Town Fire Rescue (working channel only; call on 16)
78- Abaco Regatta (4-12 July only)
80- Marsh Harbour Emergency Services (medical, fire, police)

If you are confronted by an emergency which threatens you or your vessel with grave and immediate danger, call **Mayday on channel 16**. Do not use Mayday unless you or your vessel are threatened with grave and immediate danger, and you wish to request immediate assistance. Call Mayday 3 times, give the name of your vessel and its position as accurately as possible, state the problem and the number of people on board, and describe the boat. Then repeat the entire message, and then allow time for a response. If there is no response, say everything over again. **Do not transfer to channel 22A until you are told to do so.** If you hear a Mayday call, listen. Write the information. Do not broadcast unless it is determined that you are in the best position to render assistance. If you are unable to provide assistance and no one else has acknowledged the Mayday, you must relay the Mayday by announcing Mayday Relay 3 times and repeating the information. **Please remember to broadcast your Mayday on 16, not on 22A; the latter is a working channel only and is not monitored 24 hours a day.** Also, be aware that the U.S. Coast Guard cannot hear broadcasts from Abaco on VHF; Bahamas Air Sea Rescue (BASRA), a volunteer organization, executes search and rescue in Abaco.

If you are confronted by a situation which jeopardizes the safety of a person or your vessel which is not life-threatening, call a Pan-Pan (pronounced pahn-pahn) rather than a Mayday on channel 16. Use the same general procedure outlined above for the Mayday, repeating Pan-Pan three times, giving the name of your vessel and its position, and explain the problem.

If you have called either a Mayday or a Pan-Pan and then find that you no longer require assistance, announce the cancellation several times on channel 16 so that search and rescue or assistance efforts can be cancelled.

Remember that your vessel's VHF radio is your most valuable source of assistance in any emergency. Ensure that **every** member of your crew knows how to use it and how to call for help. It should always be in good operating condition.

CELL PHONES
by Jeff Dodge

NOTE: Post Dorian most report that Aliv has been reliable.

BTC utilizes GSM and LTE for cell phone service in Abaco ALIV (www.bealiv.com) is a new competititve carrier available with LTE/3G service in Abaco. Their rates are very competitive for week-long usage and they promise to keep a "local sim" number live for a year. I recently switched to ALIV after BTC deactived the SIM / Phone number I'd had for years. Service and coverage were quite good.

Roaming

Those who visit for short periods carrying their GSM phones from the US (AT&T and T-Mobile are GSM) or have a "World Phone" will find that automatic roaming is much more likely to work than in the past. Our Florida-based AT&T phones work immediately. The current rate is $2.50/minute for calls to The Bahamas (local) or back to the US. Data roaming is outrageously expensive: AT&T's published rate is ~ 0.02 per KB - which works out to $20.00 for 1 MB of data. Roaming data on your existing plan is not a affordable way to keep in touch. Many Verizon phones will not successfully roam in Abaco, and there are daily or monthly international roaming plans, check with your carrier for details.

Aliv SIM

Aliv sims are $15, but they will currently provide a free SIM card if you purchase a $10 or above plan.

BTC SIM

A native BTC SIM provides much better pricing per minute, and reasonable data rates. SIM cards can be obtained locally from Island Care Wireless in Marsh Harbour at very reasonable prices. For those who wish to obtain the SIM card in advance, Island Care Wireless (phone 242-367-0429)will ship FEDEX to the US (see their advertisement on facing page). We also found the website mrsimcard.com which sells SIMs and allows top-up (recharge) directly from their website (see their advertisment this page). Both businesses are customer oriented and will provide assistance to customers with questions about cell service in the Bahamas.

Rates

Aliv bundles data/voice/text in 7 day and 30 day plans. They currently have 7 day plans ranging from $5 for a 0.5Gb 50 minute talk plan, a $10 1Gb/100min/100 Text plan up to a $30 70GB/17,500min/10,500text plan - currently the freedom 10 and freedom 20 plans have a promotion for doubled data allowances, 2gb and 4gb respectively. Aliv's 30 day plans include liberty 50 10gb/500min/500text for $50, liberty 90 18gb/900min/900text for $90, to liberty 120 with unlimited data,minutes and texting for $120. Note: The voice minutes include calls to the United States, so for those keeping in touch with the states, Aliv is quite a value.

BTC published prepaid rates : $0.33/min peak (7am-7pm); $0.15/min off-peak (7pm-7am); and $0.20/min weekend. Calls to the US were historically $0.50/min but are not currently published. Verify before calling if possible.

Aliv minutes are inclusive of the united states and are bundled in the plan, add ons can be purchased in store or with the Aliv app directly on your phone.

BTC has created All in one plans for minutes and data: $3.50 for 500Mb, 100Minute(Us Calls) 1 day, $10 for 2Gb 500Mins (Us Calls) for 7 days and $30 for 15Gb 1,000 Minues (us Calls) for 15 days. Straight data plans can still be activated using *203# and have daily and weekly options (which seem inferior to the all inclusive plans) and a 30 day plans from 2GB for $13 6Gb for $25, and 15Gb for $35 Visit www.btcbahamas.com for current prepaid rates.

Cellular Equipment

AT&T or Tmobile compatible unlocked phones or wifi hotspots are your best bet for Aliv and BTC service.

WIRELESS INTERNET IN ABACO
by Jeff Dodge

Fixed Wifi in Abaco was devastated by Dorian. Aliv does have a wifi hotspot available and "mifi" plans ranging from $65 to $165 per month. All plans are "unlimited" but subject to throttling after a data cap is reached. Bahamas WiMax has also resumed services in Abaco. At press time service restoration is mostly available in central and southern Abaco with expansion coming soon.

Sunset from the west deck at Abaco Inn, White Sound, Elbow Cay, 19 July 2014. Photo by Jeff Dodge.

Abaco Real Estate Agency Ltd

estab. 1973

Beachfront • Hilltop • Acreage
Residential • Commercial
Investment Properties

Abaco Real Estate Agency, Ltd.
Stratton Drive
(Adjoining the Abaco Insurance Bldg)
Marsh Harbour, Abaco

P.O. Box AB20404
www.abacobahamas.com

Abaco Sales Professional Contacts...

Bill Thompson ~ Broker 242-477-5712
Billt@abacobahamas.com

James or Donna Rees ~ Brokers 242-458-6822
Jamesordonna@gmail.com

Kyle Stevens ~ Agent 242-375-9271
Kstevens242@gmail.com

Wendie Bishop ~ Broker Eleuthera 242-577-9910
Wendiebishop@gmail.com

Ritchie & Roshanna Eyma ~ Agents Nassau.
242-699-2228
Ritchie@abacobahamas.com
Roshanna@abacobahamas.com

Abaco: The History of an Out Island and its Cays
by Steve Dodge. Expanded third edition of the only comprehensive general history of Abaco. 6" x 9" 282 pages. ISBN 0-932265-76-6 $19.95 (plus $5.00 S&H). Available at Abaco Treasures in Marsh Harbour, Vernon's Grocery, Ebb Tide Shop and Abaco Inn on Elbow Cay, www.Amazon.com and www. wspress.com.

White Sound Press
379 Wild Orange Drive • New Smyrna Beach, FL 32168
Tel 386 423-7880 • Fax 386 423-7557
www. wspress.com • orders@wspress.com

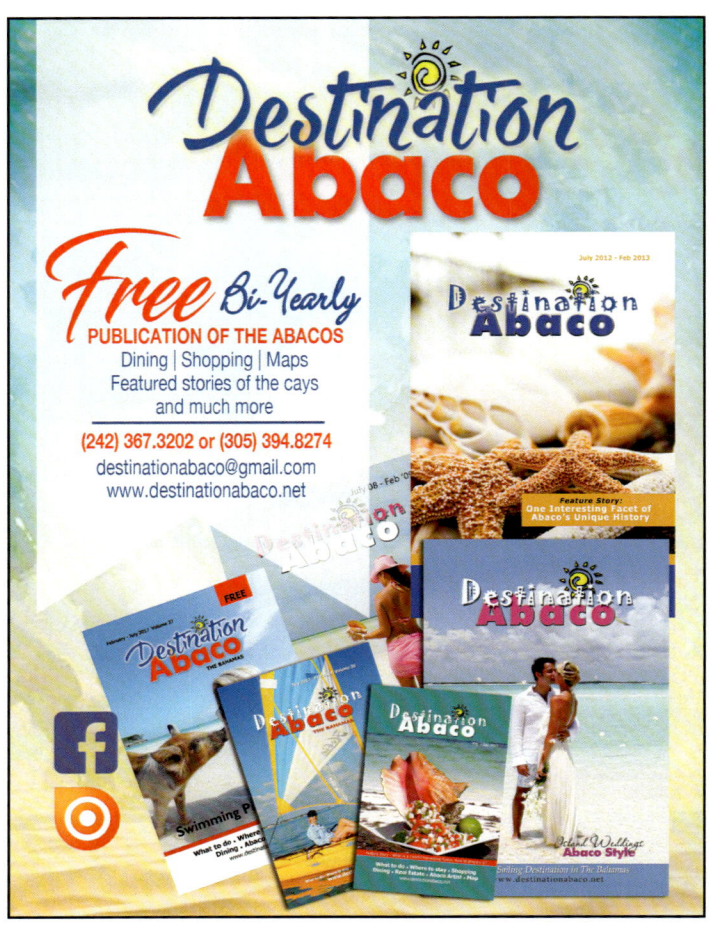

EPIRBs and SPOT

Crossing the Gulf Stream in a small boat is a lot different than cruising a few miles up the Intracoastal for lunch and a swim. Help is not readily available in the middle of the stream; on several of our crossings we did not see a single other vessel. Engines and other equipment should be thoroughly checked before departure to avoid breakdowns—belts, hoses, battery cables, etc. should all be in top notch condition. All through-hull fittings and their hoses and clamps should be in sound condition. Life preservers should be readily available to all on board, and a ditch bag should be prepared and be accessible. If a dinghy or life raft is carried, there should be a plan for deployment in an emergency, and in the unlikely event that the vessel sinks, calling for help will be very important.

If there is time before leaving the vessel, call 'May Day" on the VHF radio on channel 16; if there is no time, call on the portable VHF which should be in the ditch bag. Know your position so you can tell potential rescuers where to find you. Nearby vessels may respond and be your best chance for timely assistance, and the Coast Guard monitors channel 16 with large antennas and powerful receivers on the Florida coast.

406 EPIRBs broadcast distress signals which include your latitude, longitude, and boat identification to a constellation of satellites which relay the data to a central clearing office which verifies it and then dispatches rescuers. 406 EPIRBS are readily available at most marine stores.

Another device which can summon assistance is the SPOT by Globalstar. This pocket size device has an SOS button which, when pressed, sends a message to a different constellation of satellites which is then relayed to the Coast Guard. A very interesting feature of the SPOT is that in normal operation it is programmed to send your position every ten to twenty minutes to its constellation of satellites and that position is then relayed to the FindMeSpot website which your family and friends can use to monitor your progress on Google Maps. The InReach by DeLorme is a similar device; check both before deciding which one to purchase.

We carry both a 406 EPIRB and a SPOT when we cross the Gulf Stream; we think it is the prudent thing to do and recommend that all who cross the stream consider carrying these emergency devices. We all hope, of course, that none of us will ever have to use them to signal distress.

BASRA, TowBoatUS and SeaTow

The Bahamas Air-Sea Rescue Association (BASRA) has provided emergency rescue service in the Bahamas for over 50 years. It is not a branch of the Bahamian government; it is funded by member dues and contributions. Its Abaco base is Hope Town. BASRA can be called directly on VHF, or they respond to May-Day calls. The organization is dedicated to saving lives, not salvaging or towing boats. BASRA should be called only when lives are in danger. Situations of less significance will be handed off to others who may be willing to provide help.

TowBoatUS' service areas from south Florida bases vary from 75-130 miles and therefore include the western half of Grand Bahama Island, Bimini and almost to Great Sale Cay, but do not include any part of Abaco. If you are outside of all TowBoatU.S. service areas BoatU.S. can still assist you in locating a local service provider and will reimburse any out of pocket expense up to the member's selected service level. SeaTow's Florida bases are normally limited to 40 miles for service, but SeaTow has arrangements with Bahamian based towers and they say that membership includes towing throughout the Bahamas.

All Harbours are No Wake Zones

For many years certain harbours in Abaco, such as Hope Town Harbour, were designated as No Wake Zones. During 2015 the Port Authority declared that all harbours in the Bahamas are no wake zones and placed the notice below in several editions of *The Abaconian* newspaper. This applies to all boats except emergency vessels.

Support the Bahamas Air-Sea Rescue Association.

You are not required to take an active part in BASRA.

Send $40.00 for one year's membership dues to:

BASRA ABACO, Hope Town, Abaco, Bahamas

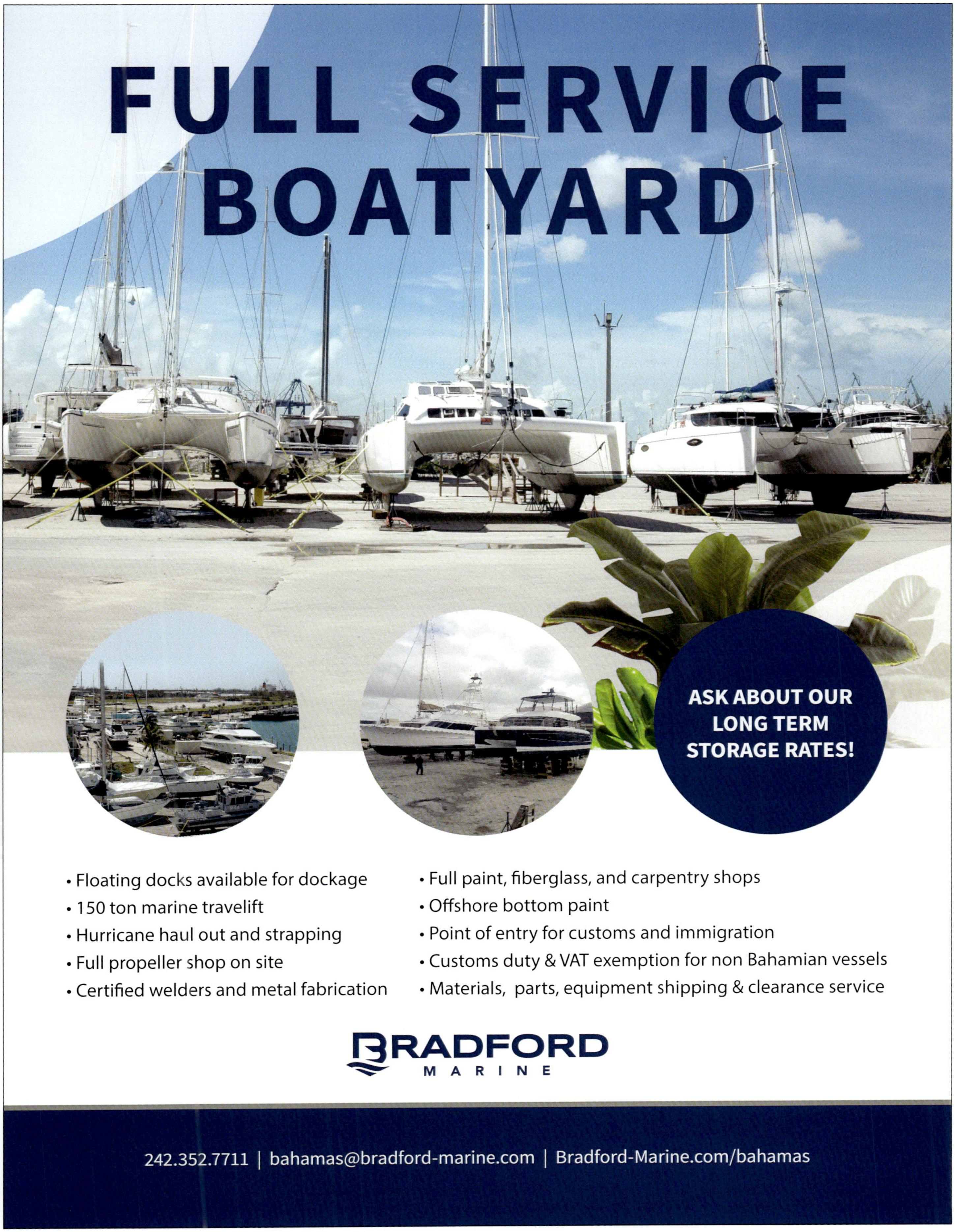

FULL SERVICE BOATYARD

ASK ABOUT OUR LONG TERM STORAGE RATES!

- Floating docks available for dockage
- 150 ton marine travelift
- Hurricane haul out and strapping
- Full propeller shop on site
- Certified welders and metal fabrication
- Full paint, fiberglass, and carpentry shops
- Offshore bottom paint
- Point of entry for customs and immigration
- Customs duty & VAT exemption for non Bahamian vessels
- Materials, parts, equipment shipping & clearance service

BRADFORD MARINE

242.352.7711 | bahamas@bradford-marine.com | Bradford-Marine.com/bahamas

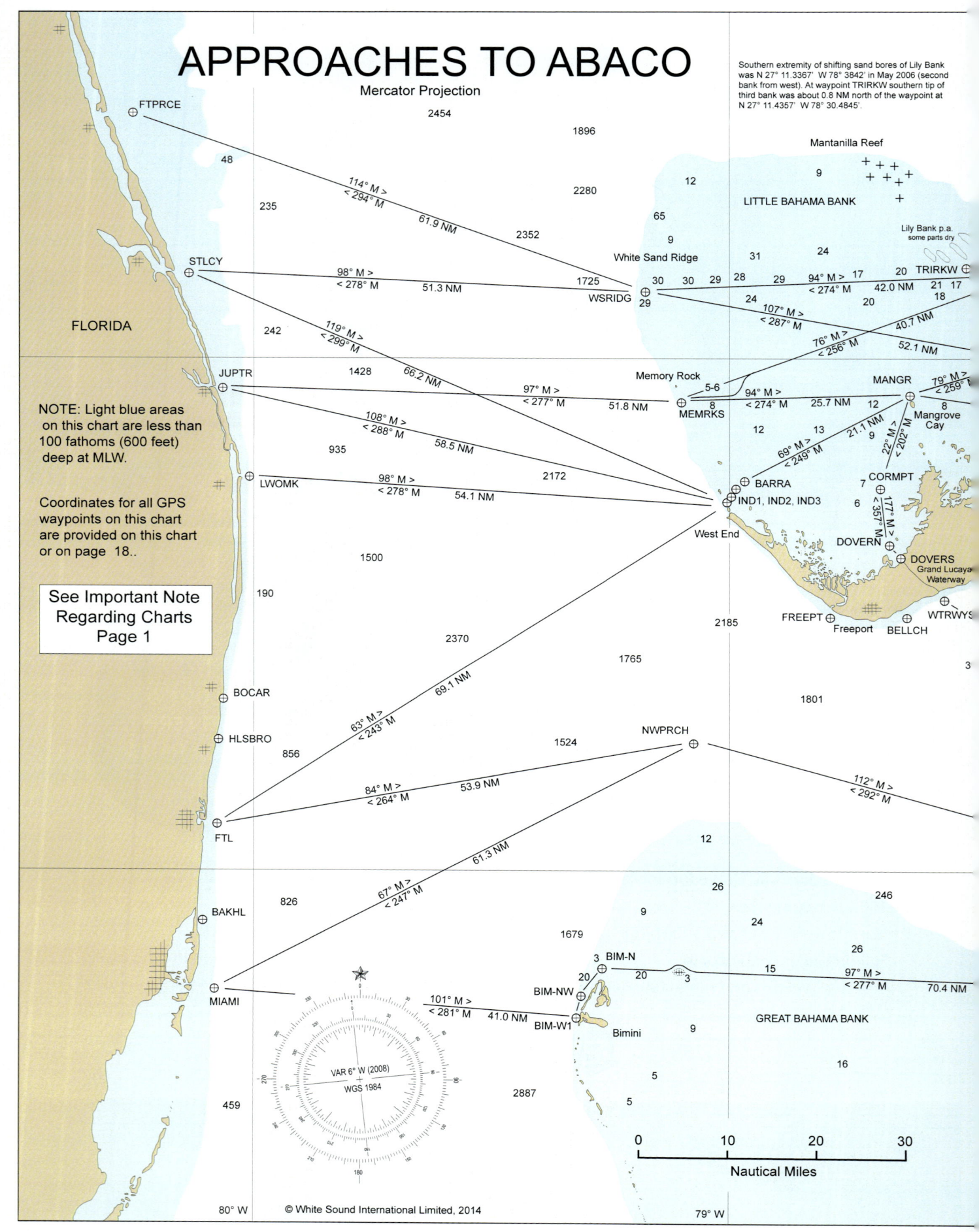

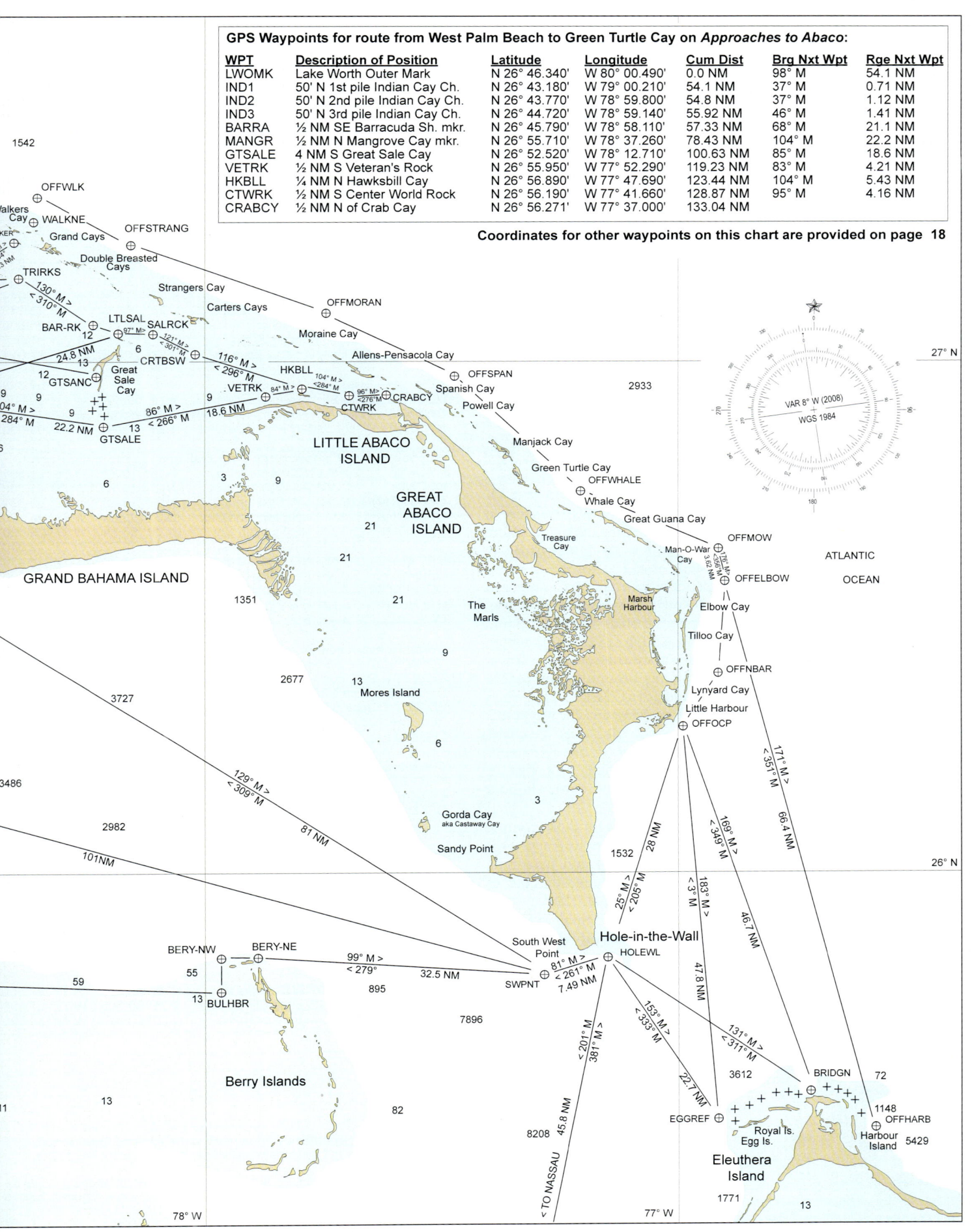

APPROACHES TO ABACO

The route from West Palm Beach to Abaco via Indian Cay Channel is all over 6' except for Indian Cay Channel itself, which carries about 5½' MLW. See the large scale chart on page 22. Boats drawing more need tide help. Planning the passage through Indian Cay Channel for 1-2 hours before high tide will provide 6½-7' on neap tides and 7½-8' on springs. Another alternative is to go north of Sandy Cay or either side of Memory Rock. The suggested course from MEMRKS to MANGR carries more than 6' MLW, but the straight-line course from MEMRKS to TRIRKS is very close to or over a 5-6' shoal which is 1-2 NM ENE of MEMRKS. If your draft is more than about 4', we suggest a course of 94° M (head for MANGR) until about 4 NM east of MEMRKS before turning to port to head for TRIRKS. White Sand Ridge is another deep water route, and is especially useful for boats departing from St. Lucie Inlet or Ft. Pierce and going to Walker's Cay. Note that we now show a route to Walker's Cay from waypoint TRIRKW; the route is north of Triangle Rocks and south of Lily Bank.

The routes north and south of Great Sale Cay both carry well over 6'; the northern route, which comes closer to visible landmarks, is 1.59 nautical miles longer. The Grand Lucayan Waterway carries 6-7' MLW, but the channel approaching it through Dover Sound at its northern end carries only about 3' MLW. Also, a bridge over the waterway limits passage to vessels under 27½' high at MHW. See the large scale chart on page 24.

Boats entering the Sea of Abaco through North Man-O-War Channel or South Man-O-War Channel should go offshore to OFFMOW (and OFFELBOW if approaching from the south) before heading for the openings. From either OFFMOW or OFFELBOW one may go to the waypoints located "east, east" of the channels (SMOWEE and NMOWEE) and then approach the "east" waypoints for the channels (SMOWE and NMOWE). These courses will keep boats off the many dangerous reefs in the area. All boats should use them unless very familiar with the area. It is very important to stay east of Elbow Reef, which extends eastward from Hope Town. **More boats ground on this reef than any other offshore reef in Abaco—please be wary of this reef and go to OFFELBOW when passing Elbow Cay and Reef.** For more detail and for waypoints and coordinates not on this small scale chart, please see the charts on pages 74 and 80. Boats leaving Abaco via these channels and heading south should use these same waypoints. Note that we now show an offshore route from Walker's Cay to Little Harbour which keeps boats well off Abaco's barrier reef.

The best entrances to the Sea of Abaco for those coming from Eleuthera are North Bar Channel (see pages 118 and 116) and North Man-O-War Channel (see page 74 and paragraph above). The waypoints at the Eleuthera end of the suggested courses provide access to Spanish Wells and Harbour Island. The waypoint BRIDGN is at the north end of the Bridge Point opening in Devil's Backbone Reef. Local knowledge and good visibility are required for this passage the first time.

Other GPS Waypoints on Approaches to Abaco (pp. 16- 17):

WPT	Description of Position	Latitude	Longitude
SEBAST	E Sebastian Inlet (not shown)	N 27° 51.674'	W 80° 26.450'
FTPRCE	E Ft. Pierce inlet	N 27° 28.680'	W 80° 15.180'
STLCY	Outer mark St. Lucy inlet	N 27° 10.000'	W 80° 08.000'
JUPTR	1 NM E Jupiter inlet	N 26° 56.605'	W 80° 03.877'
BOCAR	E Boca Raton inlet	N 26° 20.061'	W 80° 03.940'
HLSBRO	½ NM SE Hillsboro Inlet	N 26° 15.116'	W 80° 04.420'
FTL	FtL outer mark	N 26° 05.400'	W 80° 04.700'
BAKHL	½ NM E Baker's Haulover inlet	N 25° 54.011'	W 80° 06.625'
MIAMI	S Govt. Cut Outer Mark	N 25° 45.950'	W 80° 05.000'
WSRIDG	33 NM NNW West End	N 27° 08.000'	W 79° 10.500'
MEMRKS	2 NM S Memory Rock	N 26° 55.000'	W 79° 06.000'
LTLSAL	½ NM NW Little Sale Cay	N 27° 03.274'	W 78° 10.809'
SALRCK	¾ NM N Sale Cay Rocks	N 27° 03.229'	W 78° 06.552'
CRTBSW	¾ NM SW of Carters Bank	N 27° 00.994'	W 78° 01.049'
GTSANC	Great Sale Cay anchorage	N 26° 58.581'	W 78° 13.149'
TRIRKS	SE Triangle Rocks	N 27° 09.750'	W 78° 23.500'
TRIRKW	4 NM W Triangle Rocks	N 27° 10.638'	W 78° 30.045'
WALKER	S of Walker's Cay Markers	N 27° 14.077'	W 78° 24.145'
OFFOCP	1 NM ESE Ocean Point	N 26° 17.079'	W 76° 59.349'
HOLEWL*	2 NM SE Hole-in-the-Wall	N 25° 50.000'	W 77° 09.000'
SWPNT*	3 NM WSW South West Point	N 25° 48.000'	W 77° 17.000'
NWPRCH	West end NW Prov. Channel	N 26° 15.000'	W 79° 05.000'

Waypoints for off shore route from Walker's Cay to Little Harbour:

WPT	Description	Latitude	Longitude
WALKNE	2 NM ENE Walker's Cay	N 27° 16.289'	W 78° 21.598'
OFFWLK	4.2 NM NE Walker's Cay	N 27° 19.100'	W 78° 21.200'
OFFSTRANG	6.8 NM NW Strangers Cay	N 27° 13.500'	W 78° 09.337'
OFFMORAN	3.3 NM NNE Moraine Cay	N 27° 05.635'	W 77° 44.700'
OFFSPAN	3.5 NM NE Spanish Cay	N 26° 58.340'	W 77° 28.400'
OFFMANJ	3.3 NM N north tip Manjack	N 26° 53.730'	W 77° 22.940'
OFFWHALE	2.8 NM NE Whale Cay	N 26° 44.772'	W 77° 12.430'
OFFMOW	5.0 NM NE MOW Cay	N 26° 37.820'	W 76° 55.000'
OFFELBOW	3.6 NM NE Hope Twn hbr	N 26° 34.270'	W 76° 54.250'
OFFNBAR	3.6 NM E North Bar Channel	N 26° 23.410'	W 76° 55.000'
OFFLHB	1.4 NM SSE Little Hrbr Bar	N 26° 18.971'	W 76° 58.858'

Grand Bahama Island:

WPT	Description	Latitude	Longitude
CORMPT	Pole 2.5 NM NW Cormorant Pt.	N 26° 44.540'	W 78° 40.800'
DOVERN	Pole north end Dover Sound	N 26° 38.280'	W 78° 39.650'
DOVERS	south end Dover Sound	N 26° 36.800'	W 78° 38.470'
WTRWYS	Buoy S. end Grd. Luc. Wtrwy.	N 26° 31.670'	W 78° 33.270'
BELLCH	200' S buoy off Bell Channel	N 26° 29.826'	W 78° 37.791'
FREEPT	1.2 NM SE Freeprt Hbr entry	N 26° 30.000'	W 78° 47.100'

Eleuthera:

WPT	Description	Latitude	Longitude
BRIDGN**	N end Bridge Pt. reef opening	N 25° 34.298'	W 76° 43.344'
EGGREF	0.8 NM west of Egg Reef	N 25° 31.102'	W 76° 55.031'
OFFMAN	2 NM NE Man Island	N 25° 33.500'	W 76° 36.500'
OFFHARB	3.0 NM NE Harbour Mouth	N 25° 30.000'	W 76° 35.000'

Nassau:

WPT	Description	Latitude	Longitude
NASSAU	north Nassau Hbr. entrance	N 25° 05.447'	W 77° 21.340'

Bimini:

WPT	Description	Latitude	Longitude
BIM-N*	1/3 NM N of North Rock	N 25° 48.250'	W 79° 15.500'
BIM-NW	1.0 NM NW North Bimini	N 25° 45.000'	W 79° 18.450'
BIM-W1	entrance dredged channel	N 25° 42.630'	W 79° 18.450'

Berry Islands:

WPT	Description	Latitude	Longitude
BULHBR	5.0 NM WNW Bullocks Hbr	N 25° 46.000'	W 77° 57.500'
BERY-NW	1.2 NM NW Little Stirrup Cay	N 25° 50.000'	W 77° 57.500'
BERY-NE	1 NM NE entrance Grt. Hbr.	N 25° 50.000'	W 77° 53.000'

Island Queen heading west back to Florida after nine months in Abaco on the route north of Grand Bahama, 20 July 2011. Photo by Steve Dodge.

* Waypoints designated by an asterisk were acquired from reliable sources, but have not been personally checked on-site by the author.

**This waypoint is at the north end of the Bridge Point opening in Devil's Backbone Reef. Local knowledge and good visibility are required for this passage the first time.

From Florida to Abaco -- Crossing the Gulf Stream

by Marcel Albury and Steve Dodge

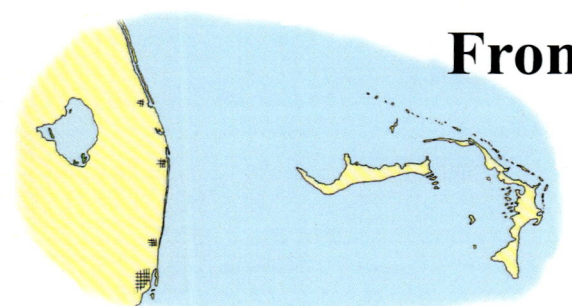

The crossing from Florida to Abaco is about 135 nautical miles—55 miles across the Florida Straits from West Palm Beach to West End, Grand Bahama Island, and then 80 miles across Little Bahama Bank from West End to Crab Cay, where one enters into Abaco Sound, sometimes called the Sea of Abaco. It is another 15 nautical miles to Green Turtle Cay, and then another 20 to Marsh Harbour. A planing powerboat can make the trip in one day; a sailboat generally requires 3 to 5 or more days. There are good overnight anchorages or dockage at West End (Old Bahama Bay Marina), Great Sale Cay, Fox Town, Spanish Cay (Spanish Cay Marina), Powell Cay/Cooperstown, and, of course, Green Turtle Cay.

The most challenging part of the trip is crossing the Florida Straits. The Gulf Stream flows northward through the Straits at a speed of about 3 knots. It is about 20-25 miles wide, and is usually located in the center of the Straits. If the wind blows hard (15 or more knots) from the north—against the current—the equivalent of a tide rip 25 miles wide is created, with short, steep, treacherous waves. This condition often exists during the winter months after the passage of cold fronts, and makes the Gulf Stream almost impassable for small boats. Add to this the navigation problem created by the current sweeping one's vessel to the north when the destination is east and, of course, the usual challenges of any 50-mile open ocean crossing, and it should be clear that the trip across the Florida Straits must be taken seriously. But it is not difficult, and most anyone with some open water experience can do it successfully if they follow the general rules of good seamanship, and pay attention to certain special aspects of this crossing.

The single most important factor affecting the comfort and safety of crossing the Gulf Stream is the weather. One should make certain that there will be adequate time to cross before any bad weather moves in. Marcel Albury, who crossed the Gulf Stream well over 100 times, drove over to the beach to look at the ocean before leaving. He did this even if the weather report was good: "If you see elephants out there on the horizon, forget it. It should look nice and flat. I realize that what you can see is not all that you are going to run into, but it gives you a pretty good idea. The weather report, along with what I can see—the two of these things together—is what makes me decide. And then I leave within about 2 hours. It takes about 6 hours to cross, and I know the weather will be good for that long, so I leave right away."

The boat and the boat's equipment should be in good condition with all standard Coast Guard equipment including life jackets, flares, etc. Fuel should be ample, which like an airplane, should be about 50% more than what you need for the trip. It may be necessary to reduce speed because of sea conditions, making the boat less efficient and the extra fuel essential. The most important extra piece of equipment is a VHF radio, which should be in good operating condition. Some boats carry a portable or a spare. The safety of the crossing can be greatly enhanced by traveling with another boat. Then if problems develop, help is close at hand. Crossing alone in a small open boat—a runabout—is not recommended. Larger boats may cross alone, but Marcel Albury did not recommend single-handed crossings, unless it is an emergency: "I have done it, but you get different as you get older. There are just too many things that can go wrong with me, or it, or that, or them, or what have you. I want somebody else; I just like company. I might twist my ankle and not be able to get up. When one thing happens, it causes something else to happen; it always seems to snowball. It's not in the best interest of anyone to cross the Gulf Stream single-handed."

Notify someone that you are making the crossing and arrange to call them after arrival. The Coast Guard can serve in this way, but it is probably better to call a relative or friend who will be more immediately concerned if you do not telephone on schedule indicating your arrival (also, see discussion of EPIRBs, SPOT and InReach on page 14).

Do not depart from any point north of Ft. Pierce, because you will be fighting the current of the Gulf Stream. Embarkation from West Palm Beach puts the current on the beam, and departure from Fort Lauderdale gives the boat a boost getting to the north with the current helping. The Gulf Stream flows at about 3 knots, but you are not in it all the time as you are crossing. I figure 2 knots drift and usually that works out about right. So, if you figure the crossing to West End will take 6 hours, set your course for a spot 12 nautical miles south of West End. You should be able to see the condominiums at West Palm Beach for 20-30 miles, and you will pick up West End when still about 8 miles west of it, so you will only be out of sight of land for about 25 miles.

The landfall is an easy one—before you see the land you should be able to see the water tower at West End from about 8 miles out. If you make a little too much to the north, then you would probably see Sandy Cay, which lies about 6 miles north of West End and has a very high clump of casuarinas (Florida or Australian Pines) visible for about ten miles. So you've got two good landfalls. You can hardly be so far one way or the other that you're not going to pick up either Sandy Cay or the water tower at West End. You can see the tower if you are 6-8 miles south, and you can see Sandy Cay if you are 6-8 miles north, so you have a broad area there. Its not like going back to the states, when you can't miss it, but if you get within this 18-20 mile area, you will see one or the other landfall. If you go too far south, you will realize it because you are not in the shallow water of the bank, so if you turn and head north you will find Grand Bahama Island and Freeport. So, you probably are not going to miss land.

Memory Rock, which is about 8 miles north of Sandy Cay, is a fairly small rock and is therefore difficult to distinguish from a distance. You can enter on to Little Bahama Bank on either side of it. It is almost on a straight-line course to Sale Cay from West Palm Beach, but most small boats will need to re-fuel—they will not be able to make the additional 100 miles to Green Turtle Cay without re-fueling at West End. Other possible re-fueling stops are at Fox Town and Spanish Cay.

Finally, all boats entering The Bahamas are required to clear Customs and Immigration at a Port of Entry as soon as possible after arriving in Bahamian waters. This can be done at West End, Freeport, Walker's Cay, Spanish Cay, Green Turtle Cay, or Marsh Harbour.

Note: Marcel Albury passed away in 2005. He is missed.

Grand Bahama Island

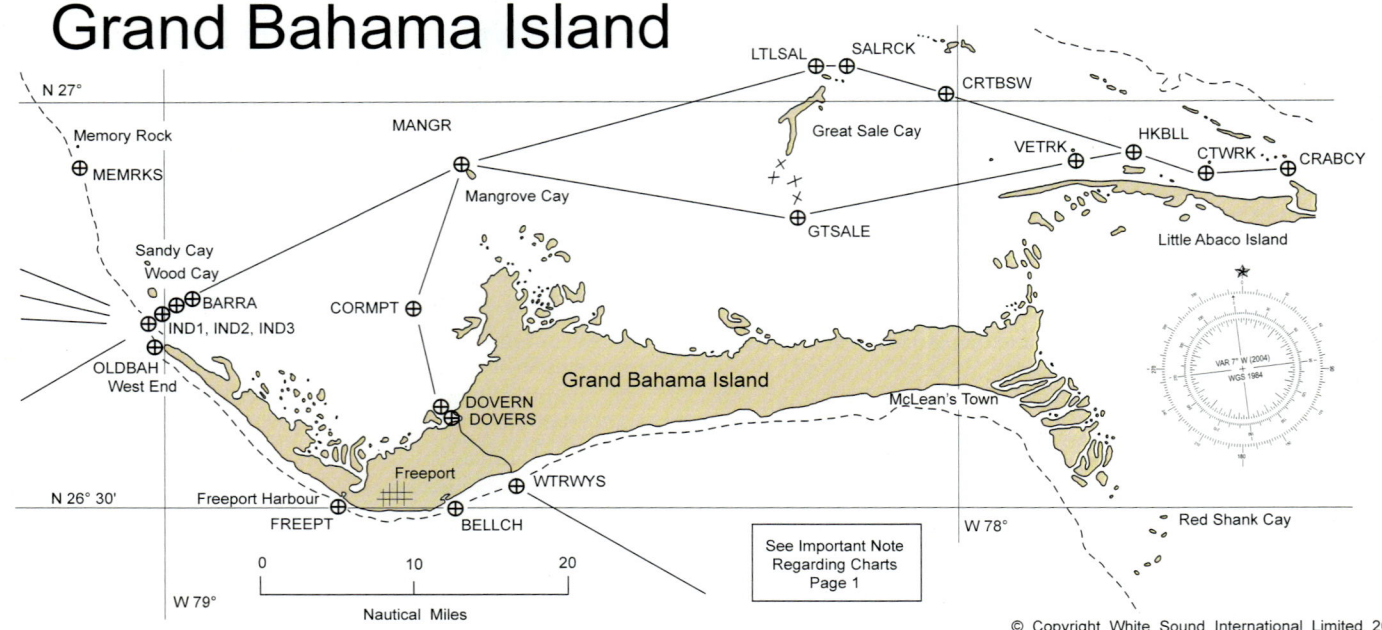

Boats departing from Lake Worth Inlet (West Palm Beach), Jupiter or St. Lucie Inlets bound for Abaco will find that Grand Bahama Island is a logical first landfall. Legal entry to the Bahamas can be made at Old Bahama Bay Marina at West End or at several harbours located on the island's south coast. Dockage fuel and other marine services are available.

The island is about sixty nautical miles long and six nautical miles wide. Its northern coast is very shallow and not approachable in cruising boats for much of its length. Old Bahama Bay at West End is the only marina on the north coast of Grand Bahama Island and is strategically located for boats arriving in The Bahamas or departing for Florida. It is a full service marina/resort (see chart p. 22). Those transiting to Abaco north of Grand Bahama can find some protection at Mangrove Cay (see chart p. 23) or Great Sale Cay (see chart p. 25). The Grand Lucayan Waterway bisects the island about 20 nautical miles east of West End (see the chart in this section on page 24).

The southern coast is close to the southern edge of Little Bahama Bank. A barrier reef parallels the coast for much of its length a short distance offshore, and just beyond that there is a steep drop-off to deep ocean water at the edge of the bank. Freeport Harbour is a commercial harbour with some facilities for cruisers (see chart on facing page). There are several harbours with marinas east of Freeport Harbour--Xanadu Beach Marina and Resort, Sunrise Resort and Marina, the Ocean Reef Yacht Club, and Grand Bahama Yacht Club at Bell Channel. McLean's Town is near the eastern end of Grand Bahama.

GPS Waypoints for Grand Bahama Section (generally from west to east):

WPT	Description	Latitude	Longitude
MEMRKS	2 NM S Memory Rock	N 26° 55.000'	W 79° 06.000'
OLDBAH	500' W ent. Old Bah Bay Mar.	N 26° 42.256'	W 78° 59.818'
IND1	50' N 1st pile Indian Cay Ch.	N 26° 43.180'	W 79° 00.210'
IND2	50' N 2nd pile Indian Cay Ch.	N 26° 43.770'	W 78° 59.800'
IND3	50' N 3rd pile Indian Cay Ch.	N 26° 44.720'	W 78° 59.140'
BARRA	½ NM SE Barracuda Sh. mkr.	N 26° 45.790'	W 78° 58.110'
FREEPT	1.2 NM SE Freeprt Hbr entry	N 26° 30.000'	W 78° 47.100'
'MANGR	1/2 NM N Mangrove Cay mkr.	N 26° 55.710'	W 78° 37.260'
CORMPT	pole 2½ NM NW Cormorant Pt.	N 26° 44.540'	W 78° 40.800'
DOVERN	pole north end Dover Sound	N 26° 38.280'	W 78° 39.650'
DOVERS	south end Dover Sound	N 26° 36.800'	W 78° 38.470'
WTRWYS	buoy S. end Grd. Luc. Wtrwy.	N 26° 31.670'	W 78° 33.270'
BELLCH	200' S buoy off Bell Channel	N 26° 29.826'	W 78° 37.791'
GTSALE	4 NM S Great Sale Cay	N 26° 52.520'	W 78° 12.710'
LTLSAL	1/2 NM NW Little Sale Cay	N 27° 03.274'	W 78° 10.809'
SALRCK	3/4 NM N Sale Cay Rocks	N 27° 03.229'	W 78° 06.552'
CRTBSW	3/4 NM SW of Carters Bank	N 27° 00.994'	W 78° 01.049'
VETRK	1/2 NM S Veteran's Rock	N 26° 55.950'	W 77° 52.290'
HKBLL	1/4 NM N Hawksbill Cay	N 26° 56.890'	W 77° 47.690'
CTWRK	1/2 NM S Center World Rock	N 26° 56.190'	W 77° 41.660'
CRABCY	½ NM N of Crab Cay	N 26° 56.271'	W 77° 37.000'

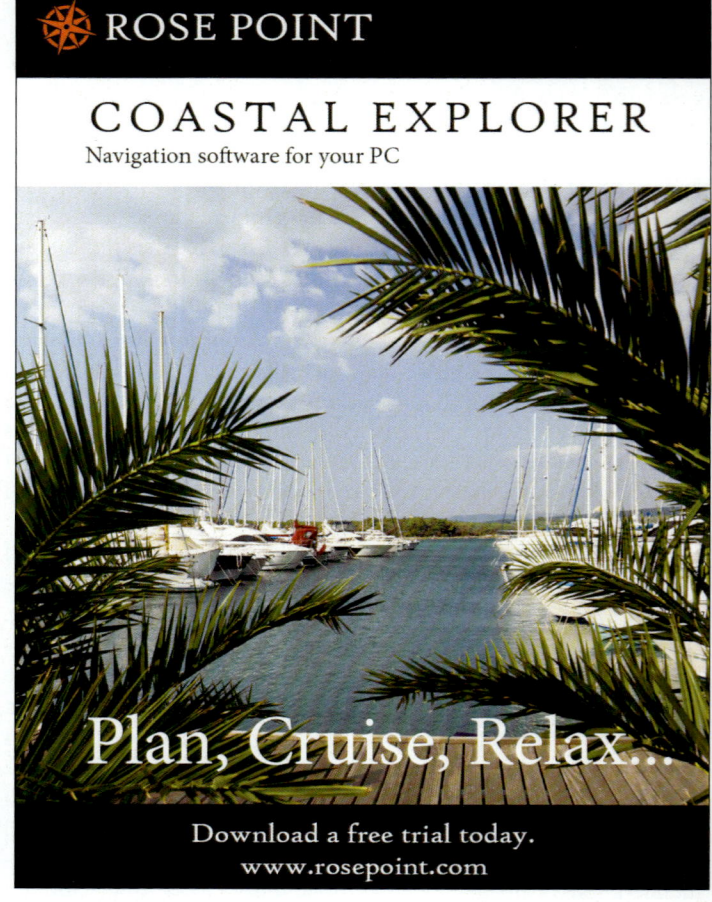

Freeport Harbour

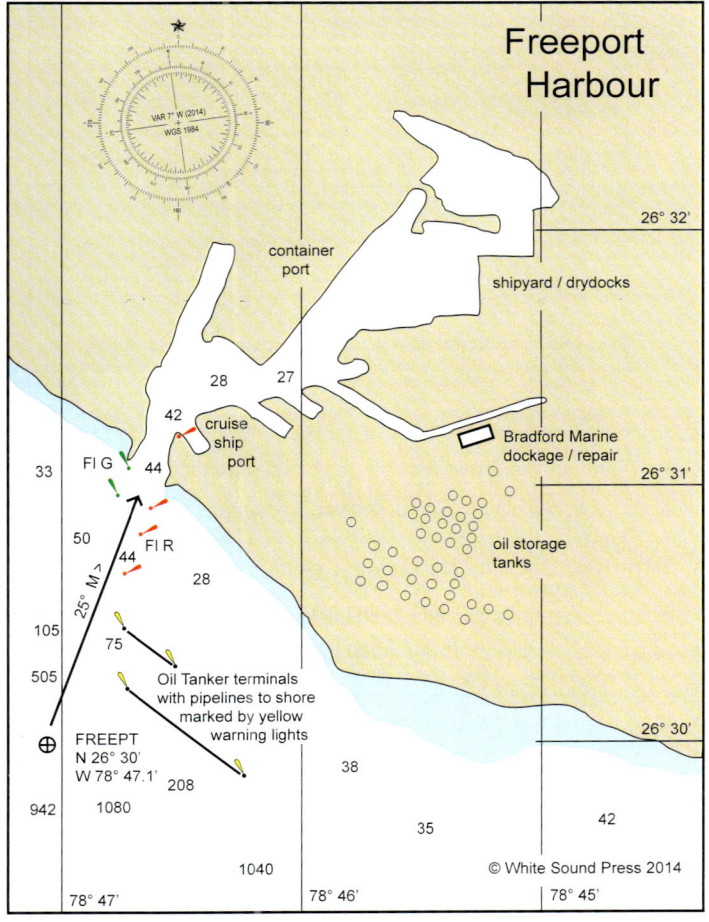

Freeport Harbour

Freeport is the Bahamas' second largest city and its harbour is a major commercial harbour with a large container port, a cruise ship pier, a shipyard with dry dock facilities for commercial vessels and a major oil storage and transhipment facility. But it is certainly not off limits to cruisers. Bradford Marine is not only a full service boat yard, but offers dockage on three easily accessible floating docks. The daily rate for boats up to 49' is $1.25/foot plus $10. and includes wifi, daily water, security and garbage removal. Taxi service is available to Freeport. The entire harbour is deep and entry is straightforward and well marked. All should be aware of the offshore oil tanker terminals on the SW side of the approach to the harbour and stand clear of it (see photo below). Also, commercial vessels may be moored or anchored west of the harbour entrance awaiting permission to enter the harbour. Call Freeport Harbour Control on VHF 16 to request permission to enter the harbour about 20-30 minutes before your arrival.

The BORCO oil transhipment facility's offshore terminals is located just SW of the entry to Freeport Harbour. Approaching vessels should stand clear of it. Photo by Bahamas Oil Refining Company (BORCO).

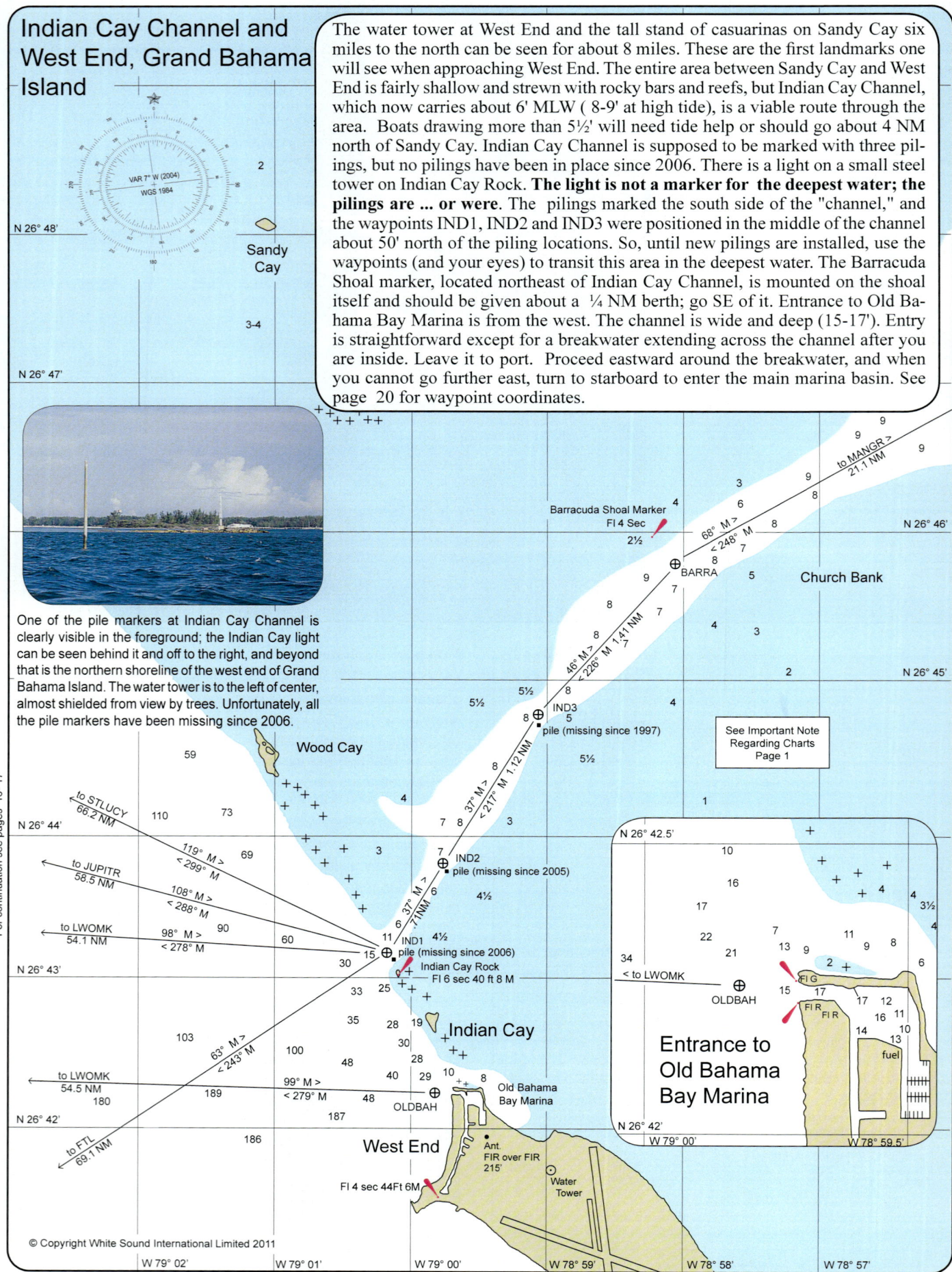

Entrance to Old Bahama Bay

Approach from the west. After entering between the breakwaters, move to the starboard side to avoid the spur breakwater, the end of which is marked with a white sign in the above photo. After passing it and the branch canal which goes to the south, turn to starboard to enter the marina basin. The fuel dock is on the starboard side as you enter. **These photos are a few years old—the rock jetties have turned to gray and grass, plants and trees have made the area greener.**

MANGROVE CAY

Mangrove Cay is located about halfway between West End / Memory Rock and Great Sale Cay, and therefore is a convenient anchorage for some boats transiting the area. It can provide good protection from the SW and W, and from the NE and E, marginal protection from SE winds, and little protection from NW winds. The cay is appropriately named—it consists of mangroves with some other trees on slightly higher land in the center of the cay, and a single palm tree at the north end. The flashing white light is mounted on a tall pole; unfortunately it is unreliable. The waypoint MANGR is located on the principal east/west routes and is located about 0.6 NM north of the pole.

Sailboat anchored at Mangrove Cay,. Photo taken several years ago before Palm tree grew at the northern end. Photo by Steve Dodge.

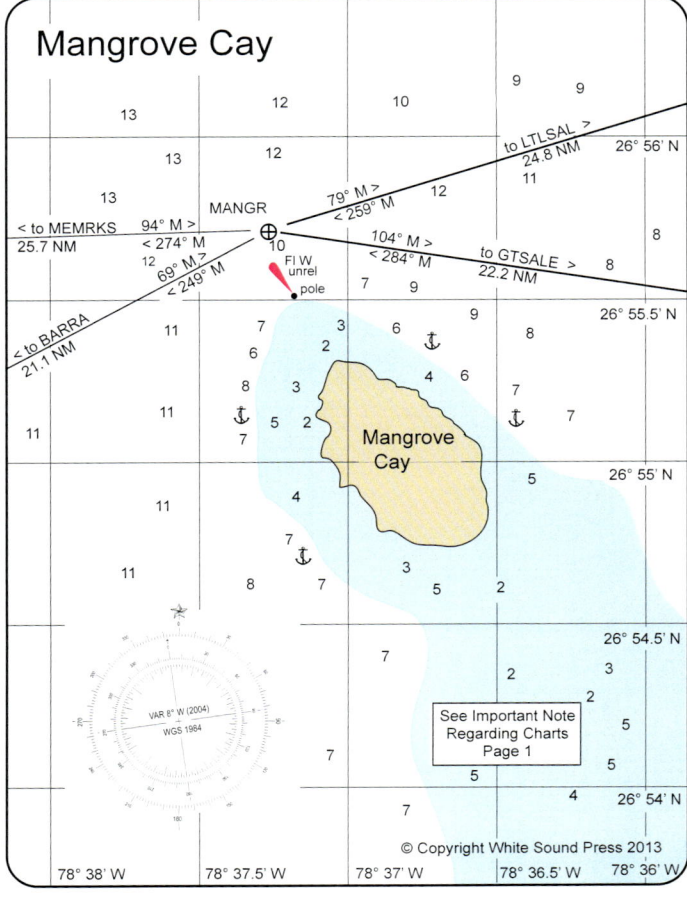

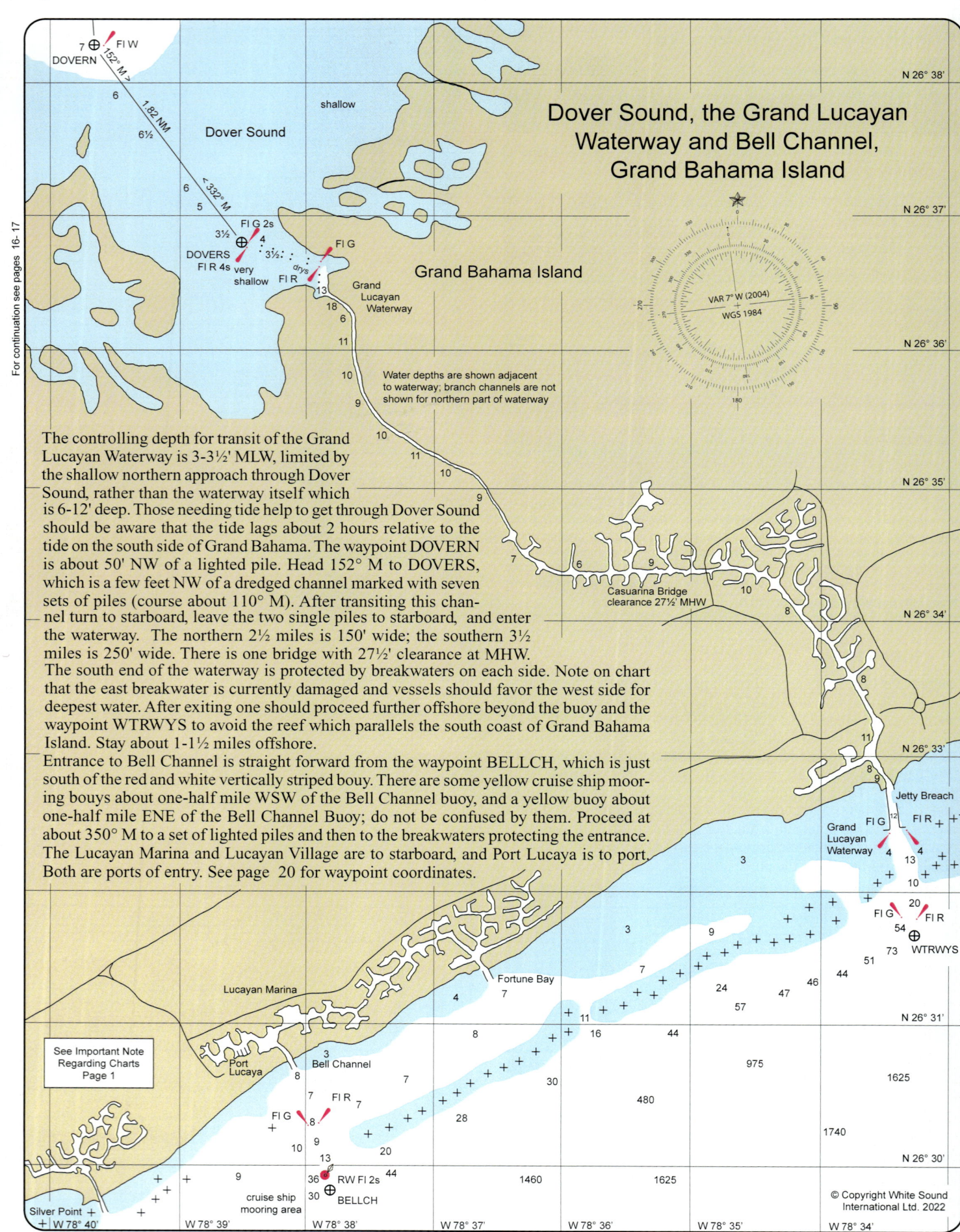

GREAT SALE CAY

Great Sale Cay provides conveniently located anchorages roughly half-way between the western edge of Little Bahama Bank and Green Turtle Cay. The cay is generally low lying with mangroves, but there is some elevation at the northern end. Anchorages can be found in the bight on the western side which is generally known as Northwest Harbour. The holding is best in sand at and around the waypoint GTSANC; further north in the harbour the bottom is mud, but, of course, there is more protection. The anchorage along the northwestern shore of the cay is good for southeast winds, and the anchorage on the east side of the cay is good for northwest winds. The shoals extending from the southern point stretch for about 3 NM. It is possible ro carry up to 6' MLW between them, but it should only be attempted in settled weather with good visibility on a rising tide. The waypoint GTSALE is on the suggested east-west route south of Great Sale Cay and is located about 4 NM south of the southern point (see the chart on page 26). At the northern end of the cay rocky shoals extend north to Little Sale Cay and the Sale Cay Rocks. Vessels transiting the area should use the waypoint LTSAL. Great Sale Cay is not particularly pretty; its greatest asset is its location on the route between Florida and Abaco.

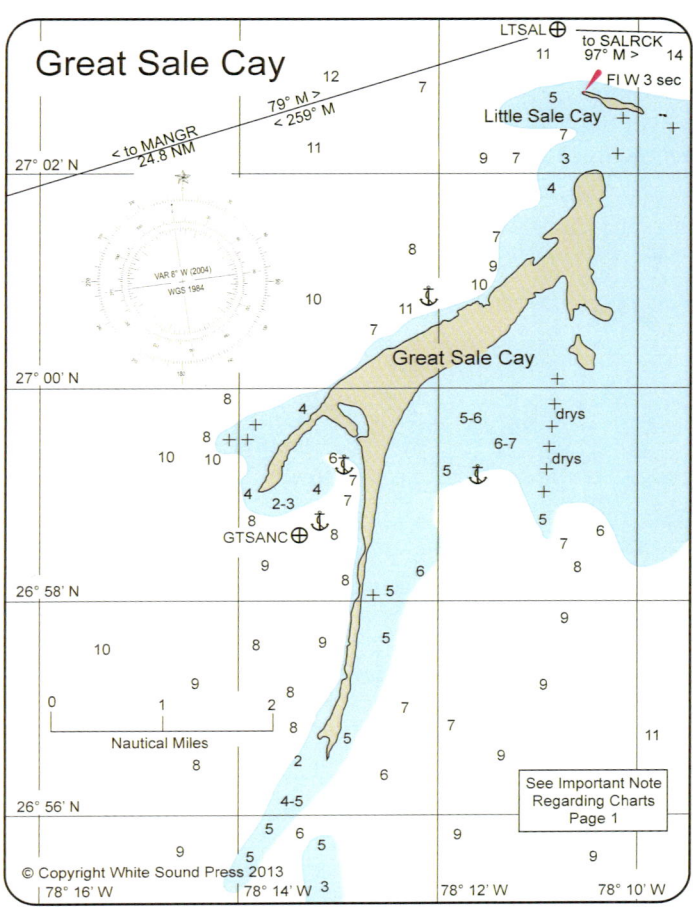

Fish muds are common on Little Bahama Bank in the area north of Grand Bahama Island. This one was photographed from the air in July, 2002. When approaching them in a boat they often appear, at first, to be a shoal area, but homogenous colour and sometimes fuzzy edges give them away as fish muds rather than shoals. There are several theories regarding their cause; the most common being schools of bottom feeding fish.

GPS Waypoints for *Walker's Cay to Carters Cays* (generally from north to south):

WPT	Description of Position	Latitude	Longitude	WPT	Description of Position	Latitude	Longitude
OFFWLK	4.2 NM NE Walker's Cay	N 27° 19.100'	W 78° 21.200'	CRTBSW	Southwest of Carter Bank	N 27° 00.994'	W 78° 01.049'
WALKNE	2.0 NM ENE Walker's Cay	N 27° 16.289'	W 78° 21.598'	GRAND	South of Grand Cays	N 27° 11.884'	W 78° 18.970'
WALKER	South of Walker's Cay markers	N 27° 14.077'	W 78° 24.145'	DBLBRE	South of Double Breasted Cays	N 27° 11.000'	W 78° 16.500'
TRIRKN	Northeast of Triangle Rocks	N 27° 10.766'	W 78° 25.056'	STCHN	N end Stranger Cay Channel	N 27° 12.400'	W 78° 09.770'
TRIRKW	4 NM W Triangle Rocks	N 27° 10.638'	W 78° 30.045'	STCHS	S end Stranger Cay Channel	N 27° 10.500'	W 78° 10.500'
TRIRKS	Southeast of Triangle Rocks	N 27° 09.750'	W 78° 23.500'	STRANG	1¾ NM S of W tip Stranger Cay	N 27° 06.000'	W 78° 06.350'
BAR-RK	Southwest of Barracuda Rocks	N 27° 04.258'	W 78° 14.071'	CARTER	2 NM SW of Carters Cays	N 27° 03.528'	W 78° 01.087'
LTLSAL	Northwest of Little Sale Cay	N 27° 03.274'	W 78° 10.809'	GTSALE	4 NM south of Great Sale Cay	N 26° 52.520'	W 78° 12.710'
SALRCK	¾ NM North of Sale Cay Rocks	N 27° 03.229'	W 78° 06.552'	GTSANC*	Great Sale Cay anchorage	N 26° 58.581'	W 78° 13.149'

WALKER'S CAY TO CARTERS CAYS
(including Great Sale Cay)

All vessels operating in the area SW of Walker's Cay should note the abandoned drill rig located approximately 2 NM SW of Walker's Cay. It is indicated on the chart.

Boats drawing 4' or more and transiting the area from Walker's Cay to Carters Cays must take care to avoid the shoal between Walker's and Grand Cays, the Double Breasted Bars which are about 5 NM S of Double Breasted Cays, and the large shoal extending from the Rhoda Rocks and Pelican Rock. GPS waypoints are shown on the chart for this route. It extends generally S from Walker's Cay to Triangle Rocks, then SE to Barracuda Rocks, ESE to Little Sale Cay, and then E to Carters Cays. This route is not the shortest distance between Walker's and Carters, but it is clear of obstacles and carries over 6' MLW (except for the final approach to Walker's over the bank there, which carries about 4-5' MLW). Waypoints for this route are listed below the chart.

Possible overnight anchorages along the way (within about 5 NM) include Grand Cays, Double Breasted Cays, Strangers Cay and Great Sale Cay. Grand Cays is the next anchorage to the SE. Grand Cays has a settlement with restaurants and stores, and fuel service is available. Beaches on the east side of the cays are beautiful, and bone-fishing is good in the entire area. See the chart on page 30 for more detail.

Double Breasted Cays is a beautiful collection of small cays and rocks. An anchorage offering protection from the west, north, and east is available near the NW end of the archipelago. See the chart on page 32 for more detail.

Strangers Cay has a settled weather anchorage near its NW tip. See the chart on page 34 for more detail.

Great Sale Cay has a bight on its west side which offers good protection from west, north, and east winds, but is open to the south. It is a favorite overnight stop for boats making the Abaco-Florida passage. The approach to it is straightforward—the only obstacle is a shoal extending westward from Great Sale Cay. Give it a wide berth. Another possible anchorage is just east of the cay—but this offers protection only from the west and north, being exposed to the east and south (see the chart on page 25).

Note that the old Elephant Rock route between Walker's Cay and Grand Cays close to Burying Piece Rocks now carries only about 2' MLW. An alternative route further off Burying Piece Rocks carries over 6' MLW. See the Grand Cays chart on page 30.

Double Breasted Cays can be approached directly from the waypoint GRAND or from the SW tip of Big Grand Cay on the Atlantic side. See pages 30-32 for larger scale charts and a detailed description.

From the waypoint DBLBRE note that a straight course line to LTLSAL, the waypoint north of Little Sale Cay, passes near the edge of the bank extending south from the Rhoda Rocks and Pelican Rock. Watch cross track error carefully here, or just alter course to the west to make certain that you avoid the edge of the bank.

There is a deep and wide channel from the Sea of Abaco to the Atlantic Ocean NW of Strangers Cay. See page 34 for more details.

This blue hole is located on the shoal extending from the southern tip of Great Sale Cay. Blue holes are located in the shallow waters (or on the land areas) of the Bahama Banks. They are connected to deep ocean waters through a tunnel or tunnels cut through the limestone base of the banks by rainwater during the ice ages when sea level was several hundred feet lower than it is today.

The anchorage at Carters Cays from the south. Photo 27 May 2011 by Steve Dodge.

A sand bar in northern Abaco. Sand bars, which are beautiful from the air and from your boat when it is in deep water, are not fun when you are aground on one. Photo by Steve Dodge, 4 July 2008.

Walkers Cay

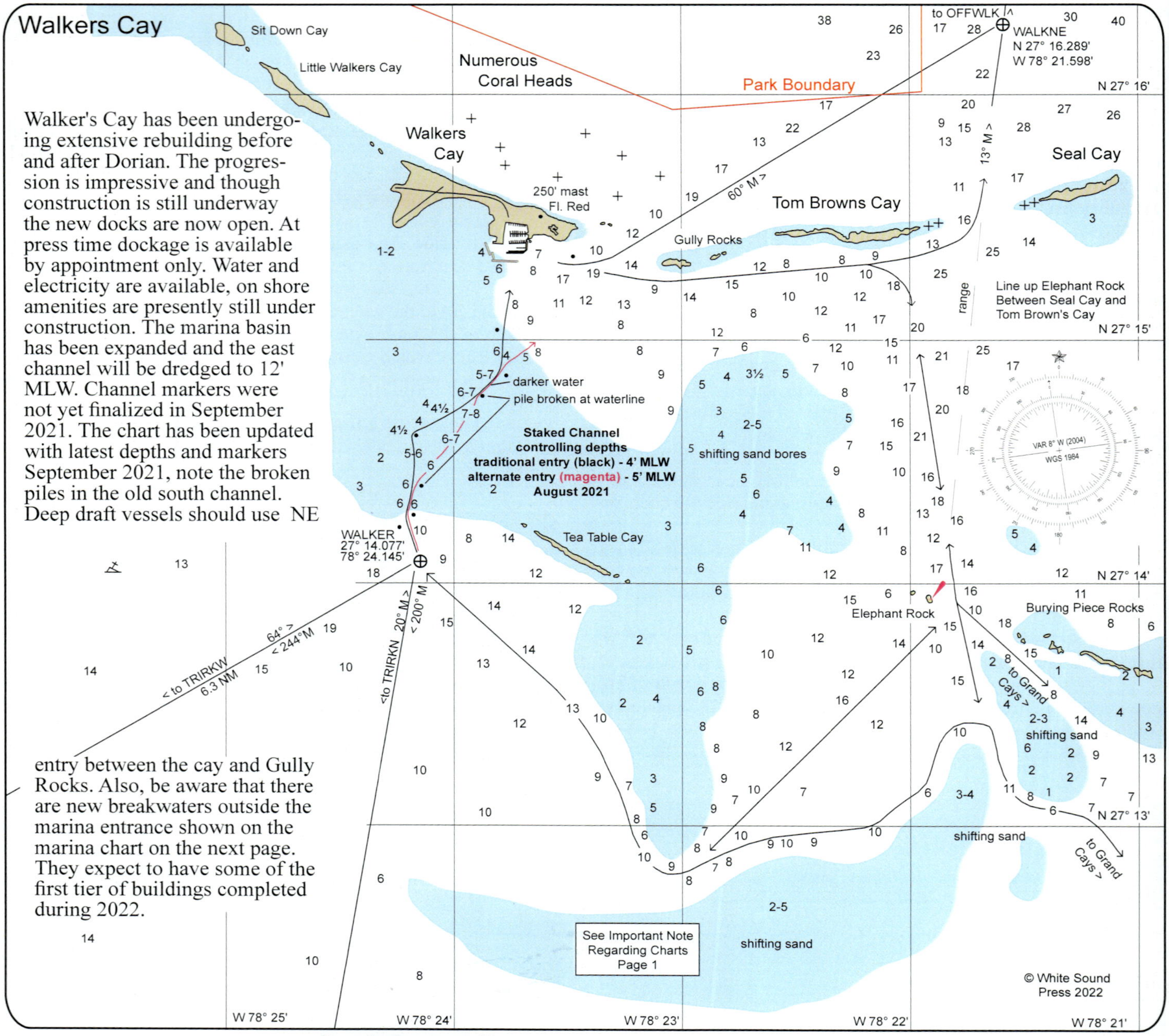

Walker's Cay has been undergoing extensive rebuilding before and after Dorian. The progression is impressive and though construction is still underway the new docks are now open. At press time dockage is available by appointment only. Water and electricity are available, on shore amenities are presently still under construction. The marina basin has been expanded and the east channel will be dredged to 12' MLW. Channel markers were not yet finalized in September 2021. The chart has been updated with latest depths and markers September 2021, note the broken piles in the old south channel. Deep draft vessels should use NE entry between the cay and Gully Rocks. Also, be aware that there are new breakwaters outside the marina entrance shown on the marina chart on the next page. They expect to have some of the first tier of buildings completed during 2022.

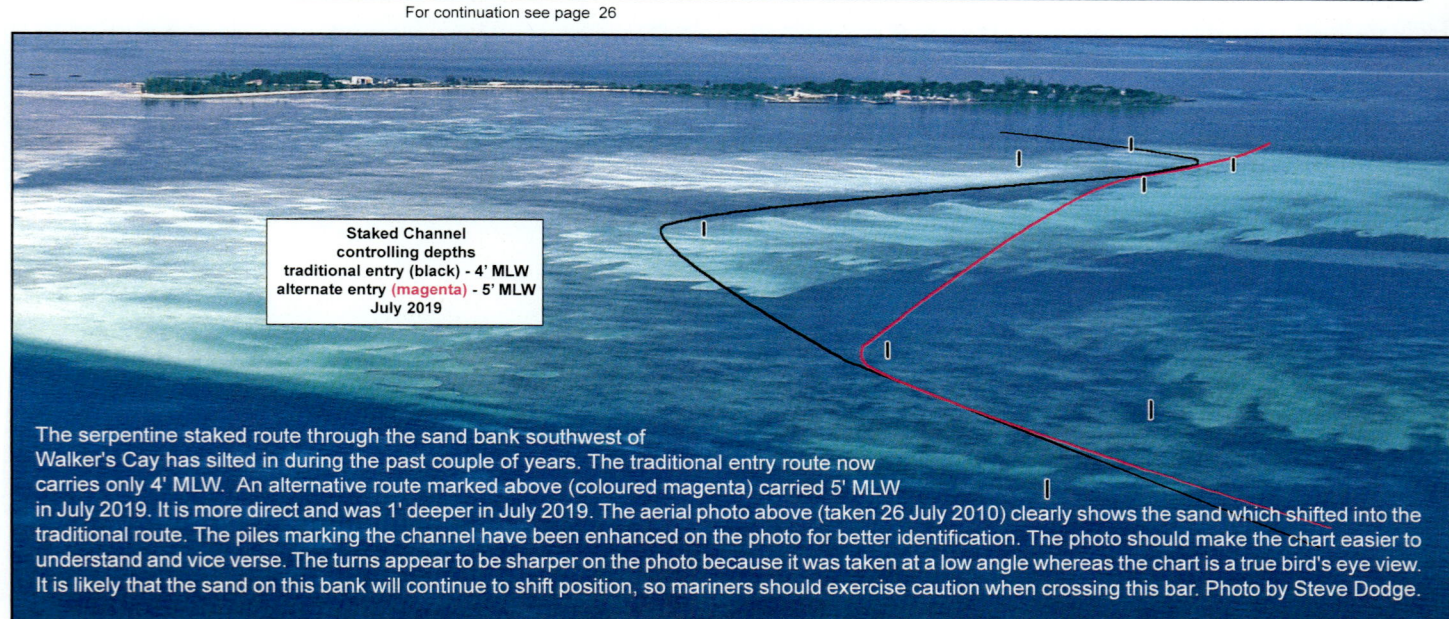

Staked Channel controlling depths
traditional entry (black) - 4' MLW
alternate entry (magenta) - 5' MLW
July 2019

The serpentine staked route through the sand bank southwest of Walker's Cay has silted in during the past couple of years. The traditional entry route now carries only 4' MLW. An alternative route marked above (coloured magenta) carried 5' MLW in July 2019. It is more direct and was 1' deeper in July 2019. The aerial photo above (taken 26 July 2010) clearly shows the sand which shifted into the traditional route. The piles marking the channel have been enhanced on the photo for better identification. The photo should make the chart easier to understand and vice verse. The turns appear to be sharper on the photo because it was taken at a low angle whereas the chart is a true bird's eye view. It is likely that the sand on this bank will continue to shift position, so mariners should exercise caution when crossing this bar. Photo by Steve Dodge.

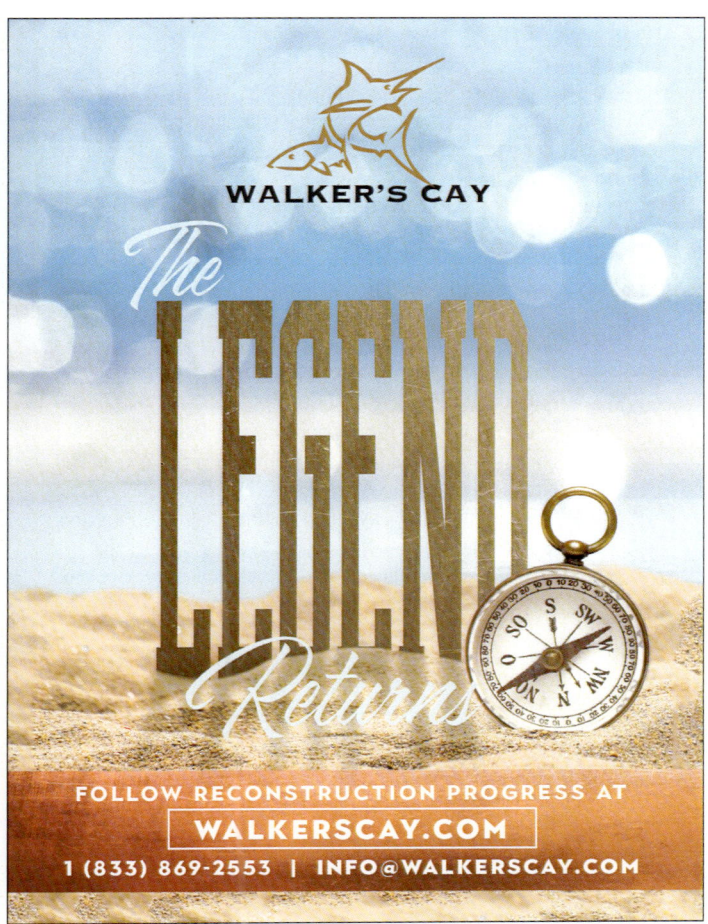

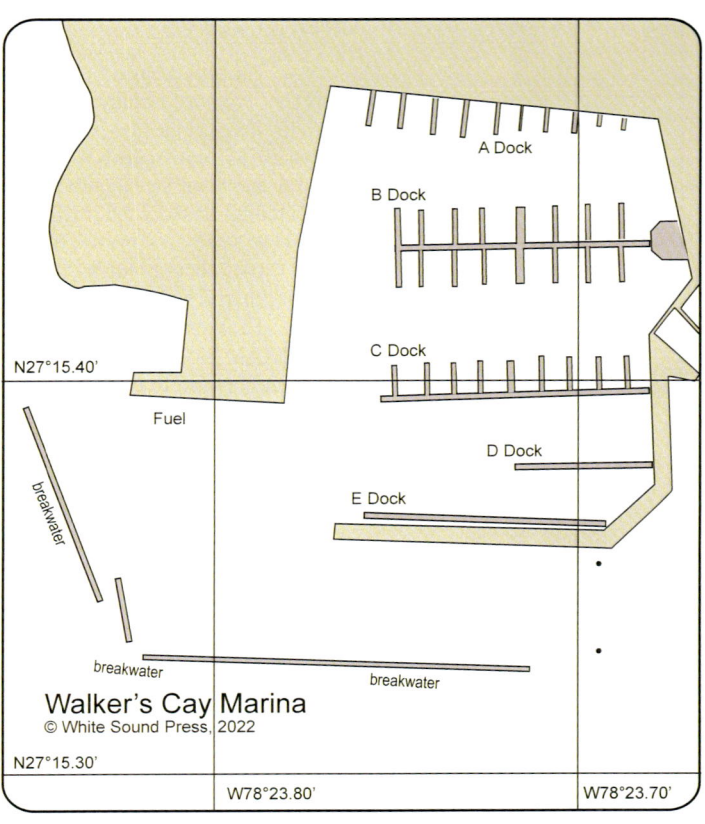

Walker's Cay Marina
© White Sound Press, 2022

Marina Contact: VHF 16 or 74 or phone 833 869 2553

The Elephant Rock route between Walker's Cay and Grand Cays from the south (27 May, 2011). This area continues to be very volatile; the best channel has changed several times. The best route between Walkers and Grand runs NW-SE and carries over 6' MLW; it is marked on the photo above and is accurately shown on the chart (next page). You should be able to see the deeper water based on water colour. Note that there is a second and wider deep water route southwest of the one marked on this photo; is also clearly marked on the chart. All turns appear to be sharper on the photo because it was taken at a low angle whereas the chart is a true bird's eye view.

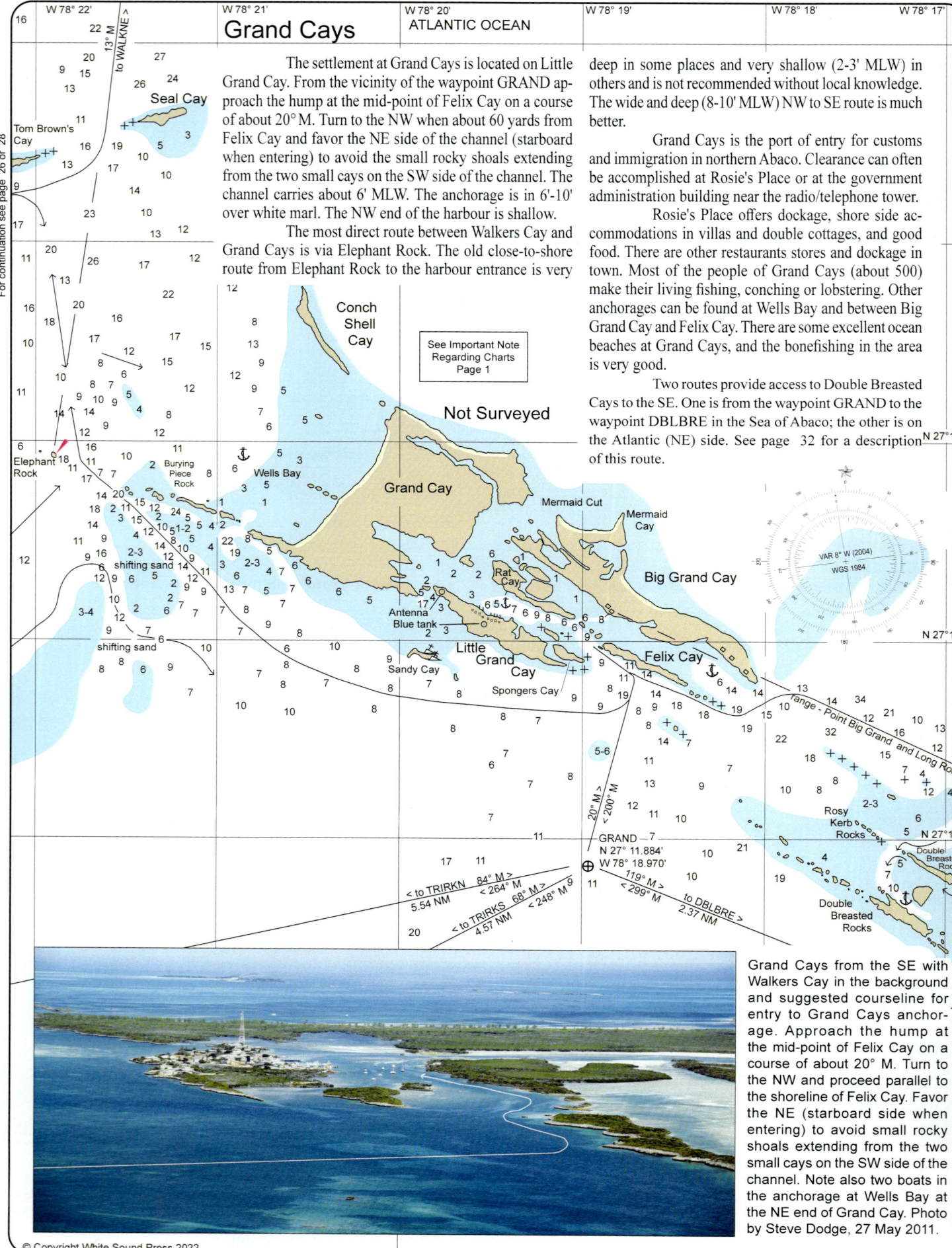

Grand Cays

The settlement at Grand Cays is located on Little Grand Cay. From the vicinity of the waypoint GRAND approach the hump at the mid-point of Felix Cay on a course of about 20° M. Turn to the NW when about 60 yards from Felix Cay and favor the NE side of the channel (starboard when entering) to avoid the small rocky shoals extending from the two small cays on the SW side of the channel. The channel carries about 6' MLW. The anchorage is in 6'-10' over white marl. The NW end of the harbour is shallow.

The most direct route between Walkers Cay and Grand Cays is via Elephant Rock. The old close-to-shore route from Elephant Rock to the harbour entrance is very deep in some places and very shallow (2-3' MLW) in others and is not recommended without local knowledge. The wide and deep (8-10' MLW) NW to SE route is much better.

Grand Cays is the port of entry for customs and immigration in northern Abaco. Clearance can often be accomplished at Rosie's Place or at the government administration building near the radio/telephone tower.

Rosie's Place offers dockage, shore side accommodations in villas and double cottages, and good food. There are other restaurants stores and dockage in town. Most of the people of Grand Cays (about 500) make their living fishing, conching or lobstering. Other anchorages can be found at Wells Bay and between Big Grand Cay and Felix Cay. There are some excellent ocean beaches at Grand Cays, and the bonefishing in the area is very good.

Two routes provide access to Double Breasted Cays to the SE. One is from the waypoint GRAND to the waypoint DBLBRE in the Sea of Abaco; the other is on the Atlantic (NE) side. See page 32 for a description of this route.

Grand Cays from the SE with Walkers Cay in the background and suggested courseline for entry to Grand Cays anchorage. Approach the hump at the mid-point of Felix Cay on a course of about 20° M. Turn to the NW and proceed parallel to the shoreline of Felix Cay. Favor the NE (starboard side when entering) to avoid small rocky shoals extending from the two small cays on the SW side of the channel. Note also two boats in the anchorage at Wells Bay at the NE end of Grand Cay. Photo by Steve Dodge, 27 May 2011.

Rosie's Place

- Overnight Dockage •
- Water and Electricity
- Fuel Dock •
- Gasoline and Diesel
- Air Conditioned Marina Villas and Cottages •
- Good Bahamian Food •

Grand Cays • Abaco • Bahamas
VHF 68 "Rosie's Place"
242 727 6051 (Rosie)   242 533 7709 (Mekiva)
www.rosiesplace.com   rosie@rosiesplace.com

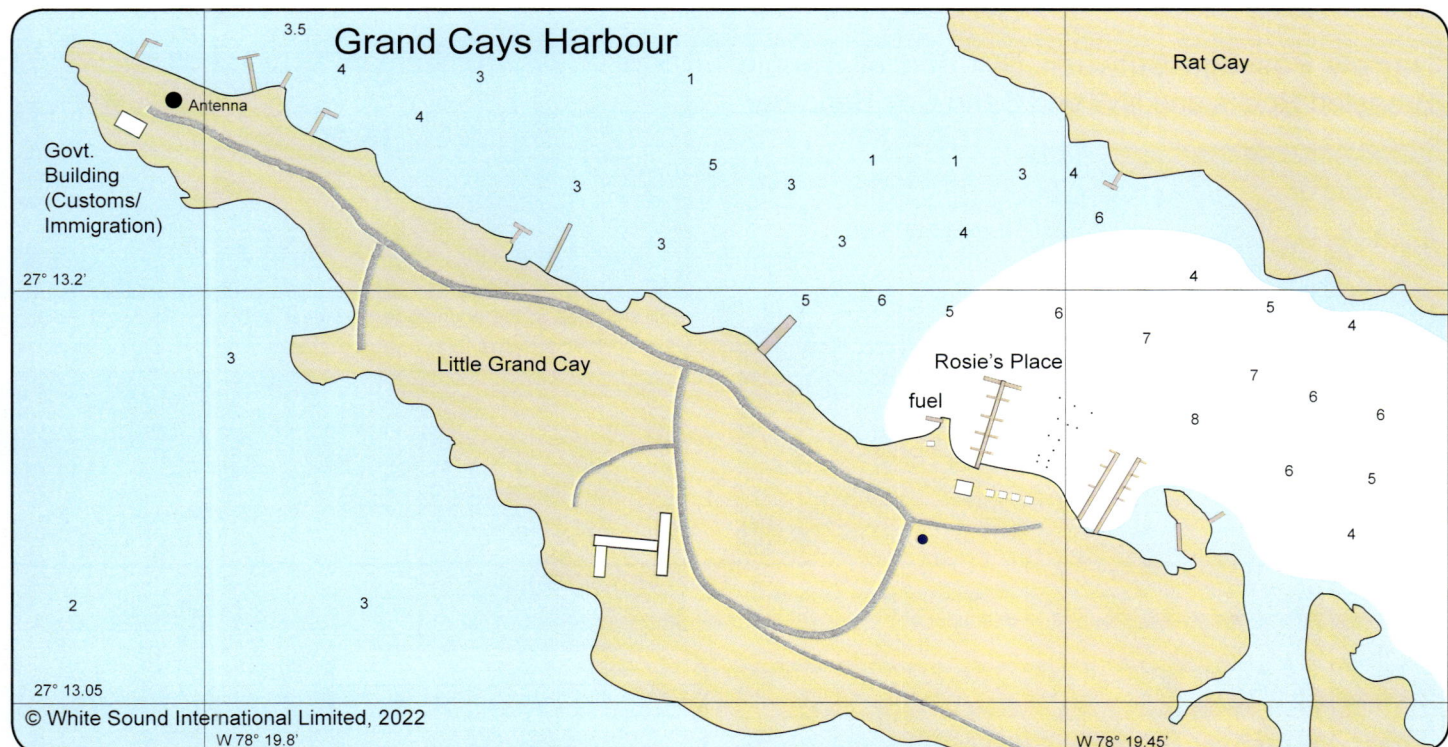

Grand Cays Harbour accommodates about 6' draft at mean low water. Deepest water for entry is just SW of Felix Cay (see chart on facing page) and continues to favour the NE side until reaching the harbour itself where there is deep water (6'-7') to the docks at Rosie's Place. The SW side of the harbour beyond Rosie's Place carries 3'-5' and will accommodate many outboard powered boats.

Page 32

Double Breasted Cays

From the waypoint DBLBRE head toward the long narrow Double Breasted Rock to the NE (52° M). There is a settled weather anchorage in the lee of this long rock. For more protection turn to the NW and go to the anchorage SW of Sand Cay. Favor the dark water just NE of the shallow white bar extending from Sand Cay. At the NW end of the Double Breasted Rocks there is a strong current, and the deepest water (about 5-6' MLW) is about 60' off the rock—execute during slack water or flow to avoid being pushed onto the rock. An alternative route to this beautiful anchorage is to approach from the NW from Grand Cays on the course line shown which is on a range between the SE point of Big Grand Cay and Long Rock (approx. 113° M). When you reach about W 78° 16.800' longitude make a wide sweeping turn to the S and SW. Leave the white patch to starboard. This is an area of shifting sand bores—watch for shoal spots. We now suggest to enter the protected area close to Rosy Kerb Rocks; there is usually a strong current here. The old entrance close to Double Breasted Rocks was still viable but has become very narrow in recent years. Note this is a recent change and may continue to vary. Proceed to the anchorage leaving the large shallow bar to port. Controlling depth for this approach is about 6' MLW. There are viable anchorages between the Double Breasted Cays and the Double Breasted Rocks. Round the SE end of Double Breasted Rocks by staying close to the shore for about 6-7' MLW. Access to the NW sector between Double Breasted Cays and Double Breasted Rocks is best gained from the northwest with good visibility.

Narrow Passage Between NW end of Double Breasted Rocks and NW end Sand Cay Sand Bar

1 - Approach from SE; best to attempt at slack water just before high tide.

2 - Best route is just to west of second dark spot

3 - Almost abeam second dark spot.

4 - After passing northern extremity of the sand bar, turn to port and head for the anchorage.

Four sailboats in the anchorage northeast of Double Breasted Rocks at Double Breasted Cays.

Sand Cay anchorage a Double Breasted Cays from the WNW

Double Breasted Cays is clearly one of the most beautiful pristine places in the Bahamas. It is a place you will never forget. Double Breasted Cays from the south, 27 May 2011, Photo by Steve Dodge

Double Breasted Cays from the northwest, 26 July 2010
Photo by Steve Dodge

Strangers Cay Channel and Anchorage

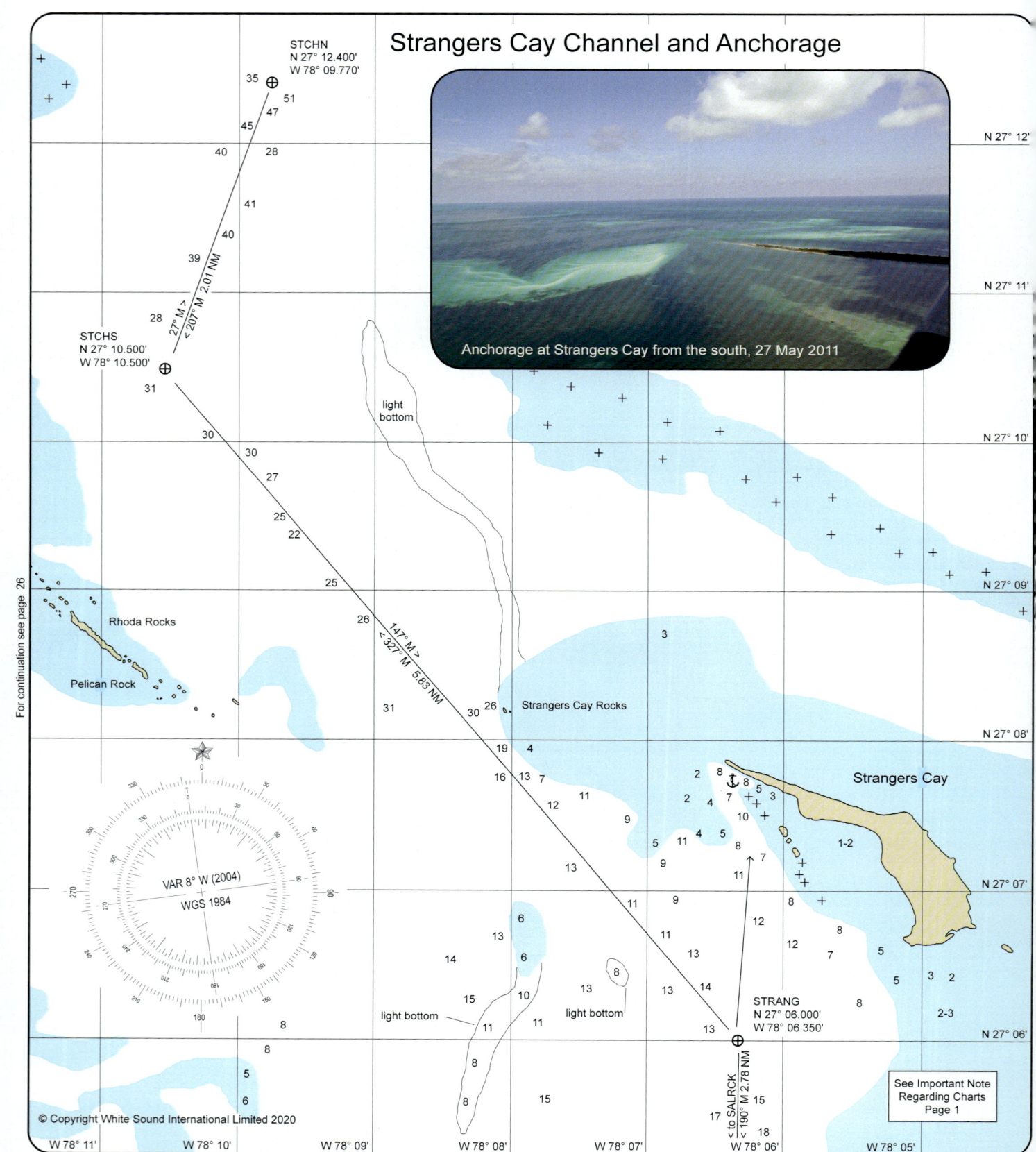

Anchorage at Strangers Cay from the south, 27 May 2011

STRANGERS CAY

Strangers Channel is a deep and wide route between the Sea of Abaco and the Atlantic Ocean. It is not frequently used because Strangers Cay has no development and only a marginal anchorage. The channel is remote from Bahamian communities, secure anchorages and marinas. The waypoints and routes should keep one in deep water, but please remember to keep a sharp lookout for stray coral heads (we looked, but found none close to the routes).

The anchorage at Strangers can be approached from the waypoint STRANG. The shoal water on both sides should be clearly visible. The anchorage is in 8' MLW, but it is small and completely exposed to winds from SSE to NW. Use it as a daytime anchorage, or stay overnight in settled weather. There are some nice beaches on the NE side of the cay, but the anchorage presents only a rocky shoreline.

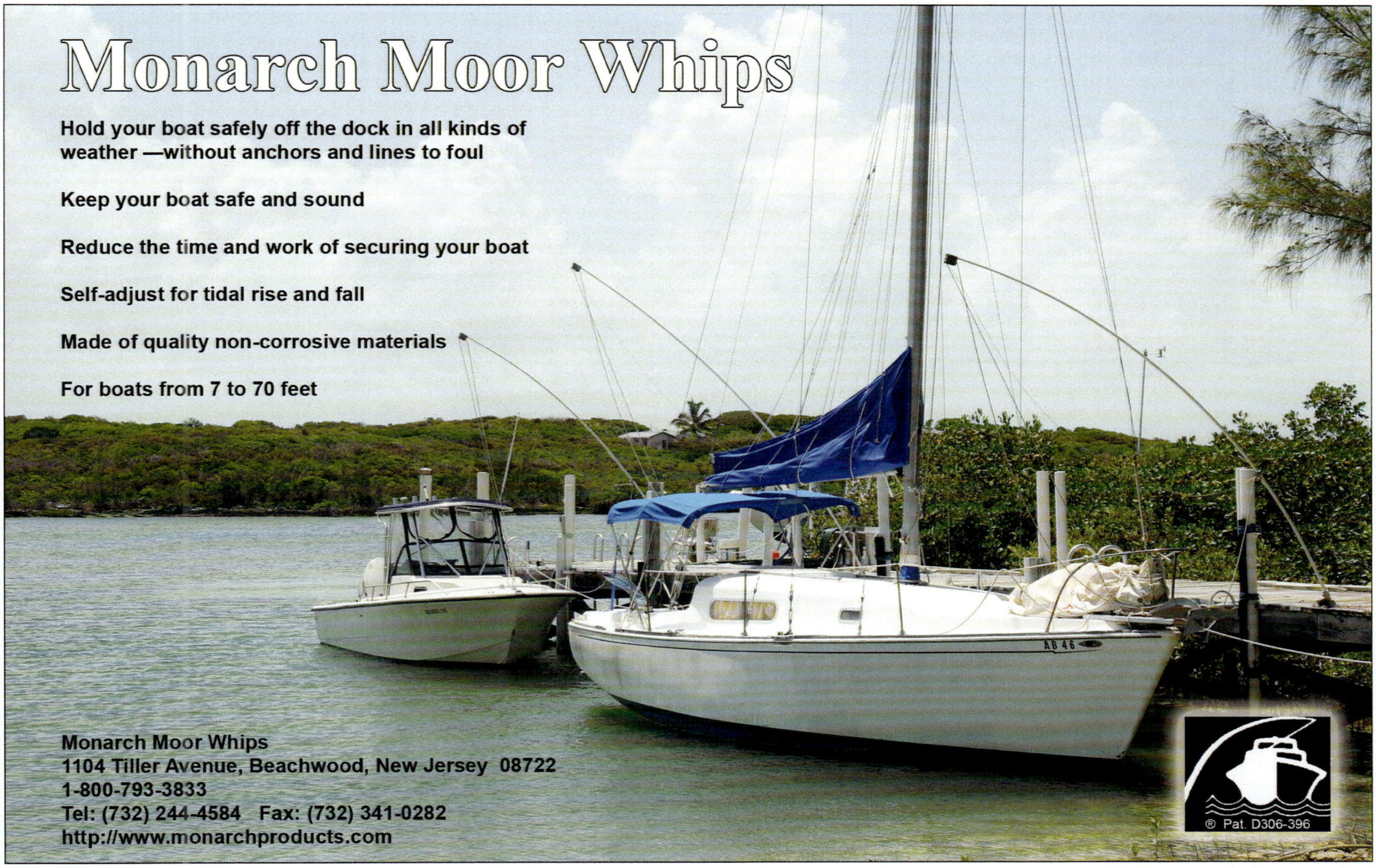

Monarch Moor Whips

Hold your boat safely off the dock in all kinds of weather —without anchors and lines to foul

Keep your boat safe and sound

Reduce the time and work of securing your boat

Self-adjust for tidal rise and fall

Made of quality non-corrosive materials

For boats from 7 to 70 feet

Monarch Moor Whips
1104 Tiller Avenue, Beachwood, New Jersey 08722
1-800-793-3833
Tel: (732) 244-4584   Fax: (732) 341-0282
http://www.monarchproducts.com

® Pat. D306-396

If you want it, we have it.

ABACOBUZZ.COM

UP TO DATE "GO TO" SITE, LIVE 24/7.
FOR EVERYTHING AND ANYTHING IN ABACO.

info@abacobuzz.com

ABACO GLOW

Photo by KP Carroll

The crew of Abaco Glow would like to wish Godspeed and good luck to the people who are rebuilding their homes, businesses, and lives in the Bahamas. Our thoughts and prayers are with everyone dealing with the aftermath of Dorian and Covid-19.

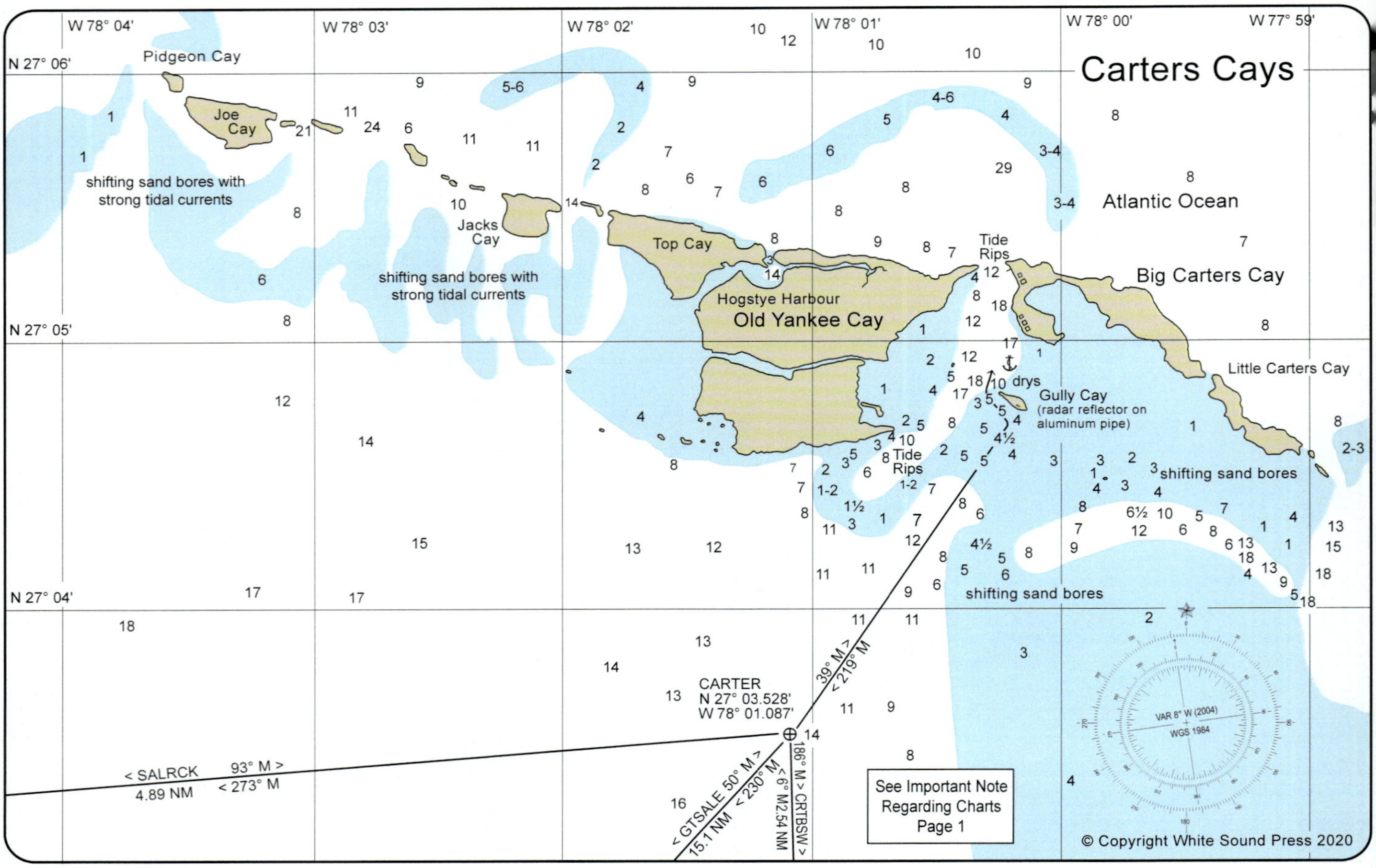

Carters Cays

Proceed from the waypoint CARTER toward the marker on Gully Cay (a radar reflector on an aluminum pipe - not vertical, leaning) on a course of about 39° M. The approach had a controlling depth of 4½' MLW when last surveyed in July 2019. When about 50' off Gully Cay turn to port and head roughly NW until clear of the end of Gully Cay. Anchor between Gully Cay and Big Carters Cay to avoid the swift current which runs in the main part of Carters Cay Harbour. The anchorage area is not large, and shoals rapidly as you go east. An alternative entrance across the bar on the SW side of the "harbour" carries only about 2-3' MLW and is less desirable because of stronger current flows and shifting sand. Big Carters Cay has some temporary houses on the SW point which are inhabited during the crawfishing season, and it has the remnants of a US missile tracking station and helicopter landing pad. A small hurricane hole called Hogstye Harbour is located between Old Yankee Cay and Top Cay. The entrance carries 3' MLW; there is 14' inside.

Joe Cay and Jack's Cay along with several smaller cays and rocks lie to the west of Old Yankee and Top Cays. Very strong tidal currents run through the openings between them and large sand bars have built up to the south of these openings and cays, making beautiful settled weather anchorages which of course require Bahamian moors because of the strong reversing tidal flows. Some cruisers who have found these beautiful sand banks return to them every year. The sand bores change frequently so we have made no attempt to chart them accurately. Good visibility and slack water is probably essential for first timers here. In good weather entry to the inside anchorages can be made from the ocean side—again, slack water is desirable.

Carters Cays from the SSE with boats in the anchorage. Gully Cay is in the foreground, Big Carters Cay on the right, the east tip of Old Yankee Cay on the left, and the Atlantic Ocean in the back. By anchoring on the extreme east side of the cut, the boats have avoided the strongest current in the center.

This is the deep cut between Top Cay and Jacks Cay in the Carter Cays area viewed from the north, or Atlantic Ocean side. These complex sand banks are built by strong tidal current flows through openings between cays (called cuts or passages in Abaco and often inlets in the US) along the edge of the Little and Great Bahama Banks. These areas are usually volatile because storms combined with strong current flows can move tons of sand in just a few hours. A single boat has found a private and serene anchorage here. Photo by Steve Dodge, 27 May 2011.

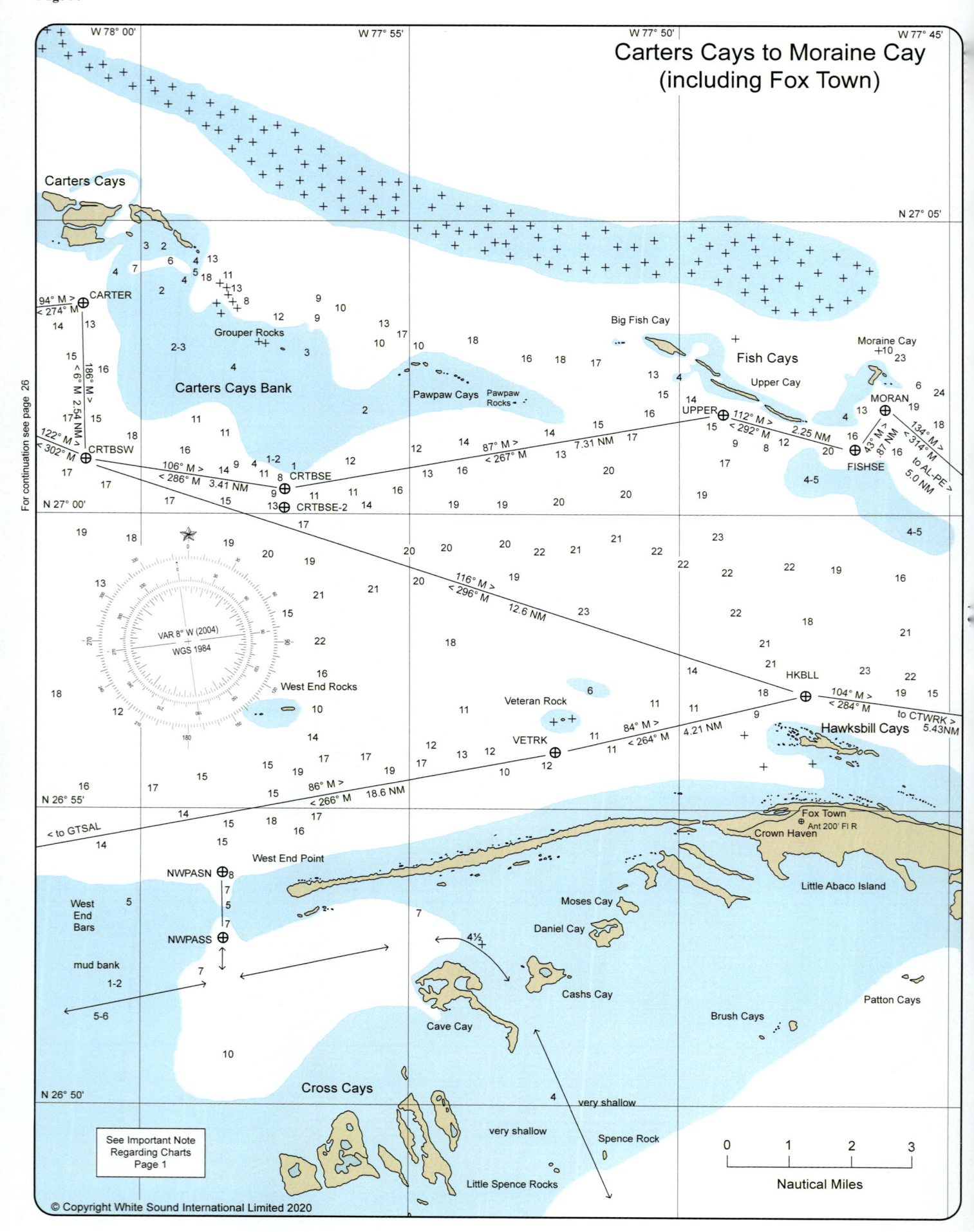

Carters Cays to Moraine Cay (including Fox Town)

CARTERS CAYS TO MORAINE CAY (including Fox Town)

Boats transiting this area from Carters Cays to Moraine Cay or beyond must avoid the Carters Cays Bank and also the shoals stretching southeast from the Fish Cays. Waypoints for a suggested route are shown on the chart, and coordinates are printed below.

The preferred route from the Carters Cays to the Fish Cays requires a detour to the south around the Carters Cay Bank, which extends about 7 nautical miles ESE from the Carters Cays. There are several islets and rocks along its northern edge—the Pawpaw Rocks, the Pawpaw Cays, and Grouper Rocks. It is possible to go on the Atlantic side of the bank, but access to Carters Cays is more difficult from this side because of the shifting sand bank south of Big and Little Carters Cays, so the Sea of Abaco route is generally better. Please note that the waypoint CRTBSE is only about .25 NM from the edge of Carters Cays Bank. During the past ten years several cruisers have reported that Carters Bank has expanded and moved closer to the waypoint. We do check this waypoint and the bank each year, and we have found that the edge of the bank has **not** moved south. The edge of the bank is shallower than it used to be—it now consists of a series of ridges which are only about 1'-2' deep at MLW (a couple of years ago it was 3' MLW). The waypoint CRTBSE is a good waypoint located over 1500' away from the edge of the bank, but because it has led to some discomfort, we have added waypoint CRTBSE-2 to the chart. It is located about .6 NM south of the tip of the bank. Those who wish to stay a little further from Carters Bank should substitute CRTBSE-2 for CRTBSE. Anchorages can be found at the Fish Cays (for more detail see p. 40) and Moraine Cay (see page 42).

Boats transiting the southern portion of the chart are also provided with GPS waypoints. The suggested route passes south of Veteran Rock and West End Rocks, and north of the Hawksbill Cays. West End Rocks are generally plainly seen, but Veteran Rock is low-lying and difficult to see—we passed it several times going back and forth from Abaco to Florida before we saw it. Pay close attention and keep a sharp lookout when near it.

Along this route the only reasonable stop is Fox Town, which is on Little Abaco Island south of the Hawksbill Cays. See the large scale chart on page 41. Go west of the outermost rocks extending from Hawksbill Cays and proceed SE toward Fox Town. Avoid taking the western "short cut" when approaching or leaving Fox Town from the west because of several submerged rocks and heads in this area. Fuel, groceries and restaurants are all available at Fox Town. Anchor off or tie up at Fox Town Shell. It is also possible to anchor just south of the Hawksbill Cays and dinghy over to Fox Town. This provides better protection from the north.

Note that approximate course lines are provided for the Cave Cay/Spence Rock route to the Bight of Abaco. Give West End Point a 4.5 mile berth (off chart to west) to round West End Bars, then head for the northern tip of Cave Cay. Keep a sharp lookout and negotiate on a rising tide if you draw more than 4½'; controlling depth for this part of the route is about 5-6' MLW. A shorter route from the north to the south side of Little Abaco Island was recently found a little less than one nautical mile west of West End Point. Called the NW Pass, it carries 5' MLW over a hard rock and coral bottom. The course is true north and south (7°M/187°M). Waypoints are provided for it; attention should be given to cross track error. The route around the east side of Cave Cay and south to Spence Rock and the deeper waters of the Bight of Abaco will carry only about 4' MLW.

GPS waypoints for *Carters Cays to Moraine Cay*:

WPT	Description of Position	Latitude	Longitude
Northern route, west to east:			
CARTER	1 NM SSW Carters Cays	N 27° 03.528'	W 78° 01.087'
CRTBSW	SW Carters Bank	N 27° 00.994'	W 78° 01.049'
CRTBSE	SE corner of Carters Bank	N 27° 00.440'	W 77° 57.277'
CRTBSE-2	.6 NM S of SE corner Crts Bk	N 27° 00.080'	W 77° 57.277'
UPPER	¼ NM S Upper Cay	N 27° 01.683'	W 77° 49.210'
FISHSE	1 NM SE Fish Cays	N 27° 01.085'	W 77° 46.779'
MORAN	½ NM S Moraine Cay	N 27° 01.781'	W 77° 46.201'

Southern route, west to east (This is a portion of route from Florida to Abaco; for the entire route see page 17):

WPT	Description	Latitude	Longitude
VETRK	½ NM S Veteran Rock	N 26° 55.950'	W 77° 52.290'
HKBLL	¼ NM N Hawksbill Cays	N 26° 56.890'	W 77° 47.690'

NW Pass waypoints:

WPT	Description	Latitude	Longitude
NWPASN	N end NW Pass	N 26° 53.900'	W 77° 58.150'
NWPASS	S end NW Pass	N 26° 52.830'	W 77° 58.150'

Veteran Rock is difficult to see from the surface. It lies about halfway between Hawksbill Cays and West End Rocks, both of which are easily seen. It is located about .5 NM north of waypoint VETRK. The waypoint is located here to minimize cross track error in this area. This photo taken from the NE in July 2007 shows the western extension of Little Abaco Island in the background.

Cave Cay and Cashs Cay from the south with western extension of Little Abaco Island in the background. The route to the back side of Abaco is between these two cays; it carries about 4- 4 ½' MLW. See the chart on the facing page.

Fish Cays (North)*

Three or four anchorages can be found here which offer protection from winds from a specific direction, but none of the anchorages are fully protected. They are for settled weather or daytime stops. The most protected is the 8' MLW hole between Upper Cay and the unnamed cay to the NW of it. Although deep, the anchorage is small, and the entry to it carries only 3-4' MLW so many cruising boats will need tide help to enter and to leave. Strong tidal currents flow between these cays. There are some small beaches on the northern side of Upper Cay and the unnamed cay, and another beach in the bight at the SE end of Big Fish Cay.

See Important Note Regarding Charts Page 1

UPPER
N 27° 01.683'
W 77° 49.210'

FISHSE
N 27° 01.085'
W 77° 46.779'

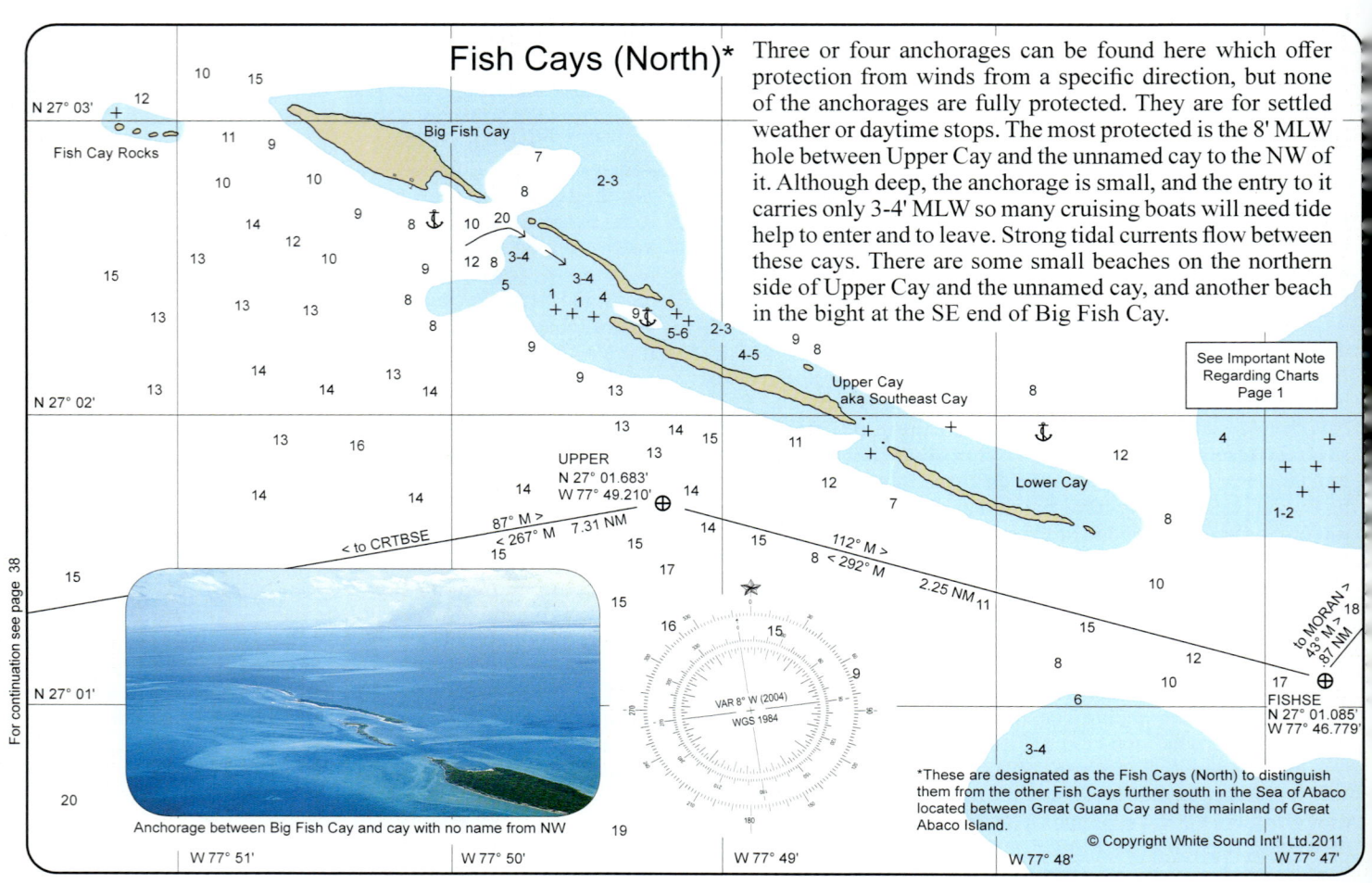

VAR 8° W (2004)
WGS 1984

*These are designated as the Fish Cays (North) to distinguish them from the other Fish Cays further south in the Sea of Abaco located between Great Guana Cay and the mainland of Great Abaco Island.

© Copyright White Sound Int'l Ltd. 2011

Anchorage between Big Fish Cay and cay with no name from NW

Crown Haven on Little Abaco Island with Foxtown and Hawksbill Cay in the background. Photo by Steve Dodge, 27 May 2011.

Hawksbill Cays and Fox Town

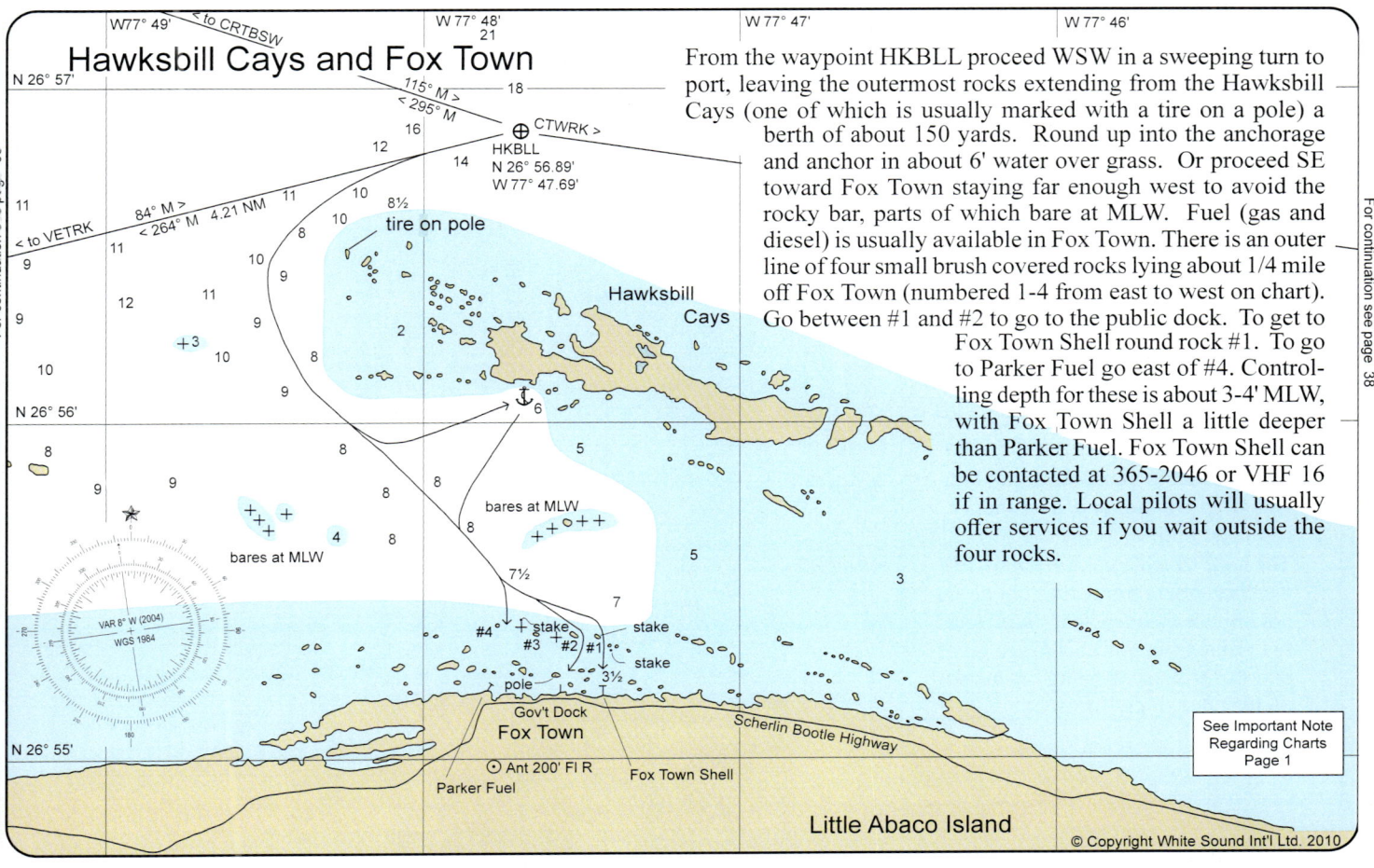

From the waypoint HKBLL proceed WSW in a sweeping turn to port, leaving the outermost rocks extending from the Hawksbill Cays (one of which is usually marked with a tire on a pole) a berth of about 150 yards. Round up into the anchorage and anchor in about 6' water over grass. Or proceed SE toward Fox Town staying far enough west to avoid the rocky bar, parts of which bare at MLW. Fuel (gas and diesel) is usually available in Fox Town. There is an outer line of four small brush covered rocks lying about 1/4 mile off Fox Town (numbered 1-4 from east to west on chart). Go between #1 and #2 to go to the public dock. To get to Fox Town Shell round rock #1. To go to Parker Fuel go east of #4. Controlling depth for these is about 3-4' MLW, with Fox Town Shell a little deeper than Parker Fuel. Fox Town Shell can be contacted at 365-2046 or VHF 16 if in range. Local pilots will usually offer services if you wait outside the four rocks.

For continuation see page 38

See Important Note Regarding Charts Page 1

© Copyright White Sound Int'l Ltd. 2010

Fox Town

BRIGITTE Bowyer CAREY

Watercolours & Acrylics

bowyerart@gmail.com
watercolours.faso.com
fb: Island Watercolors-Brigitte Bowyer Carey

Moraine Cay

Proceed directly toward the midpoint of the beach on Moraine Cay from the waypoint MORAN and enter the anchorage in about 7-8' MLW. Anchor in about 6-7' MLW over grass. This reef protected anchorage offers protection from west, north, and east winds, but is fully exposed to the south. Moraine Cay is a delightful daytime or (good weather) overnight stop. The beach is just a few feet from the anchorage, and the reef to the east is pristine and beautiful. The island is private, and a residence has been built there by the owner. The reef, which breaks in almost all weather, offers protection but does not impede the view to the east, and the vistas from this anchorage give one the feeling of being anchored on the edge of civilization.

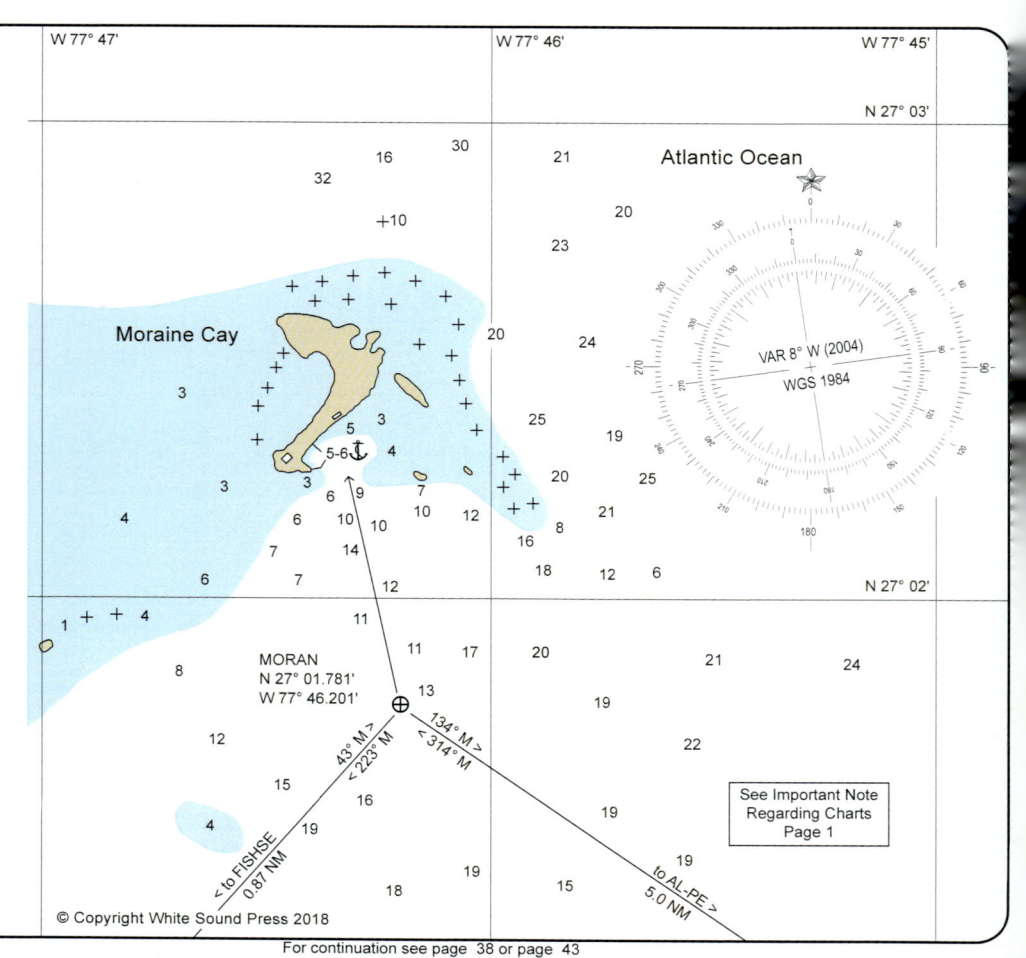

For continuation see page 38 or page 43

Moraine Cay from the SSW 11 July 2002.

Moraine Cay to Spanish Cay

GPS Waypoints:
FISHSE	N 27° 01.085'	W 77° 46.779'
MORAN	N 27° 01.781'	W 77° 46.201'
AL-PE	N 26° 58.796'	W 77° 41.708'
CRABCY	N 26° 56.271'	W 77° 37.000'
AFISH	N 26° 55.810'	W 77° 34.860'
CTWRK	N 26° 56.190'	W 77° 41.660'
SPAN-N	N 26° 58.169'	W 77° 32.192'
SPANSH	N 26° 55.245'	W 77° 32.578'

© Copyright White Sound Press 2018

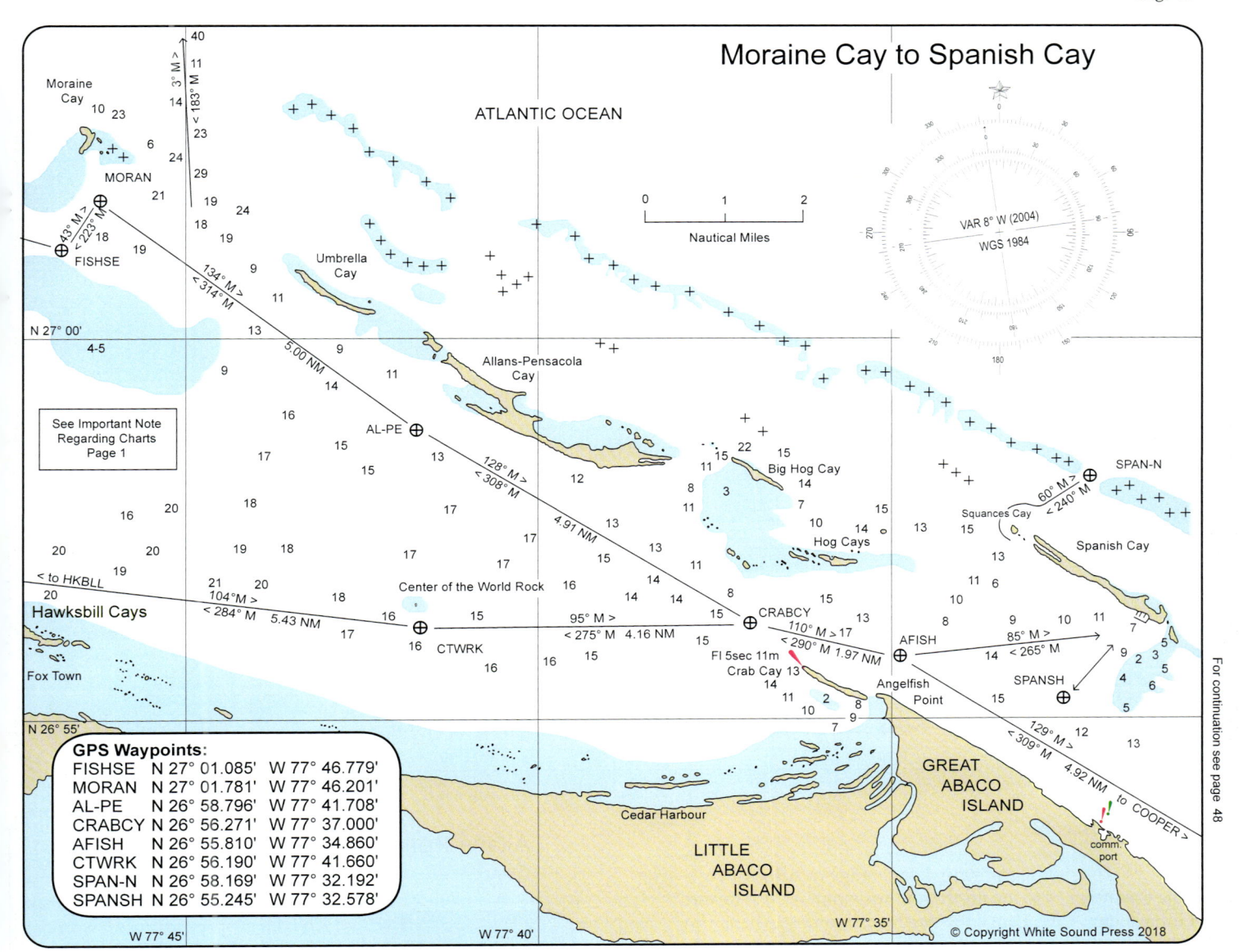

MORAINE CAY TO SPANISH CAY

Boats transiting this area need to avoid three shoal areas: the first is a very large area which extends southeastward from the area of the Fish Cays, which are off the chart west of Moraine Cay, and stretches to the south of Moraine Cay, the second surrounds the Hog Cays, and the third lies south of the southeast point of Spanish Cay. Also, the north coastline of Little Abaco Island is shoal and sprinkled with small, low islets. One should stay a mile or two off shore. Fox Town is the only settlement on Little Abaco Island which has an anchorage for boats drawing over 1-2'. Center of the World Rock, lying about two miles north of Little Abaco Island, is about halfway between Crab Cay and Fox Town. It is marked with a white post.

Moraine Cay is a beautiful reef anchorage exposed from the southeast to southwest, but offering good protection in other winds. It has a beautiful beach and the reef offers excellent snorkeling. See the chart on page 42.

Allans-Pensacola has an abandoned missile tracking station, some nice beaches, and a good harbour at its northwest end. See the chart on page 44.

The Hog Cays are a group of small cays and rocks on a shallow bank, but there is deep water and a reasonable anchorage off the southwest corner of the southeasternmost cay. The very small harbour on the north side of this same cay has shoaled in recent years and is no longer viable for boats larger than outboards.

There is an anchorage protected from the east and south located southwest of Crab Cay. Round the northern end of the cay and go either side of a shoal area (2-5' MLW) running roughly parallel to Crab Cay. Anchor in 8' MLW just SW of the SE end of Crab Cay. There are no beaches and no development in this area, but plenty of small islets and shallow water for dinghy exploration (see the chart on page 45).

Spanish Cay has a large full service marina with a well-stocked store, resort accommodations ashore, restaurant, bar, pool, beautiful beaches, an airstrip and friendly service. See page 46 for more detailed information about Spanish Cay.

Support the Bahamas Air-Sea Rescue Association.

You are not required to take an active part in BASRA.

Send $40.00 for one year's membership dues to:
BASRA ABACO, Hope Town, Abaco, Bahamas

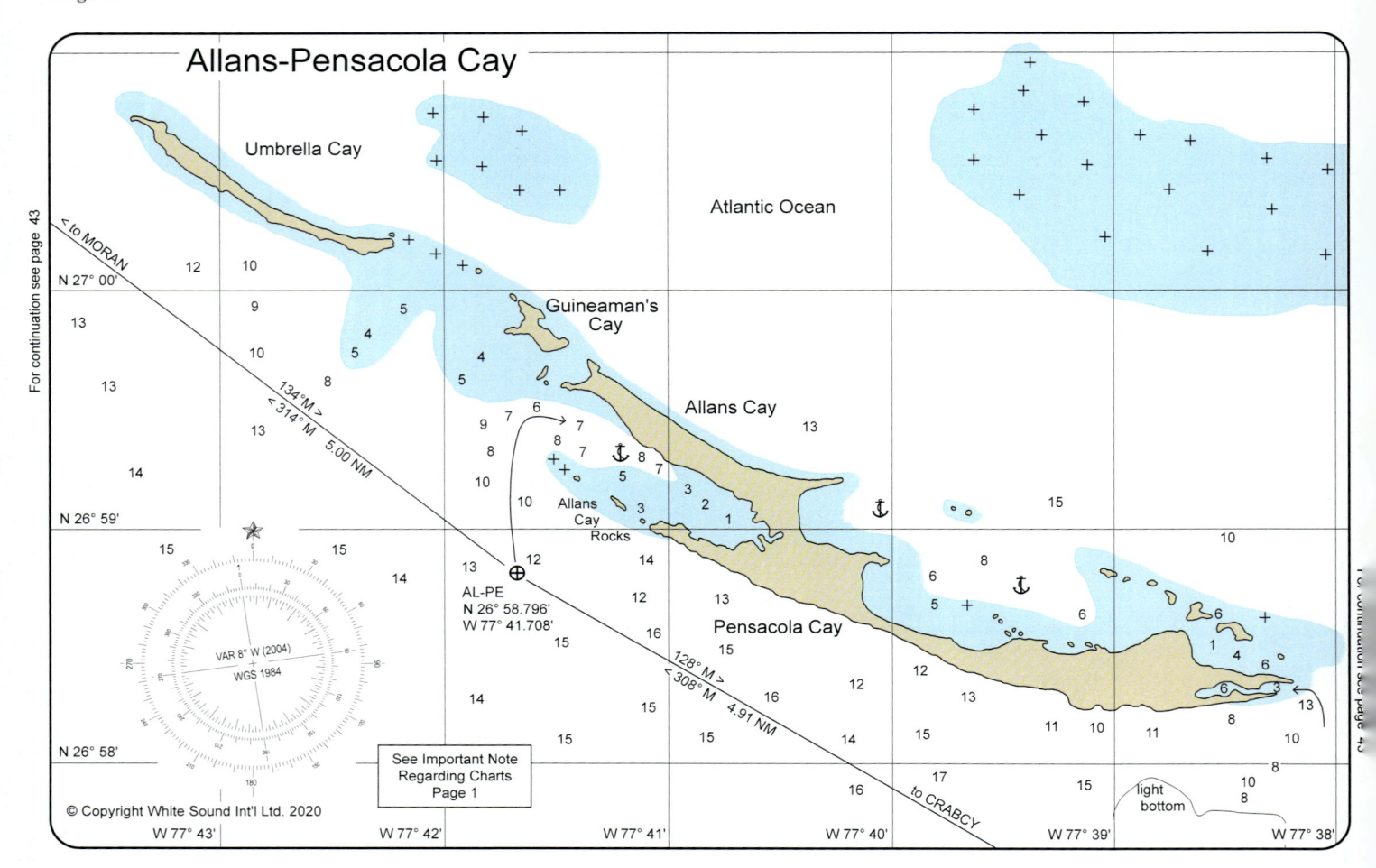

Allans-Pensacola Cay

To enter the principal anchorage at Allans-Pensacola Cay proceed to the north from waypoint AL-PE toward Guineaman's Cay. Leave the northwesternmost Allans Cay Rock about 75 yards to starboard to avoid the submerged rocks and bar extending from it, and then turn to starboard into the harbour favouring the northeast side. Anchor in 7-8' over grass and sand which is over marl. The holding ground is not the best. Allans-Pensacola's popularity is based on the easy access and good protection in all winds except W and NW. For winds in this sector, shelter can be found on the Atlantic Ocean side of the cay (see anchorages indicated on chart), but these will be exposed and unsafe if or when the NW wind clocks to the N and NE as it usually does during the winter months.

Within the past few decades Allans Cay and Pensacola Cay were two separate cays. They were joined as the result of a hurricane, and now seem to be permanently a single cay—Allans-Pensacola. The ruins of a United States missile tracking station can be found on the isthmus at the head of the harbour, which is also the site of the best beach on the island. There is a "signing tree" on the ocean beach northeast of the anchorage, where cruisers have left signed momentos of their visit here.

There is complete protection in the very small mangrove-lined hurricane hole at the east end of the cay. Controlling depth in the small creek is about 3' MLW in several places (favour the south side)—there is 6' MLW inside.

Allans-Pensacola Cay in May 2003.

CRAB CAY / ANGELFISH POINT

The anchorage at Crab Cay / Angelfish Point offers excellent protection for all winds except NW through W. It is a pleasant normally empty anchorage off a pretty beach with low scubby rocks on the western side. Enter on either side of the shoal from the waypoint CRABCY. Off this chart to the south the water narrows and ends at a causeway built to support the road connecting Great Abaco Island to Little Abaco Island. It is generally believed that this causeway has caused environmental damage, and the Bahamian government has announced that it will replace the causeway, which blocks water flow from the Sea of Abaco to the waters west of Great Abaco Island, with a bridge. When this project is completed it is likely that there will be a strong current through this area which may make a Bahamian Moor a necessity.

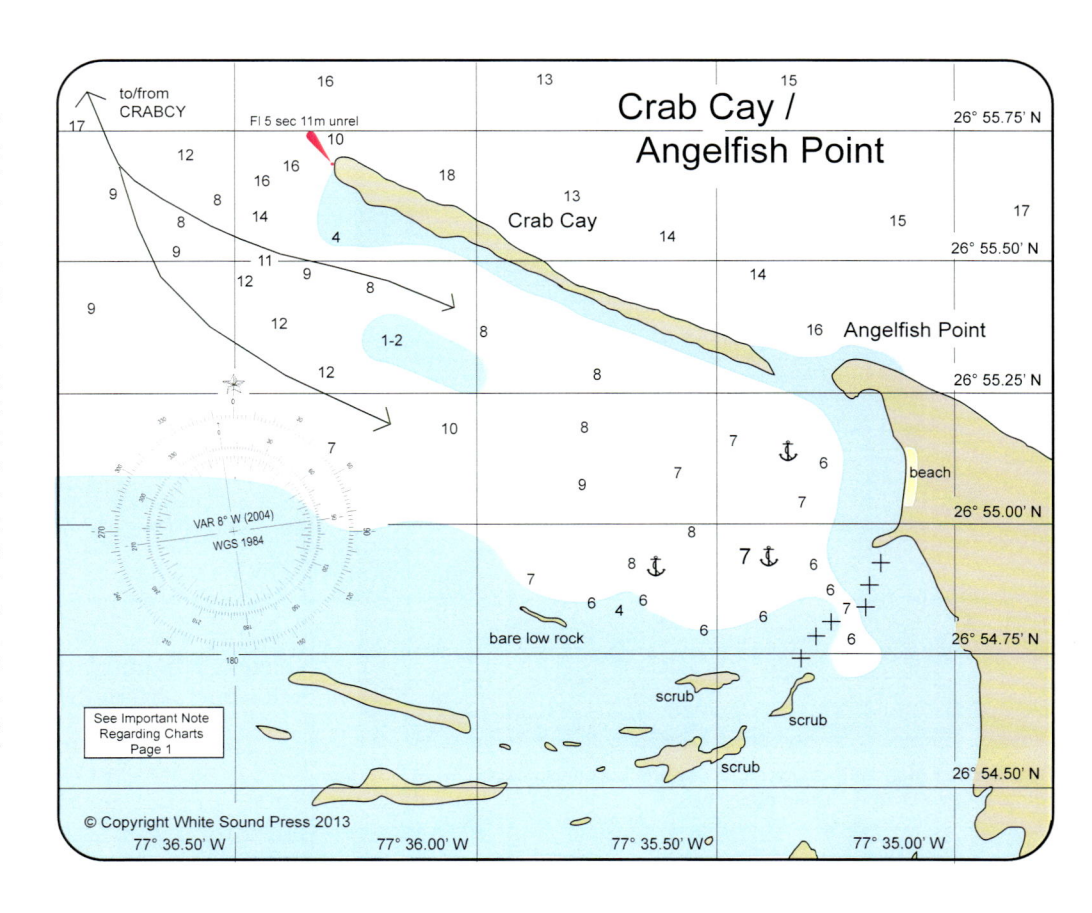

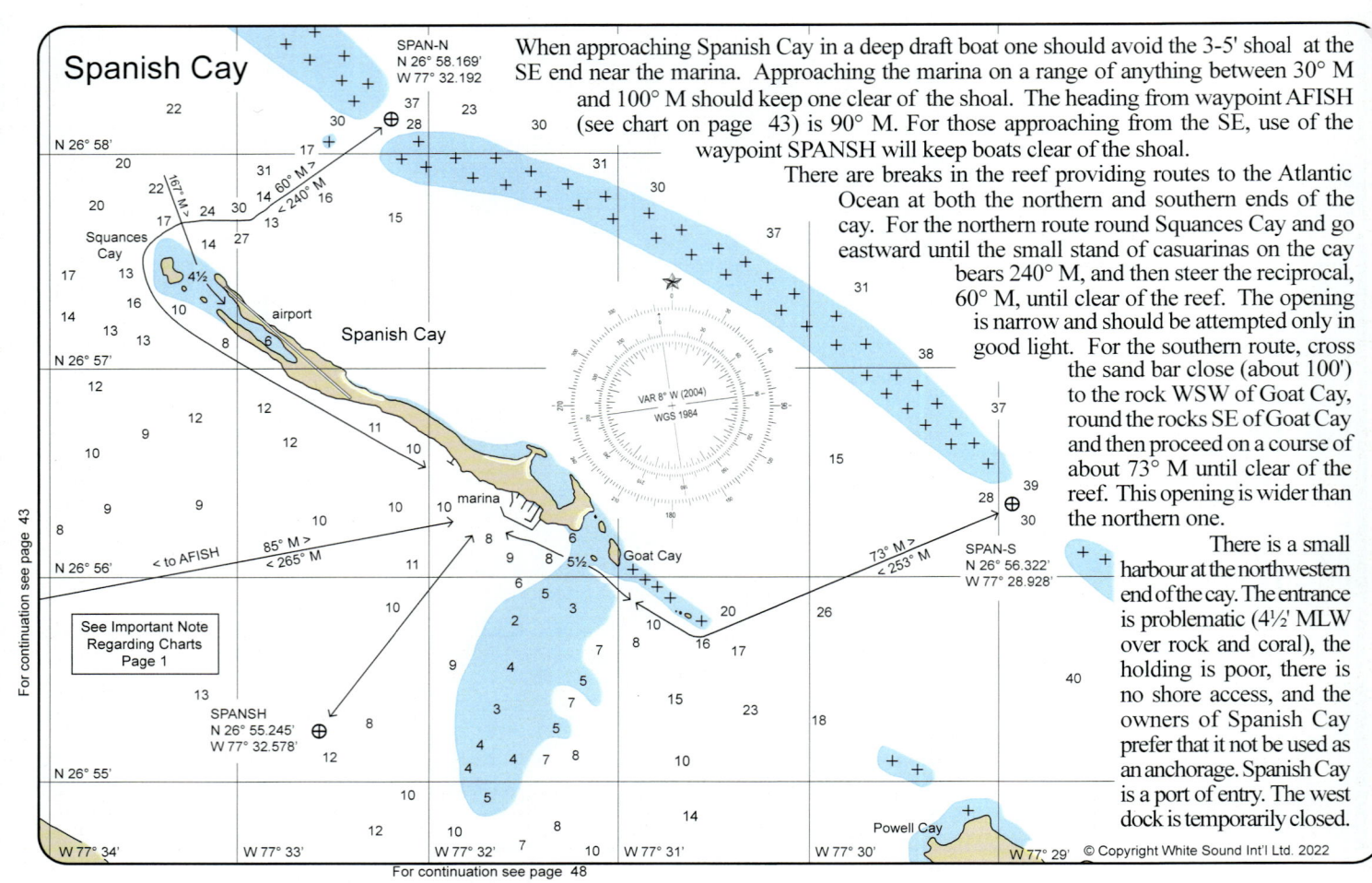

Spanish Cay

When approaching Spanish Cay in a deep draft boat one should avoid the 3-5' shoal at the SE end near the marina. Approaching the marina on a range of anything between 30° M and 100° M should keep one clear of the shoal. The heading from waypoint AFISH (see chart on page 43) is 90° M. For those approaching from the SE, use of the waypoint SPANSH will keep boats clear of the shoal.

There are breaks in the reef providing routes to the Atlantic Ocean at both the northern and southern ends of the cay. For the northern route round Squances Cay and go eastward until the small stand of casuarinas on the cay bears 240° M, and then steer the reciprocal, 60° M, until clear of the reef. The opening is narrow and should be attempted only in good light. For the southern route, cross the sand bar close (about 100') to the rock WSW of Goat Cay, round the rocks SE of Goat Cay and then proceed on a course of about 73° M until clear of the reef. This opening is wider than the northern one.

There is a small harbour at the northwestern end of the cay. The entrance is problematic (4½' MLW over rock and coral), the holding is poor, there is no shore access, and the owners of Spanish Cay prefer that it not be used as an anchorage. Spanish Cay is a port of entry. The west dock is temporarily closed.

Spanish Cay Marina Post Dorian, docks and buildings intact.
Photo by Lisa Dodge 3 December 2019

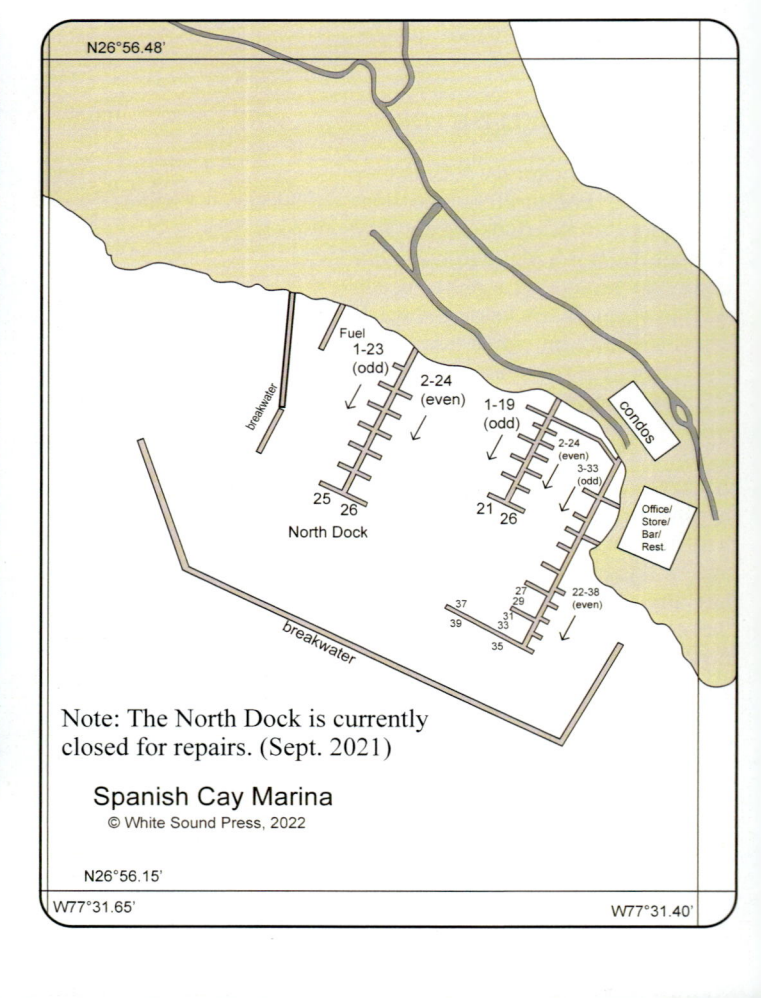

Note: The North Dock is currently closed for repairs. (Sept. 2021)

Spanish Cay Marina
© White Sound Press, 2022

Spanish Cay

Spanish Cay is a beautiful private island with a resort open to the boating world. Our facilities include 80 boat slips with full hook-ups, air conditioned bar and game room and a fresh water pool and spa. Come stay in one of our beach front rooms or marina condos. Rent a golf cart to visit our four white sand beaches. You can leave your boat at the Marina with our improved breakwater and have your pilot bring you back to paradise to our 5,000-foot asphalt airport runway. Spanish Cay is a port of entry, offering Customs and Immigration seven days a week. We offer both gas and diesel at our fuel dock. The Point House restaurant is open for breakfast lunch and dinner. There is also a grocery store and gift shop.

Marina: Water at low tide: 8½ - 9 feet. Power: 30; 50; 100; single & 3 phase. Water supply is by Reverse Osmosis. High speed Internet. Accommodation for boats up to 200 feet

Accommodations: Beachfront hotel rooms and marina condos - private homes also available

Spanish Cay   Abaco, Bahamas
1-242-807-0317 ~ 1-954-213-6195
spanishcay@aol.com   www.spanishcay.com
VHF 16

Photo by Ryan Wykoff

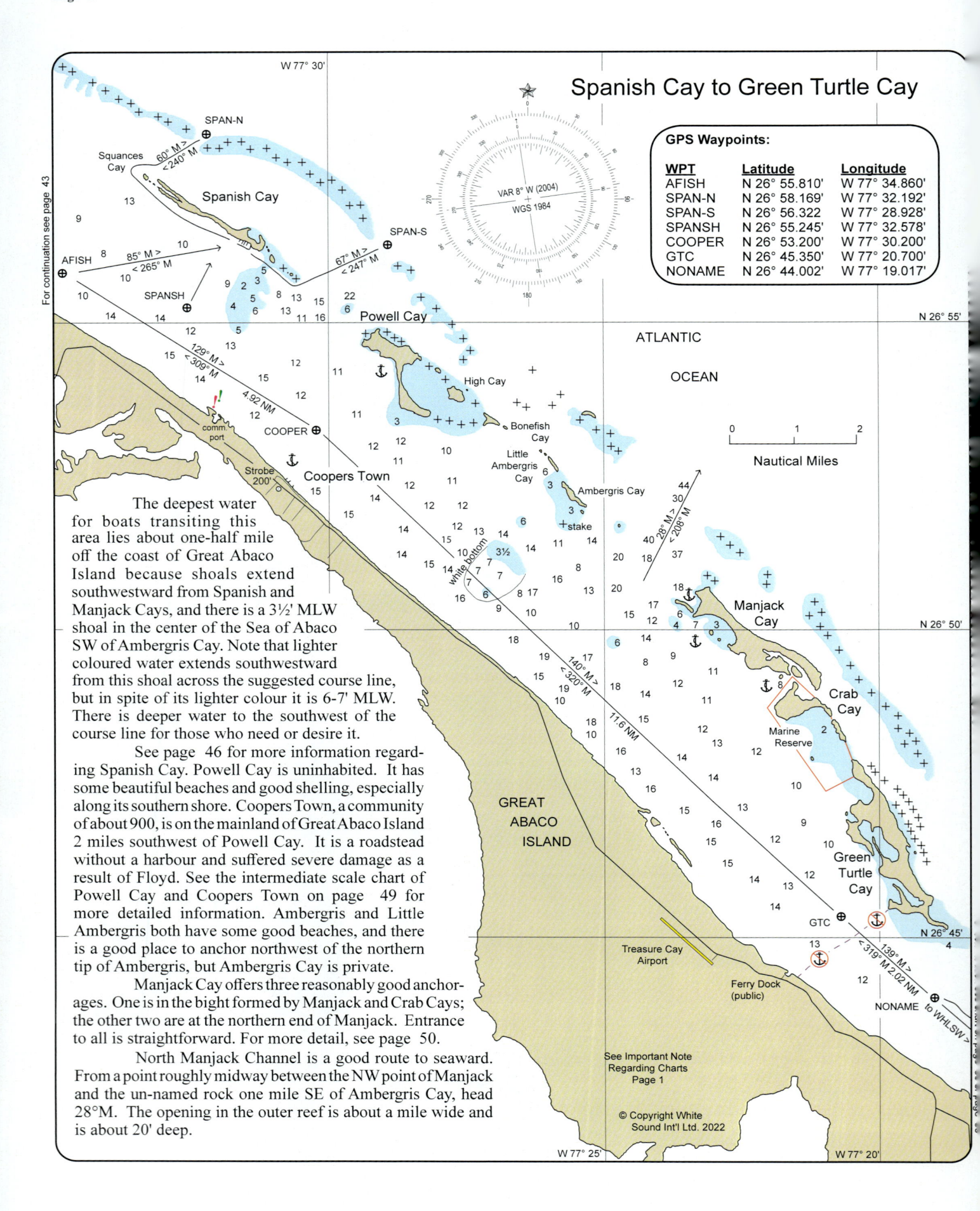

Spanish Cay to Green Turtle Cay

GPS Waypoints:

WPT	Latitude	Longitude
AFISH	N 26° 55.810'	W 77° 34.860'
SPAN-N	N 26° 58.169'	W 77° 32.192'
SPAN-S	N 26° 56.322'	W 77° 28.928'
SPANSH	N 26° 55.245'	W 77° 32.578'
COOPER	N 26° 53.200'	W 77° 30.200'
GTC	N 26° 45.350'	W 77° 20.700'
NONAME	N 26° 44.002'	W 77° 19.017'

VAR 8° W (2004)
WGS 1984

The deepest water for boats transiting this area lies about one-half mile off the coast of Great Abaco Island because shoals extend southwestward from Spanish and Manjack Cays, and there is a 3½' MLW shoal in the center of the Sea of Abaco SW of Ambergris Cay. Note that lighter coloured water extends southwestward from this shoal across the suggested course line, but in spite of its lighter colour it is 6-7' MLW. There is deeper water to the southwest of the course line for those who need or desire it.

See page 46 for more information regarding Spanish Cay. Powell Cay is uninhabited. It has some beautiful beaches and good shelling, especially along its southern shore. Coopers Town, a community of about 900, is on the mainland of Great Abaco Island 2 miles southwest of Powell Cay. It is a roadstead without a harbour and suffered severe damage as a result of Floyd. See the intermediate scale chart of Powell Cay and Coopers Town on page 49 for more detailed information. Ambergris and Little Ambergris both have some good beaches, and there is a good place to anchor northwest of the northern tip of Ambergris, but Ambergris Cay is private.

Manjack Cay offers three reasonably good anchorages. One is in the bight formed by Manjack and Crab Cays; the other two are at the northern end of Manjack. Entrance to all is straightforward. For more detail, see page 50.

North Manjack Channel is a good route to seaward. From a point roughly midway between the NW point of Manjack and the un-named rock one mile SE of Ambergris Cay, head 28°M. The opening in the outer reef is about a mile wide and is about 20' deep.

See Important Note Regarding Charts Page 1

© Copyright White Sound Int'l Ltd. 2022

Coopers Town and Powell Cay

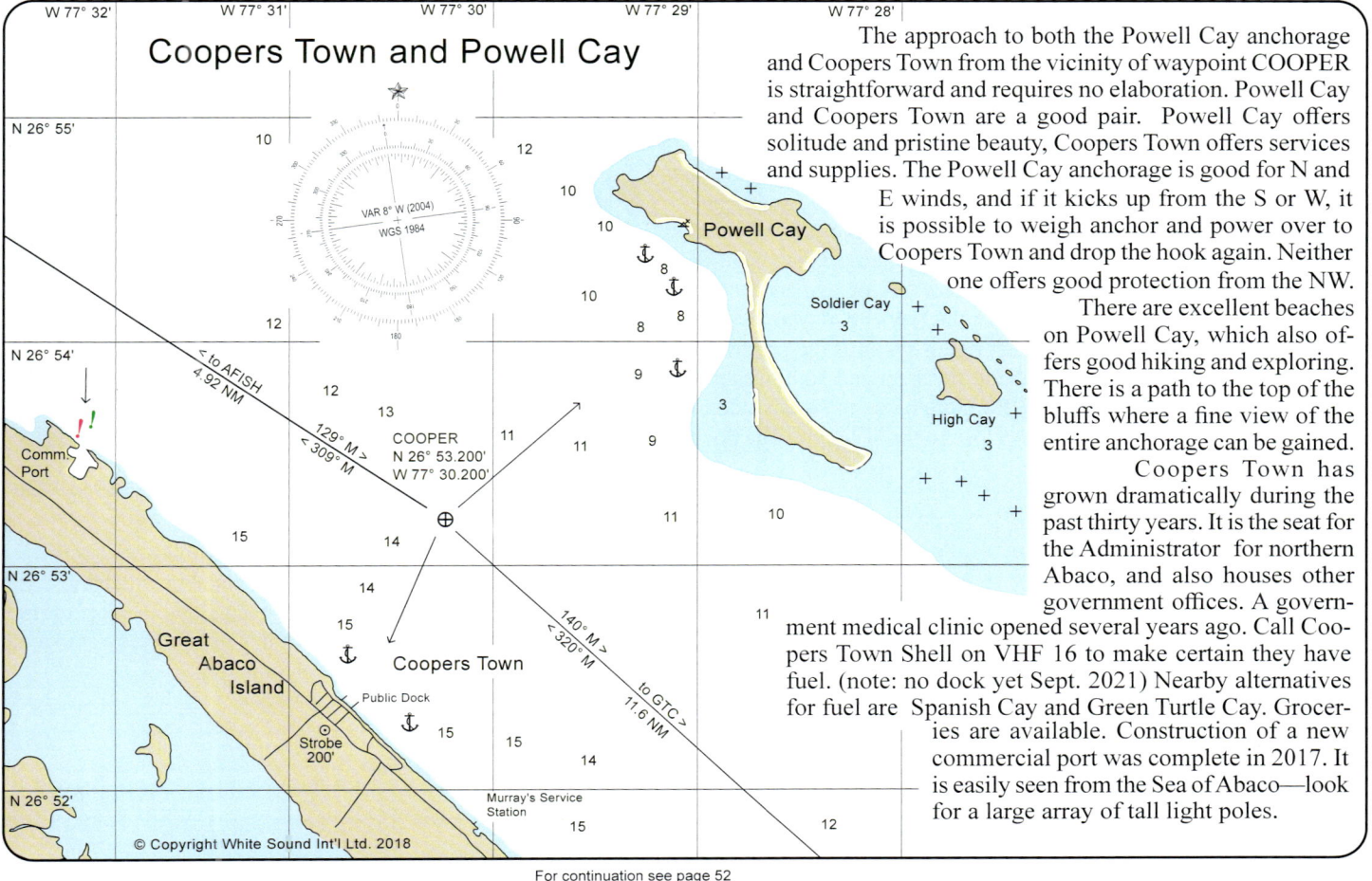

The approach to both the Powell Cay anchorage and Coopers Town from the vicinity of waypoint COOPER is straightforward and requires no elaboration. Powell Cay and Coopers Town are a good pair. Powell Cay offers solitude and pristine beauty, Coopers Town offers services and supplies. The Powell Cay anchorage is good for N and E winds, and if it kicks up from the S or W, it is possible to weigh anchor and power over to Coopers Town and drop the hook again. Neither one offers good protection from the NW.

There are excellent beaches on Powell Cay, which also offers good hiking and exploring. There is a path to the top of the bluffs where a fine view of the entire anchorage can be gained.

Coopers Town has grown dramatically during the past thirty years. It is the seat for the Administrator for northern Abaco, and also houses other government offices. A government medical clinic opened several years ago. Call Coopers Town Shell on VHF 16 to make certain they have fuel. (note: no dock yet Sept. 2021) Nearby alternatives for fuel are Spanish Cay and Green Turtle Cay. Groceries are available. Construction of a new commercial port was complete in 2017. It is easily seen from the Sea of Abaco—look for a large array of tall light poles.

For continuation see page 52

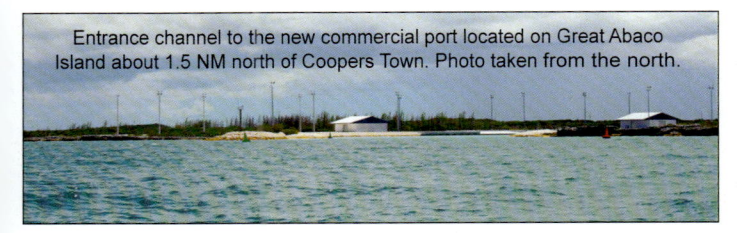

Entrance channel to the new commercial port located on Great Abaco Island about 1.5 NM north of Coopers Town. Photo taken from the north.

The new port north of Coopers Town.

Powell Cay from the north with a few boats in the anchorage. Coopers Town and Great Abaco Island can be seen in the background. Beyond Great Abaco is the Bight of Abaco.

Coopers Town from the southeast.

Manjack and Crab Cays

The large bight formed by Manjack (pronounced Munjack or sometimes Nunjack) and Crab Cays provides a delightful anchorage, though it is not protected from the south through the west. Entry is straightforward. Vessels drawing more than 4' should not go east of Rat Cay. The docks on the NW side of the anchorage are private. The mangrove creek is shallow, but is easily explored by dinghy at high tide. The beach along the northeast side of Manjack is pretty and there is some good diving and snorkeling just offshore. The two anchorages at the NW end of Manjack are both attractive. The northernmost one is open to the northwest and north, and the other is open to the west and southwest. A shallow rocky bar extends NW from the rocks at the SE side of the entrance to the latter, so stay close to the NW side. The dock

Several boats in the anchorage at Manjack and Crab Cays. This photo was taken from the SE. Generally boats drawing more than four feet should not go east of Rat Cay.

on the north side is part of a land development in which there are roads which lead to a very beautiful beach along the north shore of Manjack Cay. There is also a park in a mangrove swamp area and a nature walk. Visitors are welcome.

© Copyright White Sound Int'l Ltd. 2018

The anchorage at Manjack and Crab Cays from the northwest in 2004.

This is the limestone rock bluff near the southwest extremity of Crab Cay, and is typical of the limestone base of the Bahamian islands. The Bahama Banks were built of calcium carbonate over a period of 200 million years; they now tower about 1 1/2 miles above the floor of the sea. The calcium carbonate was extracted from the sea in a variety of ways, including the growth and death of shell fish, the growth of coral reefs, and the creation of oolitic sand. The present islands were built up higher than the rest of the banks when sea level was up to 100' higher than it is today. When the earth cooled and the polar ice caps re-formed, sea level declined leaving the limestone islands. Limestone is a soft rock which has been carved by the waves of the sea at the periphery of the islands and cays, dissolved by rainfall, and weathered by winds.

Green Turtle Cay

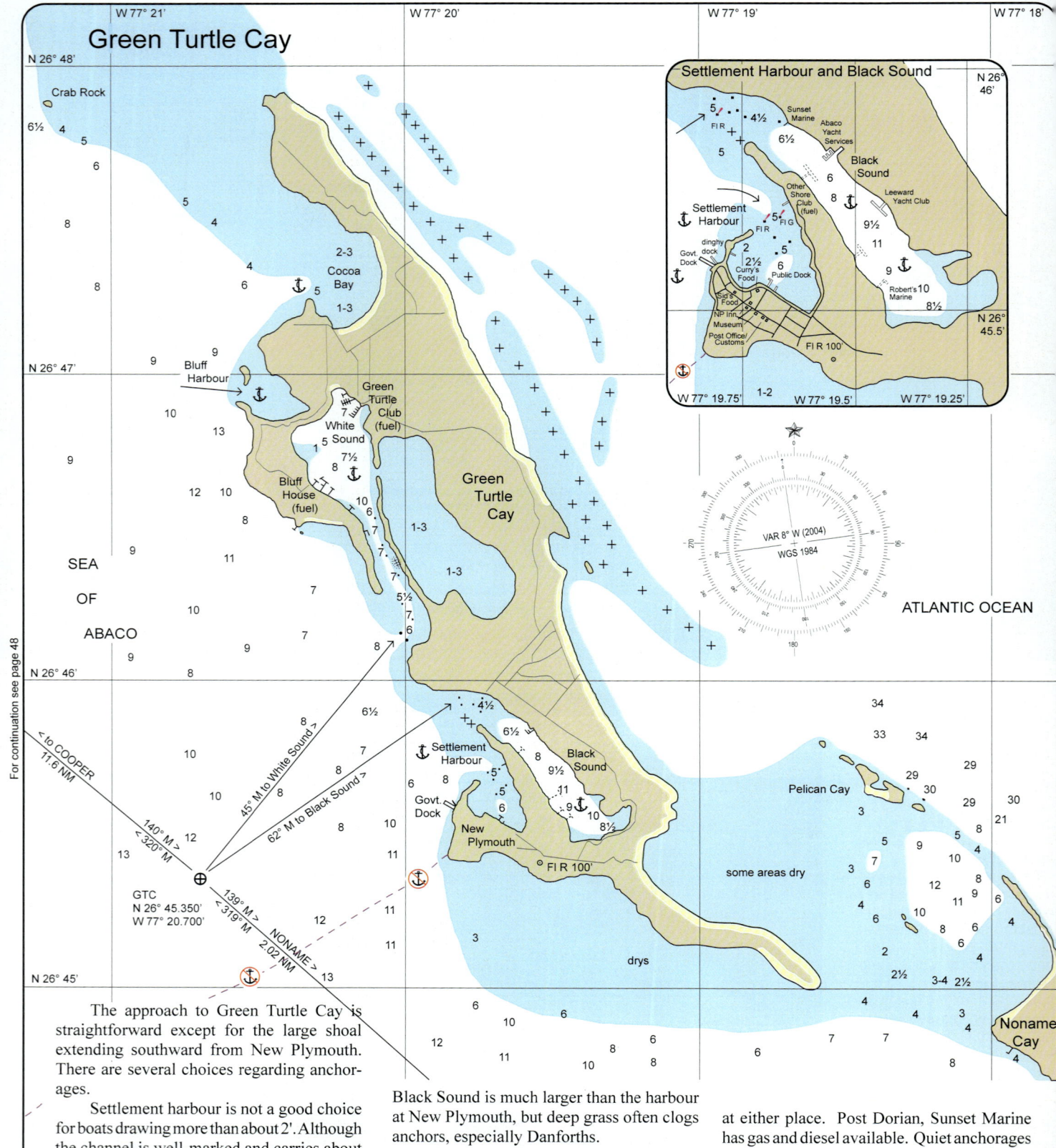

The approach to Green Turtle Cay is straightforward except for the large shoal extending southward from New Plymouth. There are several choices regarding anchorages.

Settlement harbour is not a good choice for boats drawing more than about 2'. Although the channel is well-marked and carries about 5', there is very little room inside. When it is possible to rely on easterly winds, boats often anchor in the area off the government dock rather than going into the harbour. This is not a good winter anchorage because it is exposed to the west and northwest.

The entrance to Black Sound carries about 4½-5' MLW. It is narrow but well-marked. Black Sound is much larger than the harbour at New Plymouth, but deep grass often clogs anchors, especially Danforths.

The dredged channel was widened and deepened in September 2013 and is still now about 40' wide with a controlling depth of 5½' MLW. Stay between the pairs of red and green buoys. A good anchorage can be found in the area between the Bluff House dock and the Green Turtle Club dock. Avoid the 1' MLW rocky shoal just north of the Bluff House docks. Dockage and fuel could usually be purchased at either place. Post Dorian, Sunset Marine has gas and diesel available. Quiet anchorages can be found further north at Bluff Harbour and Cocoa Bay, but Bluff Harbour is small and there is no public dinghy dock, and Cocoa Bay is shallow. See marina maps for Green Turtle Club and Bluff House on p. 54.

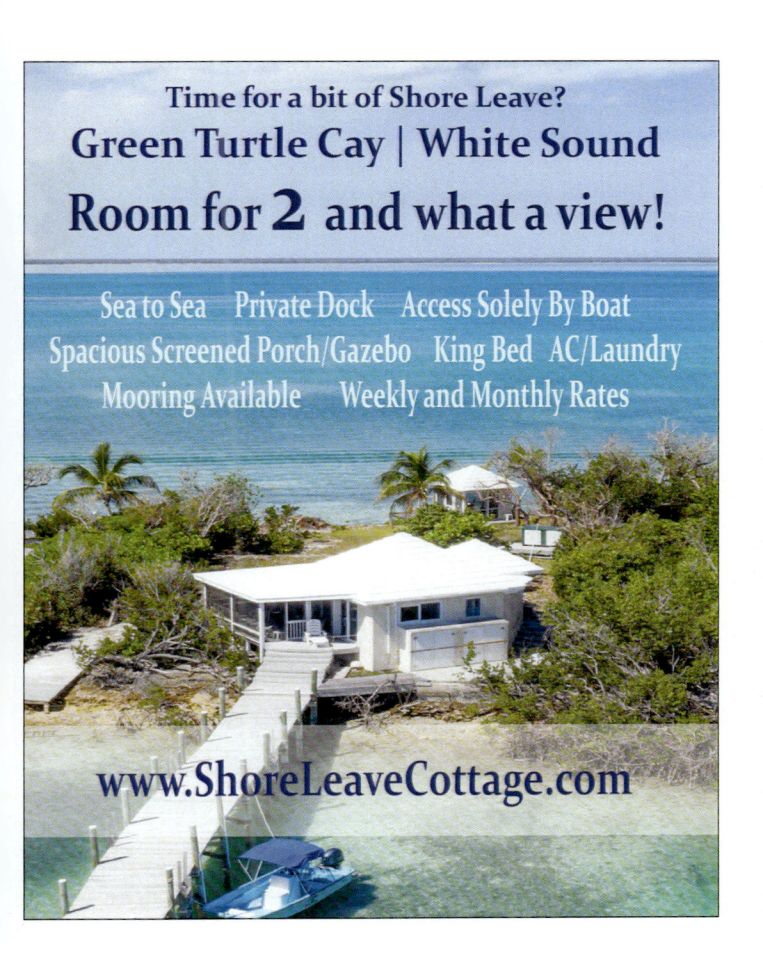

Time for a bit of Shore Leave?
Green Turtle Cay | White Sound
Room for 2 and what a view!

Sea to Sea   Private Dock   Access Solely By Boat
Spacious Screened Porch/Gazebo   King Bed   AC/Laundry
Mooring Available   Weekly and Monthly Rates

www.ShoreLeaveCottage.com

Green TurtleCay, Photo by Lisa Dodge October 2020

Approaches to Settlement Harbour, New Plymouth, Black Sound, and White Sound, Green Turtle Cay.

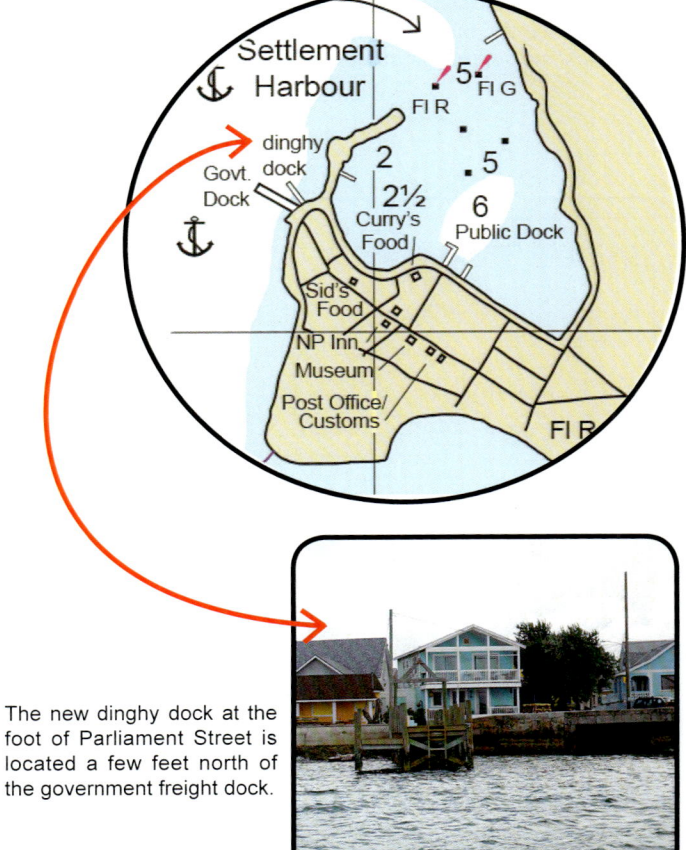

The new dinghy dock at the foot of Parliament Street is located a few feet north of the government freight dock.

NEW PLYMOUTH AND GREEN TURTLE CAY

Green Turtle Cay is a small island with a population of about 450, but it offers visiting yachtsmen exceptional variety with several different anchorages, and an excellent array of restaurants, hotels, marine services, and shopping facilities. Restaurants in New Plymouth include the McIntosh Restaurant and Bakery, the Blue Bee Bar and Restaurant, the Wreckin' Tree Restaurant and Bar, the Plymouth Rock, and Pineapples Bar and Grill. At White Sound the Green Turtle Club and Bluff House both offer excellent dining. Bluff House has re-opened it's Tranquil Turtle Beach Bar on the Sea of Abaco and again rebuilt the small boat dock. There are two hotels—Bluff House and the Green Turtle Club at White Sound. There are cottages and houses for rent throughout the island.

Abaco Yacht Services on Black Sound is a complete boat yard with a large Travelift. Marine fuel is available at the Other Shore Club, Sunset Marine and the Green Turtle Club. Abaco Yacht Services is a Yamaha dealer; Roberts Marine and Sunset Marine are also located in Black Sound.

There are two grocery stores—Sid's and Curry's, —and Roberts Hardware is open for business. At press time The Albert Lowe Museum was still reportedly closed for repairs. It houses artifacts and photographs which tell the story of the history of New Plymouth. It has ship models built by the late Albert Lowe, and paintings by Albert's talented and well-known artist son, New Plymouth native Alton Lowe. The Memorial Sculpture Garden features bronze busts of persons who have played important roles in Bahamian history, and a centerpiece sculpture depicting the arrival of loyalists from the United States. The Captain Roland Roberts House Environmental Center features the restored house itself and educational information on the ecology of local coral reefs. Also, there is a gallery with paintings on display in a section of Alton Lowe's hilltop home, which is located east of New Plymouth.

Green Turtle Cay is small enough so that one can cover a good part of the island on foot, but bicycles and golf carts can be rented. See the business directory for a more complete list of businesses and services available at Green Turtle Cay.

Entrance to Black Sound in July 2010. Note that the pilings marking the entry can be seen in this photograph. The large boat yard on the port side soon after entering is Abaco Yacht Services The dock opposite it is the Other Shore Club. Leeward Yacht Club was beyond Abaco Yacht Services on the NE shore; Black Sound Marina is about 0.5 NM from the entrance on the starboard side (SW shore). Sunset Marine is located off the starboard side of the boat exiting Black Sound.

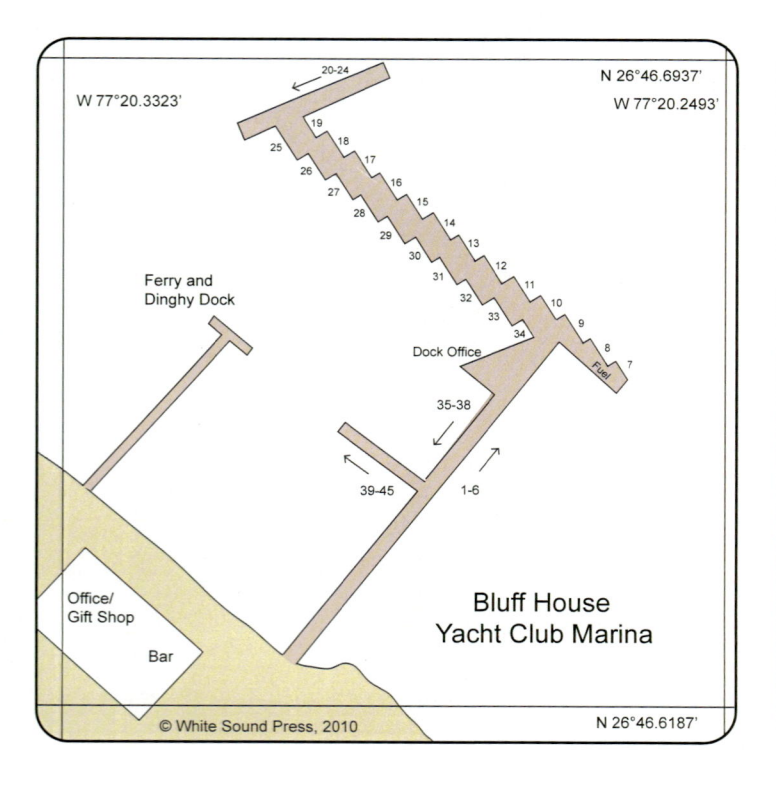

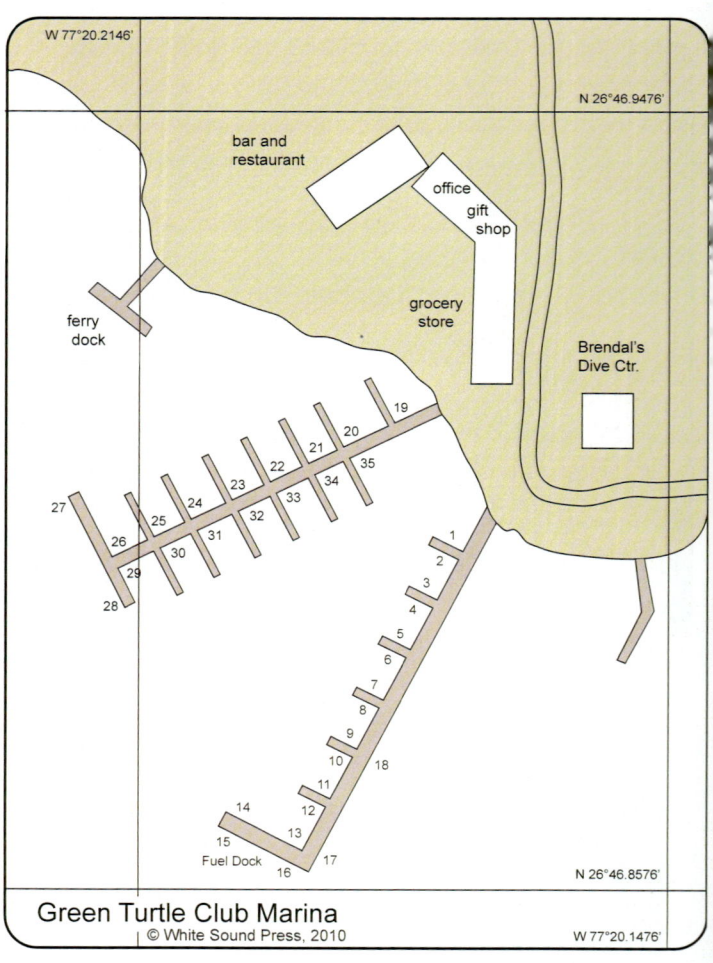

Bluff House Yacht Club Marina

Green Turtle Club Marina

Page 55

Entrance to White Sound, Green Turtle Cay

Approach from the SW. Head to the left of the beach.

Turn to the NNW following the green and red buoys.

Continue approx. NNW for about .5 NM and enter the anchorage.

Aerial of entrance to White Sound, Green Turtle Cay,

Big O's Photo by Lisa Dodge September 2021

Entrance to Black Sound, Green Turtle Cay

Approach from WSW heading just to the left of the cell tower; the deep water channel is on the north (port side when entering) of the opening. A rocky shoal extends across the rest of the opening.

Pilings with red and green arrows mark the channel, which turns to the SE (starboard when entering). See aerial of entrance below

Brendals Dive Center Adventure Tours

Established 1985   Over 30 Years of Expierence
Bahamas Tourism Cacique Award
Platnum Pro Instructor

Diving ~ Scuba Courses ~ Adventure Tours
Island Hopping ~ Deep Sea Fishing ~
Sailing ~ Private Tours

www.brendals.com   brendal@brenddal.com
Phone: 1-242-365-4411

Harbour View Cart Rentals

Green Turtle Cay · Abaco · Bahamas

www.HarbourViewCartRentals.com

Tel: 1-242-365-4411
Cell: 1-242-458-7868
VHF Ch. 16
brendal@brendal.com

© Brendal's, White Sound
Green Turtle Cay, Abaco, Bahamas

FREE PICK UP & DROP - OFF
HOURLY · DAILY · 3 DAYS · WEEKLY · LONG TERM RATES

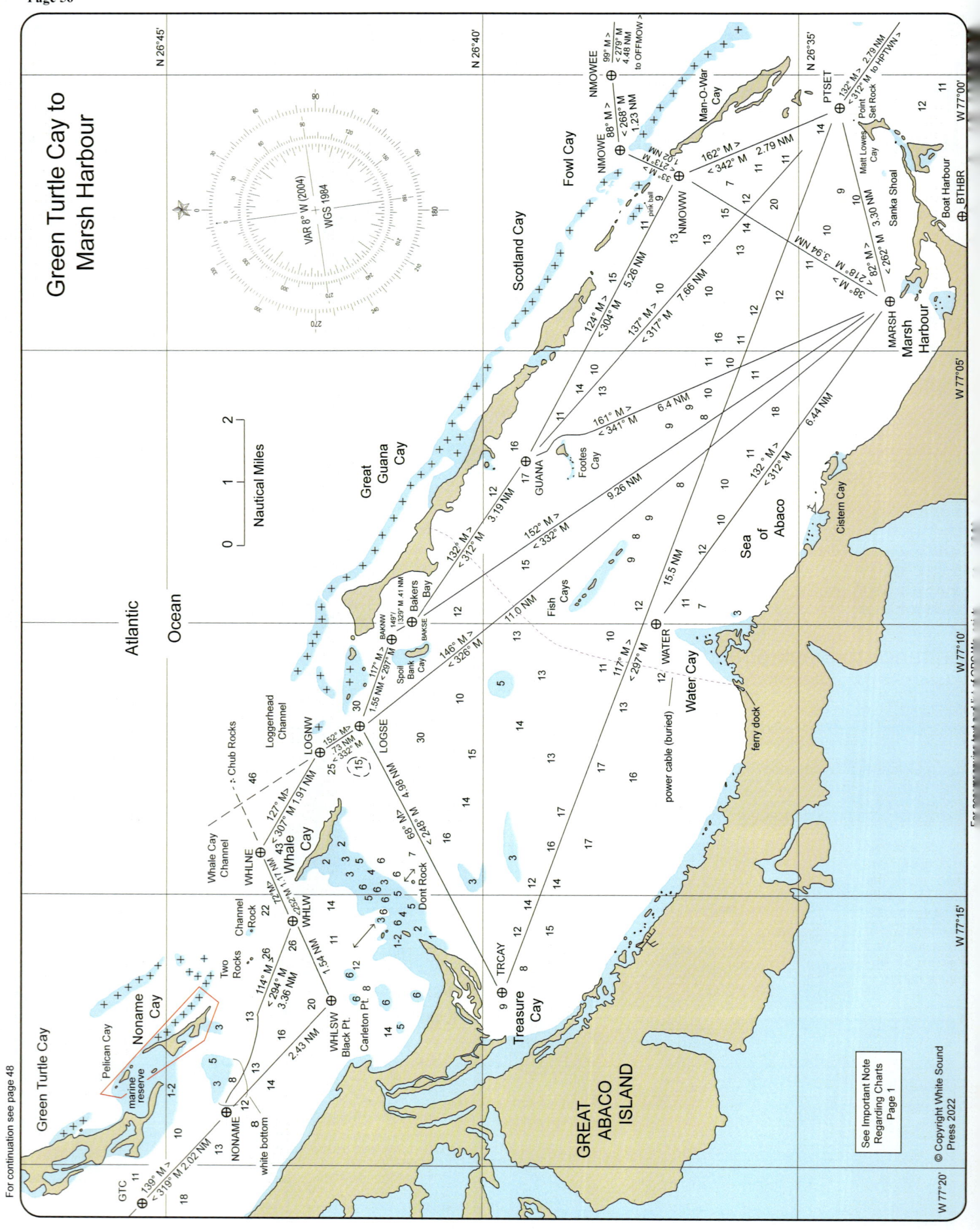

Green Turtle Cay to Marsh Harbour

GREEN TURTLE CAY TO MARSH HARBOUR

The area from Green Turtle Cay to Marsh Harbour is probably the most popular cruising area in Abaco—perhaps the most popular in the entire Bahamas. It is about 20 miles long and about 5 miles wide and offers the cruiser incredible variety—snug harbours, beautiful beaches, ocean cruising, quaint villages, good diving, excellent restaurants, good anchorages, fancy marinas, and good shopping. All continuous suggested course lines on the chart carry at least 6' MLW.

Boats drawing more than about 4' transiting the area must avoid the shallow bank extending from Treasure Cay (which is actually located on the mainland of Great Abaco Island) to Whale Cay. The preferred route in moderate weather is outside Whale Cay. The inside routes (shown as discontinuous lines) carry about 3-5' MLW. For more detailed information regarding Whale Cay passage, see pages 60.

After re-entering the Sea of Abaco there are shoals extending from Spoil Bank Cay, created when a cruise ship channel was dredged at Baker's Bay at the north end of Great Guana Cay in 1989. There are some additional small shoals between this cay and Treasure Cay. There are no other major obstacles to navigation in the area.

There is a daytime anchorage at No Name Cay, which is uninhabited but does now have a restaurant. Head for a point near the northern end of the cay on a heading of about 40 degrees to avoid the bars extending SE from Green Turtle Cay and W from the SE end of No Name Cay. When about ¼ mile offshore, turn to starboard and anchor off the entrance to the island's lagoon. A shallow rocky bar at the entrance of the lagoon bares at low water—so exploration is by dinghy at half tide or better.

Sand Bank Landing is on the mainland of Great Abaco Island north of the Treasure Cay beach, There is some dockage without amenities. The location offers an excellent view of conditions in the Whale Cay Channel. See pages 58 for more information.

There is another daytime anchorage to the west of the north tip of Whale Cay, which is also uninhabited. Like the anchorage at No Name Cay, it is exposed from the S to the NW.

continued on page 66

MARSH HARBOUR TO LITTLE HARBOUR

The Sea of Abaco narrows at its southern end, but continues to offer great variety for the visitor. Two of Abaco's principal communities—Marsh Harbour and Hope Town—are at the northern perimeter of this area. There are beautiful beaches, Pelican Cays Land and Sea Park, and three viable passages between the Sea of Abaco and the Atlantic Ocean. At its southern perimeter is Little Harbour, home of the art community founded by the late Randolph Johnston and now maintained by his son Pete.

There are several shoals in the area. The largest are Lubbers Bank, which extends about 2½ miles NW of Lubbers Quarters Cay, and Tilloo Bank, which extends 1½ to 2 miles W from Tilloo Cay. Also, most of the area west of Channel, Gorling, Sandy, and Cornish Cays is shallow. All suggested course lines on this chart carry about 6' MLW, with the exception of the course through Lubber's Quarters Channel, which carries about 4½-5', a 5½' bump on the route between White Sound and Boat Harbour, the approach to Hope Town Harbour which has several 5-5½' bumps, and the entrance to Little Harbour, which carries only 3½'.

Boat Harbour is one of the largest and finest marinas in The Bahamas. It offers complete marina services. For more information see pp.92-94.

Hope Town has a fully protected harbour. There are two marinas, one of which has fuel service. For more information, see page 96-100.

White Sound has one restaurant and one new marina just north of the sound itself. There is no room to anchor in the dredged channels in White Sound, but there is a fair weather anchorage just outside. For more information, see pages 106-112.

Lubbers Quarters Channel carries about 4½-5' MLW and requires careful piloting to avoid the shallow grassy shoals on each side of the suggested course lines. Tilloo Cut carries about 5½' MLW and is usually a viable passage to the Atlantic Ocean. There are some good fair weather anchorages in the area. For more detail, see pages 112.

There is a popular summer anchorage just north of Tilloo Bank and close to Tilloo Cay. Boats drawing more than about 2' need to go west

continued on page 66

Green Turtle Cay to Marsh Harbour, continued from page 57

Treasure Cay is a resort community. The marina was heavily damaged and has not yet been rebuilt. There are condominiums, privately owned villas and homes, stores, various services, and one of the most beautiful beaches in the world. Some dockage may be available along the old marina sea wall, or you may choose to pick up a mooring or anchor in the fully protected basin on the way to the marina site. For more information, see page 64.

Great Guana Cay also has one of the most beautiful ocean beaches in the world. It is long, wide, and sparsely developed. A favorite anchorage at Guana Cay is Baker's Bay. It was developed as "Treasure Island" for cruise ship visitors, but the "Big Red Boat" stopped visiting in 1993. It has been developed by Discovery Land Company as the Baker's Bay Club. The marina is only available for club members. Great Guana Cay has two more viable anchorages. Settlement harbour offers excellent protection from the prevailing easterlies, but is exposed from the S through the W. Orchid Bay Marina, located on the south side of Settlement Harbour near the entrance, has a breakwater and offers good protection at its docks. Fisher's Bay, the harbour immediately north of the settlement, offers good protection from the SW, but is exposed to the NW. There is a dock at the north end of the harbour. Dive Guana maintains moorings for transients in Fisher's Bay and Settlement Harbour. For more information, see page 66.

The Man-O-War/Marsh Harbour/Hope Town area forms the Hub of Abaco. For a larger scale chart of the area and some more detailed information, see page 80.

The harbour at Man-O-War Cay offers complete protection, and Man-O-War Marina has slips for transients. Complete repair and maintenance services are available from Edwin's Boat Yard, which has a sail loft as well. There is a grocery store, and several clothing and gift shops. The harbour is a busy place, and it can sometimes be difficult to find swinging room. For more information, see pages 74-80.

Marsh Harbour is the largest protected deep water anchorage in Abaco. It is the third largest city in The Bahamas, and the commerce hub of Abaco. For more information see pages 80-94.

Waypoints: G*reen Turtle Cay to Marsh Harbour* **(generally north to south):**

WPT	Description of Position	Latitude	Longitutde
GTC	1 NM W of Green Turtle Cay	N 26° 45.350'	W 77° 20.700'
NONAME	1 NM WSW Noname Cay	N 26° 44.002'	W 77° 19.017'
WHLSW	Whale Cay Channel SW end	N 26° 42.380'	W 77° 17.000'
WHLW	W of N tip Whale Cay	N 26° 43.009'	W 77° 15.426'
WHLNE	Whale Cay Channel NE end	N 26° 43.510'	W 77° 14.250'
LOGNW	Loggerhead Channel NW end	N 26° 42.560'	W 77° 12.400'
LOGSE	Loggerhead Channel SE end	N 26° 41.960'	W 77° 11.930'
TRCAY	SE of entrance Treasure Cay	N 26° 39.570'	W 77° 16.800'
BAKNW	northwest side Baker's Bay	N 26° 41.430'	W 77° 10.300'
BAKSE	southeast side Baker's Bay	N 26° 41.110'	W 77° 10.020'
GUANA	SW Guana Cay settlement	N 26° 39.310'	W 77° 07.080'
WATER	½ NM N Water Cay	N 26° 37.200'	W 77° 10.000'
NMOWW	Abaco Sd. end NMOW Chan.	N 26° 36.900'	W 77° 01.860'
NMOWE	Atlantic end NMOW Chan.	N 26° 37.820'	W 77° 01.360'
NMOWEE	ENE of NMOW Channel	N 26° 38.000'	W 77° 00.000'
PTSET	¼ mile NE Point Set Rock	N 26° 34.370'	W 77° 00.550'
MARSH	near entrance Marsh Harbour	N 26° 33.520'	W 77° 04.110'
BTHBR	near entrance Boat Harbour	N 26° 32.410'	W 77° 02.550'

Support the Bahamas Air-Sea Rescue Association.

You are not required to take an active part in BASRA.

Send $40.00 for one year's membership dues to:
BASRA ABACO, Hope Town, Abaco, Bahamas

Marsh Harbour to Little Harbour, continued from page 57

of Tilloo Bank. See page 116 for a detailed description of the Middle Passage through Tilloo Bank as well as the entire region of the Pelican Cays Land and Sea Park, where there are moorings for daytime use by small boats (28' or less) and a daytime anchorage in Pelican Harbour NW of the reef. North Bar Channel is the best passage to the Atlantic in this area. See pages 116 and 118.

Boats proceeding south to Little Harbour should stay about 1/3 mile off the coast of Great Abaco Island in order to avoid shoals extending W from Lynyard Cay. The entrance to Little Harbour carries only about 3½' MLW, and boats drawing more will need tide help. It is possible to anchor west of Tom Curry's Point in the Bight of Old Robinson or in the lee of the point on which the remnants of the old lighthouse is located to wait for the tide. For more information, see pages 119-120.

Waypoints: *Marsh Harbour to Little Harbour* **(generally north to south**

WPT	Description of Position	Latitude	Longitutde
PTSET	1/4 mile NE Point Set Rock	N 26° 34.370'	W 77° 00.550'
MARSH	Near entrance to Marsh Hrbr	N 26° 33.520'	W 77° 04.110'
HPTWN	Near entrance to Hope Town	N 26° 32.608'	W 76° 58.063'
WSMK	Near entrance White Sound	N 26° 31.130'	W 76° 58.870'
BTHBR	Near entrance to Boat Hrbr	N 26° 32.410'	W 77° 02.550'
LQN	N end Lubbers Quarters Chan	N 26° 30.330'	W 76° 59.110'
LQMID	Mid Lubbers Quarters Chan	N 26° 29.990'	W 76° 59.460'
LQS	S end Lubbers Quarters Chan	N 26° 29.100'	W 76° 59.720'
WITCHN	N of Witch Point	N 26° 30.630'	W 77° 02.550'
WITCHE	E of Witch Point	N 26° 29.550'	W 77° 01.550'
MIDNW	Middle Channel NW end	N 26° 25.830'	W 77° 01.010'
MIDSE	Middle Channel SE end	N 26° 25.280'	W 77° 00.090'
TBANK	SW of end of Tilloo Bank	N 26° 25.160'	W 77° 01.220'
PELICY	SW of the N Pelican Cay	N 26° 25.150'	W 76° 59.290'
SANDY	SE of Sandy Cay	N 26° 23.590'	W 76° 59.090'
NBAR	Atlantic End North Bar Chan	N 26° 23.410'	W 76° 58.470'
PELIPT	NE Pelican Point	N 26° 23.110'	W 76° 59.730'
LTHBW	Abaco Sd. end Little Hrbr Chan	N 26° 20.470'	W 76° 59.660'
LTHBE	Atlantic end Little Hrbr Chan	N 26° 19.900'	W 76° 59.390'

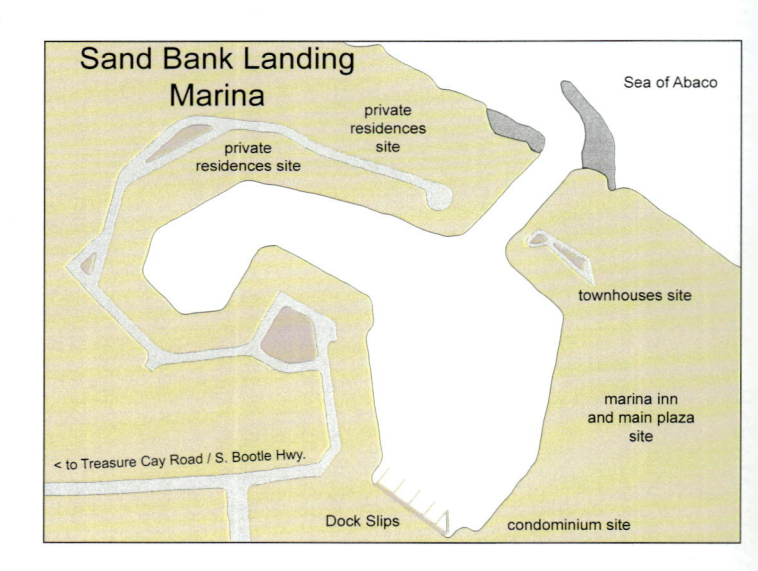

Sand Bank Landing has been under construction for several years and several slips became available in 2015. It is located north of the Treasure Cay beach along the shore of Great Abaco Island near the original loyalist settlement in Abaco at Carleton. Its location at the northern end of the Whale Cay passage makes it a strategically useful stop (see charts on pages 60, 62 and 64). The entry and the approach are deep and the marina will eventually be able to accommodate vessels up to 150'. A small hotel, restaurant, condominiums, townhouses and private residences are all in the plans for the future; the beautiful beach is there now ... just south of the marina basin.

Big O's
Swimming Pigs
Bar & Restaurant

Amazing Food & Drinks
Brand New Pool Bar
Home of Big O's Gift Shop
Tie Up to Our Newly Built Dock
Make Friends with Some Pigs
Just Minutes from Green Turtle Cay
bigosabaco@gmail.com
242-699-3281   VHF 16

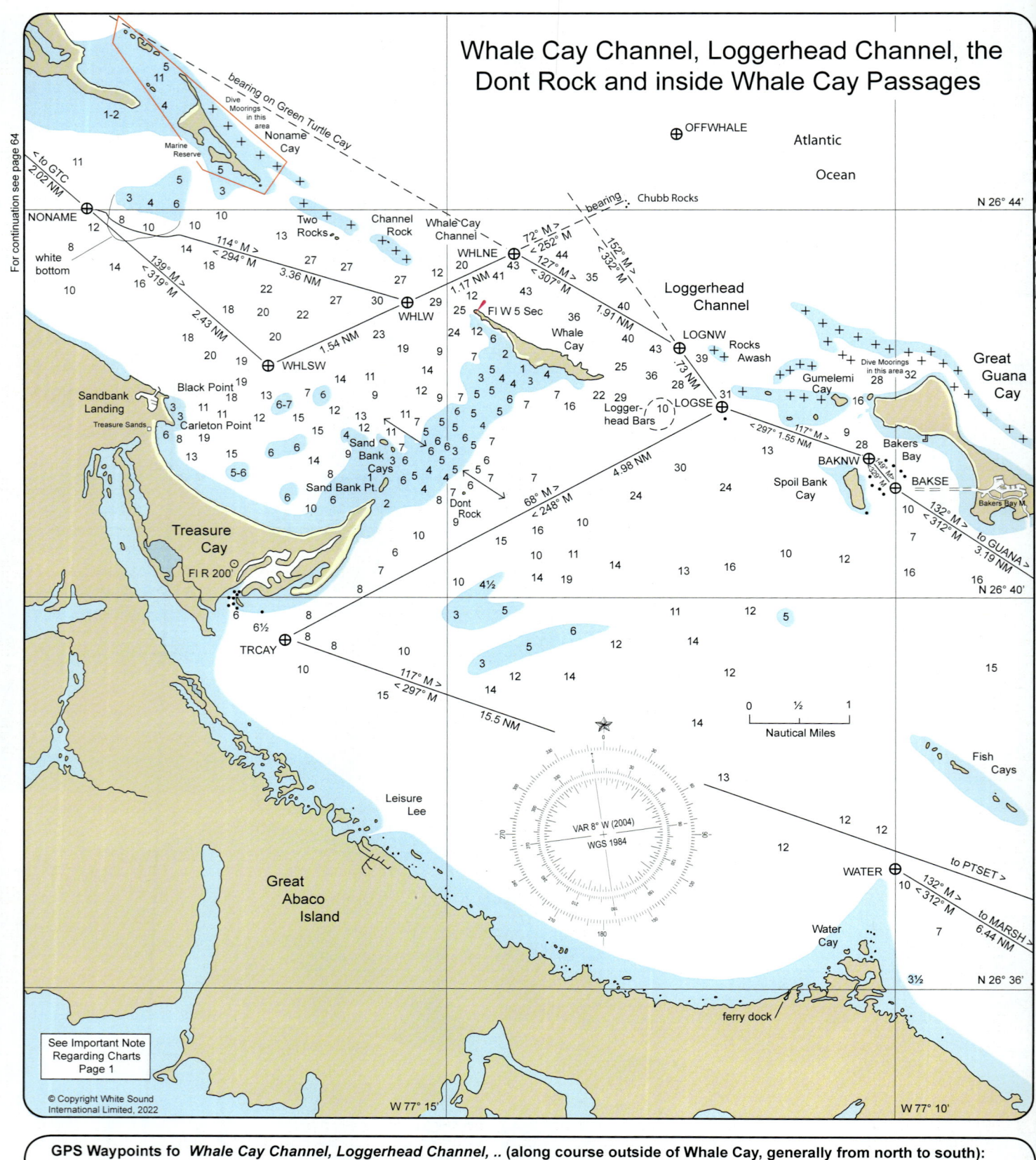

Whale Cay Channel, Loggerhead Channel, the Dont Rock and inside Whale Cay Passages

GPS Waypoints for Whale Cay Channel, Loggerhead Channel, .. (along course outside of Whale Cay, generally from north to south):

ID	Description	Latitude	Longitude
NONAME	1 NM WSW No Name Cay	N 26° 44.002'	W 77° 19.017'
WHLSW	Whale Cay Channel SW end (Abaco Sound end)	N 26° 42.380'	W 77° 17.000'
WHLW	west of north tip of Whale Cay	N 26° 43.009'	W 77° 15.426'
WHLNE	Whale Cay Channel NE end (Atlantic Ocean end)	N 26° 43.510'	W 77° 14.250'
LOGNW	Loggerhead Channel NW end (Atlantic Ocean end)	N 26° 42.560'	W 77° 12.400'
LOGSE	Loggerhead Channel SE end (Abaco Sound end)	N 26° 41.960'	W 77° 11.930'
BAKNW	northwest side of Baker's Bay	N 26° 41.430'	W 77° 10.300'
BAKSE	southeast side Baker's Bay	N 26° 41.110'	W 77° 10.020'
TRCAY	southeast of entrance to Treasure Cay	N 26° 39.570'	W 77° 16.800'
WATER	½ NM N Water Cay	N 26° 37.200'	W 77° 10.000'

© Copyright White Sound International Limited, 2022

See Important Note Regarding Charts Page 1

WHALE CAY CHANNEL AND LOGGERHEAD CHANNEL —THE OUTSIDE ROUTE AROUND WHALE CAY

The Whale Cay / Sand Banks area is clearly the most challenging part of the Abacos for cruisers. Certain weather conditions may make it impossible to traverse the area for several days, though at other times transit can be easily accomplished.

The difficulties are the result of the fact that a shallow bank extends all the way from Whale Cay to "Treasure Cay" on the mainland of Great Abaco Island, and the passage across it can be challenging for vessels drawing more than about 3-4'. Many cruising boats decide to go outside in the Atlantic and pass outside Whale Cay. Although both Loggerhead Channel (southeast of Whale Cay) and the Whale Cay Channel (northwest of Whale Cay) are wide, the Whale Cay Channel is fairly shallow (about 12') and is susceptible to a rage sea condition (breaking waves all the way across) when ocean swells come from the northeast. This most often occurs during a strong northeaster after the passage of a cold front, but can also be the result of storms hundreds of miles away, which can cause a rage during deceptively sunny and light wind days in Abaco.

The single greatest problem is deciding whether or not the Whale Cay and Loggerhead Channels are passable. Of the two, the Whale Cay Channel is the most critical. Boats contemplating the passage often consult with one another in the morning on the VHF, so it is sometimes possible to get information about conditions just by listening, or by calling "any boat in the Whale Cay area." The single best source is the cruiser's net, which airs each morning at 8:15 am on VHF 68, and almost always reports on conditions at Whale Cay as well as other passages between the Sea of Abaco and the Atlantic Ocean.

If conditions are appropriate for going around Whale Cay, follow the course lines on the chart. When heading out Whale Cay Channel (from WHLW to WHLNE) you will be heading directly toward Chubb Rocks (white Water). When you reach WHLNE turn and head 127° M (which will put Green Turtle Cay on your stern) and head toward Gumelemi Cay (which will be difficult to distinguish because Great Gauana Cay lies directly behind it). When you reach LOGNE turn and head to LOGSE leaving Rocks Awash about 1/3 NM on your port side. Your heading should be 152°M, and you should be headed toward a point just to the north of the Fish Cays, which appear as 4-5 lumps on the horizon SE of the land mass of Great Abaco Island When you readh LOGSE you may continue into the Sea of Abaco or turn to 117° and head to BAKNW which will follow the old cruise ship channel into Bakers Bay. Use the reciprocal headings if you are going SE to NW..

The inside passages are not necessarily viable alternatives to the outside passage on rough days, because high wind or rage conditions usually make the inside passages impassable also. A swell running across the shallow bank with a hard sand bottom can make it as treacherous as the outside route. See the next page (page 62) for a new chart of the inside route.

Whale Cay Channel from the West Northwest with Channel Rock in the foreground. The shoal area extending Southwestward from Whale Cay to Treasure Cay on the mainland of Great Abaco Island makes it necessary for deep draft cruising boats to go outside Whale Cay when transiting the area. Note that the best passage is approximately midway between Channel Rock and the Northwest tip of Whale Cay. The suggested course line for this Channel using the waypoints provided in this cruising guide is in the deepest water, but all should be aware that in a rage sea breakers can extend all the way across the opening. Cruisers can listen to the Cruiser's Net on channel 68 at 8:15 each morning for a report on conditions in the Whale Cay Channel. Photo by Steve Dodge March 2004.

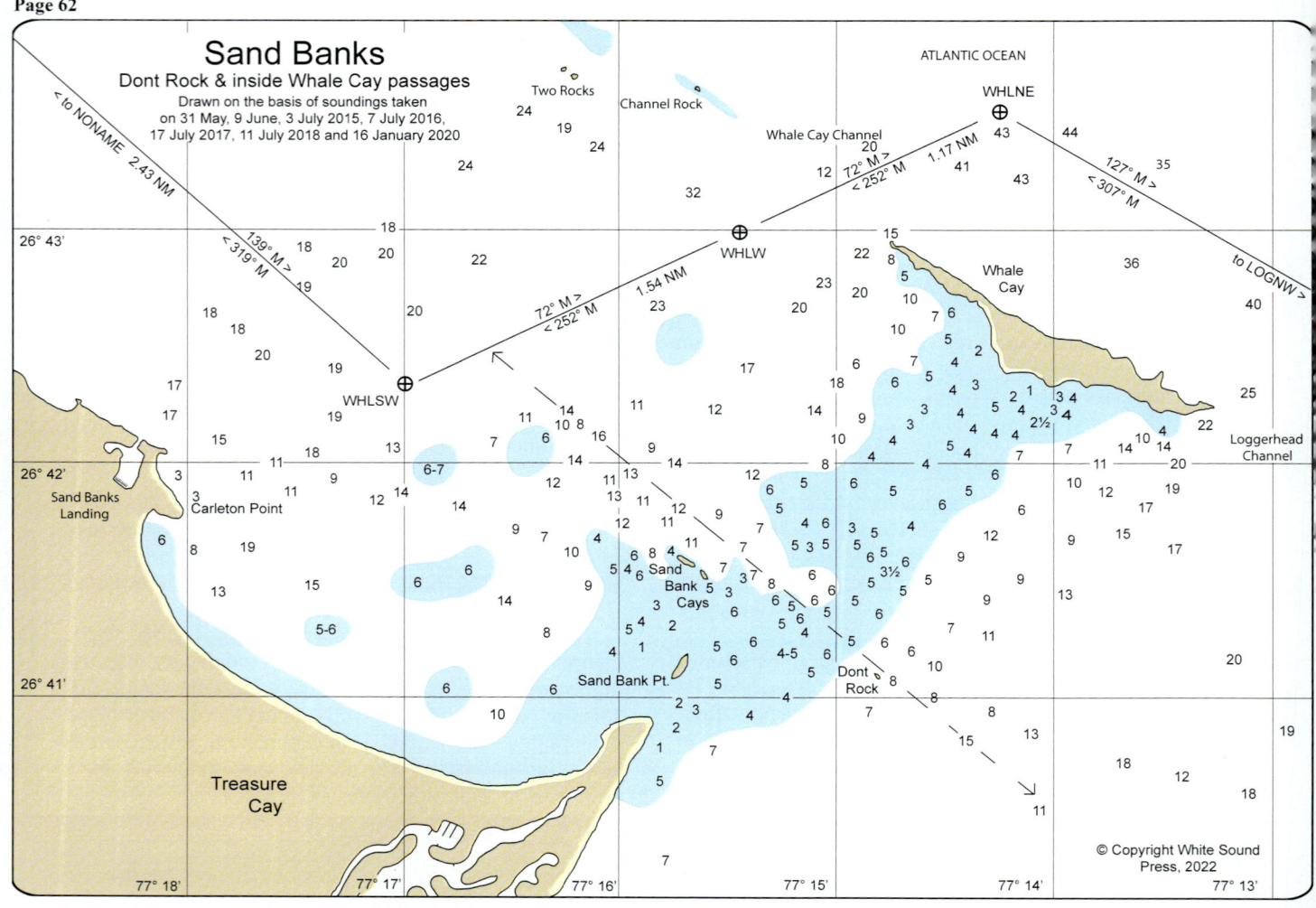

SANDBANKS AND THE DONT ROCK PASSAGE

If you choose to use the inside passage you must cross Sand Banks—a large area of shifting sand extending all the way from Whale Cay to Great Abaco Island at Treasure Cay (which is part of Great Abaco Island; not a separate cay). The Sand Banks were formed as a result of unusual wide and deep openings in the barrier reef from north Great Guana Cay to No Name Cay (about 5 NM). This allows ocean swells to roll into the Sea of Abaco, spreading sand within the Sea of Abaco and shifting it around on a regular basis. The satellite photo of the area clearly shows how the banks were built.

The Sand Banks are beautiful, but they are also a major obstacle to navigation. Vessels drawing more than 3-4' have typically gone out into the Atlantic to move SE or NW of the Sand Banks and Whale Cay. Sand Banks has not been charted in detail in the past because of their volatility and because ocean swells rolling on to the Banks can make crossing them particularly hazardous. But the inside route over the banks has its advantages on settled days—it is shorter and makes entering and leaving the Atlantic unnecessary.

We are aware that Sand Banks changes on a regular basis and therefore cannot guarantee the accuracy of the chart. Note that the chart provides the specific dates on which the hydrographic data was recorded and that the suggested course is a segmented course line (exercise caution). The Dont Rock route we show may well not be the deepest route across Sand Banks, but it has good visuals at each end which is why we suggest it. Post Dorian it was deeper than it's historic 3-4' controlling depth. However, we expect this is somewhat temporary and suggest caution. Although the area is constantly changing, most of the significant changes in the banks occur over a reasonably long time frame as well as one or more episodes of rage conditions (breaking waves at Whale and Loggerhead Channels), so this chart may well serve to help boats find their way across Sand Banks for several months. Mid-tide rising with no swells is obviously the best time to cross Sand Banks.

We resurvey this chart each year for the following year's book, and we hope this will make it easier and safer for some cruisers to use the inside route when the weather and the tide are suitable.

Portion of *Abaco From Space* Showing Whale Cay area courtesy of Denny Parker, TCB and NASA, and Sinclair Frederick, creator of the Abaco Message Board and originator of Out Island Internet (OII) in Abaco..

Sand Banks and Treasure Cay from the east with Dont Rock and the Sand Bank Cays.

Dont Rock

The Sand Bank Cays and Dont Rock from the NNW with the Fish Cays and Great Abaco Island in the background. The shallow bars of Sand Banks are clearly visible. The suggested course line is not always in the deepest water, but the principal advantage of this route are the clearly visible references at each end—Dont Rock and the Sand Bank Cays. When there is a rage in Whale Cay or Loggerhead Channels, the inside passages are often not viable either.

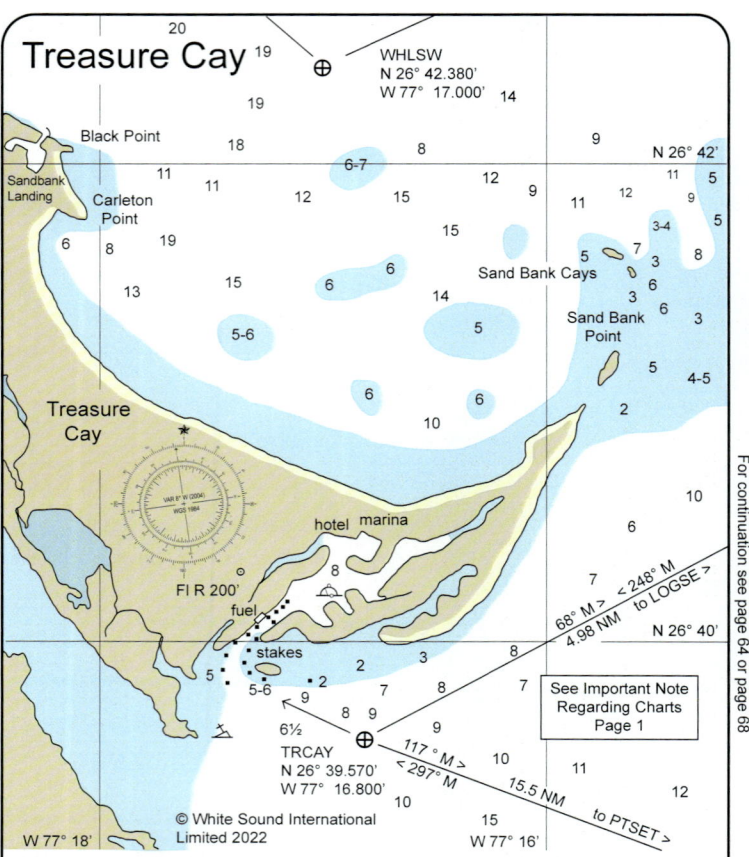

When approaching Treasure Cay from the east or southeast, head for the low part of Great Abaco Island. There is a radio tower near this point. Head NW from the waypoint TRCAY and go between the stakes, making a sweeping turn to starboard, and then proceed NE through the entrance channel. Controlling depth is 5-6' MLW. The marina has not yet been rebuilt. There are still some moorings available in the basin to starboard on the way in, or anchor there. Fuel is available at the fuel dock on the port side of the main entrance channel.

Treasure Cay, Photo by Lisa Dodge 08 October 2020

Entrance to Treasure Cay from the southwest.

TREASURE CAY

Treasure Cay started as a hotel/marina development and has grown into a medium-sized vacation community. The main attraction at Treasure Cay is its beach, which is surely one of the loveliest in the world—it extends for about 3 miles in a beautiful semi-circle. The marina and the buildings including office and restaurants have not yet been rebuilt. There were rumours of a change in ownership but no confirmation. The only marina dock remaining presently is the old dinghy dock and along the sea wall in the NW corner of the marina basin. A restaurant, Cafe La Florence is open as well as the mini-mart grocery and Treasure Boat Rentals. There are villas, private homes, and condominiums for rent.

Treasure Cay also has an 18-hole golf course and several tennis courts. Current reports are these are still closed at this time. The Treasure Sands Club is located near the north end of the beach near Carleton Point (by road just outside the Treasure Cay entrance gate). They were not yet reopened at press time but reports are they have completed repairs and intend to reopen soon. They serve lunch, dinner, drinks, have a pool, and of course, the beautiful beach. Visiting boats should anchor off in about 6' MLW; Treasure Sands may provide dinghy service to their dinghy dock.

Walking the beach is pleasant, and those who want a good bit of exercise can walk all the way to the northern end and through the brush to a path leading to the rocky point extending northeast from the beach. This point was named Carleton Point in 1983 in honor of the bicentennial of the arrival of the first loyalist settlers in Abaco. They left New York and the United States because they opposed independence; they travelled to Carleton to found a new British colony which they believed would prosper because it would gain the British trade which the new United States would lose. The settlement lasted only a few years. A plaque cemented in the rocks at Carleton Point commemorates this first settlement in Abaco.

The northwest end of Great Guana Cay is part of the private Bakers Bay development which has enjoyed rapid growth during the past few years. All shoreline in the Bahamas is public property up to the high tide line but if you visit this area please respect the privacy of the shore front homes as well as the beauty of this special place. The reef is accessible for snorkeling or SCUBA; see the dive chart on page 166. Photo by Steve Dodge, 12 July 2013.

Great Guana Cay

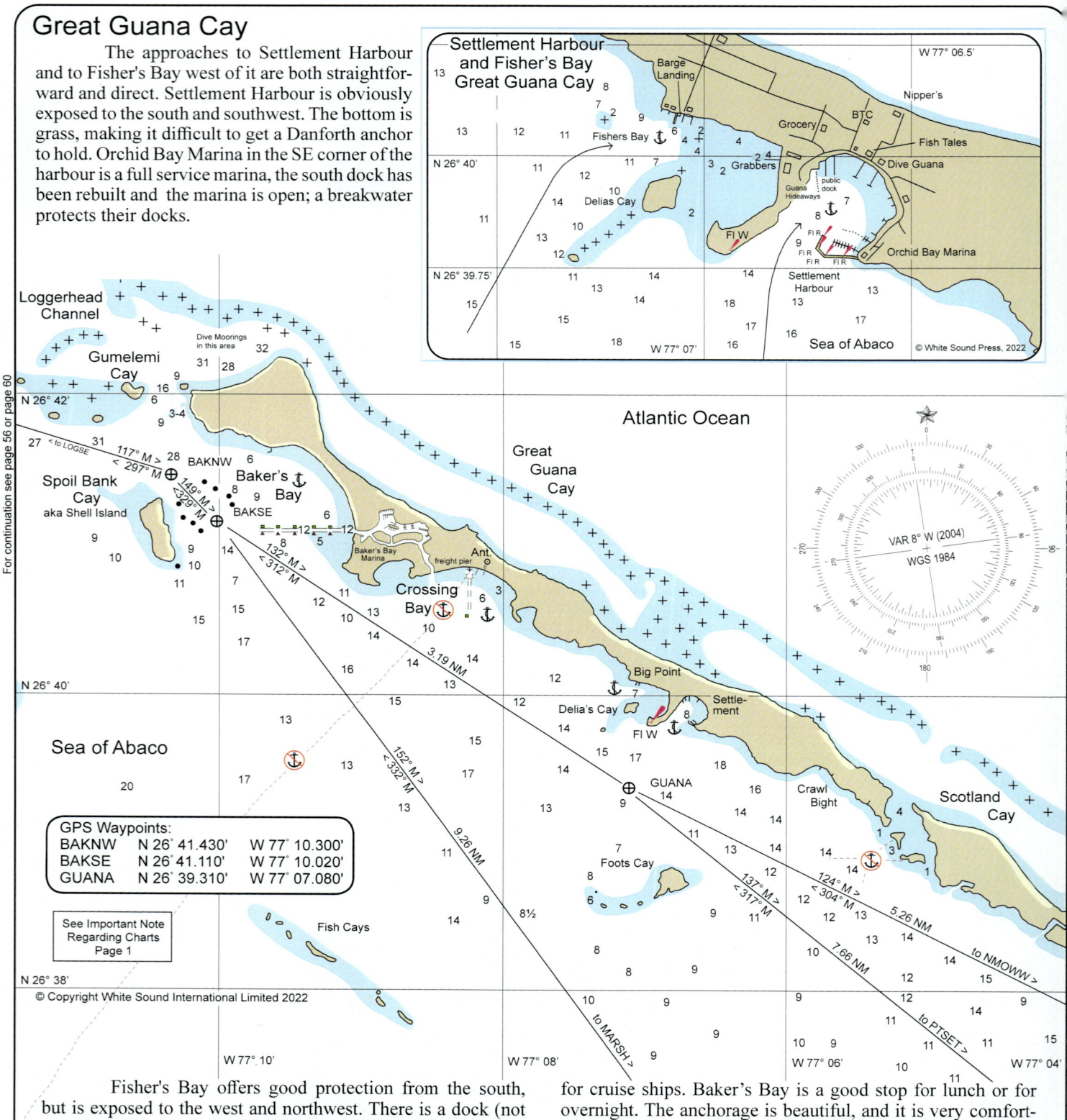

The approaches to Settlement Harbour and to Fisher's Bay west of it are both straightforward and direct. Settlement Harbour is obviously exposed to the south and southwest. The bottom is grass, making it difficult to get a Danforth anchor to hold. Orchid Bay Marina in the SE corner of the harbour is a full service marina, the south dock has been rebuilt and the marina is open; a breakwater protects their docks.

Fisher's Bay offers good protection from the south, but is exposed to the west and northwest. There is a dock (not a marina) at Big Point at the NW corner of the harbour. Moorings for transients in Fisher's Bay (6) as well as in Settlement Harbour (6) are maintained by Dive Guana, which is based in the settlement. There is a submerged rock off Big Point at the north side of the harbour. It is sometimes marked with a white pipe. A shallow rocky bar runs from Delia's Cay southwest to the off-lying rock. All boats should avoid trying to cross the bar and should go to the southwest of the off-lying rock, which is usually marked with a pole with a ball at the top.

The northwestern end of Great Guana Cay is also of interest to cruisers. The cruise ship channel is no longer in use for cruise ships. Baker's Bay is a good stop for lunch or for overnight. The anchorage is beautiful, and it is very comfortable in the prevailing winds. It does not offer protection from the south through the northwest. The spoil bank cay created by dredging the channel and mooring basin for the cruise ship is said to be a good place for shelling. Baker's Bay Club Marina as well as the golf course and other amenities are available to members only. See the Orchid Bay and Bakers Bay marina maps on page 69.

Crossing Bay, to the southeast of Baker's Bay, offers only modest protection and is shallow quite far from shore. The concrete pier is a freight dock for the Baker's Bay development.

GPS Waypoints:
BAKNW   N 26° 41.430'   W 77° 10.300'
BAKSE   N 26° 41.110'   W 77° 10.020'
GUANA   N 26° 39.310'   W 77° 07.080'

GREAT GUANA CAY

The settlement at Great Guana Cay is one of the smallest in the central part of Abaco, but it has grown. The 1990 census reported only 95 persons living on the cay and the 2010 census reported 127. The cay's principal asset has long been its beautiful ocean beach, which is one of the widest in Abaco and extends almost the entire 5½ mile length of the island. The beach made Guana a popular stop for cruisers for many years.

During the past two decades Guana has experienced a boom, and several new developments have made the cay even more attractive for visitors. The opening of Nipper's Beach Bar and Grill during summer 1996 brought large numbers of cruisers, tourists, and local residents to the cay. Nipper's did not escape damage in Dorian and though they intend to reopen they have not yet set a timeline.

The opening of Orchid Bay Marina in 1999 provided well protected dockage at Guana for the first time. It is also a residential development with lots for sale. The south dock has been rebuilt and dockage and fuel are available.

Grabbers Bar and Grill, located on the site of the old Guana Harbour Club is on the peninsula between Settlement Harbour and Fisher's Bay. The hallmark "Guana Grabber" rum drink and strikingly beautiful sunsets make this a choice lunch or dinner stop. Their shallow draft dock is located at the east end of Fischer's Bay on the beach. Overnight lodging is available and rebuilding is continuing.

Kidd's Cove is currently under reconstruction. It should soon again provide a restaurant and bar located in town on Front Street at the intersection of the street which goes north to the school and the ocean beach. A few yards further east is Dive Guana—they are open for dive trips and more. Other facilities in the settlement include a new grocery and liqour store located a couple hundred yards north of the public dock. Guana Lumber is located northwest of the settlement near the opening of Fisher's Bay.

If you want to walk, swim, snorkel, or picnic, cross to the ocean side at the settlement, and then walk southeast on the beach to High Rocks, where the reef is just off the beach. It will be obvious when you reach High Rocks.

The NW end of Great Guana Cay—Baker's Bay— has been and continues to be a favorite anchorage for cruisers. The Bay and adjacent land was developed as a cruise ship destination in 1989-90; that operation was terminated in 1993. It is now the Baker's Bay Club, an up-scale community which is planned for 358 residential units. There is a 158-slip marina which can accommodate vessels to 250' and a Marina Village, which is patterned after Caribbean port towns of the 1700s. The entire development including the marina is private and closed to the public.

Fisher's Bay and Settlement Harbour, Great Guana Cay, viewed from the Northwest. The cruising boats in Fisher's Bay are anchored or are on moorings maintained by Dive Guana. Orchid Bay Marina offers full services and their dock, protected by a breakwater, can be seen on the south side of Settlement Harbour. Since this photo was taken, they have added a second dock located northeast of the dock shown here. There is a public dock in the northwest corner of Settlement Harbour which services local needs as well as visitors. This photo was taken by Steve Dodge in March 2004.

The Atlantic Ocean beach on Great Guana Cay. Photo by Steve Dodge. 14 December 2013.

Page 69

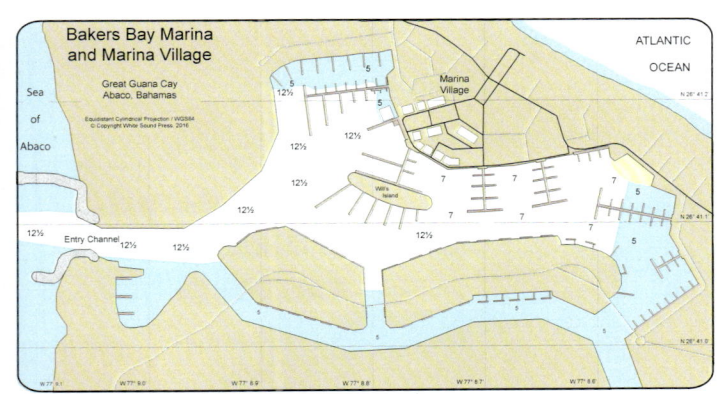

Great Guana Cay, Photo by Lisa Dodge 8 October 2020

Bakers Bay Marina and Village is a private club which is closed to the public.

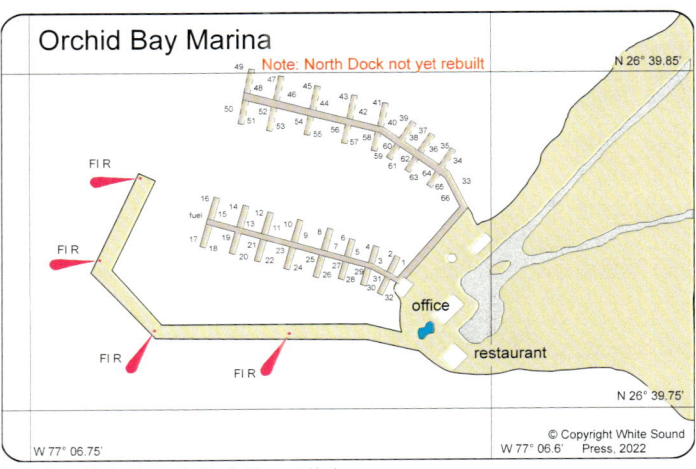

Orchid Bay Marina is located in Settlement Harbour.

★ M&B SHIPCANVAS CO. ★

sizes & colors available

WORLD'S FINEST SEABAGS & DITTY BAGS

Wool Sweaters & Watchcaps, Breton Shirts
Rope Bracelets. Oil Lamps & Gifts
Heaving Lines, Sounding Leads & Leadlines
+ PLUS + Marine Project Leather + Full Hides
US Navy Surplus & Supplies
Rigging Knives & Tools...

shipcanvas.com

WWW.SHIPCANVAS.COM   (US) +1 305.396.8535

The Abaco Tourist Office

THE ISLANDS OF THE bahamas

ISLAND HOPPING MADE EASY

Island-hopping intel is at your fingertips. From resorts and marinas to fishing charters and tournaments, find everything you need for a thrilling adventure across this 120-mile chain of islands and cays on the all-new Bahamas.com website. Discover what's in store.

THE ISLANDS OF THE bahamas — fly away

Visit Bahamas.com

Call the Abaco Tourist Office at (242) 699-0152/0153

Download on the App Store · GET IT ON Google Play

The cut between Great Guana Cay and Scotland Cay is shallow with rocky ledges and sand bars and is best used for ocean access only by shallow draft outboards with local knowledge at high tide, but the shallow sand banks have some deep holes which are beautiful and are a great place to stop for a swim. Enter carefully and anchor in one of the holes or beach the boat (on rising tide only). Enjoy the quiet beauty of this unique spot. Be aware that at mid-tide current will be moderate to strong and swim up current rather than with the current to make certain that you will be able to swim back to your boat.

Avoid anchoring over high voltage power cables.

All shoreline in the Bahamas is public property up to the high tide line but if you visit this area please respect the privacy of the shore front homes as well as the quiet beauty of this special place.

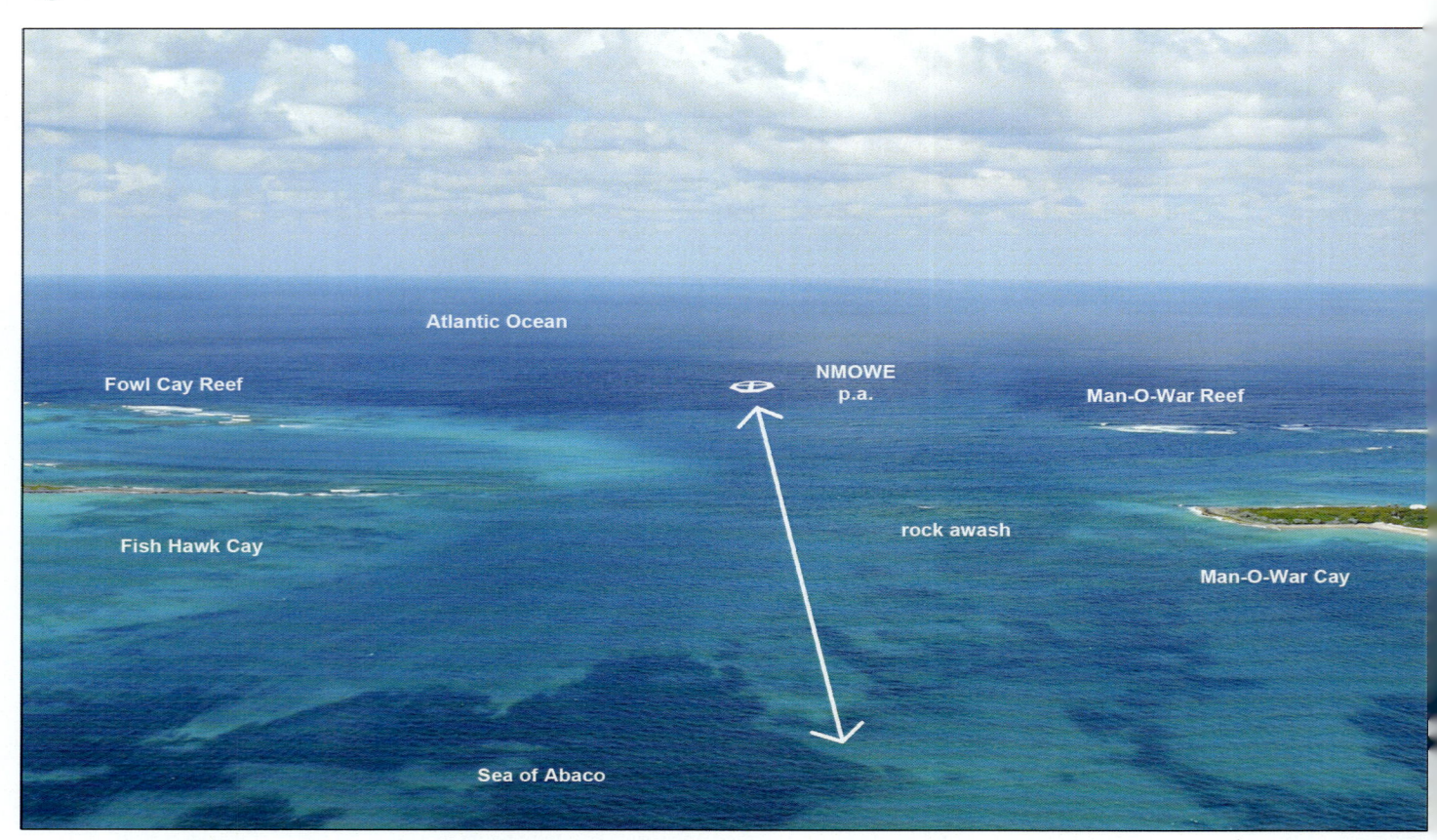

North Man-O-War Channel from the southwest. It is the widest and deepest passage between the Sea of Abaco and the Atlantic Ocean in central Abaco. Note the southeast tip of Fish Hawk Cay and a Fowl Cay Reef on the left, and the northwest tip of Man-O-War Cay with the rock which almost always breaks, as well as a portion of the barrier reef off Man-O-War Cay on the right. See the top photo on the next page, and the charts and descriptions on page 74, and also on pages 16-17 and 18. Abbreviation "p.a." is for "position approximate." Photo by Steve Dodge, 19 March 2010.

South Man-O-War Channel from the west. This passage is narrower than North Man-O-War Channel and entry is not straight forward. Note the southeastern tip of Man-O-War Cay on the left and the barrier reef offshore. The opening is clearly visible. Vessels approaching this channel from the south must use extreme caution to avoid Elbow Reef; it is recommended that all vessels coming from the south go to the waypoint OFFSMOWE before approaching SMOWE. See the bottom photo on the next page and the charts and descriptions on pages 16-17, 18, 74 and 80. Abbreviation "p.a." is for "position approximate." Photo by Steve Dodge, 19 March 2010.

North Man-O-War Channel from the northnorthwest. Fowl Cay reef is in the foreground with the darker blue water of the channel beyond it and Man-O-War Cay beyond that. Abbreviation "p.a." is for "position approximate." Photo by Steve Dodge, 4 February 2008.

South Man-O-War Channel from the eastnortheast with Man-O-War Cay in the background. The opening in the reef is clearly visible, and the darker water is the deepest entry route. Abbreviation "p.a." is for "position approximate." Photo by Steve Dodge 4 February 2008.

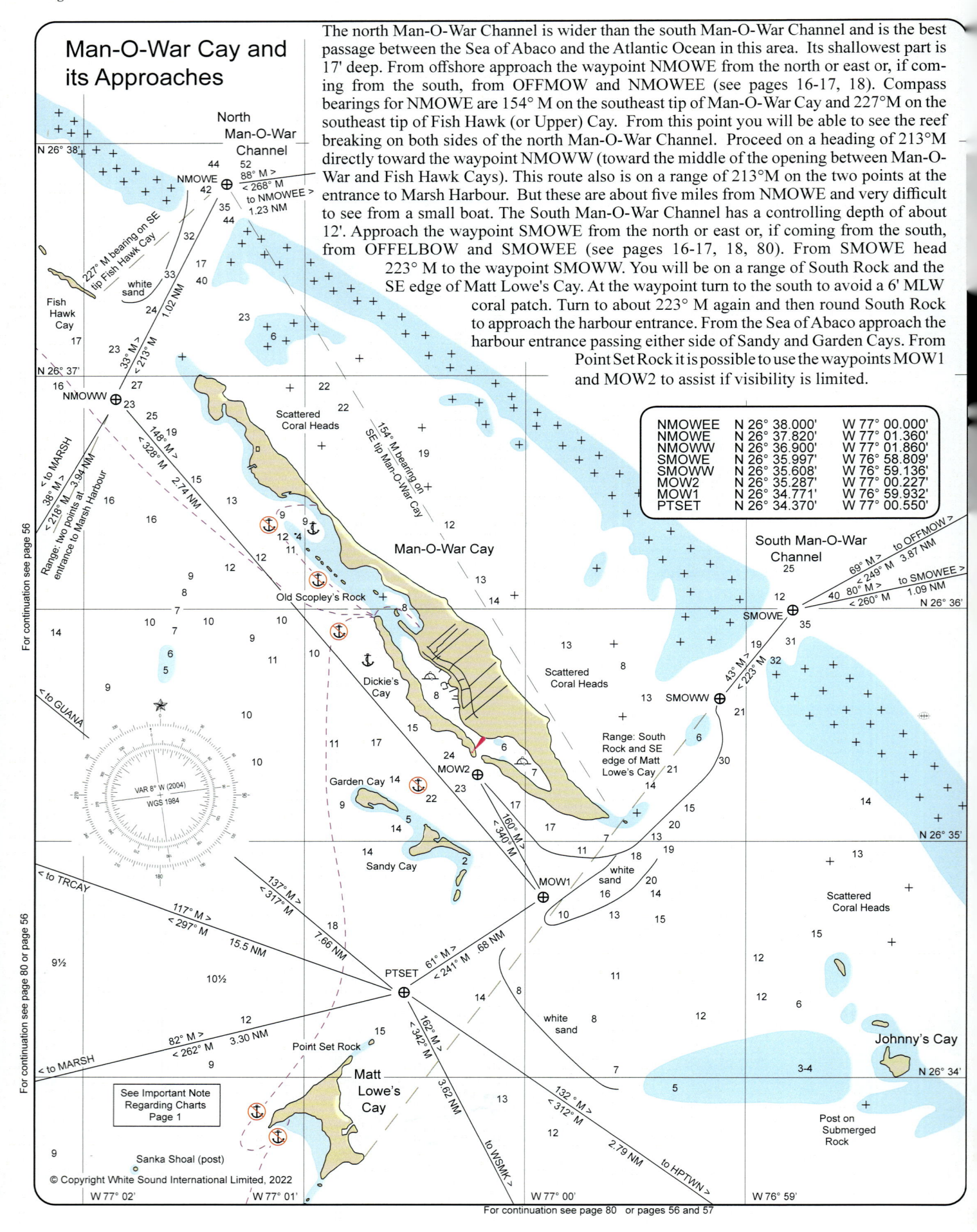

Man-O-War Cay and its Approaches

The north Man-O-War Channel is wider than the south Man-O-War Channel and is the best passage between the Sea of Abaco and the Atlantic Ocean in this area. Its shallowest part is 17' deep. From offshore approach the waypoint NMOWE from the north or east or, if coming from the south, from OFFMOW and NMOWEE (see pages 16-17, 18). Compass bearings for NMOWE are 154° M on the southeast tip of Man-O-War Cay and 227°M on the southeast tip of Fish Hawk (or Upper) Cay. From this point you will be able to see the reef breaking on both sides of the north Man-O-War Channel. Proceed on a heading of 213°M directly toward the waypoint NMOWW (toward the middle of the opening between Man-O-War and Fish Hawk Cays). This route also is on a range of 213°M on the two points at the entrance to Marsh Harbour. But these are about five miles from NMOWE and very difficult to see from a small boat. The South Man-O-War Channel has a controlling depth of about 12'. Approach the waypoint SMOWE from the north or east or, if coming from the south, from OFFELBOW and SMOWEE (see pages 16-17, 18, 80). From SMOWE head 223° M to the waypoint SMOWW. You will be on a range of South Rock and the SE edge of Matt Lowe's Cay. At the waypoint turn to the south to avoid a 6' MLW coral patch. Turn to about 223° M again and then round South Rock to approach the harbour entrance. From the Sea of Abaco approach the harbour entrance passing either side of Sandy and Garden Cays. From Point Set Rock it is possible to use the waypoints MOW1 and MOW2 to assist if visibility is limited.

Waypoint	Latitude	Longitude
NMOWEE	N 26° 38.000'	W 77° 00.000'
NMOWE	N 26° 37.820'	W 77° 01.360'
NMOWW	N 26° 36.900'	W 77° 01.860'
SMOWE	N 26° 35.997'	W 76° 58.809'
SMOWW	N 26° 35.608'	W 76° 59.136'
MOW2	N 26° 35.287'	W 77° 00.227'
MOW1	N 26° 34.771'	W 76° 59.932'
PTSET	N 26° 34.370'	W 77° 00.550'

Man-O-War Cay Harbour

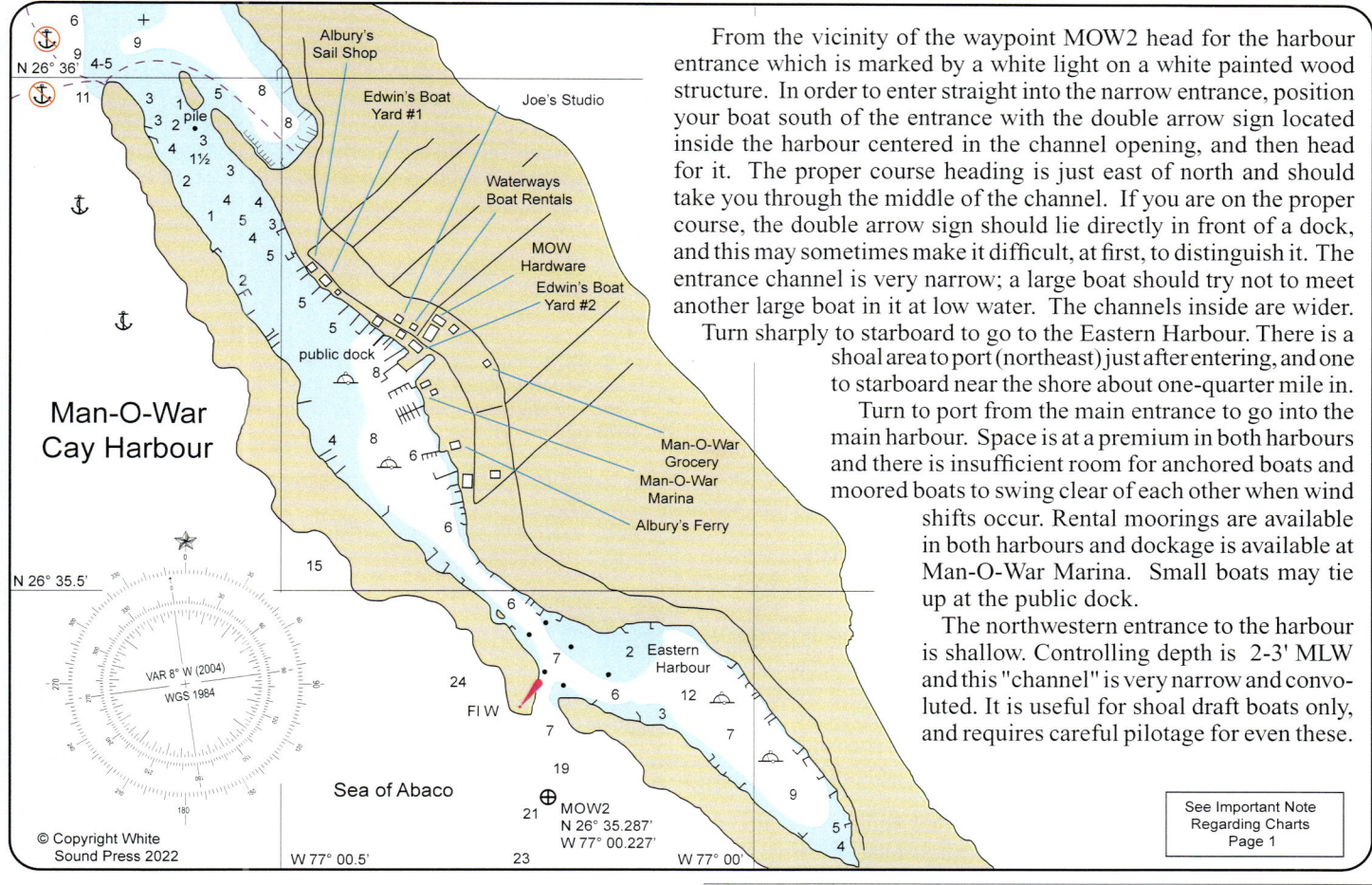

From the vicinity of the waypoint MOW2 head for the harbour entrance which is marked by a white light on a white painted wood structure. In order to enter straight into the narrow entrance, position your boat south of the entrance with the double arrow sign located inside the harbour centered in the channel opening, and then head for it. The proper course heading is just east of north and should take you through the middle of the channel. If you are on the proper course, the double arrow sign should lie directly in front of a dock, and this may sometimes make it difficult, at first, to distinguish it. The entrance channel is very narrow; a large boat should try not to meet another large boat in it at low water. The channels inside are wider. Turn sharply to starboard to go to the Eastern Harbour. There is a shoal area to port (northeast) just after entering, and one to starboard near the shore about one-quarter mile in.

Turn to port from the main entrance to go into the main harbour. Space is at a premium in both harbours and there is insufficient room for anchored boats and moored boats to swing clear of each other when wind shifts occur. Rental moorings are available in both harbours and dockage is available at Man-O-War Marina. Small boats may tie up at the public dock.

The northwestern entrance to the harbour is shallow. Controlling depth is 2-3' MLW and this "channel" is very narrow and convoluted. It is useful for shoal draft boats only, and requires careful pilotage for even these.

See Important Note Regarding Charts Page 1

© Copyright White Sound Press 2022

Approach from the south. Line up the piling with the double arrow (points left and right) in the center of the opening.

The opening is narrow; do not meet another large boat here. Note the piling with the double arrow in front of the powerboat at the dock. It should be centered in the opening.

When about 50-60' from the piling with the double arrow, turn to port and proceed toward the main harbour.

MAN-O-WAR CAY

During the early twentieth century the Commissioner, who at that time was based in Hope Town, described Man-O-War Cay as a small island which had a few enterprising men. The same could be said today, though there are undoubtedly more enterprising men (and women). Until recently Man-O-War was the home base for Albury's Ferry. Marcel Albury, who ran it, was one of the most experienced pilots in Abaco. See his article on crossing the Gulf Stream to Abaco on page 19. Man-O-War has been a center for boat building and repair for many years. Edwin's Boat Yard does excellent work and maintains a good stock of marine parts. They actually have two yards—boat yard #1 is near the Sail Shop at the northwest end of town; boat yard #2 is located near the center of town. Albury Brothers Boat Building, located just northwest of Edwin's Boat Yard #2, builds sturdy round bilge deep-V fiberglass outboard boats.

Man-O-War Marina was severely damaged and no rebuilding plans are known at time of publication. Man-O-War Grocery is at the top of the hill back from Man-O-War Marina. They will deliver groceries to all docks at Man-O-War.

Man-O-War Hardware is located across the road from Edwin's Boat Yard #2. They continue to provide well stocked hardware and building materials.

Joe's Studio is one of the most unique gift shops in Abaco because Joe Albury's hand-crafted items made of Abaco hardwoods are sold there. At this time they are open a few days a week. They also offer jewelry, T-shirts and other gift items.

Emerson's Shop is now operated by his son Andy Albury, who builds beautiful half models as well as the same sturdy rocking chairs his father built for many years.

Another very unique shop—the Sail Shop—is located at the far northwestern edge of the settlement just past Edwin's Boat Yard #1. Their dock is rebuilt and the shop is presently located just across the road. Durable and colorful canvas duffle bags, sewn on the premises, are available. Hats, jackets, purses and a variety of other canvas goods are also sewn and sold there.

The ocean side of Man-O-War Cay is worth a visit—there are some beautiful beaches alternating with rock outcroppings. The northwestern and southeastern ends of the cay are well developed with private residences. Explore by walking the road, or by bicycle or golf cart.

Man-O-War's long boat building tradition was well represented by Maurice Albury during the 1960s and 1970s. A dinghy was under construction in his shed in 1973 (below). Photos by Steve Dodge.

The rebuilt Man-O-War public dock, January 2021

NEW!

A history of Man-O-War Cay by Man-O-War resident Jeremy Sweeting with a chapter on boat building, genologies and collected stories about Man-O-War

Man-O-War
From Shipwreck to Boat Building Capital
by Jeremy Sweeting

$29.95

Avaiable
Man-O-War
Elbow Cay
Marsh Harbour
White Sound Press
Amazon.com

Post Dorian Photograph of Man-O-War Cay. Notice all of the buildings with blue tarps. Photo by Lisa Dodge 3 December 2019

EDWIN'S BOAT YARD
Man-O-War Cay • Abaco, Bahamas

- Hauling up to 65' or 50 tons
- Painting
- Varnishing
- Carpentry
- Mechanical

SAIL LOFT
- Sails
- Sail Repairs
- Rigging
- Splicing
- Canvas Tops and Covers

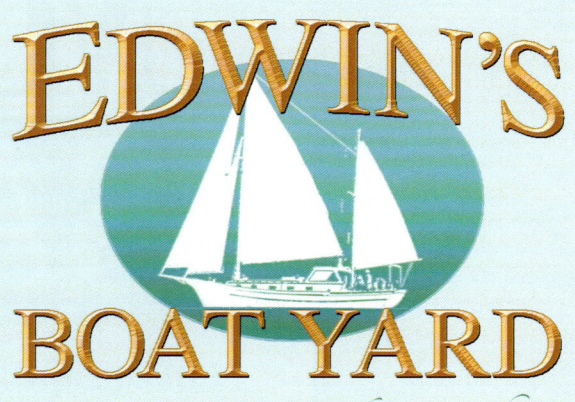

A Full Service Yard on Man-O-War Cay

One of Abaco's Largest Marine Stores

Complete Haulout Services

Wet & Dry Storage Available

VHF Channel 16
242-365-6006

Email: edwinsboatyard@hotmail.com

YANMAR marine

Sea Hawk PREMIUM YACHT FINISHES

The Sail Shop is at the extreme left with Edwin's Boatyard #1 (yellow buildings) to its right; Edwin's Boatyard #2 is at the extreme right with Albury Brothers Boats (white building) to its left. Photo by Steve Dodge, 19 March 2010.

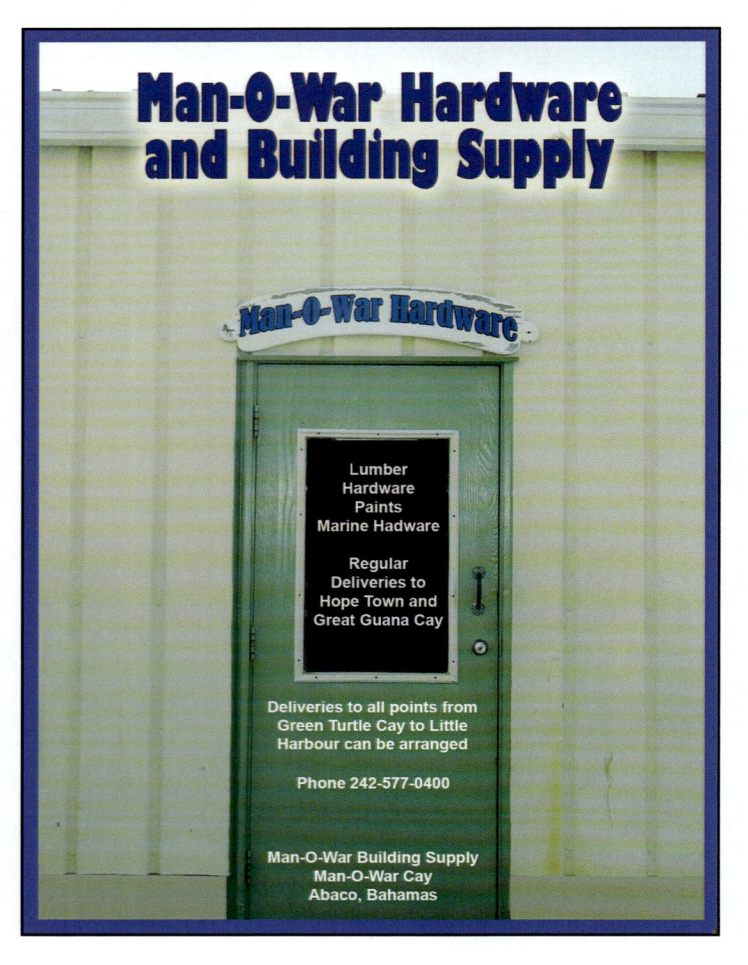

Man-O-War Hardware and Building Supply

Man-O-War Hardware

Lumber
Hardware
Paints
Marine Hadware

Regular
Deliveries to
Hope Town and
Great Guana Cay

Deliveries to all points from
Green Turtle Cay to Little
Harbour can be arranged

Phone 242-577-0400

Man-O-War Building Supply
Man-O-War Cay
Abaco, Bahamas

MACK SAILS

Handling all of your sailmaking and rigging needs, before during and after your cruise.

Call or stop by our loft in Stuart, FL or our service loft in Man O War, Abaco.

Mack Sails
(772) 283 2306
(800) 428 1384
info@macksails.com

Man O War
Jay Manni
(242) 375 8740
jjmanni@hotmail.com

The Sail Shop

We make fine sturdy handcrafted canvas duffle bags, toiletry bags, carry-ons, jackets, hats, and canvas goods of all kinds. Made in our waterfront shop at the north end of town. Come visit us!

Man-O-War Cay Abaco, Bahamas

242-824-0326

The Sail Shop dock is rebuilt, they are currently open across the steet. Photo by Jon Dodge 26 January 2021

Dickie's Cay and Man-O-War Cay form the main harbour at Man-O-War

DRIFTWOOD NEWS & GIFTS
MARSH HARBOUR AIRPORT

LOCALLY DESIGNED T-SHIRTS & HATS
BAHAMIAN MADE PRODUCTS & SOUVENIRS
HOPE TOWN CANVAS
PHARMACY ITEMS
BAHAMIAN BOOKS & AUTHORS
COLD DRINKS, HOT COFFEE, CHOCOLATES & SNACKS

**LOCATED IN DEPARTURE LOUNGE OF
LEONARD M THOMPSON INTERNATIONAL AIRPORT
MARSH HARBOUR, ABACO**

HUB OF ABACO

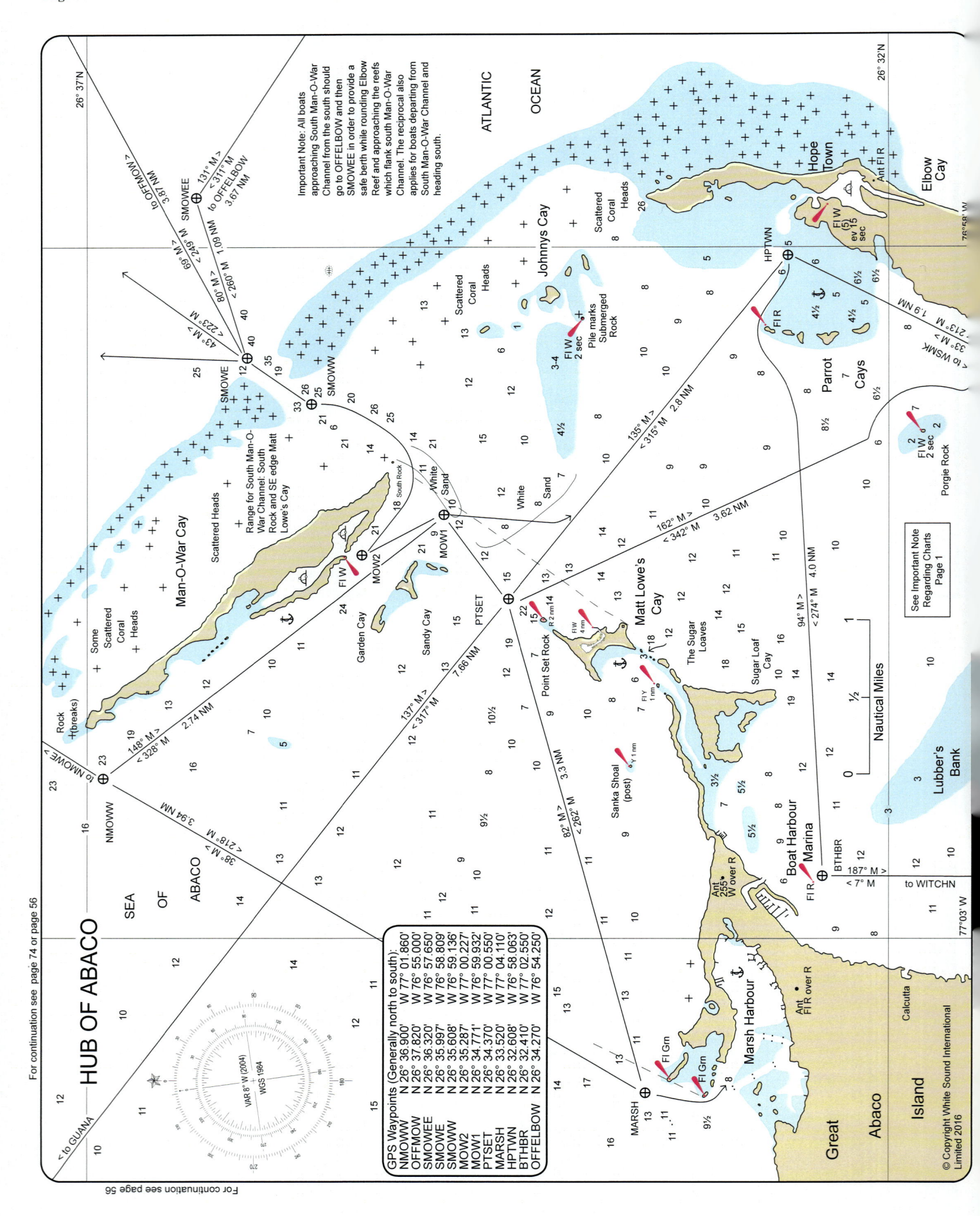

Important Note: All boats approaching South Man-O-War Channel from the south should go to OFFELBOW and then SMOWEE in order to provide a safe berth while rounding Elbow Reef and approaching the reefs which flank south Man-O-War Channel. The reciprocal also applies for boats departing from South Man-O-War Channel and heading south.

GPS Waypoints (Generally north to south):	
NMOWW	N 26° 36.900' W 77° 01.860'
OFFMOW	N 26° 37.820' W 76° 55.000'
SMOWEE	N 26° 36.320' W 76° 57.650'
SMOWW	N 26° 35.997' W 76° 58.809'
MOW2	N 26° 35.608' W 77° 59.136'
MOW1	N 26° 35.287' W 77° 00.227'
PTSET	N 26° 34.771' W 76° 59.932'
MARSH	N 26° 34.370' W 77° 00.550'
HPTWN	N 26° 33.520' W 77° 04.110'
BTHBR	N 26° 32.608' W 76° 58.063'
OFFELBOW	N 26° 32.410' W 77° 02.550'
	N 26° 34.270' W 76° 54.250'

VAR 8° W (2004) WGS 1984

© Copyright White Sound International Limited 2016

HUB OF ABACO

Most passages in this part of the Sea of Abaco are straightforward with few unmarked shoals. The shoal extending westward from the small cay south of Johnny's Cay is marked with a pile, as is Sanka Shoal, about ½ mile west of Matt Lowe's Cay. Lubber's Bank is clearly visible. Please see larger scale and harbour charts for Man-O-War Cay (pp. 74-75), Marsh Harbour (p. 82), Boat Harbour (p. 92 and 94) and Hope Town (pp. 96-97).

The straight-line route from Hope Town to Man-O-War passes over a 3-4' bank. Boats needing more water should head 306° M from Hope Town toward a point east of Point Set Rock, which lies just NE of Matt Lowe's Cay. When the entrance to Man-O-War bears roughly magnetic north, turn and head for it. This will keep you well west of the bank. The final approach to Man-O-War will take you over a white bank which is, however, 8' deep.

The route from Hope Town to Marsh Harbour is simple. Head 315° M from Hope Town toward Point Set Rock; leave it to port. Then head about 262° M toward Outer Point, leaving Sanka Shoal far to port. The route from Hope Town to Boat Harbour is also straightforward and simple. Leave the Parrot Cays and Lubber's Bank to the south.

The south Man-O-War Channel is a narrow passage from Abaco Sound to the Atlantic Ocean. Its controlling depth is 12 feet. Round South Rock giving it a good berth because of the submerged rock lying about a hundred yards northeast of it. Head seaward on a course of about 45° for about ¾NM to avoid the 6' coral head ½NM northeast of South Rock. Then head north to get on the range of South Rock and the southeast edge of Matt Lowe's Cay. Then head through the channel on that range (course should be about 43°M). This course will take you between the two extensive reefs to the northwest and southeast of this channel. Alternatively, use the waypoints. Enter from the Atlantic heading toward South Rock and southeast shoreline of Matt Lowe's Cay on a heading of 223° M. See the chart on page 74 for a larger scale view of this route.

The north Man-O-War Channel is wider than the south Man-O-War Channel and is the best passage between the Sea of Abaco and the Atlantic Ocean in this area—it is clearly the preferred passage. Its shallowest point is 17 feet deep. See the chart on page 74 for a detailed description.

Some good snorkeling areas can be found northeast of Johnny's Cay (see snorkeling maps on page 136, 137 and 142). There are some scattered heads between Johnny's Cay and the main reef, so one should not enter the area unless the sun is high so as to make the heads visible beneath the water. Johnny's Cay is private. There are also scattered heads between Man-O-War Cay and the barrier reef. Exercise extreme caution in these areas.

Matt Lowe's Cay was developed into 17 residential lots with a deep water canal system for private dockage several years ago. The electrical distribution hub for the outer cays was moved to the western point of Matt Lowe's Cay with several high voltage cables buried in the northern third of the anchorage. Cruisers should anchor only in the southern two-thirds of the anchorage west of Matt Lowes Cay. The cay is now owned by Montage Hotels & Resorts; the company announced plans to open a resort in 2023.

Point Set Rock lies off the NE point of Matt Lowe's Cay and is seen here with Hope Town, on Elbow Cay, in the background. The small white shack which housed electrical junction equipment was removed in early 2010. Point Set Rock is the crossroads of the Hub of Abaco; all vessels travelling between Hope Town or Man-O-War and Marsh Harbour pass in the vicinity of Point Set Rock.

The anchorage at Matt Lowe's Cay from the northeast with Sugar Loaf Creek and Eastern Shores behind and to the left and Marsh Harbour in the background to the right. The development of this cay has included the laying of high voltage electrical cables in the northern third of the anchorage. Cruisers should anchor only in the southern two-thirds of the anchorage.

MARSH HARBOUR

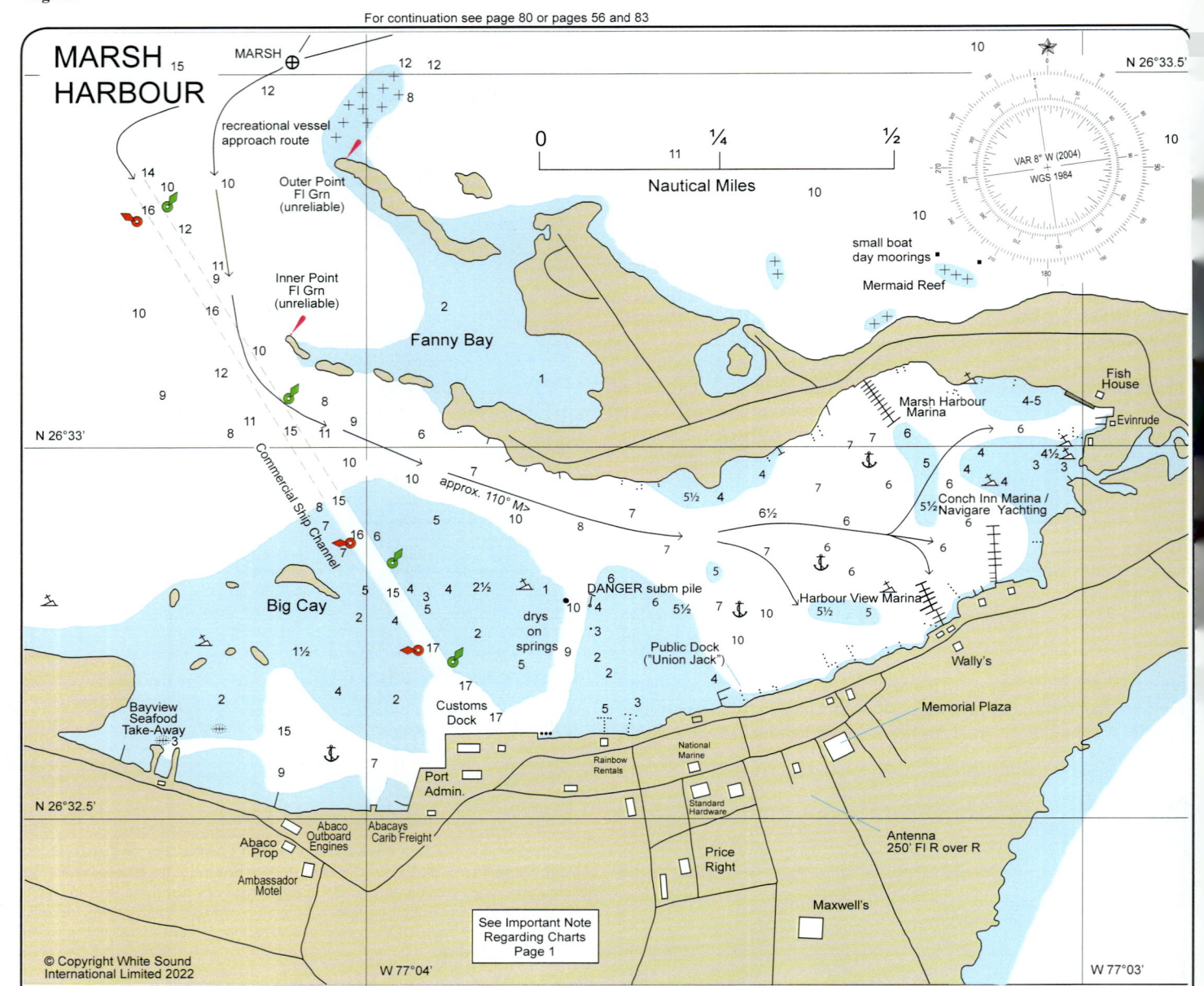

Though entry to Marsh Harbour is basically simple, there are two possible difficulties. The first is finding it. The landmarks are not very distinctive, and a newcomer to the area may wish to go to the waypoint Marsh or follow a rough compass course toward it until Outer Point can be distinguished. Entry itself is simple and direct. Stay about 200 yards off the outer point and about 50 yards off the inner point, and proceed into the harbour favoring the north shore in order to avoid the large shoal area extending from Big Cay at the western end of the harbour. Even though this is simple enough, there is a potential problem. When the new commercial port facility was built in 2002/2003, a new commercial ship channel was dredged. It is now marked with about 6 pair (changes from time to time) of large red and green steel buoys. This commercial ship channel has led to some confusion. Some cruisers have decided to enter via this straight channel. When they realize that they are headed toward the commercial port rather than the anchorage and the marinas, some have turned to port to head for the main part of the harbour and grounded on the 1-3' MLW shoal shown on the chart. We recommend that recreational cruising vessels ignore the commercial channel and the large steel buoys which mark it.

After rounding Inner Point, recreational vessels should head approx. 110° M toward the anchorage. Note that the four smaller red and green buoys which have marked the harbour entry for the past few years are no longer in place, but the entry is straightforward and clearly shown on the chart above as well as the photos on the two following pages. The main harbour is mostly 6-8-10' deep. Debris and wrecks are marked around several former docks. At press time, several wrecks were still in the harbour as shown on chart. Also, be aware of a submerged piling shown in the east customs dock channel. Shoals are clearly marked—two shoals flanking the old (east) channel leading to the commercial port and customs dock, a small shoal area extending from the small point on the north shore, and the two shoals flanking the channel leading to the Fish House, a commercial fishing facility with a retail store, at the east end of the harbour. The holding ground is generally good.

Boats should avoid anchoring within about 150' of the approach lines shown on the chart to allow all vessels easier ingress to and egress from the marinas. Anchoring is not permitted in either of the channels leading to the commercial port.

MARSH HARBOUR

Marsh Harbour is the largest town in Abaco—in fact it is the third largest in the Bahamas, exceeded in size only by Nassau and Freeport. The population was about 6000 pre-Dorian, many of the former businesses and stores have now opened and many are in progress. Several new or expanded businesses are also now available. Marsh Harbour has re-established itself as the provider of the central location for commerce and supplies in Abaco.

Several restaurants are presently up and running with others currently under reconstruction. A new business, Cat 5, is located in the new shopping center halfway to the airport and offers sit down lunch and dinner. Colours reopened last year on Bay Street overlooking the harbour and Boat Harbour offers two dining options. Premier Importers has a coffee shop with breakfast and lunch options. Several take out choices are available around town and in nearby Dundas and Murphy Town as well.

There are two supermarkets in Marsh Harbour. Both have expanded their product lines significantly. Abaco Groceries is located near the airport and now includes a separate full liqour store and has added hardware and appliances. Maxwells Grocery continues to also stock furniture and carries lumber and hardware. Premier Importers store offers hardware and home goods and an offsite lumber yard. Abaco Hardware is partially open during reconstruction and Standard is still currently closed. Parts City stocks a good inventory of auto, marine, and golf cart parts as well as tools and supplies. The central harbour public dock, called the Union Jack Dock (named after a restaurant which was located near the dock which burned down about 40 years ago) has not yet been rebuilt at press time. See the chart on page 82 and the street map of the Marsh Harbour Central Business District on page 90 for locations. Marsh Harbour stores offer an amazing selection of grocery products at excellent prices — clearly the best in the Out Islands.

The Conch Inn Marina and Harbour View Marina are located near town on East Bay Street, They both have newly rebuilt docks and are continuing projects with additional infrastructure. Conch Inn Marina is the base for Navigare Yachting. Harbour View Marina is also home to Blue Wave Boat Rentals. Marsh Harbour Marina is on the harbour's north side with excellent protection from northwest winds in winter cold fronts and good exposure to southeastern summer breezes. Boat Harbour Marina is in the town of Marsh Harbour, but not the harbour itself—it is located east of Marsh Harbour, directly off the Sea of Abaco. It is the largest and most comprehensive marina development in Marsh Harbour. For further information regarding Boat Harbour, see page 92. Marsh Harbour Boat Yards is located at Calcutta Creek south of Boat Harbour. They have an 85-ton travelling marine hoist and can provide most repair and re-building services. A marine store is located on the premises.

Please see the classified business directory for Marsh Harbour to learn the full extent of the goods and services available in this bustling Out Island town. It can be found on pages 168. Also see the street maps of Marsh Harbour on pages 90 and 91.

Entrance to Marsh Harbour viewed from the south. Note the commercial ship channel and the commercial port facility. Recreational vessels should ignore the channel and enter the harbour as shown above and on the chart on the facing page. The buoys have been enhanced on this photo to make them more visible; they are in the correct positions. Both of the small boats underway in this photo are in the suggested entry channel.

Continued on next page

A boat entering Marsh Harbour along the northern shoreline of the harbour viewed from the northwest. This boat has correctly turned to port out of the commercial ship channel (marked with buoys and not visible on this photo) and is heading approximately 120° M toward Conch Inn Marina. Marsh Harbour Marina can be seen along the northern shoreline, an area known as Pelican Shores. Beyond the mainland, Matt Lowe's Cay is visible on the left and Sugarloaf Cay on the right. The Hope Town lighthouse on Elbow Cay is visible in the distance on the right side of the photo.

This pair of buoys marks the entry to the commercial ship channel which should be used only by large commercial ships. **These buoys may be ignored by recreational vessels which should use the entry route shown on the chart on page 82 (note that this route does pass west of two of the green buoys marking the commercial channel.** If a foreign recreational vessel is clearing in, it should go directly to one of the commercial marinas flying a Q flag, and then phone Bahamian Customs (367-2522 or 367-2525) to arrange for clearance

Marsh Harbour is a port of entry for vessels coming to the Bahamas from foreign ports. Customs and immigration are located at the new port facility at the west end of town. This commercial port is a busy place, with two or more ships from West Palm Beach unloading each week, as well as the mail boat which arrives from Nassau early every Wednesday morning. **Recreational vessels should not go to the commercial port; they should go directly to one of the marinas** flying the Q flag if there is one on board, and then call Immigration and Customs to come to clear in. Phone numbers are 367-2522 or 367-2525.

Marsh Harbour is the seat of the Administrator for central Abaco. A new government office building in Dundas Town, the Government Complex Building (GCB) opened during 2012 and houses the Administrator as well as several ministries and other government offices. See the directory of government offices on page 168 for more detailed information.

Medical and dental services are available in Marsh Harbour, some within easy walking distance from the harbour, and a new mini hospital opened during summer, 2017. See the Business directory on pages 168.

Central Pines is a newer shopping center in Dundas Town on Forrest Drive. There are a variety of stores and services in the area and it is now the home for the BPL office.

Taxicabs are readily available in Marsh Harbour (though most no longer monitor VHF), and automobiles can be rented, making it possible to get around easily. Paved roads make it possible to drive to Treasure Cay or Cooperstown or even Little Abaco Island on a day trip, or south to Cherokee Sound or Sandy Point. See the article "Exploring Abaco by Land: ..." (p. 158).

Marsh Harbour Entrance, Photo by Lisa Dodge, August 2021

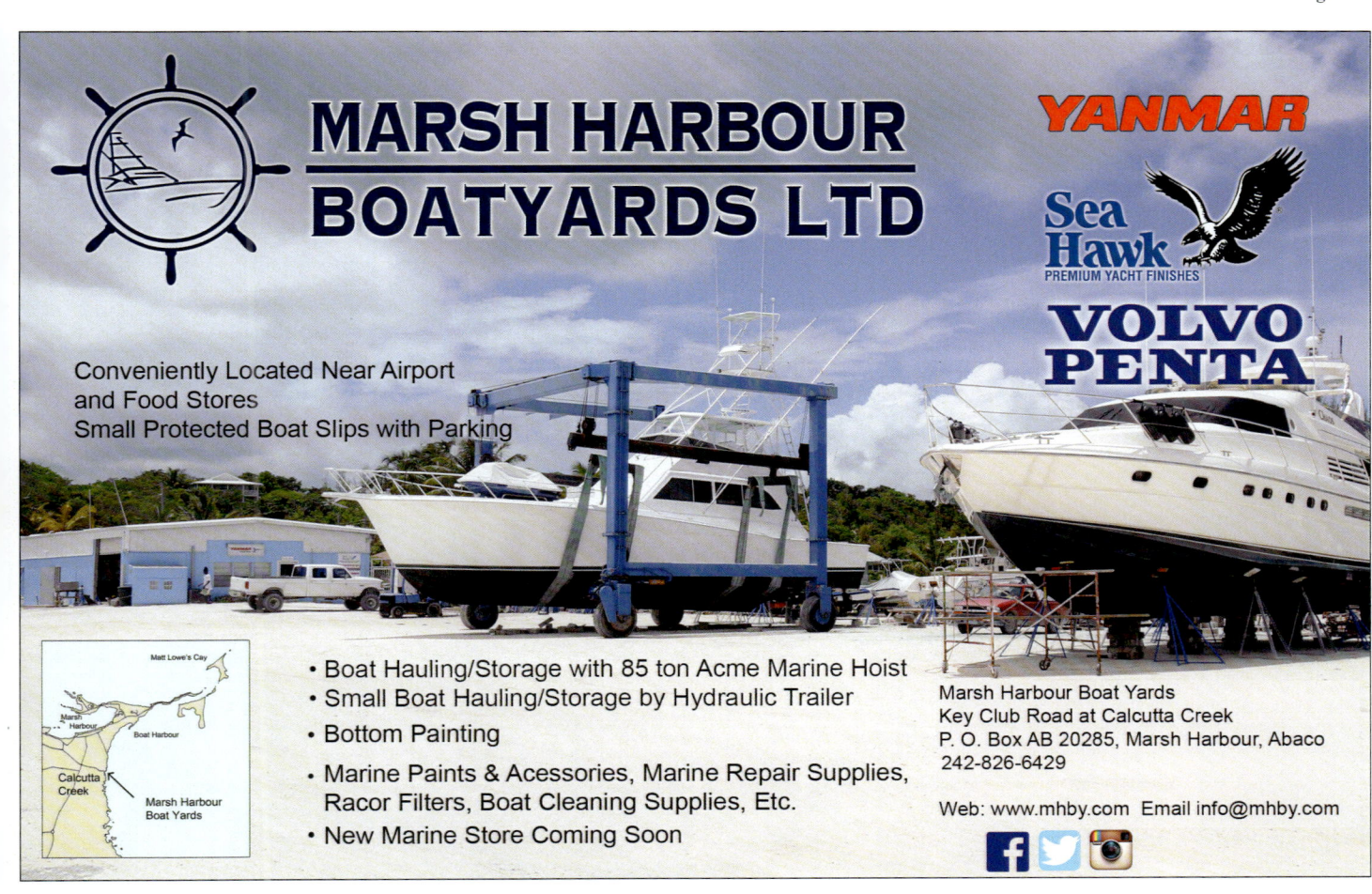

MARSH HARBOUR BOATYARDS LTD

YANMAR
Sea Hawk PREMIUM YACHT FINISHES
VOLVO PENTA

Conveniently Located Near Airport and Food Stores
Small Protected Boat Slips with Parking

- Boat Hauling/Storage with 85 ton Acme Marine Hoist
- Small Boat Hauling/Storage by Hydraulic Trailer
- Bottom Painting
- Marine Paints & Acessories, Marine Repair Supplies, Racor Filters, Boat Cleaning Supplies, Etc.
- New Marine Store Coming Soon

Marsh Harbour Boat Yards
Key Club Road at Calcutta Creek
P. O. Box AB 20285, Marsh Harbour, Abaco
242-826-6429

Web: www.mhby.com   Email info@mhby.com

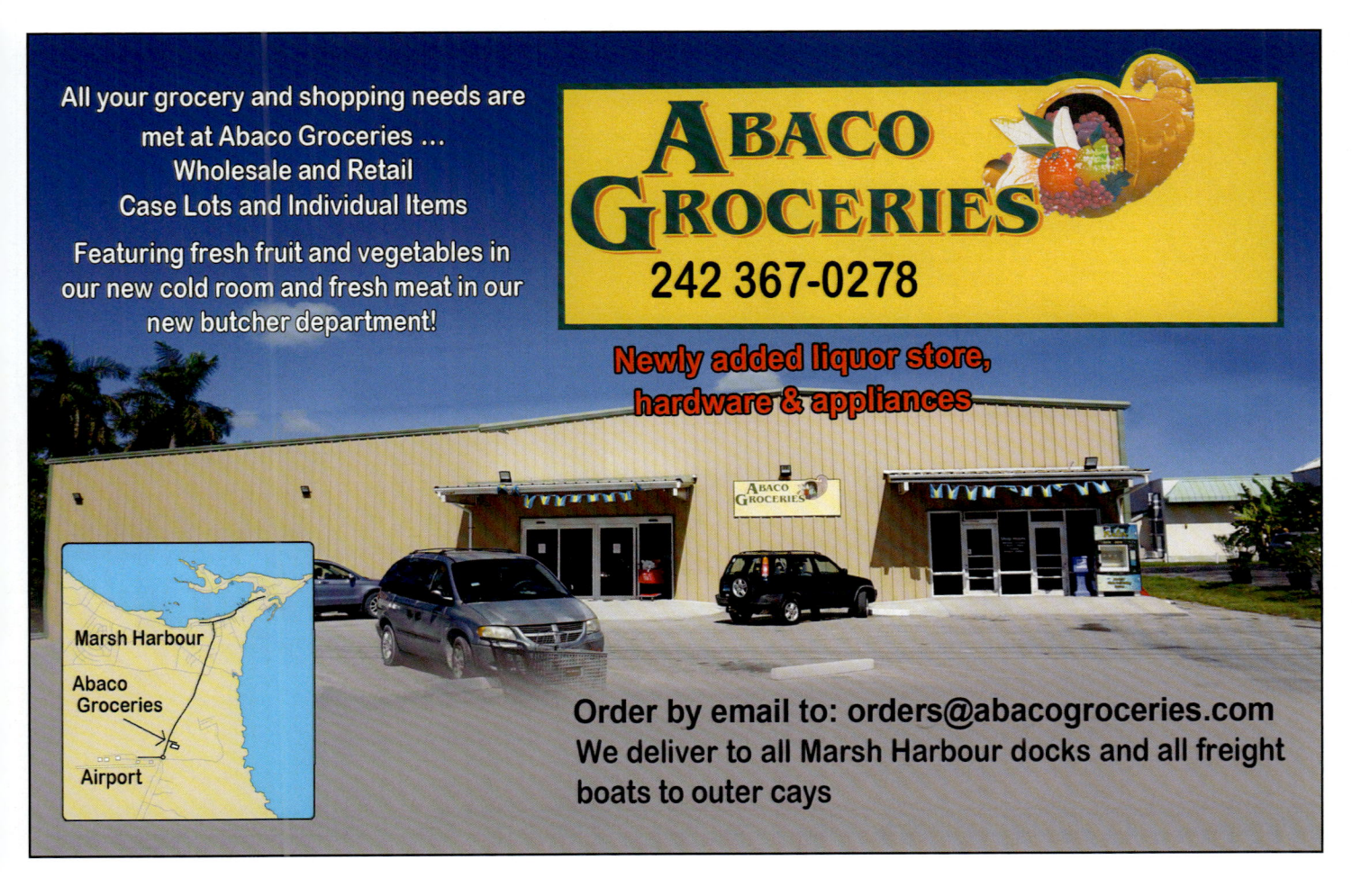

Abaco Groceries
242 367-0278

All your grocery and shopping needs are met at Abaco Groceries …
Wholesale and Retail
Case Lots and Individual Items

Featuring fresh fruit and vegetables in our new cold room and fresh meat in our new butcher department!

Newly added liquor store, hardware & appliances

Order by email to: orders@abacogroceries.com
We deliver to all Marsh Harbour docks and all freight boats to outer cays

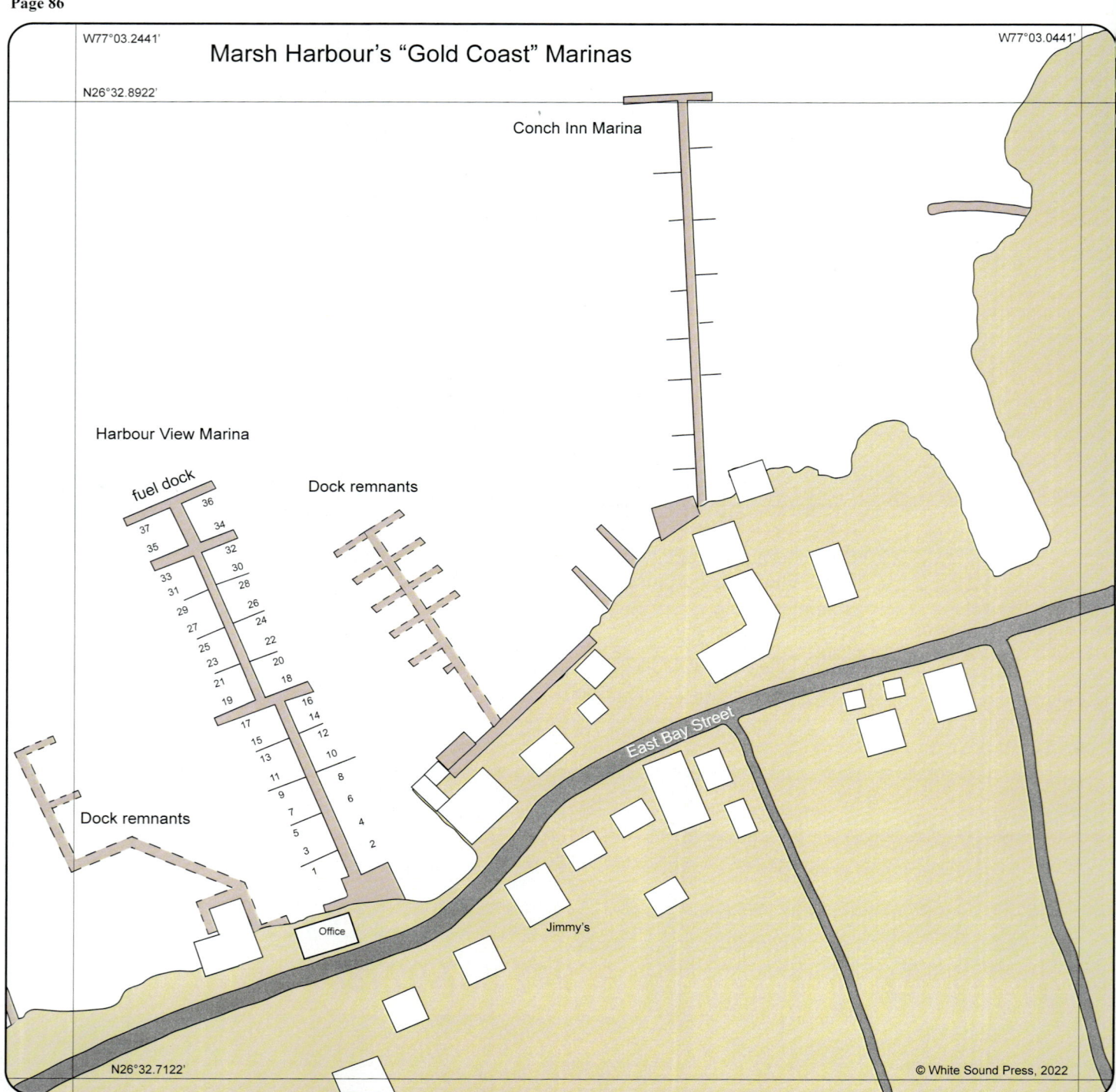

Marsh Harbour's "Gold Coast" Marinas

W77°03.2441'
N26°32.8922'

Conch Inn Marina

Harbour View Marina

fuel dock

Dock remnants

Dock remnants

East Bay Street

Office

Jimmy's

W77°03.0441'

N26°32.7122'

© White Sound Press, 2022

Parts City AUTO PARTS
DON MACKAY BLVD.
VISIT US
SEE OUR AD ON BACK COVER

ISLAND BOY TACKLE & MARINE

"The littlest, biggest tackle & marine store you'll ever see!"

- Replacement Skirts
- Bait
- Full Line of Off Terminal Tackle
- Black Bart, Mold Craft, Islander Lures & Blue Water Candy
- Ande, Sufix, Momoi Mono
- Racor Fuel Filters
- Cleaning Products
- Marinco 30amp, 50amp Electric Plugs and Accessories
- Oils, Zincs, Rope, Cable, Etc.
- Deep Drop Supplies
- VHF Radios, Antennas and GPS
- Full Line of Cable, Terminals, Switches and Bulbs
- Snorkeling Gear
- Full line of Pumps
- Charts and Navigational Aides

Sea Striker • Billfisher • Penn • Mold Craft • Black Bart • Blue Water Candy Fishing Lures • Shimano • Jabsco • Marinco • Rule • Racor Parker Filtration

Ph: (242) 367-3228 • Cell: 357-6670 • VHF Ch 16
Located just ouside Boat Harbour above Jamie's Place Restaurant Marsh Harbour, Abaco, Bahamas
islandboytackle@gmail.com

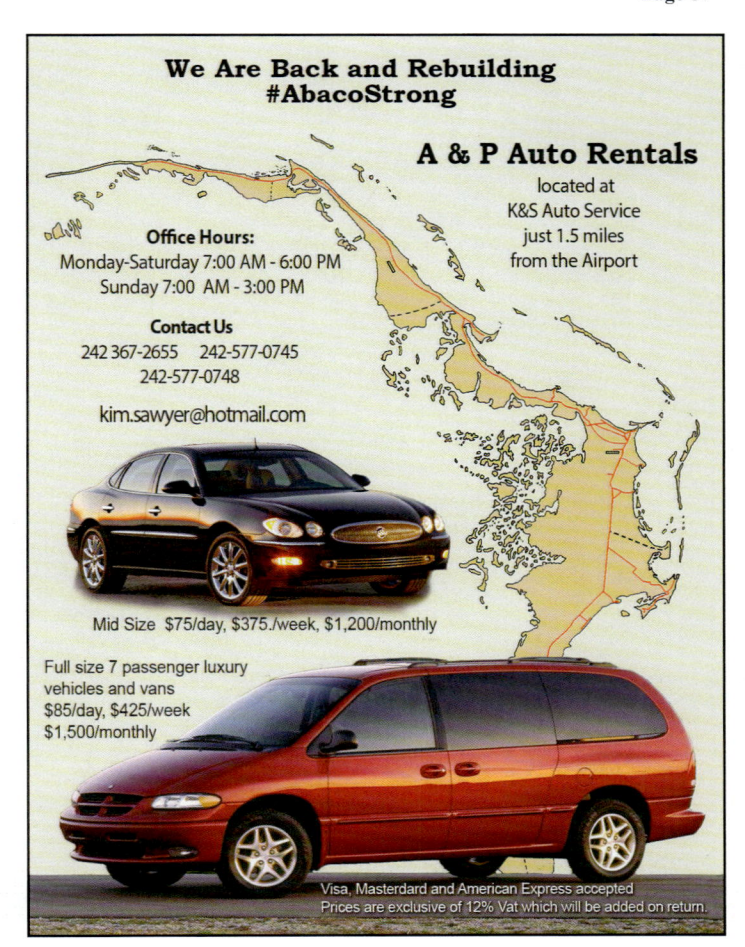

We Are Back and Rebuilding #AbacoStrong

A & P Auto Rentals
located at K&S Auto Service just 1.5 miles from the Airport

Office Hours:
Monday-Saturday 7:00 AM - 6:00 PM
Sunday 7:00 AM - 3:00 PM

Contact Us
242 367-2655   242 577-0745
242-577-0748

kim.sawyer@hotmail.com

Mid Size $75/day, $375./week, $1,200/monthly

Full size 7 passenger luxury vehicles and vans
$85/day, $425/week
$1,500/monthly

Visa, Masterdard and American Express accepted
Prices are exclusive of 12% Vat which will be added on return.

PREMIER IMPORTERS
EST. 1957

LUMBER YARD & RETAIL STORE
HOME | HARDWARE | LAWN & GARDEN

Downtown Marsh Harbour

CONTACT for orders & inquiries:
Don Mackay Blvd., Marsh Harbour
Central Abaco, The Bahamas
(242) 699-1415 | info@premierabaco.com

OPERATION HOURS:
Mon – Fri 8:00am – 3:00pm
Sat 10:00am – 1:00pm
Closed Sundays

@premierimportersabaco
www.premierabaco.com

Marsh Harbour's three principal marinas from the southwest.. Photo by Steve Dodge, 12 July 2016

Man-O-War Cay

Conch Inn Marina

Marsh Harbour Marina

Harbour View Marina

Abaco Ceramics

Lamps ~ Home & Table Decor ~ Tableware
House Signs ~ Custom Tile Work
www.abaco-ceramics.com

242.375.8774   Don Mackay Blvd.

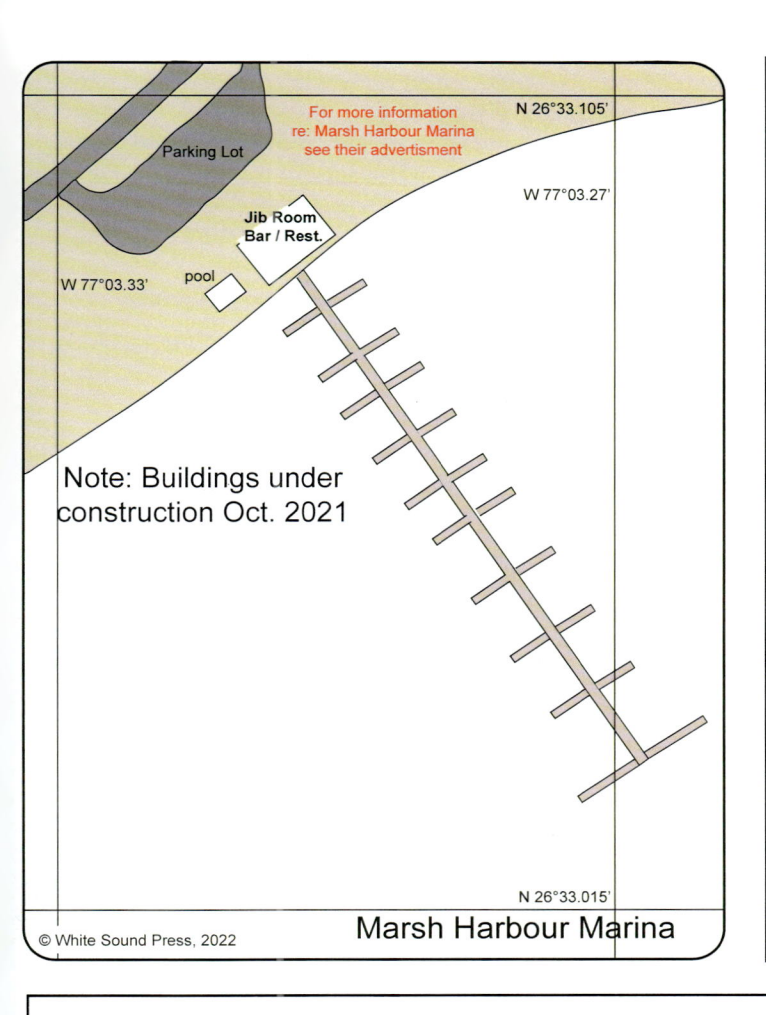

Marsh Harbour Marina

Note: Buildings under construction Oct. 2021

For more information re: Marsh Harbour Marina see their advertisment

Parking Lot
N 26°33.105'
W 77°03.27'
Jib Room Bar / Rest.
W 77°03.33'
pool
N 26°33.015'

© White Sound Press, 2022

THE CHEMIST SHOPPE

Abaco's First Complete Pharmacy
Prescriptions
O. T. C. Pharmaceuticals
Health and Beauty Supplies

"Best Selection in Town"

Located in
Maxwell's Supermarket

Pharmacists
Ted Pearce
Larry Higgs
Alana Higgs-Carroll

Marsh Harbour
Abaco, Bahamas

Phone: 242-817-3106
Fax: 367-3108
thechemist@batelnet.bs

THE FOUNDING OF MARSH'S HARBOUR

The settlement of Abaco was a result of the American Revolution which established the United States of America. Many Americans do not realize that the Revolution was a minority movement—most historians think that it was supported by about 1/3 of the population, opposed by another 1/3—with another third not "giving a damn" how it turned out. When the revolutionaries won, many of the Loyalists, whose property had been confiscated by the "patriots", had to leave the new country. One group left New York City and founded Carleton, which was located just north of Treasure Cay. These Loyalists, who opposed revolution in the United States for eight years, conspired to create a mini-revolution about two months after they had arrived in Abaco. This led to the establishment of "Marsh's Harbour."

Portion of 1817 Admiralty chart by Anthony DeMayne showing Marsh Harbour. www.heritagecharts.com

"I am sorry to inform your Lordship I found matters in a very different state at the Island of Abaco, where the colony of Refugees sent in september last from New York has settled; they had been but a few days on shore when dissention got among them, which by degrees rose to such a height they were on the point of taking arms against each other ....

"From the collected sense of the whole it appears that some of the people refusing to work at the provision store, a Court of enquiry was ordered, three of the absentees made apologies which were admitted, two refused to appear and three of them treating the Court with insolence and contempt, irritated the Officers so far they sentenced them and the two who refused to appear to depart the island in fifty-two hours. A great majority of the people justly alarmed at this violent proceeding signed an association to defend the five men, threw off the authority of all the Militia officers which Sir Guy Carleton had at their own recommendation appointed, and chose a Board of Police, consisting of three men to direct all the affairs of the settlement. Captain Stephens of the Pennsylvania Loyalists whom these people chose for their agent before they left New York does not appear to have acted with much prudence or temper,... apprehending his person in danger, he armed his servants and negros and seized two reputable inhabitants, keeping them prisoners ... Two of the militia officers became his (Stephens) sureties that he should not go out of his Town-lot till released by proper authority, where he remained from the 13th November till released by me on the 9th February. The party in opposition to the officers (and Stephens) having heard a Detachment from the garrison of Augustine was coming to support the Officers, quit the settlement and retired to Marsh's Harbour six leagues South East of Carleton,' where they have laid out a Town, and are well employed in clearing land and erecting habitations. The soil and water are better than at Carleton, and the Harbour safer though not so deep....

The numbers at Carleton and Marsh's Harbour are 658 souls, two thirds of which are at the latter."

Brig-Gen McArthur to Lord Sidney, Nassau,
1 March 1784 (CO 23, vol. 25, f. 75).

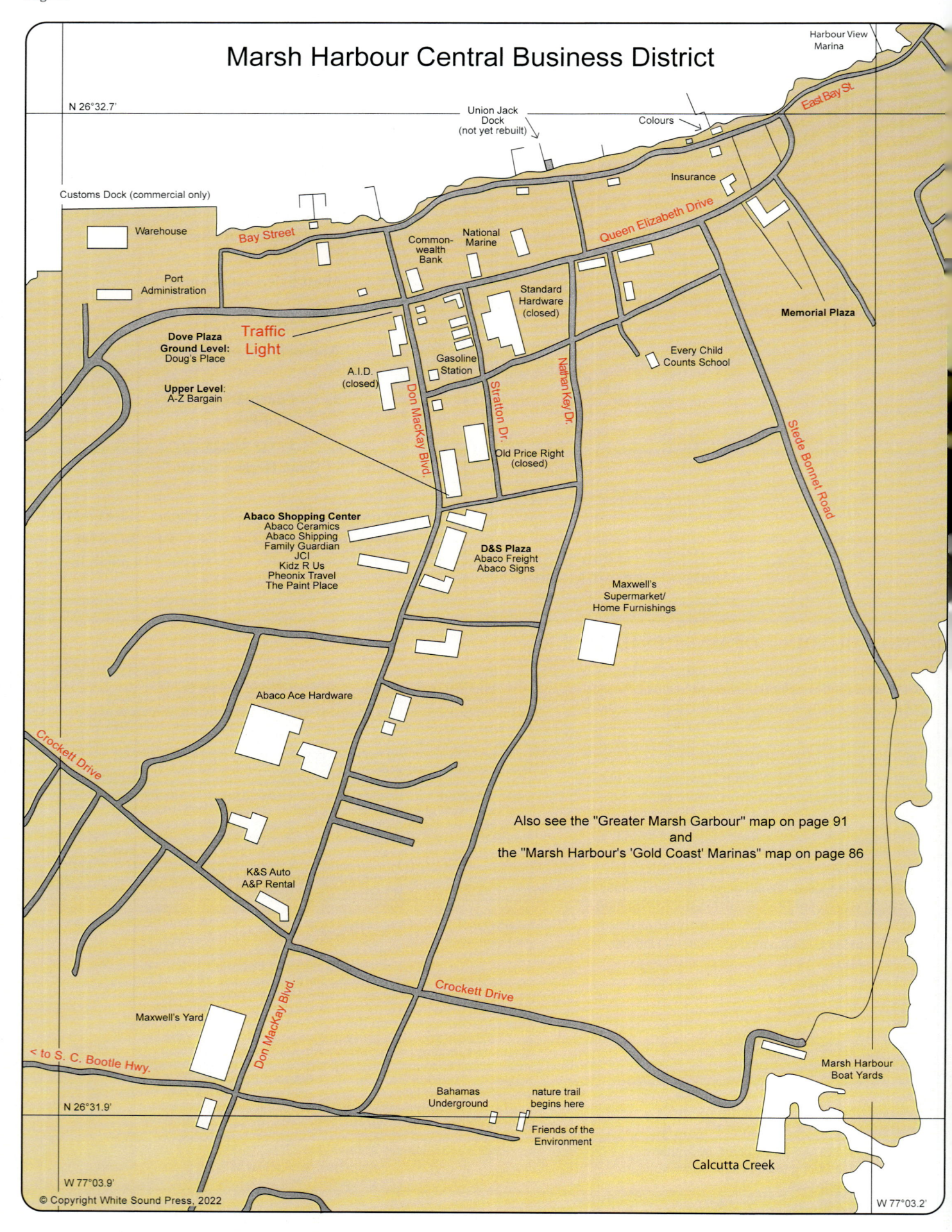

Marsh Harbour Central Business District

Page 90

N 26°32.7'

- Harbour View Marina
- East Bay St.
- Union Jack Dock (not yet rebuilt)
- Colours
- Customs Dock (commercial only)
- Warehouse
- Bay Street
- Insurance
- Queen Elizabeth Drive
- Commonwealth Bank
- National Marine
- Port Administration
- Standard Hardware (closed)
- Memorial Plaza
- **Dove Plaza**
  Ground Level: Doug's Place
  Upper Level: A-Z Bargain
- Traffic Light
- A.I.D. (closed)
- Gasoline Station
- Don MacKay Blvd.
- Stratton Dr.
- Nathan Key Dr.
- Every Child Counts School
- Stede Bonnet Road
- Old Price Right (closed)
- **Abaco Shopping Center**
  Abaco Ceramics
  Abaco Shipping
  Family Guardian
  JCI
  Kidz R Us
  Pheonix Travel
  The Paint Place
- **D&S Plaza**
  Abaco Freight
  Abaco Signs
- Maxwell's Supermarket/ Home Furnishings
- Abaco Ace Hardware

Also see the "Greater Marsh Garbour" map on page 91 and the "Marsh Harbour's 'Gold Coast' Marinas" map on page 86

- Crockett Drive
- K&S Auto / A&P Rental
- Maxwell's Yard
- < to S. C. Bootle Hwy.
- Don MacKay Blvd.
- Crockett Drive
- Bahamas Underground
- nature trail begins here
- Friends of the Environment
- Marsh Harbour Boat Yards
- Calcutta Creek

N 26°31.9'

W 77°03.9'

W 77°03.2'

© Copyright White Sound Press, 2022

Greater Marsh Harbour

Page 91

N 26°33.3'

- Murphy Town
- Dundas Town
  - BPL
  - Central Pines
- Government Sub-Division
- Dundas Town Rd.
- Forrest Drive
- Government Complex Building (GCB)
- Mini Hospital
- < to S. C. Bootle Hwy.
- < to Treasure Cay
- Pelican Shores Rd
- Marsh Harbour Marina / Jib Room
- Conch Inn
- East Bay St
- Albury's Ferry
- Harbour View
- Union Jack Dock (public)
- Port
- Traffic Light
- Nathan Key Dr.
- Stede Bonnet Rd.
- Boat Harbour
- Crockett Drive
- Parts City
- Marsh Harbour Boat Yards
- Premier Importers

For a larger scale map of the Marsh Harbour Central Business District (outlined here) see page 90

- Don MacKay Blvd.
- Resilience Square
  - Aliv
  - Cat 5
  - Island Yogurt
- School
- AMP
- Abaco Groceries
- 1st Carib Bank
- Block Plant Road
- Airport Traffic Circle
- Cherokee Aviation (FBO)
- Terminal
- Cherokee Air
- Leonard M. Thompson Int'l Airport
- Tower
- Abaco Highway to points south

W 77°05.4'   N 26°30.3'
W 77°02.43'

© Copyright White Sound Press, 2022

Abaco SIGNS Printing & Embroidery

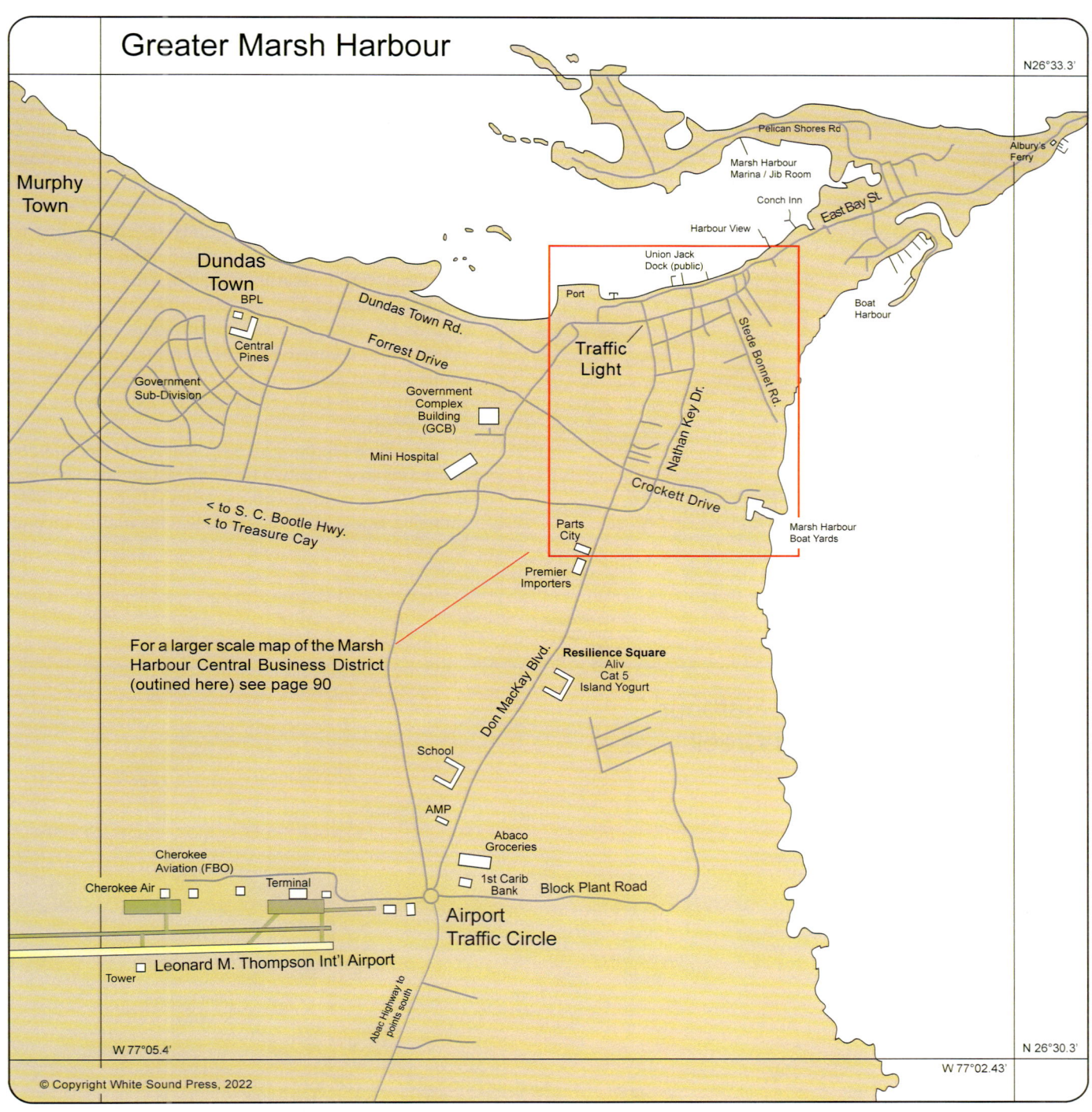

SIGNAGE
Digital Prints
Vinyl Prints
Banners
Perforated Windows, Doors
Channel Letters
A Frames

EMBROIDERY/SCREEN
Polo Shirts
T-shirts
Uniforms
Hats
Aprons

PRINTING
Business Stationery
Personal Stationery
Business Cards
Letterheads & Envelopes
Flyers & Menus
NCR Forms
Invoices
Funeral Programs
Booklets
Tickets
Laminations
and much more...

www.abacosignsandprint.com
abacosigns@gmail.com
1.242.807.8953

Dove Plaza, Don MacKay Blvd
P.O. Box AB-20968
Marsh Harbour, Abaco

The Leonard M. Thompson International Airport Terminal Building.

BOAT HARBOUR MARINA

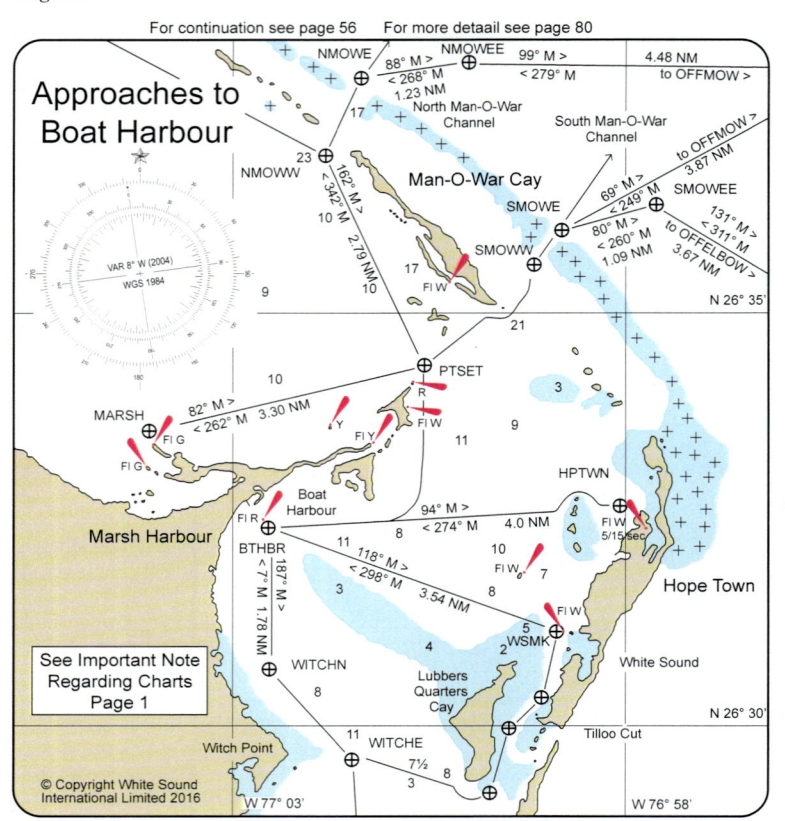

Boat Harbour Marina is conveniently located on the southeast shoreline of Great Abaco Island in the town of Marsh Harbour. Access to Marsh Harbour's business district is very good (about five minutes by car), and access by water to Hope Town, White Sound, Man-O-War Cay, or to the Atlantic Ocean via Tilloo Cut, South Man-O-War Channel or North Man-O-War Channel is easy and direct.

The waypoint BTHBR (N 26° 32.410'; W 77° 02.550') is located about 100 yards SE of the piling with the flashing red light, which is located about 100 yards ESE of the entrance to the marina. Approach the waypoint from the east on a course of 274° M, or from White Sound on a course of 298° M. Approach it from the south from the waypoint WITCHN on a course of 7° M. See intermediate scale charts of the Hub of Abaco (p. 80), the Lubbers Quarters area (p. 112), and Man-O-War Cay and its Approaches (p. 74 for more detail).

Boat Harbour offers gasoline, diesel, and complete marina services, has two bars and restaurants, and the Abaco Beach Resort on the premises. Marsh Harbour's "Gold Coast" shopping is a short walk away. See the marina map on page 94.

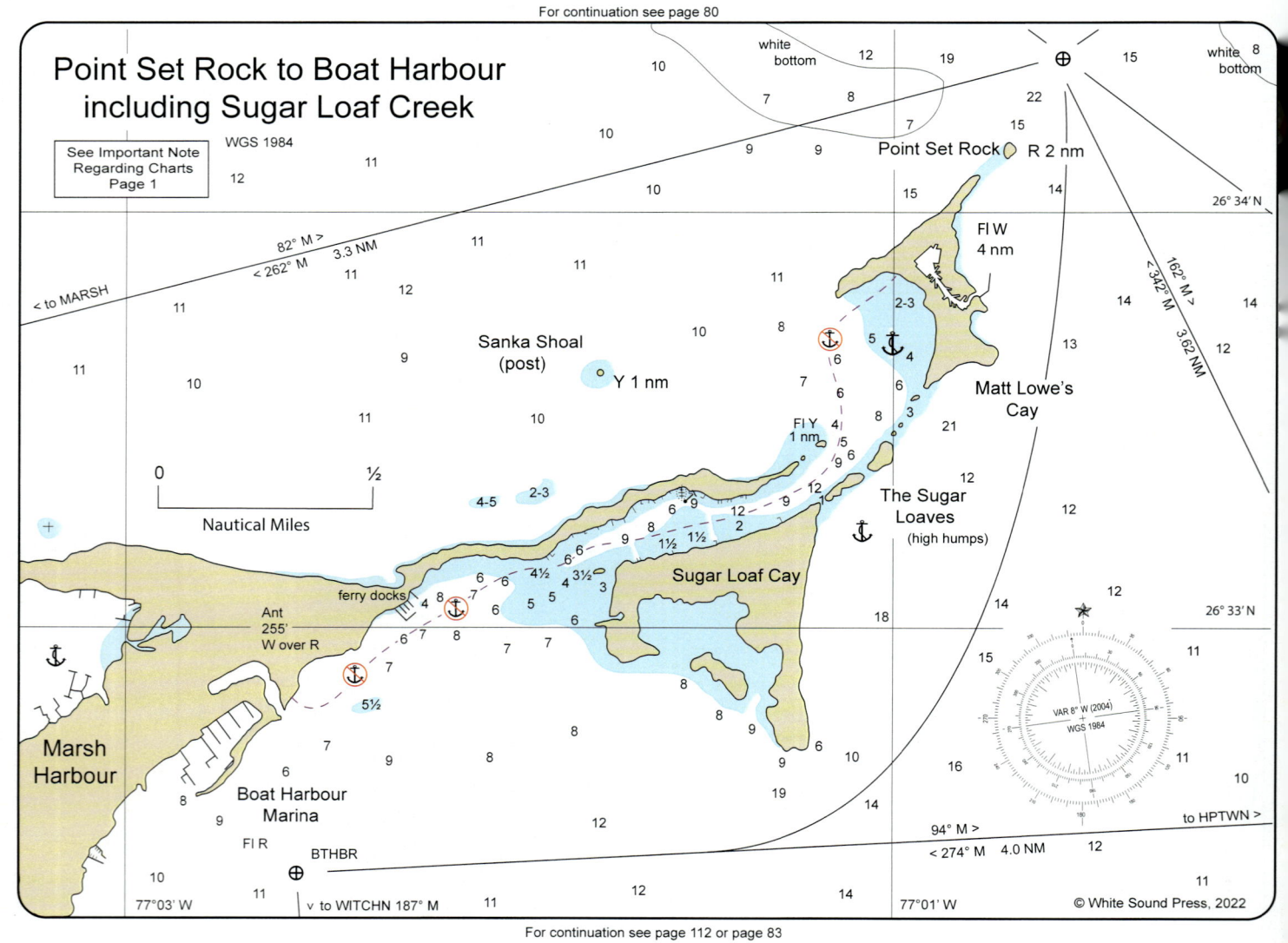

Abaco Beach Resort
AND BOAT HARBOUR MARINA
EST. 1955

EXPERIENCE CELEBRATE
REJUVENATE PLAY

Abaco's premier Oceanfront Resort and Marina in the Out Islands of the Bahamas, the ideal adventure getaway. Newly remodeled rooms, multiple dining outlets, two pools, swim-up bar, water sports, white-sand beach, and full marina amenities.

Only 165 miles from Florida by boat, 45 minutes by air.

877-533-4799 • MARSH HARBOUR • ABACO, THE BAHAMAS
WWW.ABACOBEACHRESORT.COM • RESERVATIONS@ABACOBEACHRESORT.COM

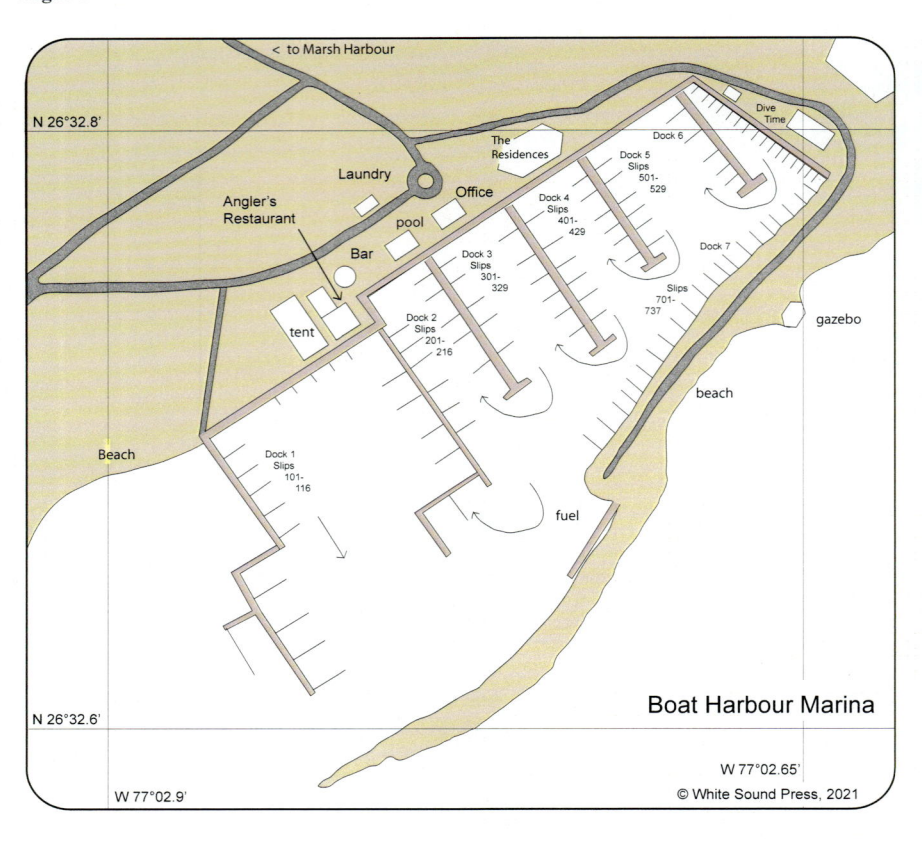

Boat Harbour Marina and Abaco Beach Resort from the southwest with Man-O-War Cay in the background. The fuel dock is to starboard after entering.

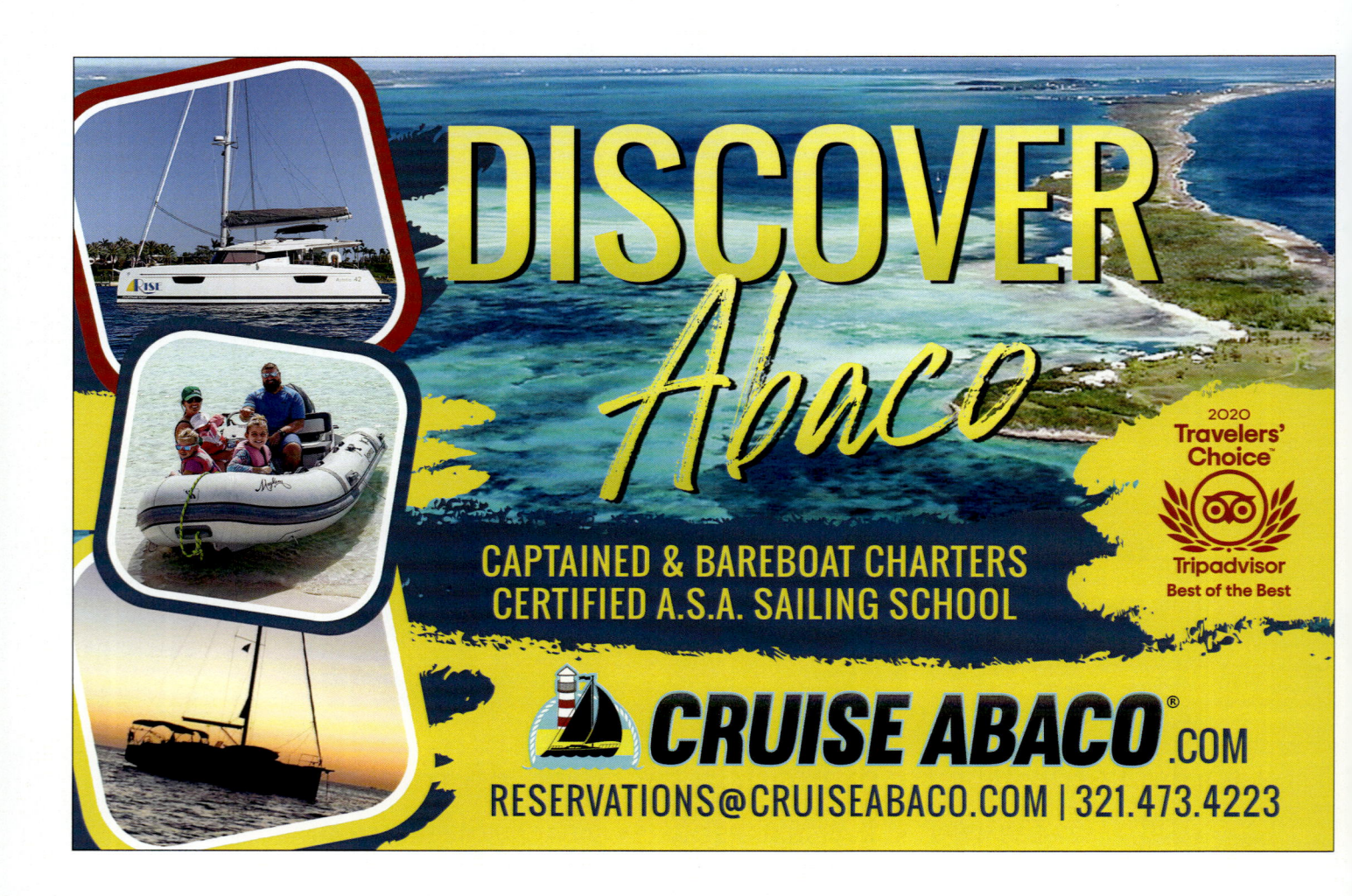

DISCOVER Abaco

CAPTAINED & BAREBOAT CHARTERS
CERTIFIED A.S.A. SAILING SCHOOL

2020 Travelers' Choice Tripadvisor Best of the Best

CRUISE ABACO®.COM

RESERVATIONS@CRUISEABACO.COM | 321.473.4223

The "back side" of Marsh Harbour looking southwest from the southwest end of Sugarloaf Creek. The land in the immediate foreground is Eastern Shores, the long narrow spit of land where most of the homes have waterfront on both sides. The wide spot in the road is at Crossing Beach. Albury's Ferry and G and L Ferry both have their Marsh Harbour terminals there for ferries bound for Hope Town, White Sound or Man-O-War Cay. Beyond the Crossing Beach ferry terminals there are a few private homes and beyond those Boat Harbour Marina is clearly visible. About a mile further along the coast Marsh Harbour Boatyards, the largest and best equipped yard in Marsh Harbour, can be seen. See a close up below. Photos by Steve Dodge, 12 July 2016.

SUGARLOAF CREEK separates Eastern Shores, Marsh Harbour, from Sugarloaf Cay and the Sugar Loaves. The top photo shows the creek with Matt Lowes Cay and Man-O-War Cay in the background from the southwest. The middle photo shows the northeastern end of the creek with Hope Town in the background; it was taken from the west. The bottom photo shows the east side of one of the Sugar Loaves. See the chart on page 92. Photos by Steve Dodge, 2008, 2010 and 2018.

Marsh Harbour Boatyards is located on the back side of Marsh Harbour. See chart page 112. Photo by Steve Dodge, 12 July 2016.

Elbow Cay and its Approaches / Hope Town

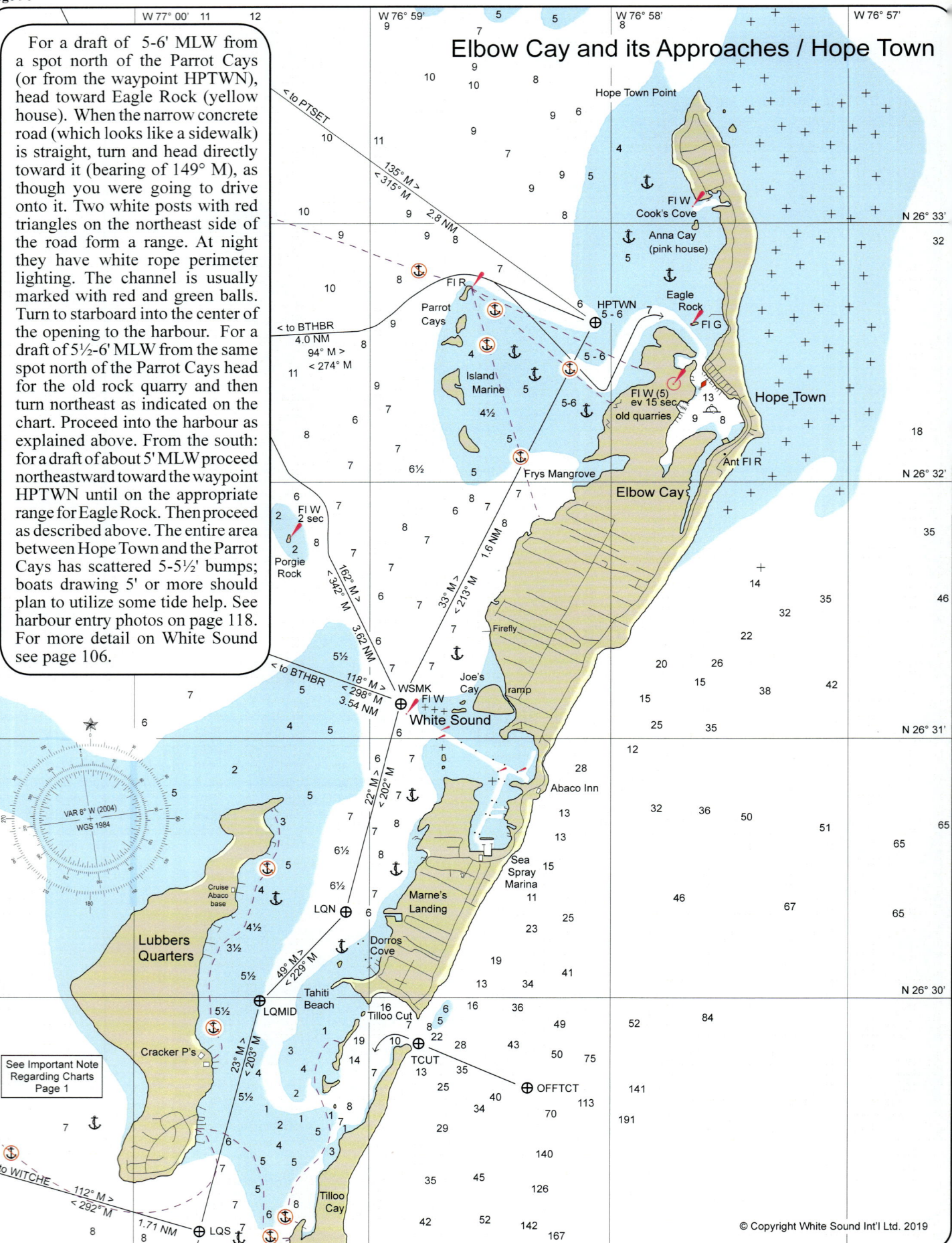

Page 96

For a draft of 5-6' MLW from a spot north of the Parrot Cays (or from the waypoint HPTWN), head toward Eagle Rock (yellow house). When the narrow concrete road (which looks like a sidewalk) is straight, turn and head directly toward it (bearing of 149° M), as though you were going to drive onto it. Two white posts with red triangles on the northeast side of the road form a range. At night they have white rope perimeter lighting. The channel is usually marked with red and green balls. Turn to starboard into the center of the opening to the harbour. For a draft of 5½-6' MLW from the same spot north of the Parrot Cays head for the old rock quarry and then turn northeast as indicated on the chart. Proceed into the harbour as explained above. From the south: for a draft of about 5' MLW proceed northeastward toward the waypoint HPTWN until on the appropriate range for Eagle Rock. Then proceed as described above. The entire area between Hope Town and the Parrot Cays has scattered 5-5½' bumps; boats drawing 5' or more should plan to utilize some tide help. See harbour entry photos on page 118. For more detail on White Sound see page 106.

For continuation see page 80 or page 83

See Important Note Regarding Charts Page 1

For continuation see page 112 or page 83

© Copyright White Sound Int'l Ltd. 2019

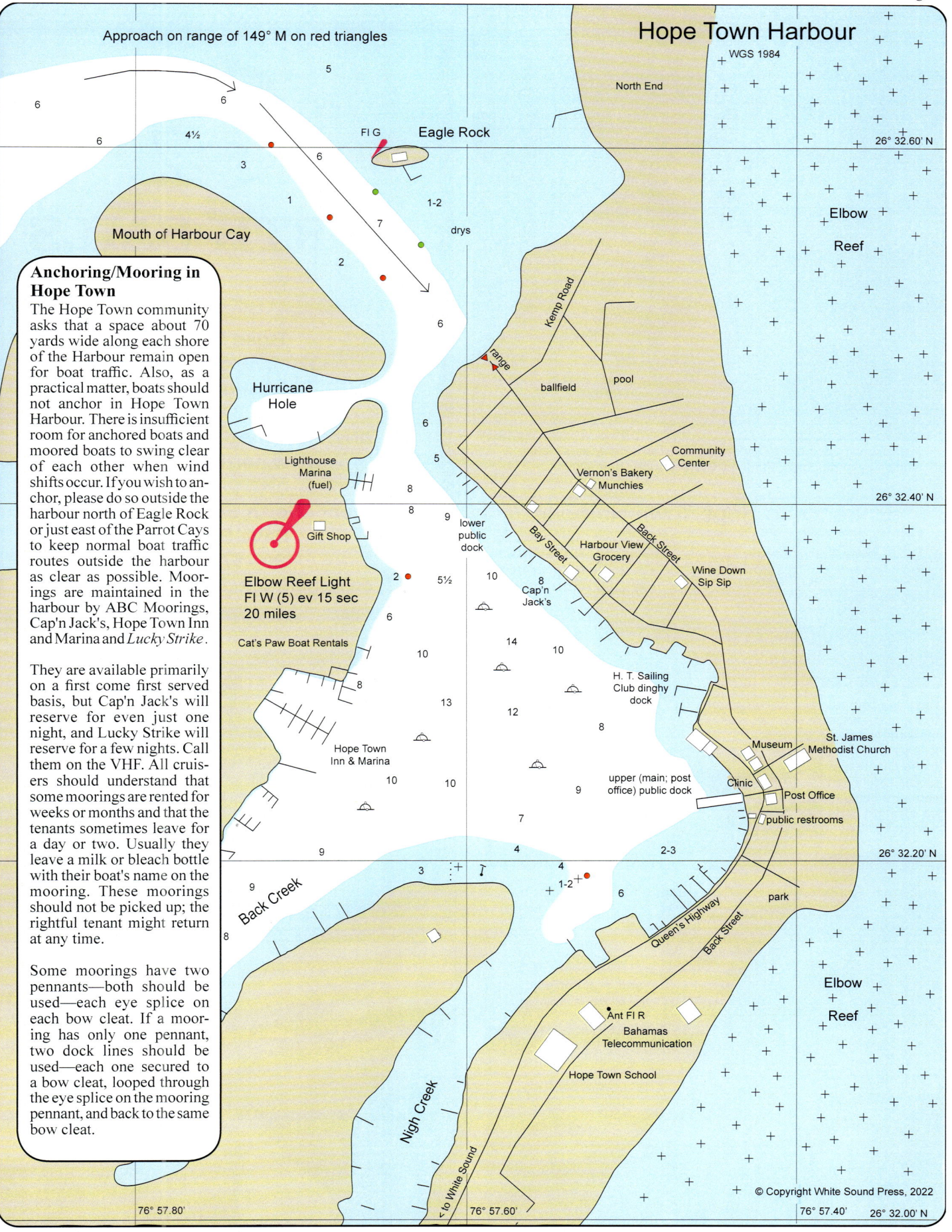

Hope Town Harbour

Page 97

Approach on range of 149° M on red triangles

WGS 1984

North End

Eagle Rock
Fl G

Mouth of Harbour Cay

drys

Elbow Reef

26° 32.60' N

Kemp Road

range

ballfield — pool

Hurricane Hole

Community Center

Lighthouse Marina (fuel)

Vernon's Bakery
Munchies

26° 32.40' N

lower public dock

Bay Street — Back Street

Harbour View Grocery

Gift Shop

Elbow Reef Light
Fl W (5) ev 15 sec
20 miles

Wine Down
Sip Sip

Cap'n Jack's

Cat's Paw Boat Rentals

H. T. Sailing Club dinghy dock

Hope Town Inn & Marina

Museum

St. James Methodist Church

Clinic

upper (main; post office) public dock

Post Office

public restrooms

26° 32.20' N

Back Creek

park

Queen's Highway — Back Street

Ant Fl R
Bahamas Telecommunication

Hope Town School

Nigh Creek

to White Sound

Elbow Reef

© Copyright White Sound Press, 2022

76° 57.80'   76° 57.60'   76° 57.40'   26° 32.00' N

Anchoring/Mooring in Hope Town

The Hope Town community asks that a space about 70 yards wide along each shore of the Harbour remain open for boat traffic. Also, as a practical matter, boats should not anchor in Hope Town Harbour. There is insufficient room for anchored boats and moored boats to swing clear of each other when wind shifts occur. If you wish to anchor, please do so outside the harbour north of Eagle Rock or just east of the Parrot Cays to keep normal boat traffic routes outside the harbour as clear as possible. Moorings are maintained in the harbour by ABC Moorings, Cap'n Jack's, Hope Town Inn and Marina and *Lucky Strike*.

They are available primarily on a first come first served basis, but Cap'n Jack's will reserve for even just one night, and Lucky Strike will reserve for a few nights. Call them on the VHF. All cruisers should understand that some moorings are rented for weeks or months and that the tenants sometimes leave for a day or two. Usually they leave a milk or bleach bottle with their boat's name on the mooring. These moorings should not be picked up; the rightful tenant might return at any time.

Some moorings have two pennants—both should be used—each eye splice on each bow cleat. If a mooring has only one pennant, two dock lines should be used—each one secured to a bow cleat, looped through the eye splice on the mooring pennant, and back to the same bow cleat.

Page 98

Correct entry and exit to and from Hope Town Harbour is clearly shown by three boats. Photo by Steve Dodge, June 2004.

Entrance to Hope Town Harbour

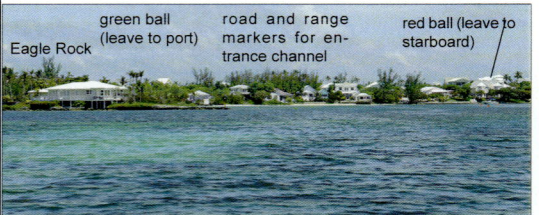

Eagle Rock — green ball (leave to port) — road and range markers for entrance channel — red ball (leave to starboard)

Approach to Hope Town Harbour from the NW showing the road and the range markers for the approach channel.

range markers (white rope light at perimeter of triangles at night)
road

Keep the two red triangular range markers lined up to stay in center of the channel, or proceed as though you were going to go straight onto the road.

Turn to starboard ...

and proceed into the harbour.

NORTH SAILS

Brian Malone
1320 20th Street North
St. Petersburg, FL 33713
727 898-1123   813 842-0401
brian.malone@northsails.com
www.northsails.com

Agent / North Sails Jacksonville
Dave Beatson
904 571-5566
dave.beatson@northsails.com

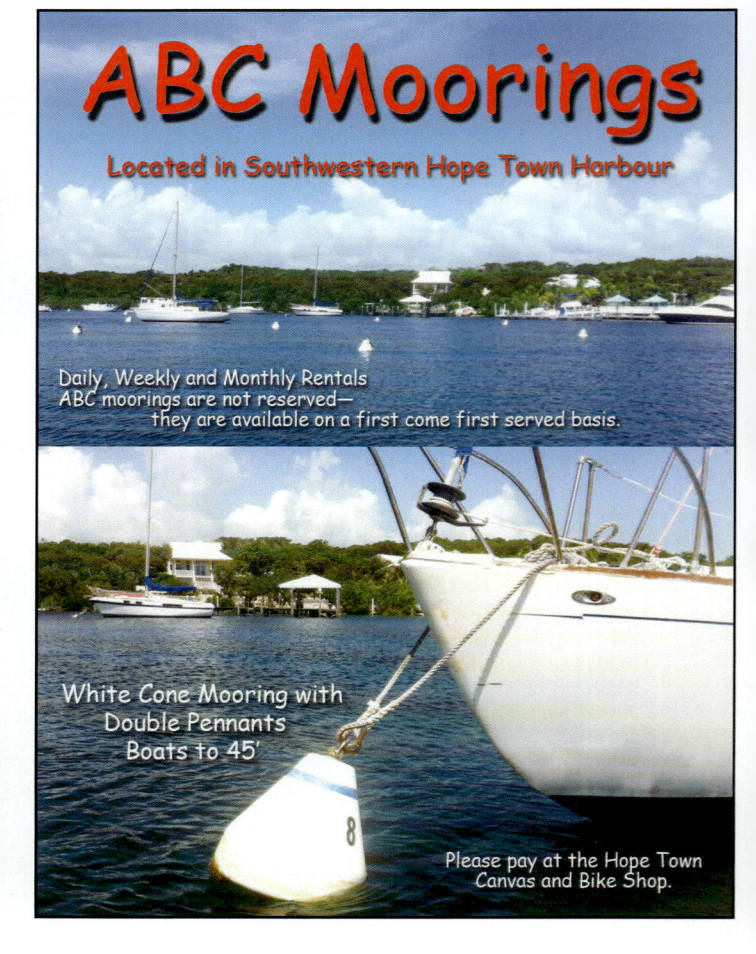

ABC Moorings

Located in Southwestern Hope Town Harbour

Daily, Weekly and Monthly Rentals
ABC moorings are not reserved—
they are available on a first come first served basis.

White Cone Mooring with Double Pennants Boats to 45'

Please pay at the Hope Town Canvas and Bike Shop.

HOPE TOWN

Hope Town is clearly one of the most picturesque settlements in the Bahamas. Its candy-striped lighthouse was built by the British Imperial Lighthouse Service in 1863, and still uses a small kerosene-fueled mantle and a huge rotating glass fresnel lens to send a beam of light which can be seen for up to 20 miles. The town has many charming old houses, some of them beautifully restored. The ocean beach, just to the east, has powdery pink sand and is protected by an extensive offshore reef. Founded by loyalists in c. 1785, the community maintains the Wyannie Malone Historical Museum, which has many interesting artifacts and photographs.

Hope Town provides many services for visitors. There are two food stores—Harbour View Grocery and Vernon's Grocery. Vernon's specializes in baked goods; pies and bread are baked daily. Harbour View Grocery is on the waterfront, and has its own dock.

There are two marinas—both on the west side of the harbour across from town. Lighthouse Marina is just inside the entrance and offers fuel, wet and dry storage, and has a well-stocked marine store. Hope Town Inn & Marina has 50 slips and a large pool/patio area with a bar, dining tables and a comprehensive lunch and dinner menu.

Cap'n Jack's bar and restaurant is located right on the harbour with their own dock in the central part of town. They are completing their rebuild and should reopen soon. They have added a liqour store across the street and Lighthouse Marina has reopened their liqour store as well. Lighthouse Liqours is no longer near the main public dock. (also called the post office dock or the upper public dock). They are currently operating out of Wine Down Sip Sip on Back Street which will require renovation before any reopening. On Da Beach Bar and Grill, located about a mile south of town at Turtle Hill Resort, is an outdoor bar and grill on a deck overlooking a beautiful ocean beach offering a grilled seafood menu. Another mile south and on the Sea of Abaco side of the island is Firefly, the newest resort on the island with a bar and restaurant open for both lunch and dinner. The menu is comprehensive, the sunset views phenomenal, and a large dock provides easy access for cruisers who anchor off. Abaco Inn is another mile further south at White Sound. They offer spectacular views of both the Atlantic Ocean and White Sound. Sea Spray Marina is just beginning their rebuilding process now(end of 2021). Abaco Inn offers breakfast, lunch and dinner. Sunset Marina is now open with a protected area just north of White Sound. Hopetown and Elbow Cay again provide the visitor with exceptional dining variety in a small town.

There are several excellent gift and souvenir shops—the Ebb Tide Shop, Sun Dried T's and the Da Crazy Crab. All have a good assortment of clothing, jewelry, T-shirts, books, and various gift items. Hope Town Canvas sews and sells authentic recycled sail bags. The Lighthouse Gift Shop located across the harbour at the lighthouse supports the Elbow Reef Lighthouse Society which maintains the lighthouse.

Golf carts are available from Island Cart Rentals, Getaway Carts, Elbow Cay Cart Rentals, Hope Town Cart Rentals, and Lighthouse Cart Rentals. White Sound is a 3-mile ride, and Tahiti Beach is another 1½ miles. Hope Town Point is a 1-mile ride or walk north of town. Motorized vehicles (including golf carts) are not allowed in town without a permit.

HOPE TOWN
Inn & Marina

We invite you to live like a local at our quaint modern island resort, with quality amenities and all the comforts of home.

Hope Town Inn & Marina is a 15-acre private estate bordered by the Sea of Abaco and Hope Town Harbour. Come stay with us at our marina, Hope Town's newest, featuring new docks and first class pedestals. We offer a variety of luxurious shoreside accomodations with striking views of the harbour and our pool. Our restaurant offers Caribbean cuisine and specialty cocktails and we are steps away from the famous candy striped Elbow Reef Lighthouse.

Call Today: 242 366-0003   US Phone: 850 588-4855   www.hopetownmarina.com   Email: office@hopetownmarina.com

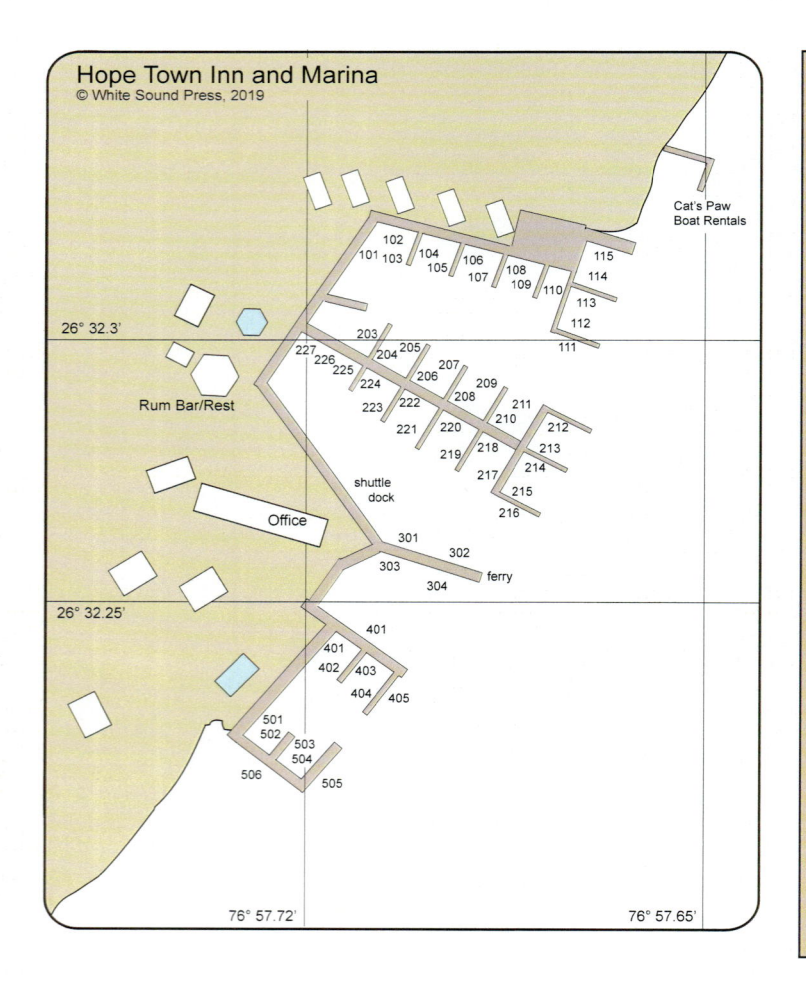

The Wyannie Malone Historical Museum

Hope Town was settled by British Loyalists who were seeking safe refuge after the American Revolution. Many of the settlers came from the Carolinas by way of East Florida after that area was turned over to Spain in the Peace of Paris in 1783. The same treaty called for the evacuation of New York by the Loyalists and many moved back to England or into Canada or down to the British Caribbean. The initial settlements were at Carleton, near the current Treasure Cay, and Marsh's Harbour. Marsh Harbour is now the largest community in Abaco and the third largest town in the Bahamas; whereas, the settlement at Carleton has disappeared. By 1785 there were over 1000 refugees in Abaco distributed in five or six settlements. The settlement at Hope Town was founded in 1785, in part, by a widow from South Carolina named Wyannie Malone. Wyannie along with her four children started a dynasty in Hope Town that spread the Malone name through the Bahamas over to Key West and other parts of Florida and outwards from there. Hence the choice of the name of: The Wyannie Malone Historical Museum. Hours of operation are Monday to Saturday, 10:00 am to 4:00 pm, November through August.

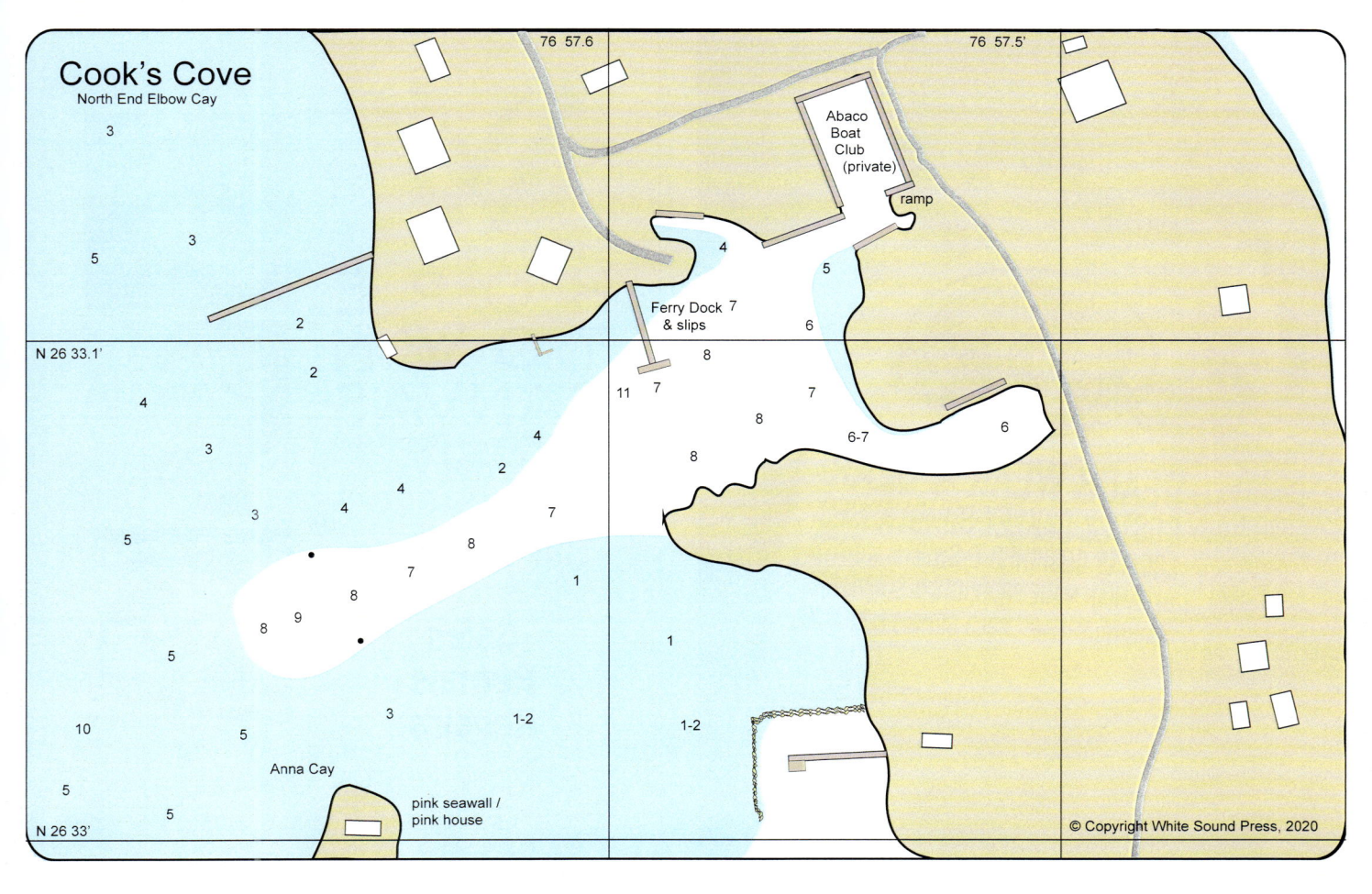

Post Dorian aerial of Hope Town, the Sea of Abaco and Great Abacol Island. Photo by Lisa Dodge 3 December 2019..

Cook's Cove
North End Elbow Cay

Abaco Boat Club (private)

ramp

Ferry Dock & slips

Anna Cay

pink seawall / pink house

© Copyright White Sound Press, 2020

VERNON'S STORE

"Let them eat key lime pie"

- Fresh Fruit
- Vegetables
- U. S. Meats
- Imported Cheeses
- Dairy Products

Justice of the Peace
Notary
Marriage Officer

Pies "R" Us

Fresh bread...
and pies...daily

Country Store
Convenience

Located at intersection of Back Street and Lover's Lane
Hope Town • Abaco • Bahamas
242 366-0037 • 242 824-7739 • vernonsgrocery37@yahoo.com

Turtle Hill Villas
On da Beach Bar and Grill

www.turtlehill.com Reservations: doug@turtlehill.com

Open Everyday at 11:30

Located downstairs at 2-storey yellow building next to Post Office dock

Sun-Dried T's Hope Town

BEACH WEAR & GEAR
COSTA & OAKLEY SUNGLASSES
LOCALLY DESIGNED T-SHIRTS & HATS
BAHAMIAN MADE PRODUCTS & SOUVENIRS
PHARMACY ITEMS, COLD DRINKS & SNACKS

Follow us on FB
email: sundriedtsht@gmail.com

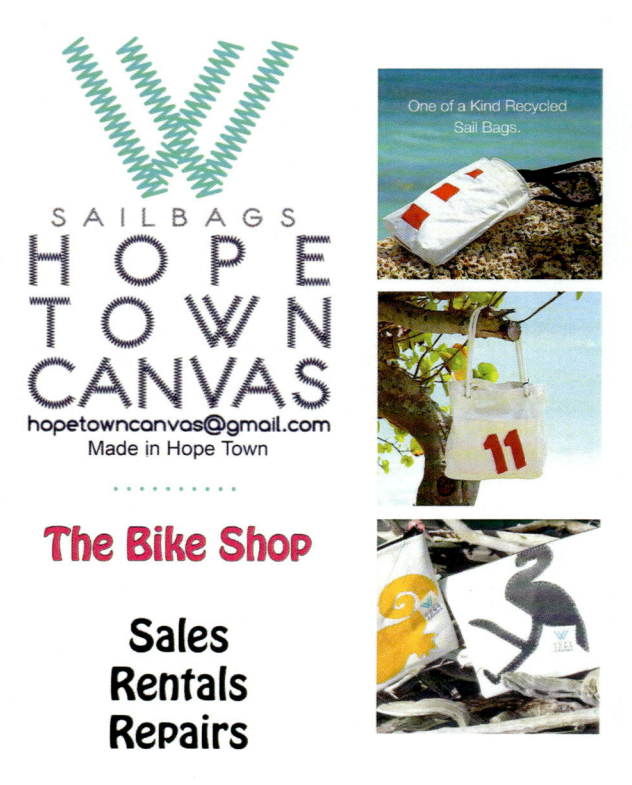

SAILBAGS
HOPE TOWN CANVAS

hopetowncanvas@gmail.com
Made in Hope Town

One of a Kind Recycled Sail Bags.

The Bike Shop

Sales
Rentals
Repairs

Tomato Paste Rental Cottages
Come Stay With Us – Our Lights Are Always On!

Located in Fry¹s Mangrove, a small quiet harbour just south of Hope Town settlement on the sea side of Elbow Cay. Our 2-2 bedroom cottages and studio-loft cottage are "island" elegant with a private dock, on site owners and island solitude.

Contact Us

242-577-0512
or
US-Toll-Free
1-888-471-1946

www.tomatopastehopetown.com
Email: tomatopasteht@cs.com

FRIENDS of the ENVIRONMENT
ABACO, BAHAMAS

Environmental education and community programs

Frank Kenyon Centre for Research, Education, and Conservation (hosting student groups of all ages and research projects)

Nature Trail and gardens

Home of the Bahamas Natural History Museum and offices of the Antiquities, Monuments and Museums Corporation

www.friendsoftheenvironment.org
242-367-2721

Come visit us!
0.6 miles south of Maxwell's Grocery Store, Marsh Harbour

Visit The Lighthouse!

ELBOW REEF LIGHTHOUSE SOCIETY

Planning a visit?
Sign in to our virtual guest book on our website and receive your pass with historical tour information to enhance your visit by applying at
www.elbowreeflighthousesociety.com/visit-the-lightstation

Elbow Reef Lighthouse Society
242 577-0542

Photo by Mary McHenry Photography

AIRGATE
AVIATION · INC

NEW SMYRNA BEACH & OTHER CENTRAL AND SOUTH FLORIDA LOCATIONS

TO

MARSH HARBOUR, TREASURE CAY, ELEUTHERA & OTHER DESTINATIONS

PET FRIENDLY

FOR RESERVATIONS CALL
386 478-0600
WWW.FLYAIRGATE.COM

WHITE SOUND

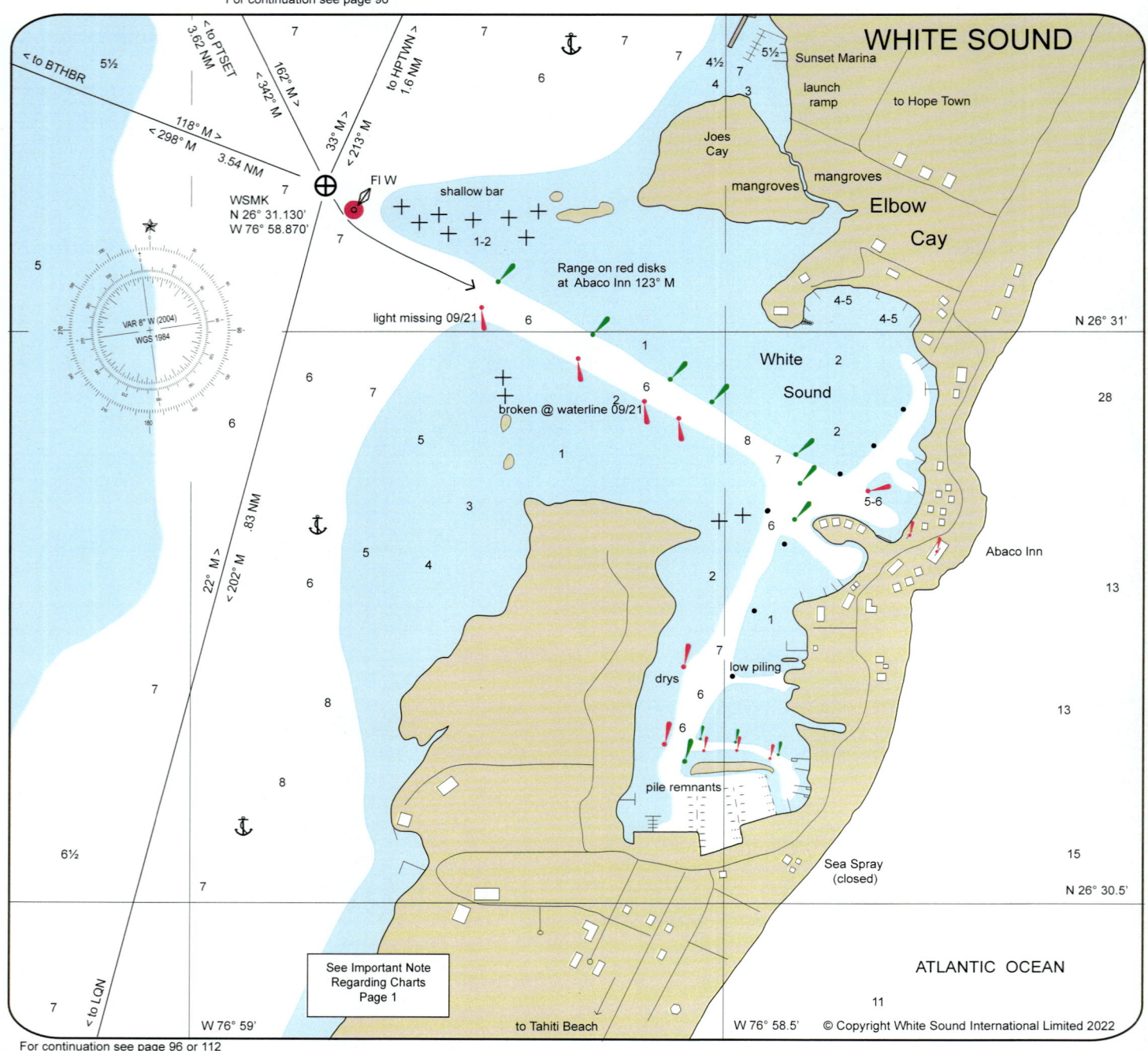

Boats transiting the area should stay west of the White Sound mark (see note below) which indicates the channel entrance and also the western end of the White Sound Bar. This rocky bank lies just to the north of the entry channel and has a depth of only about 1' at MLW, so even small outboard boats should stay west and south of the mark.

Enter White Sound in the dredged channel which carries about 5-6' at mean low water. It is marked by the White Sound mark (Fl W) at its northwestern end and a large red disk just beyond the beach at the Abaco Inn at its southeastern end. A course of 123° M heading directly toward the Abaco Inn will keep you in the channel. There is a large red disk on the beach in front of the Abaco Inn and at night there are two continuous red lights which provide a range for the channel. Most (but not all) of the channel marker pilings are now lit by flashing or fixed red and green lights. Pilings are often missing or askew because of errant barge traffic. Proceed directly to the Abaco Inn dock, or turn to starboard and follow the marked channel to the Sea Spray Marina location.

Complimentary dockage is available at Abaco Inn for restaurant and bar patrons. Space is limited, so boats should Mediterranean moor—drop an anchor off the stern or bow and secure the other end to the dock. Power and water are not available.

The channel to the south branches off the main channel with about a ninety degree turn to starboard and is marked with piles—some with fixed red and green lights. Just after entering the branch channel, there is a rock pile outside the channel off to starboard (exposed only at low water). The southern end of the channel it goes west of a free-standing sand and rock breakwater in front of the dock area at Sea Spray.

Anchoring in the dredged channels of White Sound is prohibited, and vessels drawing more than about 2 feet will be unable to find secure anchorage outside the channels in White Sound. Good anchorages in prevailing easterlies can be found just outside White Sound, both north and south of the entrance. It is a short dinghy ride into the sound.

NOTE: White Sound has more channel marker lights than any other harbour in Abaco. Some flash and some do not.

WHITE SOUND

White Sound has a residential community of about sixty homes and two resorts. The Abaco Inn is situated on a narrow strip of land between White Sound and the Atlantic Ocean, and has rooms facing each. It offers informal gourmet dining on open air patios or in the dining room and has sensational views of breaking surf to the east and placid White Sound to the west. Its swimming pool is built into a rock outcropping on the ocean side, and its bar is a friendly place. Call for complimentary transportation.

Sunset Marina is open just north of White Sound and south of Firefly offering dockage with electricity and water. Former Sea Spray patrons will recognize the smiling greeting from Junior, the marina manager. The deepest water for entry is closer to the breakwater entrance than land. See the chart on page 106. Note some dredging was underway at time of publication. Sea Spray Marina and Resort sustained major damage from Dorian. At press time rebuilding is planned to begin in late 2021.

The ocean beaches at White Sound are beautiful; the beach to the north of the Abaco Inn is better for swimming than the one to the south, which has shallow coral and rock. Because there is no offshore reef here, the area offers some of the best surfing in the Bahamas, with at least six good breaks all within half a mile of the Abaco Inn. The walk to Tahiti Beach is about 1½ miles. Hope Town is a 3-mile walk.

The ocean dune at White Sound was severely damaged by multiple hurricanes over the last 20 years. Dune reconstruction has been necessary many times, and reconstruction makes the dune fragile. Visitors are asked to stay off the recovering privately-owned dunes between the Abaco Inn and Sea Spray Resort. Access to the ocean beach is available at Abaco Inn.

Sunset Marina
Exclusive Dockage
White Sound, Elbow Cay

Conviently Located Between Abaco Inn and Firefly Resort
Accomodates Boats Up to 56 feet
Daily, Weekly, & Monthly Rates
Electric and Water Available
Flsh Cleaning Station
Enjoy Beautiful Sunsets on Your Boat or from The Gazebo

For Reservations: (242) 485-9255
Email: juniormernard@yahoo.com

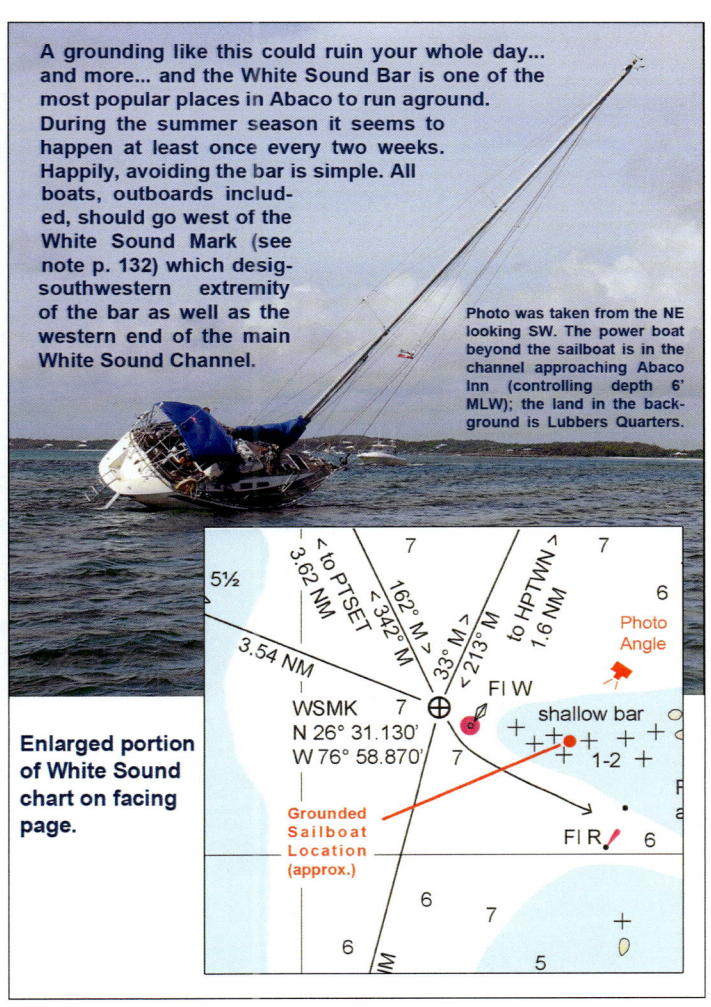

A grounding like this could ruin your whole day... and more... and the White Sound Bar is one of the most popular places in Abaco to run aground. During the summer season it seems to happen at least once every two weeks. Happily, avoiding the bar is simple. All boats, outboards included, should go west of the White Sound Mark (see note p. 132) which designates southwestern extremity of the bar as well as the western end of the main White Sound Channel.

Photo was taken from the NE looking SW. The power boat beyond the sailboat is in the channel approaching Abaco Inn (controlling depth 6' MLW); the land in the background is Lubbers Quarters.

Enlarged portion of White Sound chart on facing page.

Aids to navigation are enhanced on this photo. Most but not all pilings are lit at night (red and green fixed or flashers). Red range lights on Abaco Inn help also; the lower light is much brighter than the upper light. The turn to Sea Spray marks the beginning of the **3 mph harbour speed limit mandated by the Government of The Bahamas**.

The Candy Striped Lighthouse

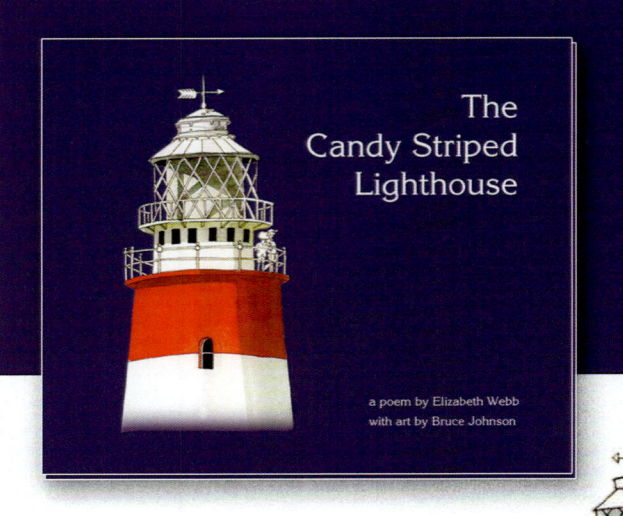

a poem by Elizabeth Webb with art by Bruce Johnson

A book of poetry by renowned English author Elizabeth Webb and art by internationally known artist Bruce Johnson. Suitable for all ages.

The candy striped lighthouse I stand on a hill
Watching over the world down below.
I gaze out to sea and around Elbow Cay
And the boats as they pass to and fro.

The Elbow Reef Lighthouse—a kerosene mantle hand wound rotating fresnel lens lighthouse sending its beacon out to sea since 1863—is the last of its kind in the world. Elizabeth Webb's poem and Bruce Johnson's art tells its story.
Available at stores in Hope Town and Marsh Harbour, The Bruce Johnson Art Gallery in Rockport, MA, www.bjohnsonltd.com, www.amazon.com and www.wspress.com. $29.95

THE VIEW
FROM HERE

ABACO INN, ELBOW CAY, THE BAHAMAS

| BEAUTIFUL VILLAS | TROPICAL ROOMS | FINE DINING |

Step into the serenity of a waterfront villa, lounge on white sand beaches or slip into the warm sea. You could lose hours trying to name all the variations of blue in the surrounding waters. You'll come to think of all this as your own private hideaway. **Discover your home is paradise!**

abaco inn
TAN YOUR TOES IN THE ABACOS

WWW.ABACOINN.COM, INFO@ABACOINN.COM
242.816.1114, 242.802.5856

Abaco Dinghies

Framed and planked like the full-size Abaco dinghies

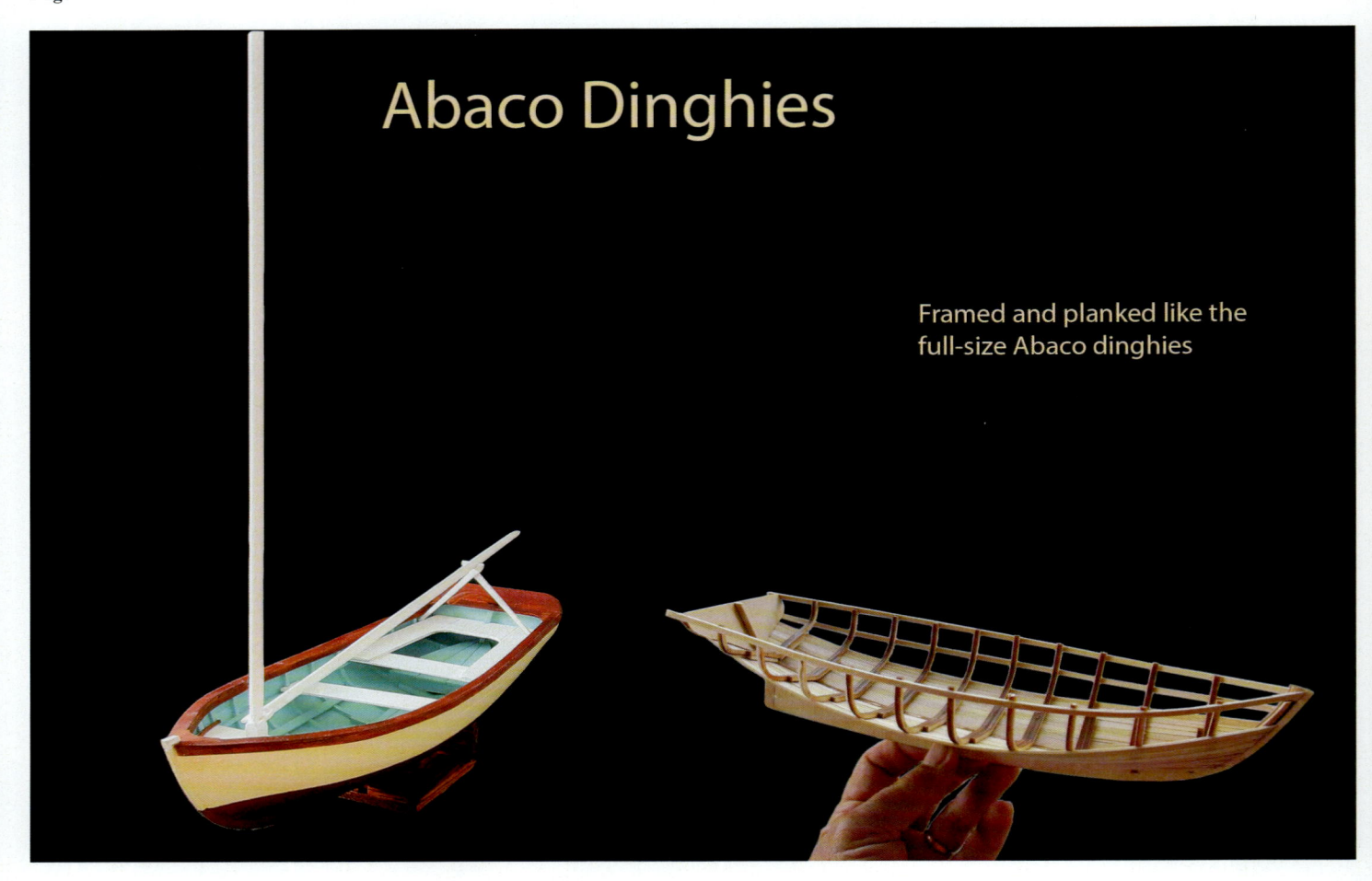

The Bahama Dinghy

The characteristic small sailing boat of the Bahamas is the dinghy—a heavy keel boat having very raking ends and a heart-shaped transom.... These boats are from 13 to 20 feet long.... Figure 89 shows a good boat of the type. She was built on Great Abaco in 1898, and was an excellent sailer in the strong Trades, and was somewhat better-looking than most boats of her type... The boats are roughly built, having sawn frames in shingle-lapped futtockes of black mangrove or local ironwood (called "horseflesh," as it looks like "salt-horse" when seasoned and weathered). The plank and keel are usually yellow pine. The boats are very heavy and also carry some sand, rock, or scrap-iron ballast.

The Bahama dinghy has a reputation, which is often warranted, for seaworthiness and speed in her home waters. The boats not only make the long jumps from island to island, but a number have crossed the Gulf Stream to Florida. However, as in the case of some modern small craft that have crossed the Atlantic, these voyages were rarely without incident, and the successful conclusion is hardly acceptable evidence that the boats were suitable or even reasonably safe for these ventures. The Bahama boatmen, white and black, are commonly skilled in the handling of these small boats, and it is this, rather than any remarkable qualities in the boats themselves, that accounts for some of the very hazardous passages that the dinghies have made.

Excerpted from Howard I. Chapelle, *American Small Sailing Craft: Their Design, Development and Construction* (New York: W. W. Norton and Company, 1951), pp. 226-228.

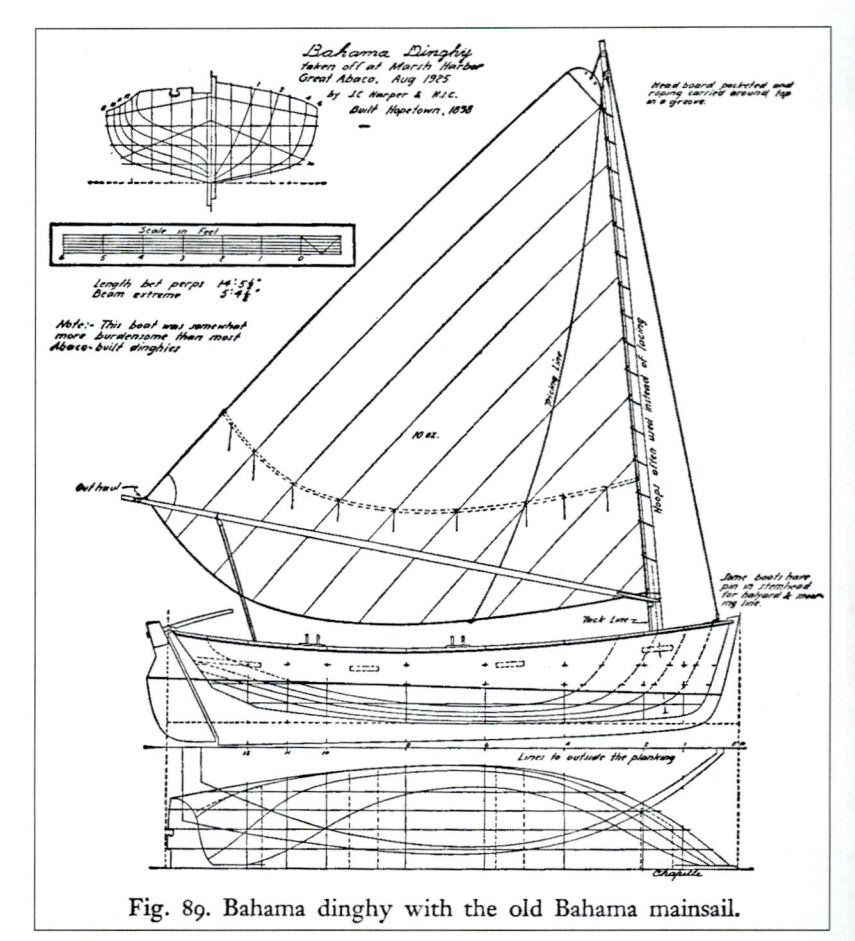

Fig. 89. Bahama dinghy with the old Bahama mainsail.

"Horizon"

"Bring The Islands Home"

Tripp Harrison
Studio & Gallery

WWW.TRIPPHARRISONGALLERY.COM

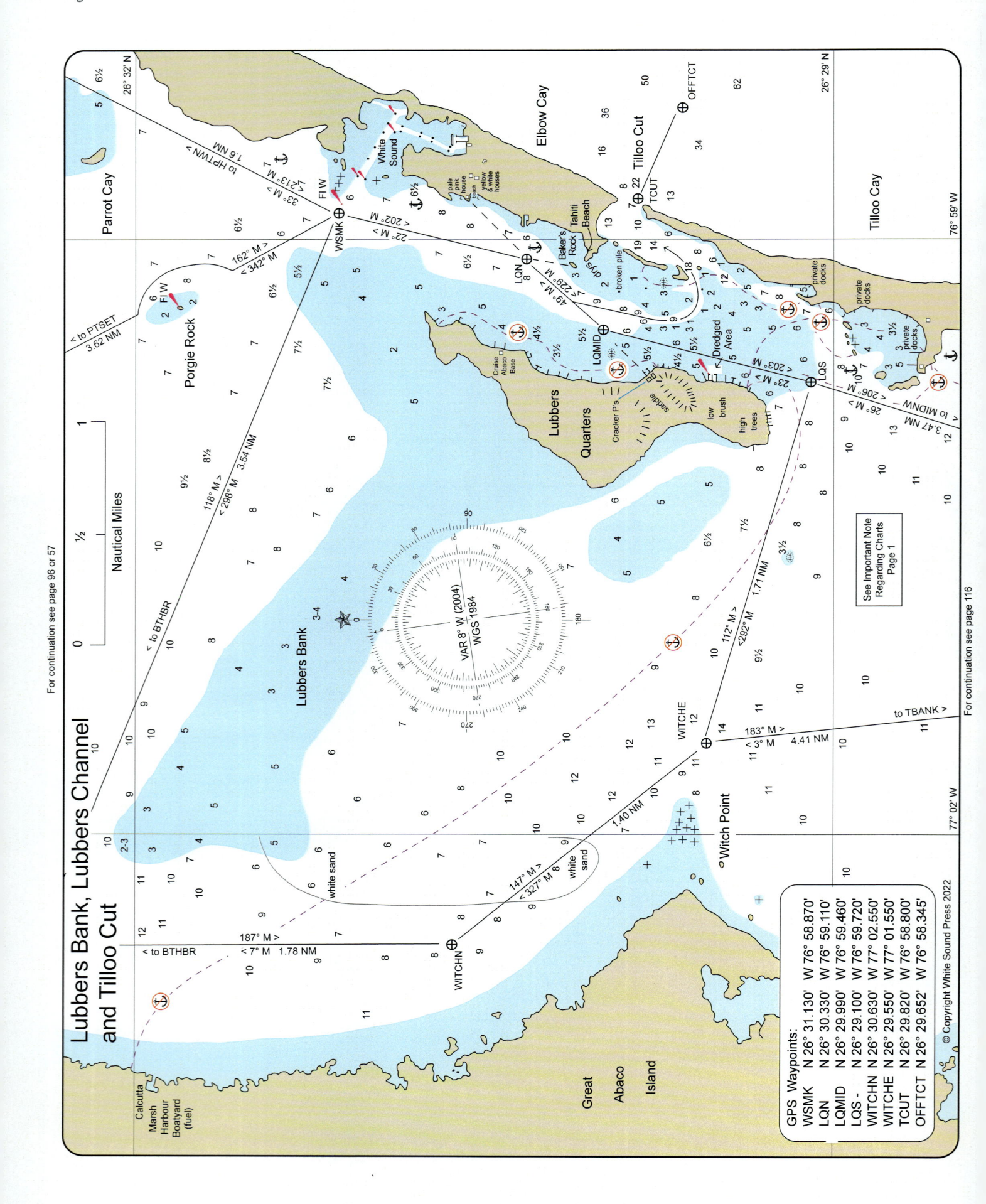

Lubbers Bank, Lubbers Channel and Tilloo Cut

Page 112

GPS Waypoints:	
WSMK	N 26° 31.130' W 76° 58.870'
LQN	N 26° 30.330' W 76° 59.110'
LQMID	N 26° 29.990' W 76° 59.460'
LQS	N 26° 29.100' W 76° 59.720'
WITCHN	N 26° 30.630' W 77° 02.550'
WITCHE	N 26° 29.550' W 77° 01.550'
TCUT	N 26° 29.820' W 76° 58.800'
OFFTCT	N 26° 29.652' W 76° 58.345'

© Copyright White Sound Press 2022

Lubbers Channel from the north with Elbow Cay, Tahiti Beach, the Cooperjack (pronounced Coopyjack) Cays and Tilloo Cay on the left and Lubbers Quarters on the right. Photo by Steve Dodge, 12 July 2016.

LUBBER'S BANK, LUBBER'S CHANNEL, AND TILLOO CUT

Lubber's Quarters and the bank extending northwest of it lie athwart the Sea of Abaco, making it necessary for boats to maneuver through Lubbers Quarters Channel or to go west of the cay and the bank. The channel is shallow and has shoaled during recent years—it is now about 4½-5' MLW—and passage through it is not straightforward. Many cruising boats make the mistake of going directly down the middle of the channel because it looks OK and the outboards sometimes do it successfully. If they draw more than 2-3', and the tide is lower than high, they usually find themselves aground on a bar which is somewhat difficult to see because it is grassy rather than sandy. To carry 4½' MLW through the channel follow the course lines as drawn on the chart. Approaching from the north, go from the White Sound Mark toward Baker's Rock on a heading of 202° M, with the Parrot Cays on your stern. When the large pale pink house located at the north end of the small beach on your port quarter bears 49°, turn to put it on your stern, heading toward the saddle on Lubbers Quarters on the reciprocal heading of 229° M (directly toward Cracker P's dock area, currently closed but new owners plan rebuild). Beware of the "false saddle" which results from the high trees and low bush at the southern end of Lubbers. Stay on this course until you are rather close to Lubbers—until the western shoreline of Tavern Cay bears 203° M, then turn and head toward Tavern Cay. If you are in the right place, you will pass over the outer edge of the dredged area at the Abaco Ocean Club's community dock. Continue on this course until you are abeam the southern tip of Lubbers Quarters.

For passage from south to north sail the reciprocals—go toward the channel area heading toward a point between the northern tip of Lubbers Quarters and the Parrot Cays on a heading of 23° M. When the large pale pink house located at the north end of the small beach bears 49° M, turn and head for it. When you reach the point at which your position and Baker's Rock are in range with the Parrot Cays, turn and go toward the Parrot Cays on a heading of 22° M, which will take you to the White Sound Mark.

There is a good route to the ocean through Tilloo Cut. From the north, proceed as though you were going to go through Lubber's Channel, but when about halfway between Baker's Rock and Lubber's Quarter's, turn and head toward the north tip of the curved natural deep channel which has a white sandy bottom and is therefore visible. Your heading should be about 200° M. Then follow the channel around Cooperjack Cay, passing between the cay and a rock to starboard. Proceed to the cut. Go close to the south side of the cut (only about 40 yards off the north tip of Tilloo Cay) and then turn southeast when in the ocean to avoid a shallow bar on which waves often break straight out and northeast of the cut. The depth at the cut itself is 7', but controlling depth is 5-6 feet inside just north of the north end of the natural curved channel.

All should be aware of the wrecked barge located a little more than .5 NM almost due west (magnetic) of the southern extremity of Lubbers Quarters (see the chart for location; coordinates are N 26° 29.173' W 77° 00.602'). It is covered by only 3½' MLW in an area which is generally 8' to 9' MLW. It is definitely a hazard to navigation, but also holds some fish.

There are several pleasant anchorages in this area. Just north of Baker's Rock near Tahiti Beach is a favorite summer anchorage for many boats; others can be found on either side of the entrance to White Sound, and a fourth can be found just north of the small shallow harbour on Tilloo. All of these offer little protection from the northwest.

Cracker P's Bar and Restaurant has been closed since the storm. New owners acquired the property in the fall of 2021 and reportedly plan to reopen. Also, next door Lubbers' Landing is rebuilding and hopes to reopen soon.. Those anchoring off are asked to stay well off to avoid fouling electrical cables. There is good protection along this shoreline when the wind is from the west and northwest.

Lubbers Quarters Cay is a developing residential community of over 60 homes. It has grown substantially since being

continued on page 140

every child counts
Starfish Enterprises/ECC Training Center

Life's important journey's start...

On faith alone...without clear knowledge of the destination.
Such was the case over 20 years ago with ECC.

As our vision crystallized, it became clear that our children with disabilities deserve:
- A specialized education
- A supportive community
- A productive life

Our journey continues as our students mature and their needs grow. It is clear now that the services at ECC must become long-lasting and permanent as we strive to meet the challenges of our children and young adults.

Please join us - your support will help us to make a difference one by one...

P.O. Box AB 20085, Marsh Harbour, Abaco, Bahamas - Ph: 242.367.2505
Website: www.everychildcountsabaco.org - Email: eccabaco.bs@gmail.com

---

continued from page 139

serviced by electricity, telephones and internet about 15 years ago. An old coral path winds its way around the south end in the Abaco Ocean Club subdivision. A small marina in the subdivision is comprised of privately owned boat slips and a small public dock for its homeowners. Throughout the entire cay there is a nice mix of well-spaced homes in peaceful settings owned by Bahamians as well as foreigners.

Tilloo Cut with Lubbers Quarters from the northeast 12 July 2016. Photo by Steve Dodge.

Tilloo Cut from the south southwest with the Cooperjack Cays, Tahiti Beach and Elbow Cay, 12 July 2016. Photo by Steve Dodge.

Tavern Cay to Lynyard Cay including North Bar Channel

Tavern Cay to Lynyard Cay

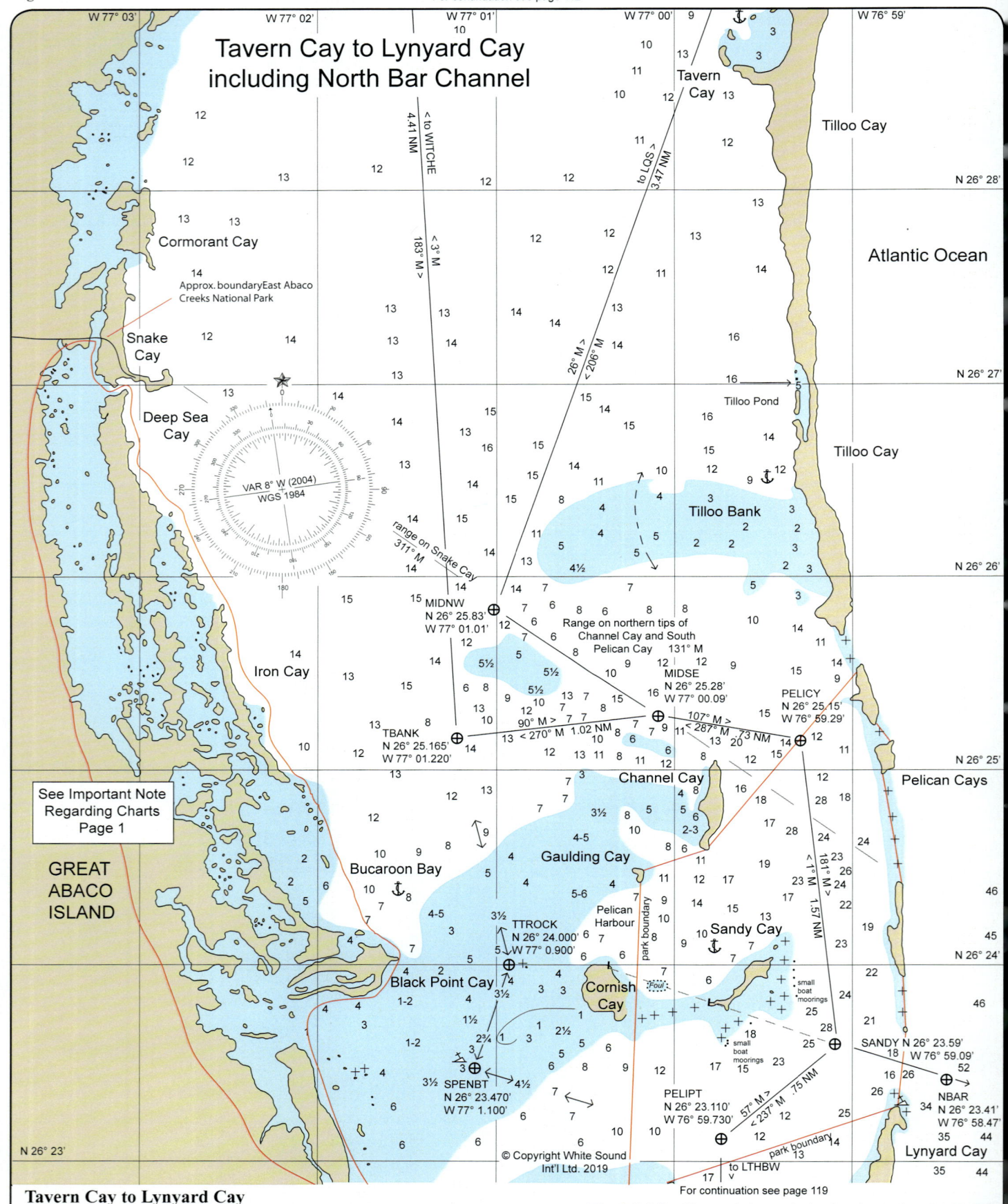

The area south of Tavern Cay down to Tilloo Bank is wide open and averages 12-14' deep. Tilloo Bank is easily seen; go west of it or use the middle channel. Boats drawing 3' or less may well be able to cross the bank on the dotted line route, but please be aware that sand banks change and move, so go slowly and look for the deepest water.

The Middle Channel through the bank carries 6' MLW. Go through on a range of the northern tips of Channel Cay and the southernmost Pelican Cay or use the GPS waypoints. Your heading should be 131° M and Snake Cay should be on your stern at 311° M. Or go around the entire bank using the waypoint TBANK.

text continued on next page

The deep water route to the south is east of the the four small cays (Channel, Gaulding, Cornish and Sandy) located in this part of the Sea of Abaco. Give Sandy Cay Reef, which is marked by a high rock near the north end and a low rock near the south end, a wide berth. Snorkeling is excellent on the reef, which is part of the Pelican Cays Land and Sea Park. All fishing is prohibited in the park and no shells or coral may be taken. See the more detailed chart on page 118 for the boundaries of the park. Holding ground off the reef is poor (smooth round rocks covered with about 2" of sand), but there are several small boat moorings (for boats 27' or less) located just east of the reef. Anchoring on the reef is prohibited; it damages the coral. Larger boats should anchor in Pelican Harbour to the west of Sandy Cay and dinghy to the small boat moorings. Holding ground in Pelican Harbour is less than ideal, and there is a swell in the area. This is a daytime anchorage only; Pelican Harbour is not really a harbour. See the separate snorkeling/diving charts on pages 137 and 143 for more detailed information about the reef.

North Bar Channel is one of the best passages from the Sea of Abaco to the Atlantic Ocean, providing about 16-17' of water at its shallowest point. The range for this channel consists of two white concrete posts, one on Sandy Cay and the other on Cornish Cay. When entering on the range, the heading should be 295° M. This course should take you about midway between the north tip of Lynyard Cay and Channel Rock, avoiding the rocky shoal area just off Lynyard Cay.

A shoal draft route (about 2' 9'" MLW) exists west of the four cays. It passes close to Tea Table Rock west of Cornish Cay, and is quite narrow at one point, so GPS waypoints are provided.

Several settled weather or daytime anchorages can be found in appropriate weather on the west side of Tilloo Cay (see page 118) and at Snake Cay (see chart this page). Anchoring in Tilloo Pond is not recommended; it is small and a Bahamian moor is necessary to hold the boat in position if the wind shifts. It can, of course, be used in an emergency, and it offers excellent shelter. The cut leading to the lagoon behind Snake Cay and Deep Sea Cay is deep with excellent protection, but it is also very small and strong tidal currents exist, so if one chooses to be anchored here during a reverse of tidal flow, a Bahamian moor is absolutely necessary.

Iron Cay and Mocking Bird Cay beyond on the right, John Doctor Cay and Deep Sea Cay on the left, with Snake Cay center/left background and Witch Point and Marsh Harbour beyond. Taken from the south July 2007. Compare this photo to the chart to the right. This pristine and serene shallow area can be explored by kayak or dinghy at half tide or higher.

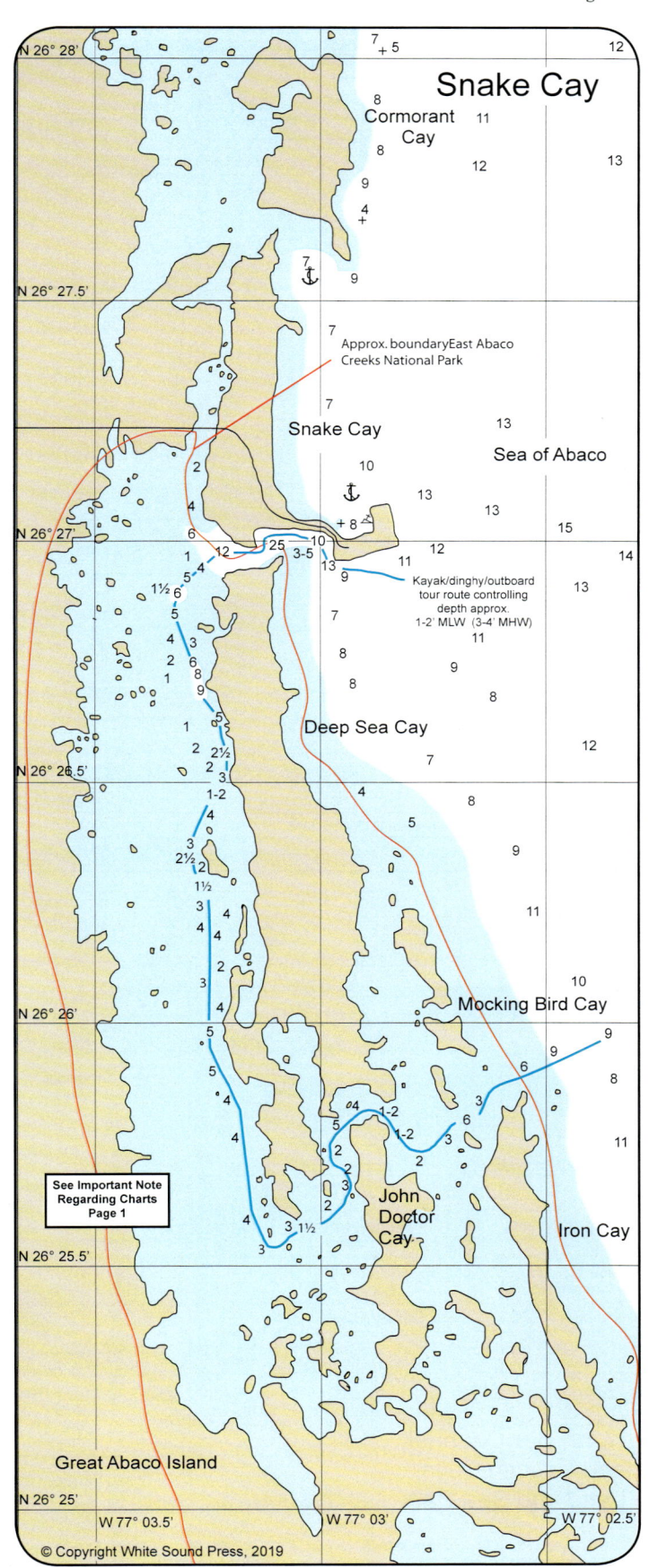

Snake Cay The cut between Snake Cay and Deep Sea Cay is deep, but very strong tidal flows make it absolutely necessary to use a Bahamian moor if one chooses to anchor there. There are two acceptable anchorages east of Snake Cay. Note the suggested route for a kayak/dinghy tour of the flats recommended for half tide or better.

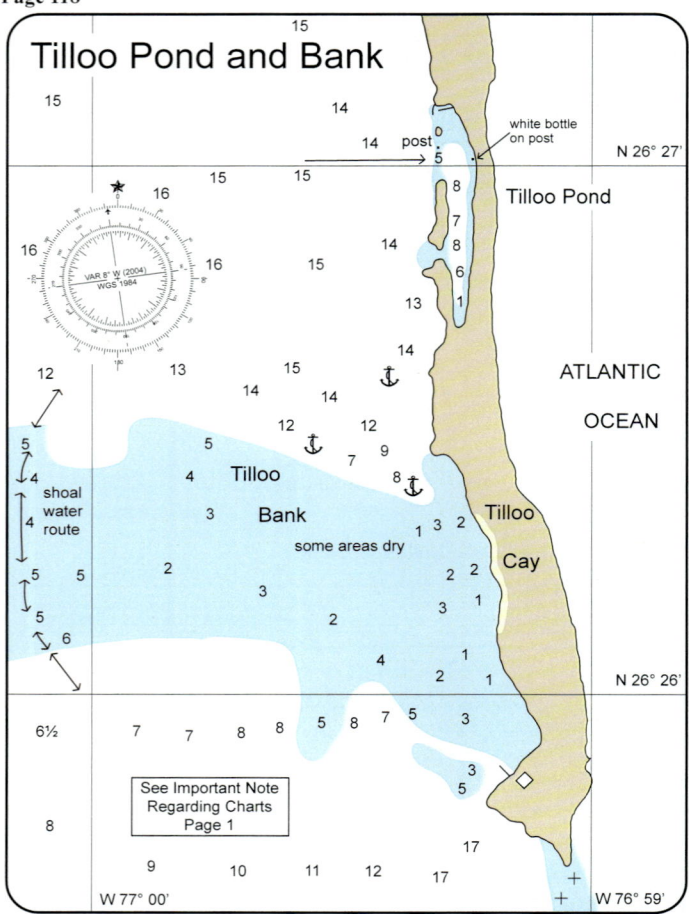

Tilloo Pond and Bank

North Bar Channel and Pelican Cays Land and Sea Park

The southern sector of the Sea of Abaco from the north. The southernmost Pelican Cay is on the left in the foreground. Moving south from there is North Bar Channel with Channel Rock clearly visible. Boats should be to the south of Channel Rock, between Channel Rock and Lynyard Cay. Little Harbour on the mainland of Great Abaco Island is beyond Lynyard and Winding Bay is visible beyond that. Continuing clockwise, another peninsula protruding eastward from Great Abaco is visible. It is the site of the old settlement of Wilson City (1906-1916). In the foreground on the right is Sandy Cay with its reef to the east. Three boats are anchored in the area known as Pelican Harbour, which usually has a surge and is not recommended for overnight, but it is a place where large boats can anchor in order to dinghy to the moorings at the reef, which are limited to boats under 27' LOA. Photo by Steve Dodge, 13 July 2008.

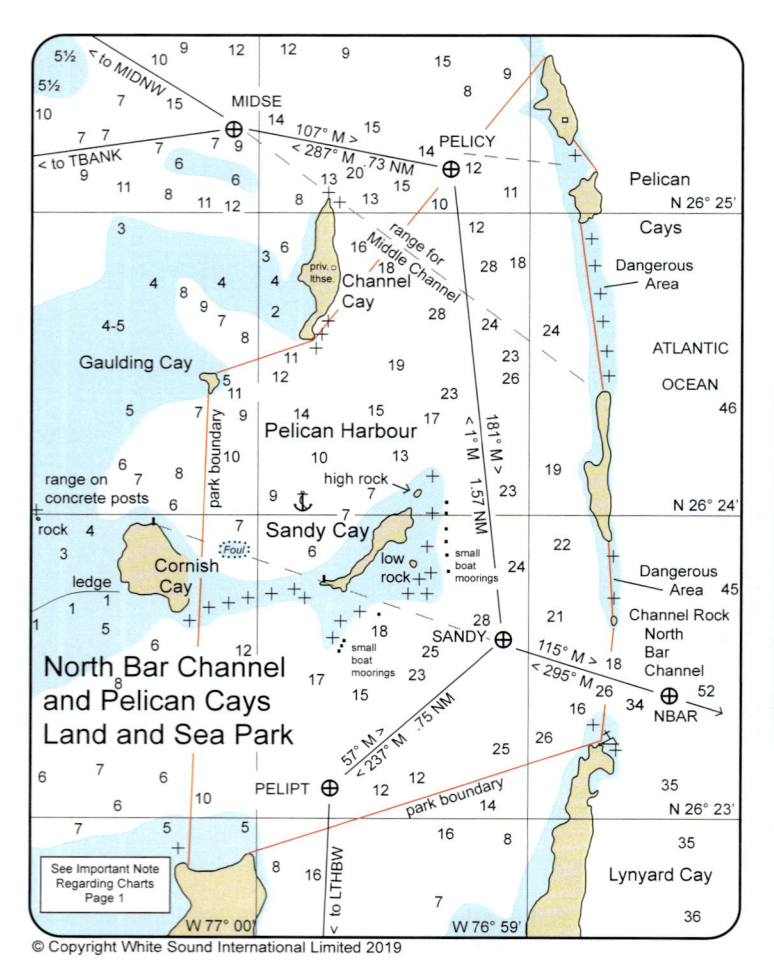

North Bar Channel is one of the best passages between the Atlantic Ocean and the Sea of Abaco. It is 18' deep at MLW and is used by the mailboat. Enter between the northern tip of Lynyard Cay and Channel Rock. The area north of Channel Rock is shallow and should be avoided. The photo above was taken from the west on a calm day during the summer 2004. Channel Rock is on the left side, and the northern tip of Lynyard Cay is on the right. Boats entering North Bar Channel must alter course about .33 NM after entering to avoid Sandy Cay reef. For waypoint coordinates see chart p. 119.

Approaches to Little Harbour

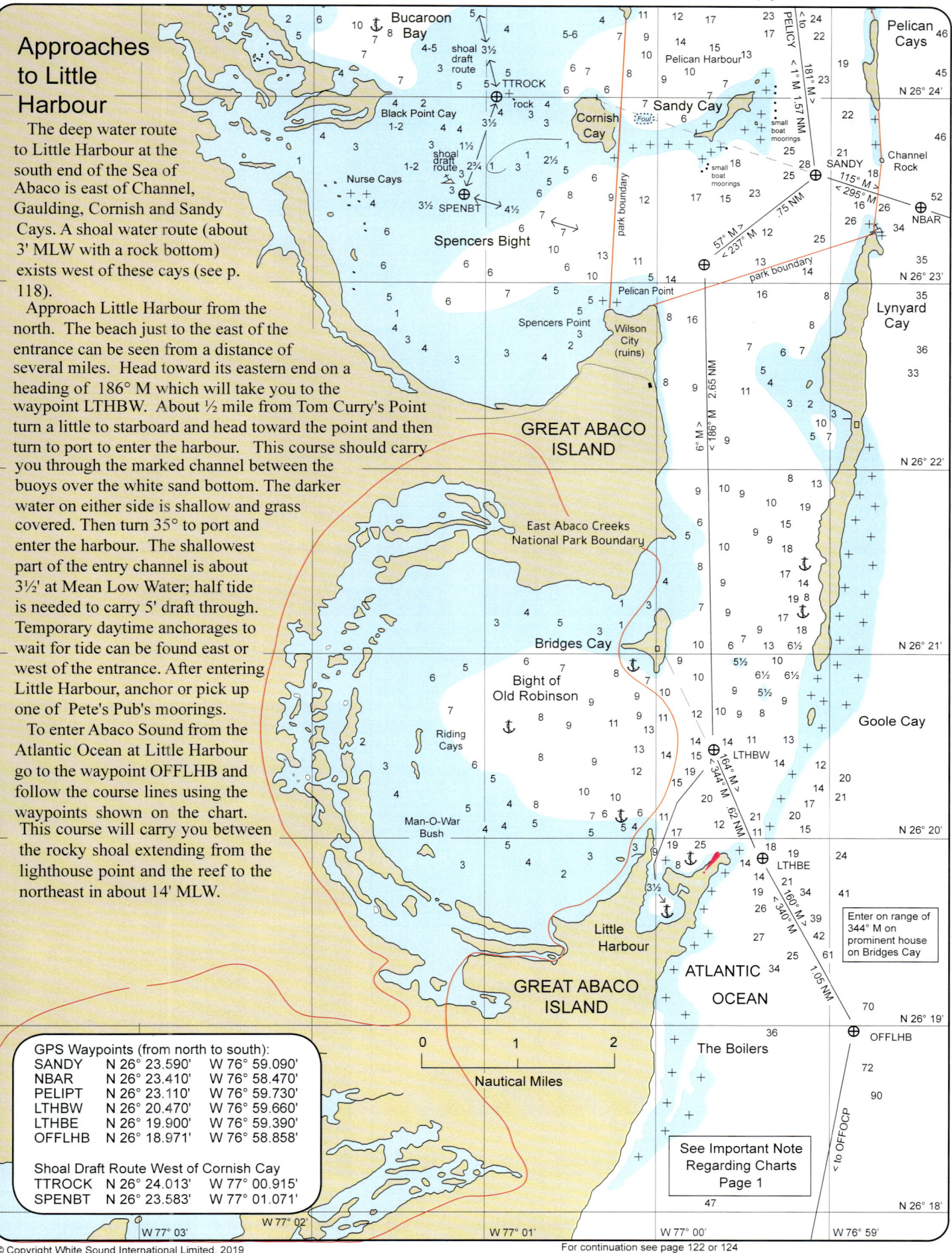

The deep water route to Little Harbour at the south end of the Sea of Abaco is east of Channel, Gaulding, Cornish and Sandy Cays. A shoal water route (about 3' MLW with a rock bottom) exists west of these cays (see p. 118).

Approach Little Harbour from the north. The beach just to the east of the entrance can be seen from a distance of several miles. Head toward its eastern end on a heading of 186° M which will take you to the waypoint LTHBW. About ½ mile from Tom Curry's Point turn a little to starboard and head toward the point and then turn to port to enter the harbour. This course should carry you through the marked channel between the buoys over the white sand bottom. The darker water on either side is shallow and grass covered. Then turn 35° to port and enter the harbour. The shallowest part of the entry channel is about 3½' at Mean Low Water; half tide is needed to carry 5' draft through. Temporary daytime anchorages to wait for tide can be found east or west of the entrance. After entering Little Harbour, anchor or pick up one of Pete's Pub's moorings.

To enter Abaco Sound from the Atlantic Ocean at Little Harbour go to the waypoint OFFLHB and follow the course lines using the waypoints shown on the chart. This course will carry you between the rocky shoal extending from the lighthouse point and the reef to the northeast in about 14' MLW.

GPS Waypoints (from north to south):

SANDY	N 26° 23.590'	W 76° 59.090'
NBAR	N 26° 23.410'	W 76° 58.470'
PELIPT	N 26° 23.110'	W 76° 59.730'
LTHBW	N 26° 20.470'	W 76° 59.660'
LTHBE	N 26° 19.900'	W 76° 59.390'
OFFLHB	N 26° 18.971'	W 76° 58.858'

Shoal Draft Route West of Cornish Cay

TTROCK	N 26° 24.013'	W 77° 00.915'
SPENBT	N 26° 23.583'	W 77° 01.071'

Entrance to Little Harbour

The opening is between the beach and Tom Curry's Point.

Get on a range with Tom Curry's point on the transom and the group of houses on the bow.

The channel is marked with buoys, and the deepest water is the light green water (approx. 3½' MLW).

Turn about 35° to port and enter the anchorage.

Pete's Pub — Little Harbour

Open mid November – mid August
Bronze Sculpture and Gold Jewelry in the Gallery
Fresh Seafood in the Pub

Moorings and Dockage Available

Mailing Address:
Pete's Pub and Gallery
P. O. Box AB 20282
Marsh Harbour, Abaco, Bahamas
Cell 242-577-5487
Email: pete@petespub.com
Web: www.petespubandgallery.com

Please contact for current hours
lunch ~ dinner (reservations required)

Little Harbour chart

For continuation see page 122 or 57

< 186° M / 6° M >
2.65 NM to PELIPT
range on house on Bridges Cay

LTHBW
N 26° 20.47'
W 76° 59.66'

< 164° M / 344° M >
.62 NM

*Note: Two inner red buoys missing 01/2020

LTHBE
N 26° 19.90'
W 76° 59.39'

< 160° M / 340° M >
to OFLHB

Tom Curry's Point

Fl W
foundry
gallery
Pete's Pub
Little Harbour
cave
prominent house
prominent house

See Important Note Regarding Charts Page 1

Nautical Miles
0 — ¼

© Copyright White Sound International Limited, 2020

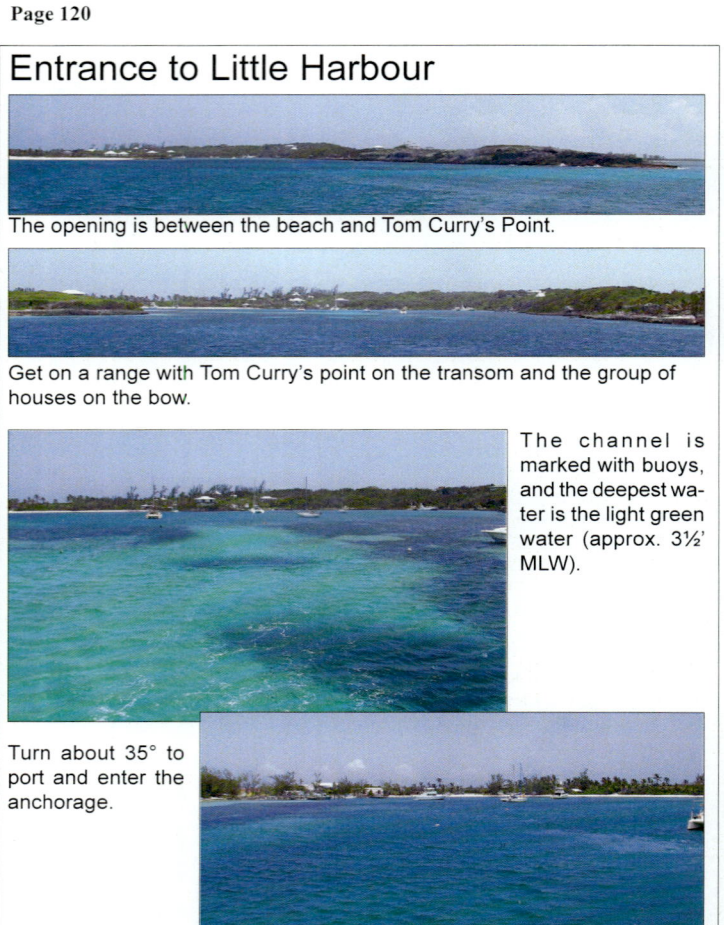

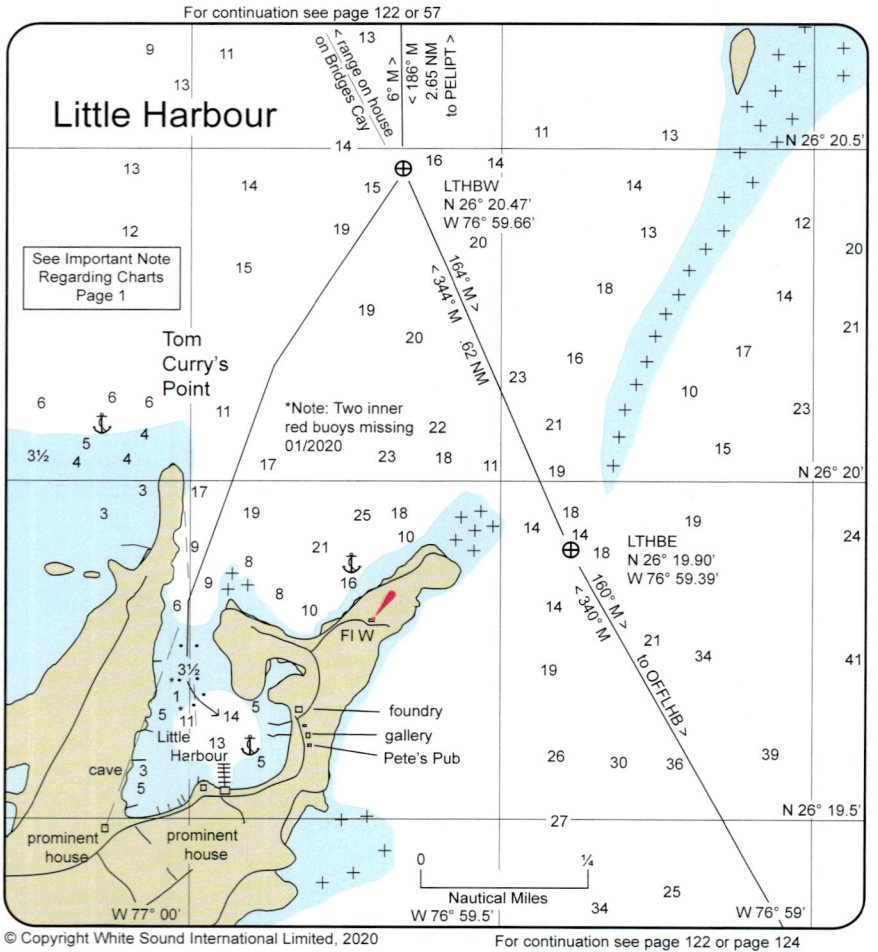

For continuation see page 122 or page 124

Entrance to Little Harbour from the north. Note that the entry should be made over the white sand bottom. The channel through that area is always marked with buoys. It carries 3½' MLW and up to 7' at the top of the tide.

Little Harbour

Little Harbour is a beautiful, small, fully-protected anchorage. Randolph and Margot Johnston made Little Harbour their home during the middle 1950s, and founded an art colony there. Randolph, who died in late 1992, was an internationally known artist renowned for his lost wax casting in bronze, and his wife Margot worked with ceramics. Their son Pete now runs Pete's Pub and Gallery, and makes life size marine bronzes and jewelry inspired by local motifs. The gallery is open seven days a week from about 11:00 to about 4:00. Foundry tours are available for a nominal fee. Pete's Pub is an open air bar on the beach. It serves hot dogs and hamburgers, fish, ribs, chicken, lobster and bouillabaisse. In season it is open seven days a week beginning at 11:00 am, serving lunch from noon to 4:00 pm, and dinner from 6:00 to 9:00 with reservations (Closed mid August - November 1 / short schedule till December). No other shopping or services are available.

The walk to the lighthouse and the ocean side is well worth it, and the caves on the west side of the harbour in which the Johnstons lived when they first came to Little Harbour, are interesting. The small reef to the east of the entrance is convenient for snorkeling, and the larger open water reef off Lynyard Cay is quite beautiful. The Bight of Old Robinson, to the west, has numerous interesting shallow creeks, some with blue holes (see the chart on page 119 for locations).

Little Harbour 21 June 2019

Pete working on a new project and a pour at the foundry. Photos by Steve Dodge, 3 June 2010.

Little Harbour from the southeast with Bridges Cay, part of Great Abaco and part of Lynyard Cay in the background. Photo by Steve Dodge, 30 June 2012..

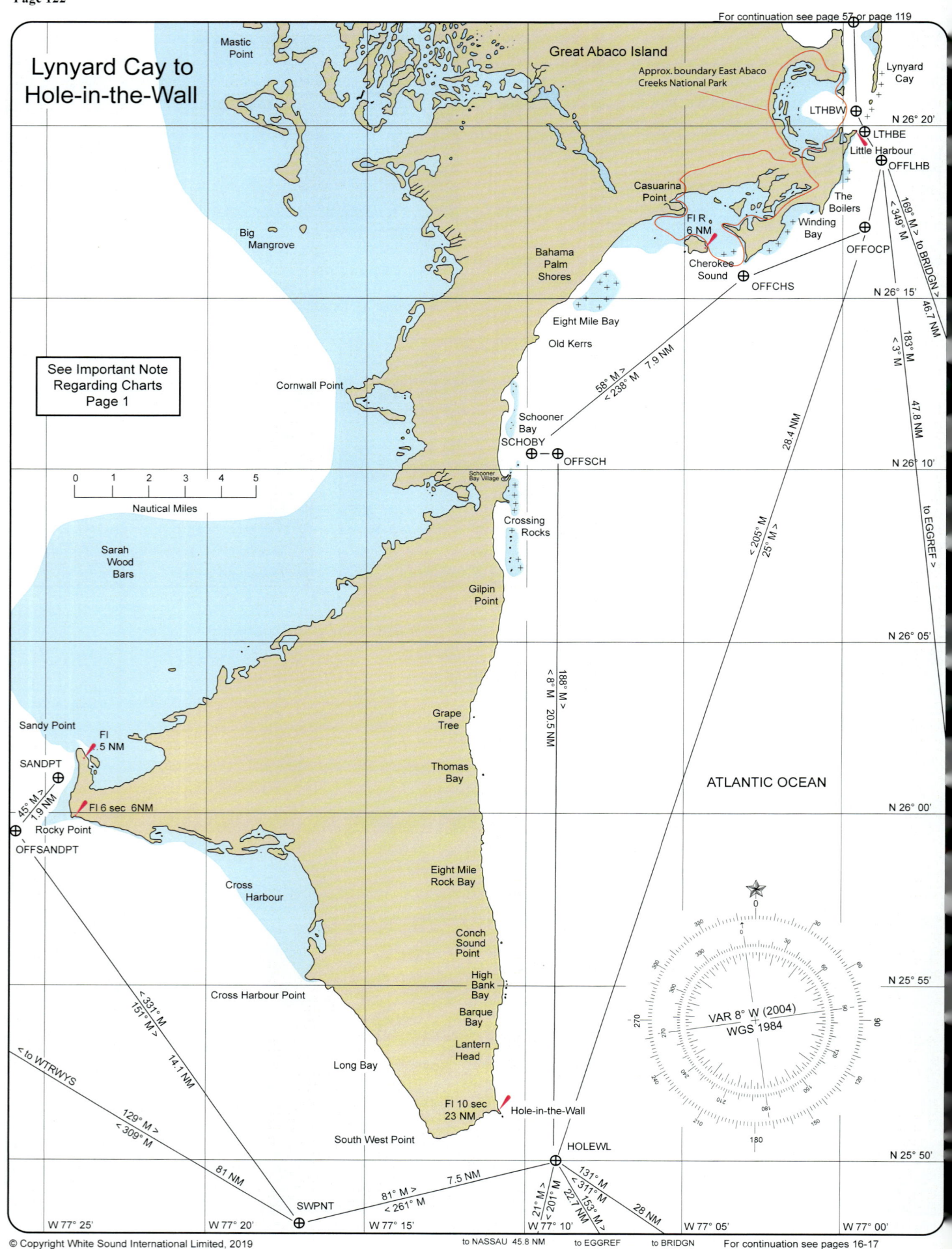

Lynyard Cay to Hole-in-the-Wall

Page 122

For continuation see page 57 or page 119

Great Abaco Island

- Mastic Point
- Lynyard Cay
- Approx. boundary East Abaco Creeks National Park
- LTHBW
- LTHBE
- Little Harbour
- OFFLHB
- Casuarina Point
- The Boilers
- Fl R 6 NM
- Winding Bay
- Big Mangrove
- Cherokee Sound
- OFFOCP
- Bahama Palm Shores
- OFFCHS
- Eight Mile Bay
- Old Kerrs
- Cornwall Point
- Schooner Bay
- SCHOBY — OFFSCH
- Schooner Bay Village
- Crossing Rocks
- Sarah Wood Bars
- Gilpin Point
- Grape Tree
- Thomas Bay
- Sandy Point
- Fl .5 NM
- SANDPT
- Fl 6 sec 6NM
- Rocky Point
- OFFSANDPT
- Cross Harbour
- Eight Mile Rock Bay
- Conch Sound Point
- Cross Harbour Point
- High Bank Bay
- Barque Bay
- Lantern Head
- Long Bay
- Fl 10 sec 23 NM
- Hole-in-the-Wall
- South West Point
- HOLEWL
- SWPNT

ATLANTIC OCEAN

Bearings/Distances:
- 169° M / 349° M to BRIDGN
- 46.7 NM
- 183° M / 3° M
- 47.8 NM to EGGREF
- 58° M / 238° M 7.9 NM
- 205° M / 25° M 28.4 NM
- 188° M / 8° M 20.5 NM
- 45° M 1.9 NM
- 331° M / 157° M 14.1 NM
- 129° M / 309° M 81 NM to WTRWYS
- 81° M / 261° M 7.5 NM
- 21° M / 201° M
- 131° M / 311° M
- 153° M / 22.7 NM
- 28 NM

to NASSAU 45.8 NM   to EGGREF   to BRIDGN

For continuation see pages 16-17

See Important Note Regarding Charts Page 1

Nautical Miles: 0 1 2 3 4 5

VAR 8° W (2004)
WGS 1984

© Copyright White Sound International Limited, 2019

Page 123

Lynyard Cay to Hole-in-the-Wall

North Bar Channel and the opening between Little Harbour and Lynyard Cay are both viable routes between the Sea of Abaco and the Atlantic Ocean. See pages 116 and 118, and page 119 respectively for more information. Once in the ocean, care should be taken to give a wide berth to the Boilers, a reef lying off the coast of Great Abaco Island between Little Harbour and Ocean Point. Use of the waypoints and course lines provided will keep boats well clear of all reefs. Cherokee Sound offers limited protection to the west of Cherokee Point, where there is often a surge, and the route to the small inner anchorage only carries about 3' MLW. For more detail see page 124.

The 27-mile coastline of Great Abaco Island from Cherokee Sound to Hole-in-the-Wall is forbidding and hostile, offering no secure anchorages or protection for boats. A new development offers relief—Schooner Bay Village at the south end of Schooner Bay (about halfway between Little Harbour and Hole-in-the-Wall) has a small harbour with deep water entrance (controlling depth 8' MLW) and a fledgling town. See the chart on page 126.

It is possible to anchor just west of Hole-in-the-Wall to gain protection from the prevailing easterlies, but this anchorage is completely exposed to the S and SW.

Sandy Point, located about 15 NM northwest of Hole-in-the-Wall offers good protection for winds from the east, but the only protection from the west is the other side of a bar which carries only 3' MLW. See the chart on page 128.

Waypoints: Lynyard Cay to Hole-in-the-Wall and beyond

LTHBW	Abaco Sd. end Little Hrbr Ch.	N 26° 20.470'	W 76° 59.660'
LTHBE	Atlantic end Little Hrbr Ch.	N 26° 19.900'	W 76° 59.390'
OFFLHB	1¼ NM SSE Little Harbour	N 26° 18.971'	W 76° 58.858'
OFFOCP	1¼ NM ESE Ocean Point	N 26° 17.079'	W 76° 59.349'
OFFCHS	0.4 NM S Cherokee Point	N 26° 15.663'	W 77° 03.152'
SCHOBY	0.75 NM E Schooner Bay	N 26° 10.500'	W 77° 09.800'
OFFSCH	0.7 NM E SCHOBY	N 26° 10.500'	W 77° 09.000'
HOLEWL	2 NM SE Hole-in-the-Wall	N 25° 50.000'	W 77° 09.000'
SWPNT	3 NM WSW South West Pt.	N 25° 48.000'	W 77° 17.000'
OFFSANDPT	3NM SW Sandy Point	N 25° 59.500'	W 77° 26.000
SANDPT	.75 NM SW Sandy Point	N 26° 1.000'	W 77° 24.650'

Eleuthera:

BRIDGN*	N end Bridge Pt. reef opening	N 25° 34.298'	W 76° 43.344'
EGGREF	0.8 NM west of Egg Reef	N 25° 31.102'	W 76° 55.031'

Nassau:

NASSAU	north Nassau Hbr. entrance	N 25° 05.447'	W 77° 21.340'

Grand Bahama Island:
See pages 16-17 and 20-24

*This waypoint is at the north end of the Bridge Point opening in Devil's Backbone Reef. Local knowledge and good visibility are required for this passage the first time. For charts and waypoints for Eleuthera, see pages 130-.

Hole-in-the-Wall Lighthouse from the northwest.

Cherokee Sound from the southwest 15 March 2010. Note the shallow reef in the foreground, and the protected deeper area west of Cherokee Point. Winding Bay and even houses at Little Harbour can be seen in the background. The long dock extending from the shore east of the town is visible: the end of it is still in water which is only 1-2' deep at MLW. Boats can find some protection by using the channel just east of Duck Cay (controlling depth is 3' MLW). This cannot be seen on this photo, but can be found on the chart of Cherokee Sound on page 124. Photo by Steve Dodge.

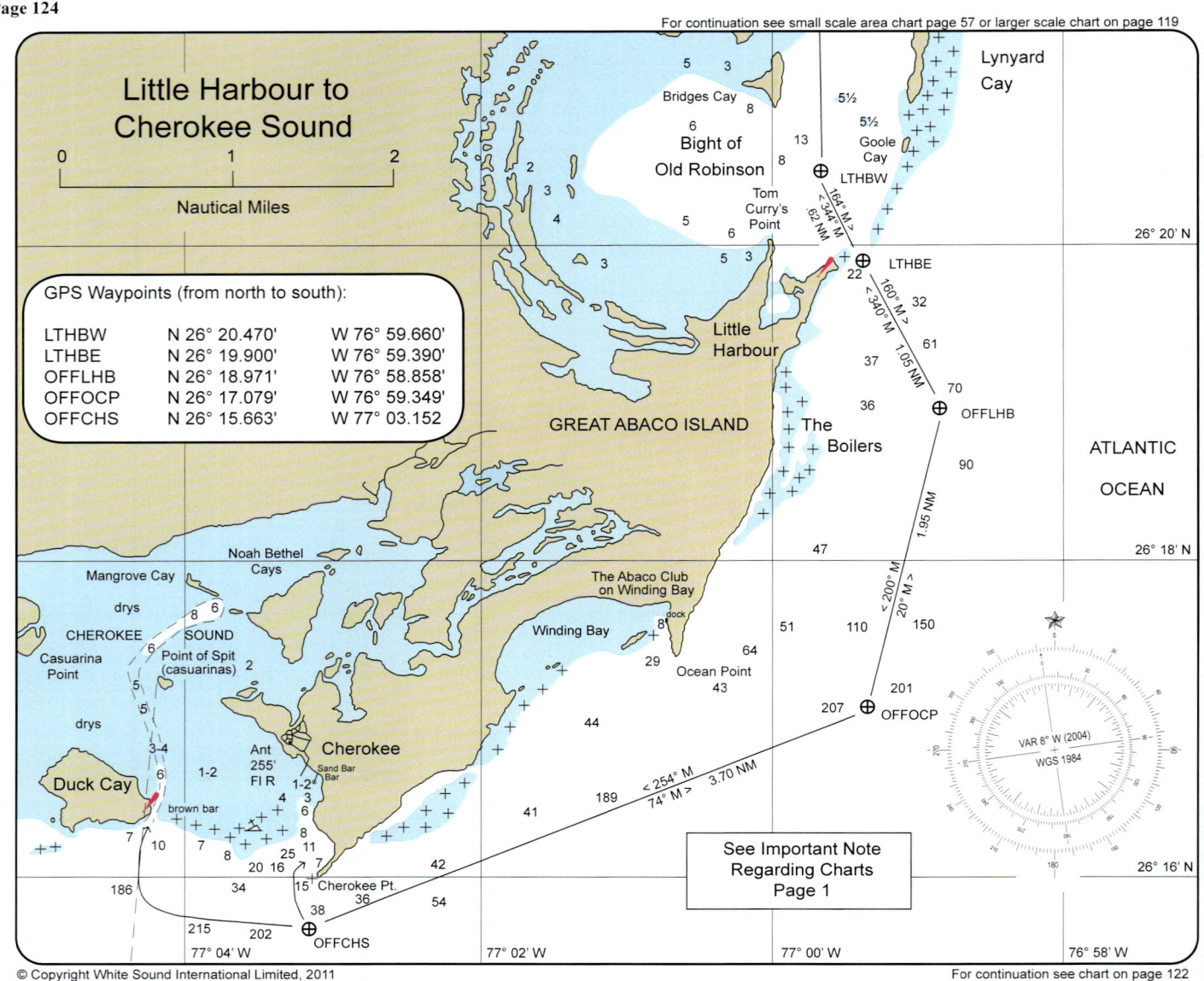

Little Harbour to Cherokee Sound

GPS Waypoints (from north to south):

LTHBW	N 26° 20.470'	W 76° 59.660'
LTHBE	N 26° 19.900'	W 76° 59.390'
OFFLHB	N 26° 18.971'	W 76° 58.858'
OFFOCP	N 26° 17.079'	W 76° 59.349'
OFFCHS	N 26° 15.663'	W 77° 03.152

LITTLE HARBOUR TO CHEROKEE SOUND

Vessels proceeding southward from Little Harbour should stay well clear of the Boilers, a breaking reef extending about ½ mile offshore from Great Abaco Island located about 1½ miles south of the Little Harbour channel. The waypoints and suggested course lines shown on the chart keep boats about 1 mile offshore. Cherokee Sound, located 5 miles SW of Little Harbour, is an extensive region of shallow water with a small settlement. Entrance to either one of the two possible anchorages there should be attempted in flat or moderate conditions only as breaking seas extend across both entrances in an easterly blow or when there is a strong surge.

From the waypoint OFFCHS proceed on a heading of about 0° toward the radio antenna located in the settlement. This should keep you well clear of Cherokee Point. Round the point, turning to starboard and head for the beach with the limestone cliff. The anchorage is just west of the beach with 7-11' MLW. This provides good shelter from the prevailing easterlies, but offers little protection from the SW to W, and there is often a surge in this area. Shoal draft vessels may be able to get to the dock which may well be the longest in The Bahamas, but still has only 1-2' MLW at its end. Stay fairly close to shore in order to avoid the reef to port. Proceed slowly toward the dock and look for the deepest water. Plan your visit for a tide which offers sufficient water for departure as well as arrival.

A second anchorage in the center of Cherokee Sound offers better protection, but access is not straightforward, and the anchorage is about a mile away from the settlement. Approach Duck Cay from the south on a range which lines up the lighthouse on Duck Cay with the W shoreline of Point of Spit, which has a stand of casuarinas. When about 100-150 yards off Duck Cay, turn about 20-25° to starboard and pass between Duck Cay and the brown bar to starboard. You should pass over two or three black spots. Then turn gradually to port to assume a course which will leave Point of Spit well to starboard. The shallowest spot is near where you make this turn—it is between a grassy patch (west side) and a sand bar (east side)—and it carries about 3' MLW. The remainder of the route to the anchorage is a narrow dredged channel clearly visible in good light which carries about 5' MLW. The anchorage is about 7' MLW and is just SE of Mangrove Cay and W of Noah Bethel Cays. From this anchorage you can take the dinghy to small boat docks on the creek which borders the NW side of the town.

The settlement at Cherokee Sound is small, but there is a grocery store, a new (2017) shell museum (phone 475-7868 for admission), and a road which goes to Marsh Harbour. Cherokee Sound was formerly a center for boat building and a thriving fishing community. The people are friendly and welcome visitors.

Winding Bay is about midway between the Little Harbour channel and Cherokee Sound. A private member community of town houses and homes is centered on Ocean Point where there is a clubhouse with a commanding view of the area. The community is managed by Southworth Development and features a scenic links golf course. Casual visitors are generally not welcome. There is one small fair weather dock on the west side of Ocean Point.

The Boilers on a very calm day with Little Harbour and the Bight of Old Robinson in the background. The Cessna 152's horizontal stabilizer was unintentionally included in the photo by Steve Dodge, 30 June 2012.

Winding Bay is the site of The Abaco Club on Winding Bay, now managed by Southworth Development. It has a beautiful beach and a highly rated links golf course, but has no significant provision for boating on site. Photo by Steve Dodge 30 June 2012.

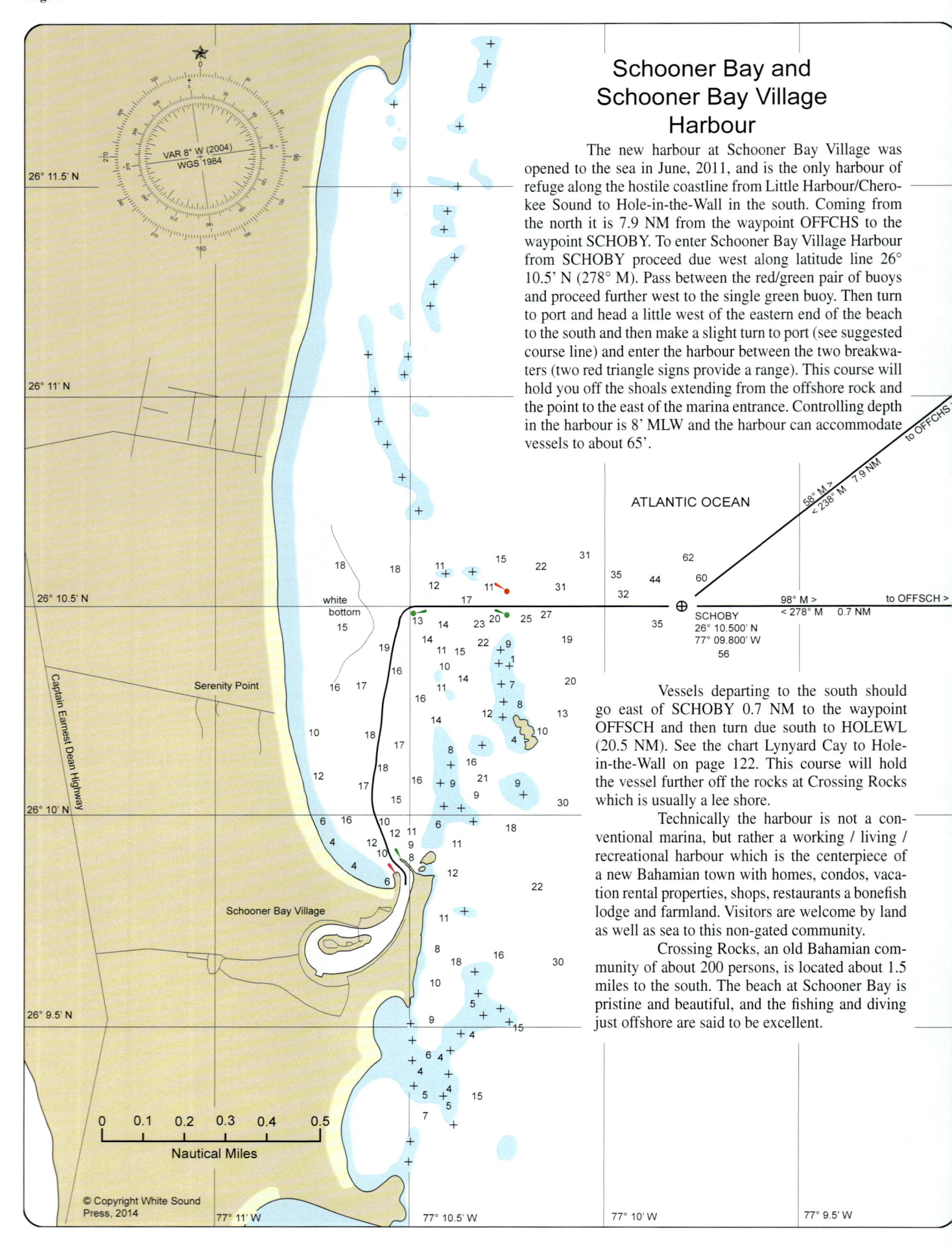

Schooner Bay and Schooner Bay Village Harbour

The new harbour at Schooner Bay Village was opened to the sea in June, 2011, and is the only harbour of refuge along the hostile coastline from Little Harbour/Cherokee Sound to Hole-in-the-Wall in the south. Coming from the north it is 7.9 NM from the waypoint OFFCHS to the waypoint SCHOBY. To enter Schooner Bay Village Harbour from SCHOBY proceed due west along latitude line 26° 10.5' N (278° M). Pass between the red/green pair of buoys and proceed further west to the single green buoy. Then turn to port and head a little west of the eastern end of the beach to the south and then make a slight turn to port (see suggested course line) and enter the harbour between the two breakwaters (two red triangle signs provide a range). This course will hold you off the shoals extending from the offshore rock and the point to the east of the marina entrance. Controlling depth in the harbour is 8' MLW and the harbour can accommodate vessels to about 65'.

Vessels departing to the south should go east of SCHOBY 0.7 NM to the waypoint OFFSCH and then turn due south to HOLEWL (20.5 NM). See the chart Lynyard Cay to Hole-in-the-Wall on page 122. This course will hold the vessel further off the rocks at Crossing Rocks which is usually a lee shore.

Technically the harbour is not a conventional marina, but rather a working / living / recreational harbour which is the centerpiece of a new Bahamian town with homes, condos, vacation rental properties, shops, restaurants a bonefish lodge and farmland. Visitors are welcome by land as well as sea to this non-gated community.

Crossing Rocks, an old Bahamian community of about 200 persons, is located about 1.5 miles to the south. The beach at Schooner Bay is pristine and beautiful, and the fishing and diving just offshore are said to be excellent.

The entrance to Schooner Bay Village Harbour from the north.

SCHOONER BAY AND SCHOONER BAY VILLAGE

Schooner Bay Village is an interesting development in several ways. First, those cruising between Hole-in-the-Wall and the Little Harbour Cut have a possible harbour of refuge—a place to stop on the way from Abaco to North Eleuthera, Nassau, Florida or elsewhere. It will make the southern route between Florida and Abaco more comfortable by providing relief from the 100+ mile run without viable protection.

Second, the development itself is interesting. It was not planned as just another residential development—the goal was to create a new village—in the tradition, generally speaking, of the Puritans in Boston and the loyalists at Carleton, Abaco. Envisioned as a business center serving southern Abaco, it was to have a bank, a post office and a supermarket which was to sell produce grown on adjacent farmland. Mom and Pop businesses were envisioned to surround the harbour housed in two-storey buildings with the business at street level and the owner's living quarters above—similar to Manhattan 200 years ago. Those who purchased land were required to build within a certain time frame (1-3 years)—in order to achieve a reasonable critical mass for the town in a short period of time, and to avoid land purchase for speculative reasons. Much of what was planned has not been achieved, but the village still has a chance of success—it could become an alternative to Marsh Harbour for residents of Crossing Rocks and Sandy Point for employment as well as retail shopping and other business.

It is also interesting from an environmental point of view. Designed as a green community, a large area of coppice has been left in its natural state to accommodate local as well as migrating birds, and energy and water systems have been designed with protection of the environment in mind. That said, it should also be noted that the harbour basin itself is the product of a dredge and fill. But almost every new marina in the Bahamas is built this same way—all the really good natural deep water harbours were settled and developed many years ago (Nassau, Marsh Harbour, Hope Town). Every development takes away something that can never be recovered, but adds something that didn't previously exist. In the case of Schooner Bay Village, it seems that the positives may eventually outweigh the negatives.

One of the two range markers for the entry channel at Schooner Bay (right) and both of the markers taken from the west side of the channel below. Photos by Steve Dodge.

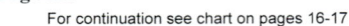

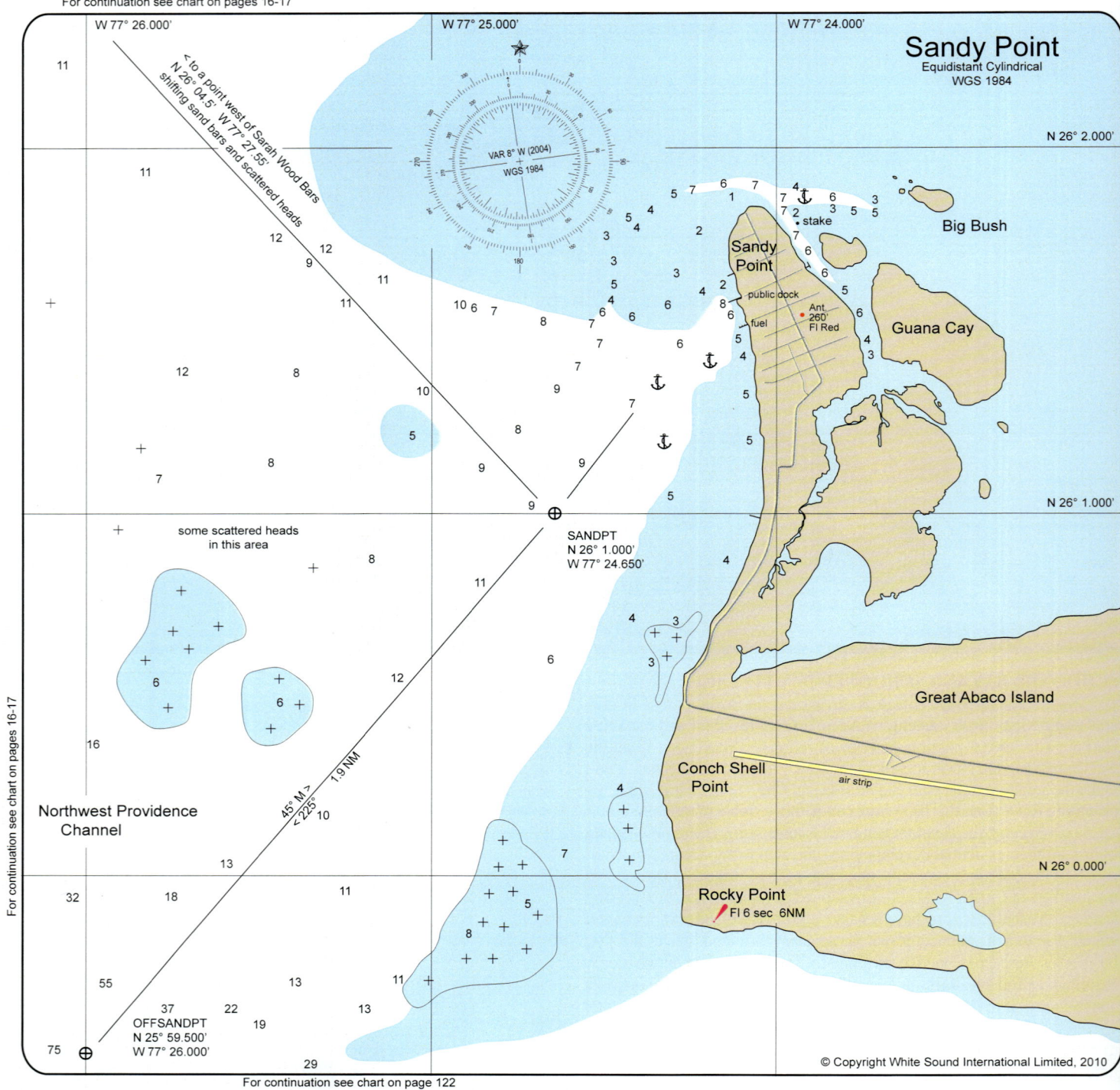

SANDY POINT

This small community, located on the SW side of the southern extremity of Great Abaco Island, is a possible stop for boats travelling between Florida and the Sea of Abaco by the southern route which rounds Hole-in-the-Wall about 20 NM SE of Sandy Point. Its advantage is its location close to this route; its disadvantage is that it has no real harbour. There is protection from SE to NE—anchor off the west side of the town. For protection from the S and SW go to the creek north of the town over a bar which carries about 3' MLW. Lightbourne's Marina is the dock south of the government dock and has fuel, power and water and room for 4 boats to about 40'. Like the anchorage, it is fully exposed to the W, actually from S through W to N. There are a couple of grocery stores and restaurants in town. Nancy's is the best known restaurant, and seems to be open more often than the others. Bahamas Fast Ferries had scheduled service to and from Nassau on Mondays and Wednesdays during Fall 2015; check regarding current schedule (www.bahamasferries.com). Flights to Nassau are scheduled several times a week and there is a shuttle service for travel to Marsh Harbour via the highway.

LOVE THE LOOK OF THIS HELM?
JOIN THE CLUB

GARMIN

GPSMAP® 8600 SERIES WITH WITH AUTO GUIDANCE†

- 10", 12" OR 16" TOUCHSCREEN HD IPS DISPLAYS
- FULLY NETWORK CAPABLE
- PRELOADED MAPPING WITH NAVIONICS DATA BLUECHART G3 + LAKEVÜ G3
- ACTIVECAPTAIN APP READY WITH BUILT-IN WIFI

Auto Guidance is for planning purposes only and does not replace safe navigation operations. Wi-Fi is a registered trademark of the Wi-Fi Alliance. ©2021 Garmin Ltd. or its subsidiaries.

Page 130

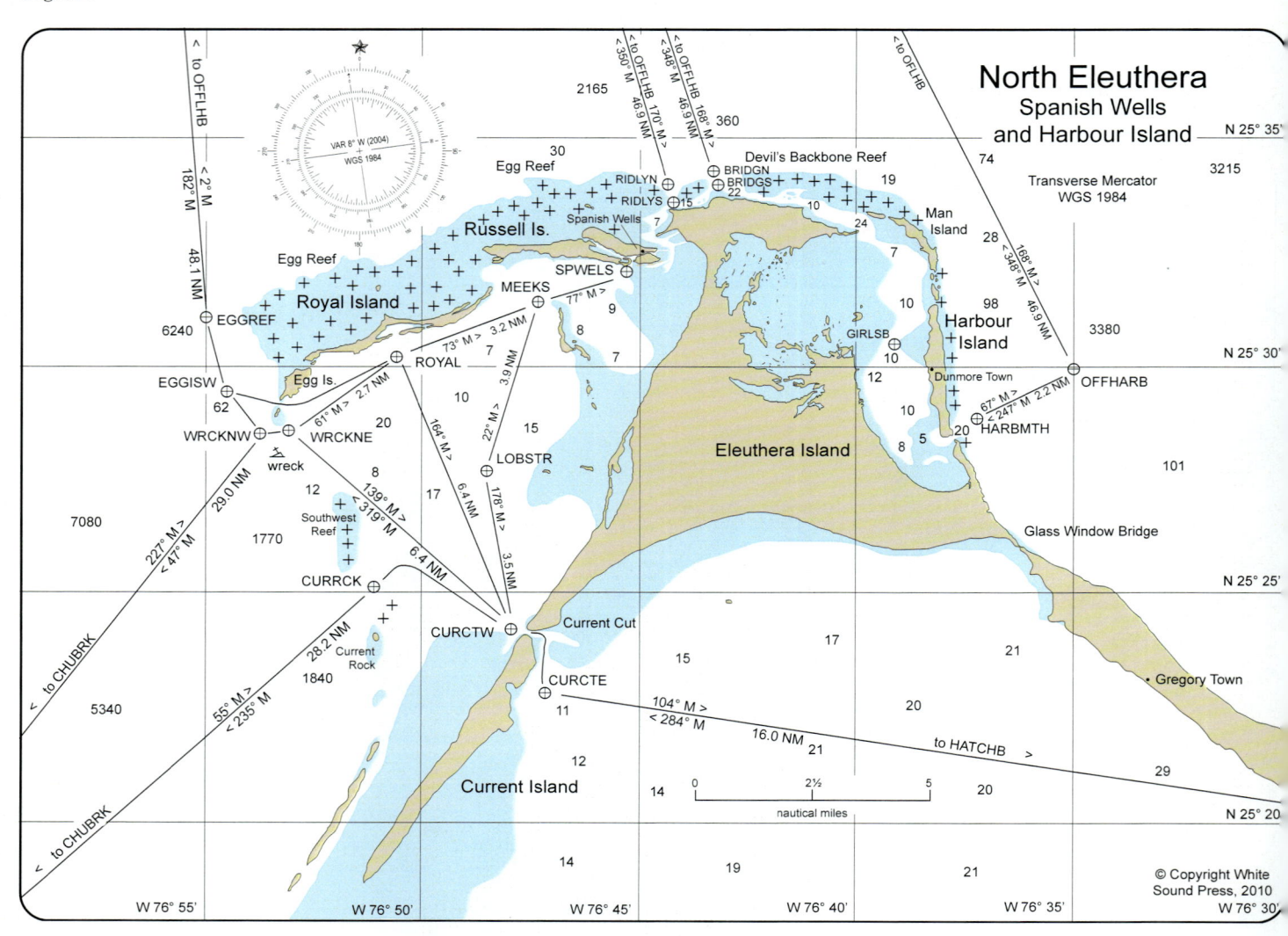

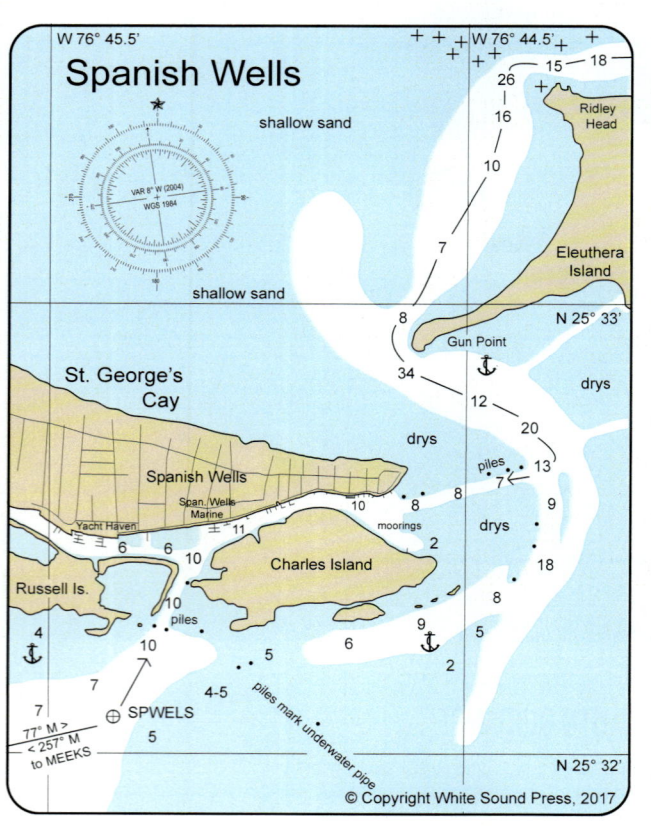

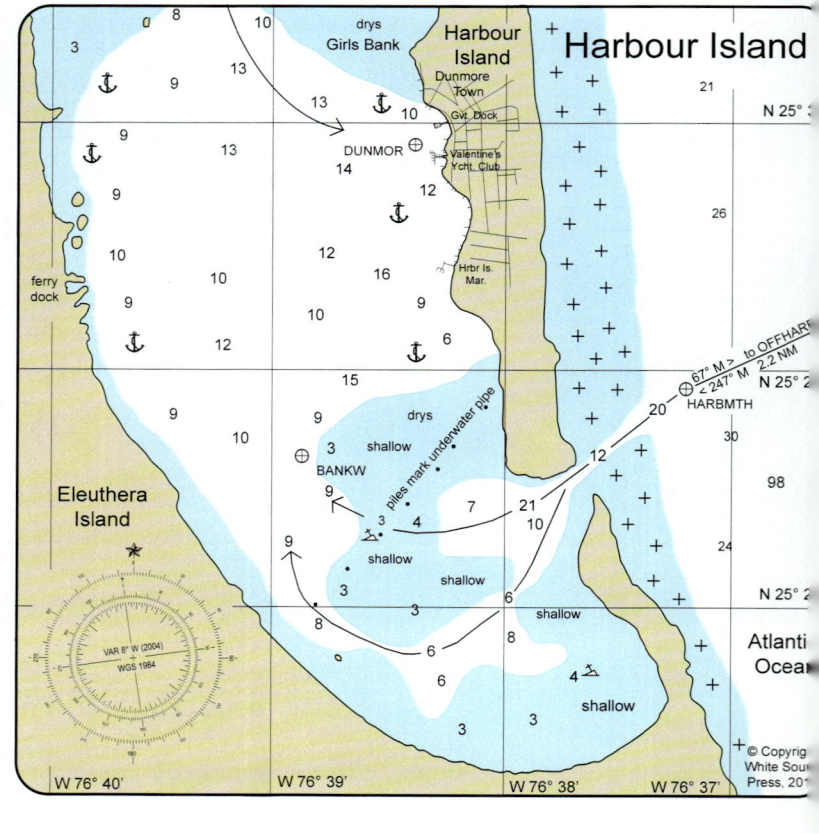

North Eleuthera
Spanish Wells and Harbour Island

Transverse Mercator
WGS 1984

© Copyright White Sound Press, 2010

Spanish Wells (inset)
© Copyright White Sound Press, 2017

Harbour Island (inset)
© Copyright White Sound Press, 2010

Approaches to North Eleuthera

The northern tip of Eleuthera Island is situated about 30 NM SE of Hole-in-the-Wall, Abaco. The two principal communities—Spanish Wells and Dunmore Town—are located on relatively small land masses—St. George's Cay and Harbour Island—on opposite sides of Eleuthera Island. Passage from one to the other inside Devil's Backbone Reef is challenging with a circuitous and in some places very narrow deep water channel between the beach and the reef. Local pilots are readily available and highly recommended for the first time or two. They will come to your boat in their outboard and tow it through behind yours, and then return home in their boat. Call them on VHF 16.

There are two openings in the reefs which ring the northern tip of Eleuthera—one north of Ridley Head and the other north of Bridge Point. Waypoints for these passages are provided. These are fair weather good visibility passages only. If the weather is not suitable, go west around Egg Reef and Egg Island to get to Spanish Wells, or east around Man Island and Harbour Island to get to Harbour Mouth (inlet) at the south end of Harbour Island. Royal Island, about 5 NM west of Spanish Wells, offers a good anchorage, and Current Cut, which is aptly named, is the most direct route to the various harbours and communities located further south on the west side of Eleuthera.

Spanish Wells

The harbour is long and narrow—formed by St. George's Cay on the north and Russell and Charles Islands on the south. Entry is through dredged channels at the eastern end and in the middle between Russell and Charles Islands. There is a lot of traffic in the harbour, and no room to anchor. Yacht Haven and Spanish Wells Marine have dockage, and moorings are available in a small area east of Charles Island. Anchorages can be found south of Charles Island or east of St. George's Cay. Spanish Wells is an old Bahamian fishing and boat building community.

Harbour Island

Harbour Island is most easily approached through Harbour Mouth, which has strong tidal flows. Waypoints for the approach are provided. Two routes through the sand banks on the inside are shown, one providing about 3' MLW and the other about 6'. Alternatively, the northern approach is via the natural channel between Devil's Backbone Reef and the beach on Eleuthera Island for which a local pilot is recommended. Anchorages can be found along the west shore of Harbour Island. Moorings are available as well, and Valentine's Yacht Club and Harbour Island Marina both have full service dockage available. Dunmore Town is a charming old hillside community with a beautiful beach on the eastern shore of Harbour Island. There are several resorts, restaurants and shops in this vibrant resort town.

Waypoints: *Eleuthera* (generally listed WNW to ESE):

WPT	Description of Position	Latitude	Longitutde
EGGREF	0.8 NM W of Egg Reef	N 25° 31.210	W 76° 55.031'
EGGISW	1.1 NM W Egg Island	N 25° 29.500'	W 76° 54.500'
WRCKNW	0.75 NM NW wreck of *Arimora*	N 25° 28.550'	W 76° 53.757'
WRCKNE	0.75 NM ENE wreck of *Arimora*	N 25° 28.680'	W 76° 53.093'
ROYAL	0.5 NM S Royal Island harbour	N 25° 30.226'	W 76° 50.635'
MEEKS	0.4 NM NNW Meeks Patch	N 25° 31.489'	W 76° 47.290
SPWELS	0.2 NM S of south ent. SpWells	N 25° 32.082'	W 76° 45.340'
LOBSTR	1 NM W of Lobster Cays	N 25° 27.734'	W 76° 48.507'
CURRCK	1.4 NM N of Current Rock	N 25° 25.180'	W 76° 51.160'
CURCTW	0.35 NM W of Current Cut	N 25° 24.275	W 76° 47.982'
CURCTE	1.2 NM S of E end Current Cut	N 25° 22.875'	W 76° 47.141'
RIDLYN	N end Ridley route thru reef	N 25° 33.986'	W 76° 44.340'
RIDKYS	S end Ridley route thru reef	N 25° 33.611'	W 76° 44.270'
BRIDGN	N end Bridge Pt. route thru reef	N 25° 34.298'	W 76° 43.344'
BRIDGS	S end Bridge Pt. route thru reef	N 25° 33.970'	W 76° 43.300'
GIRLSB	W of Girls Bank	N 25° 30.560'	W 76° 39.120'
DUNMOR	W of Govt Dock, Dunmore Twn	N 25° 29.918'	W 76° 38.389'
BANKW	W of bank N of Harbour Mouth	N 25° 28.634'	W 76° 38.897'
OFFHARB	3.0 NM NE Harbour Mouth	N 25° 30.000'	W 76° 35.000'
HARBMTH	0.5 NM NE Harbour Mouth	N 25° 28.900'	W 76° 37.200'

Waypoints not shown on charts

OFFLHB	1 NM SE ent. Little Harbour*	N 26° 18.971'	W 76° 58.858'
HATCHB	0.25 NM S of entr Hatchet Bay	N 25° 20.531'	W 76° 29.649'
CHUBRK	0.4 NM NW Chub Rock **	N 25° 06.700'	W 77° 14.700'

*Little Harbour, Abaco
**Chub Rock is N of the east end of Salt Cay about 5 NM NE Nassau

Spanish Wells and northern Eleuthera Island from the south with Gun Point, Ridley Head and part of Devil's Backbone Reef. Photo by Steve Dodge.

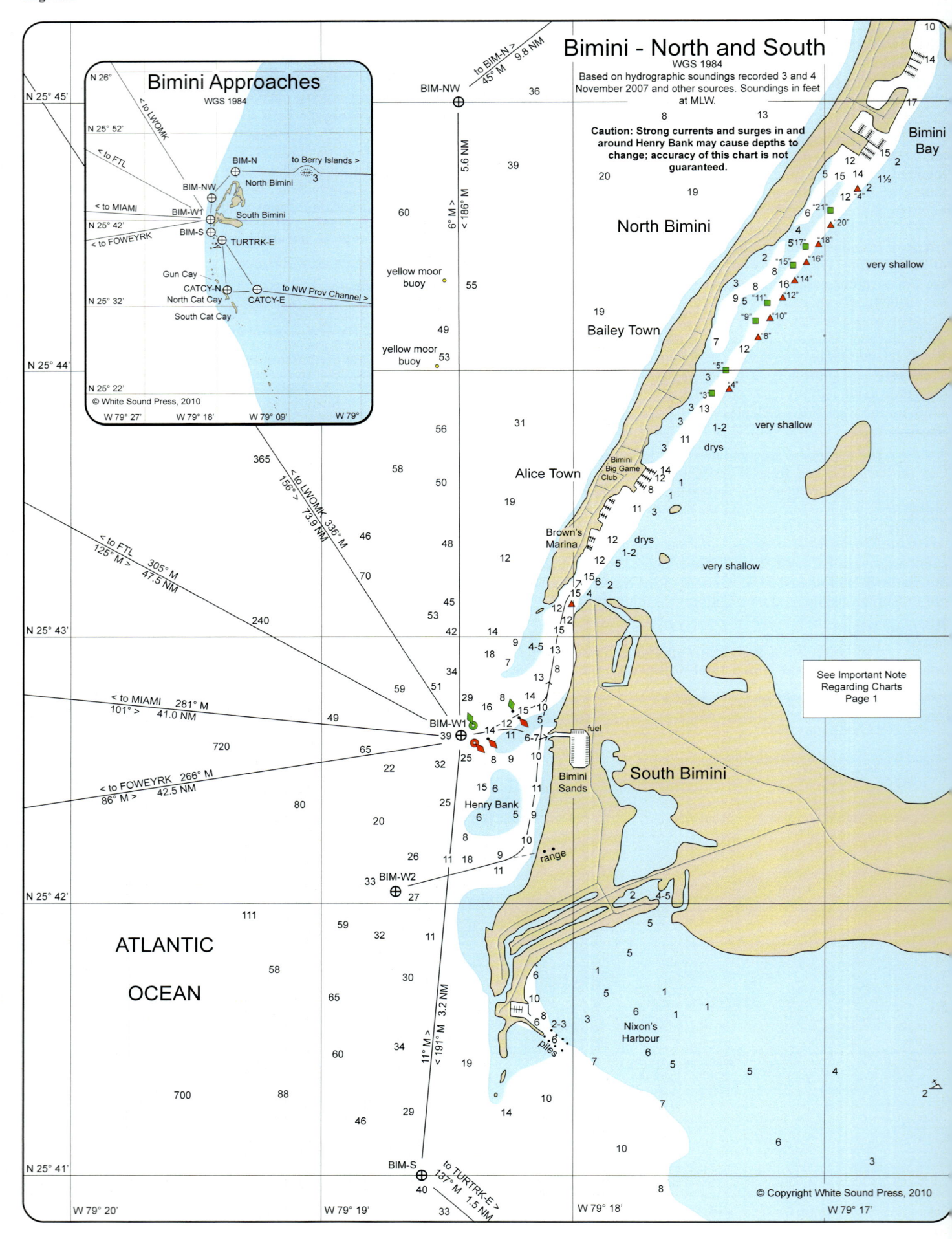

Bimini - North and South

WGS 1984

Based on hydrographic soundings recorded 3 and 4 November 2007 and other sources. Soundings in feet at MLW.

Caution: Strong currents and surges in and around Henry Bank may cause depths to change; accuracy of this chart is not guaranteed.

See Important Note Regarding Charts Page 1

Bimini Approaches
WGS 1984

© White Sound Press, 2010

© Copyright White Sound Press, 2010

BIMINI

There are two ways to enter protected areas at North and South Bimini. The "old" natural channel is marked with a range on the beach on South Bimini. from the waypoint BIM-W2 approach the beach on the range and then turn to port and parallel the shore. Enter Bimini Sands on South Bimini (short breakwaters on both sides of the entrance) or continue northward and enter the main harbour at North Bimini where Alice Town is located.

The other entry is via a dredged channel marked with red and green buoys. Go to the waypoint BIM-W1 and proceed between the buoys, and then enter Bimini Sands or turn north to North Bimini and Alice Town. This channel, which is exposed to the ocean, periodically shifts. It is best to call one of the marinas on VHF 16 and ask for advice regarding entering.

Bimini Sands is a marina/condo development with a restaurant and a store on site. Marinas at North Bimini (in order of appearance for entering vessel) are Brown's Marina, the Bimini Big Game Club, and Bimini Bay.

Entrance to harbour at Alice Town, North Bimini from the south. Photo by Steve Dodge, November, 2007.

Waypoints shown on these charts (generally from north to south)

WPT	Description	Latitude	Longitude
BIM-N	0.3 NM N of North Rock	N 25° 48.250'	W 79° 15.500'
BIM-NW	1.0 NM NW cntr.North Bimini	N 25° 45.000'	W 79° 18.450'
BIM-W1	West of dredged channel	N 25° 42.630'	W 79° 18.450'
BIM-W2	entrance old channel	N 25° 42.050'	W 79° 18.700'
BIM-S	0.5 NM SSW South Bimini	N 25° 41.000'	W 79° 18.600'
CATCY-N	0.5 NM N Harbr North Cat Cy	N 25° 33.800'	W 79° 16.700'
CATCY-E	3.5 NM E of Cat Cay	N 25° 34.000'	W 79° 13.000'

Waypoints beyond area shown on these charts (generally from north to south)

WPT	Description	Latitude	Longitude
LWOMK	Lake Worth outer mark	N 26° 46.340'	W 80° 00.490'
FTL	Fort Lauderdale outer mark	N 26° 05.400'	W 80° 04.700'
MIAMI	S of Govt. Cut outer mark	N 25° 45.950'	W 80° 05.000'
FOWEYRK	1NM E Fowey Rock light	N 25° 35.400'	W 80° 04.700'

Natural channel looking SSW from beach on South Bimini near Bimini Sands. Henry Bank is clearly visible with breakers on right side of photo. Range markers are on beach north of point on photo and are not clearly discernible on this photo. Photo by Steve Dodge, November, 2007.

A sting ray cruising along Sandy Cay Reef. String rays are not aggressive—they do have a sharp barb near the base of the tail which can be used to cut and inject toxin in a threatening opponent—but aggressive attacks against non-threatening humans are almost unknown. When sting rays rest they usually go to the bottom and flap their wings to stir up the sand; the result is a partially buried sting ray on the bottom (see photo below). When walking in shallow water off the beach it is wise to make some noise—splash so as to wake any resting sting ray. However, if stepped on the sting ray will swim away and may cut a bare foot with its barb and toxin. Photos by Katie Dodge at Sandy Cay Reef, July, 2014.

A pair of spotted eagle rays cruising along just beyond the eastern edge of Sandy Cay Reef. Note the remora swimming beneath the second spotted eagle ray. Photo by Katie Dodge, July, 2011.

Snorkeling/Dive/Fishing Chart Section

South Abaco Sound	136-137
Walkers Cay Dive Chart	138
Manjack, Green Turtle and No Name Reefs	139
Great Guana Cay, Northwest end	140
Fowl Cay Preserve Dive Moorings	141
Johnnys Cay Reef	142
Sand Sandy Cay Reef	143

Fowl Cay reef has moorings installed and maintained by Friends of the Environment for use by snorkelers and SCUBA divers. This head is near the northwest area of the reef.

Coral Courtesies
by Friends of the Environment

- Corals are live animals that are incredibly important to reefs. Standing on, kicking, or touching could injure the coral, spread disease, or you may get stung.
- Help protect the reef by always using mooring buoys or anchoring in sand away from reef.
- Only small boats (up to 28 feet) should tie up to moorings at North Guana, Fowl Cay, Mermaid, and Sandy Cay reefs. There is a danger of the moorings breaking if larger boats tie up.
- Tie your bow line to the pick-up line of the mooring buoy and let out enough rope to give a horizontal pulling on the mooring. (Ultimately, you are responsible for your boat. It is always a good idea to dive the mooring and assess its condition).
- Please pick up debris.
- Please dispose of fishing line responsibly.
- Please leave live corals, shells, sea stars, sand dollars, or sea fans in the sea.
- Support restaurants and fishermen selling seafood that is in season and up to measure.
- Do not discharge holding tanks or bilge water within 3 miles of land.
- Report dumping or other illegal activities to the police (367-2560); report poaching to the Bahamas National Trust Park Warden (367-6310) or Department of Marine Resources (699-0202).

Photo Fowl Cay Reef by Steve Dodge 4 July 2008.

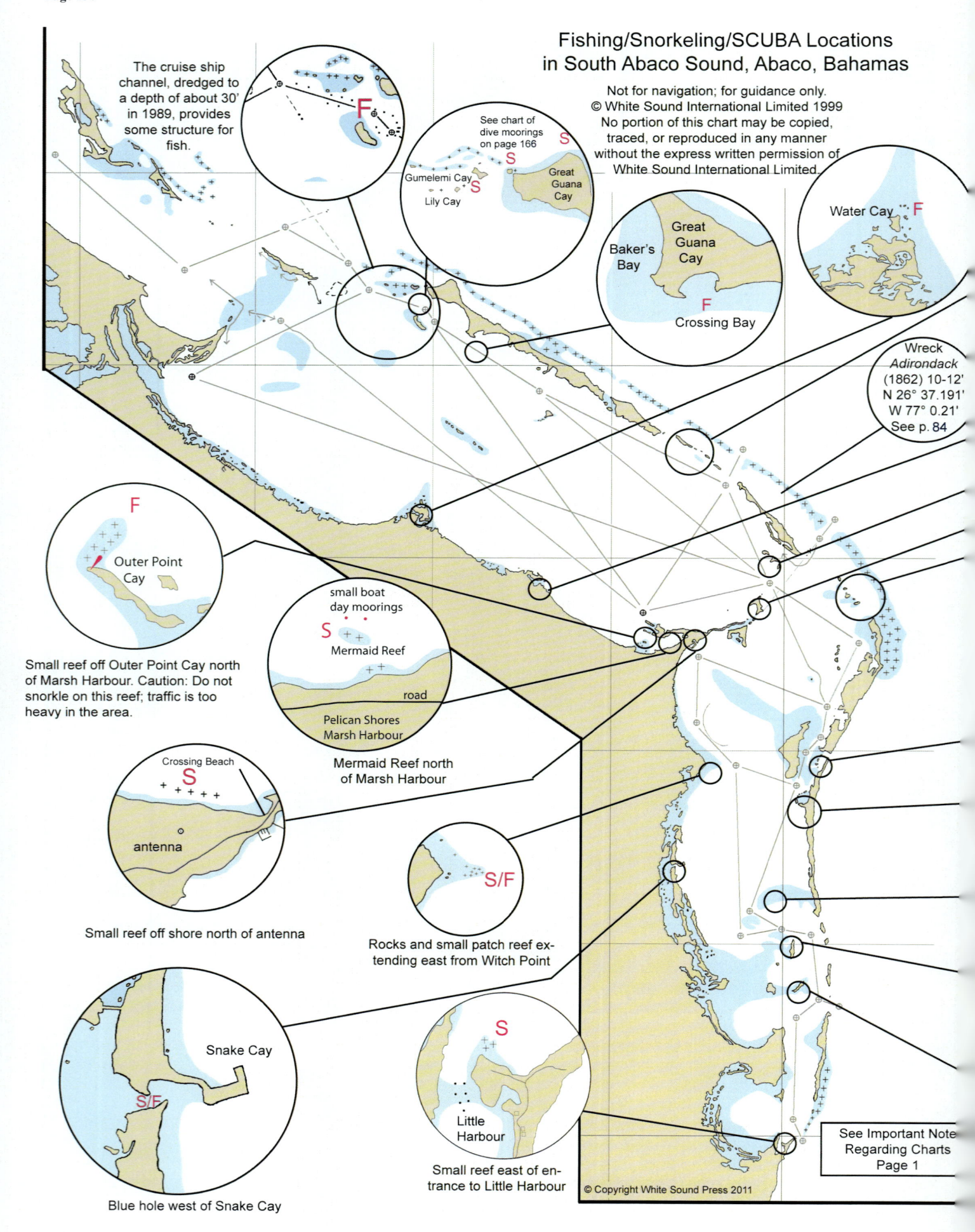

Fishing/Snorkeling/SCUBA Locations in South Abaco Sound, Abaco, Bahamas

Not for navigation; for guidance only.
© White Sound International Limited 1999
No portion of this chart may be copied, traced, or reproduced in any manner without the express written permission of White Sound International Limited.

The cruise ship channel, dredged to a depth of about 30' in 1989, provides some structure for fish.

See chart of dive moorings on page 166

Gumelemi Cay
Lily Cay
Great Guana Cay

Baker's Bay
Great Guana Cay
Crossing Bay

Water Cay

Wreck *Adirondack* (1862) 10-12'
N 26° 37.191'
W 77° 0.21'
See p. 84

Outer Point Cay

Small reef off Outer Point Cay north of Marsh Harbour. Caution: Do not snorkle on this reef; traffic is too heavy in the area.

small boat day moorings
Mermaid Reef
road
Pelican Shores
Marsh Harbour

Mermaid Reef north of Marsh Harbour

Crossing Beach
antenna

Small reef off shore north of antenna

Rocks and small patch reef extending east from Witch Point

Snake Cay

Little Harbour

Small reef east of entrance to Little Harbour

Blue hole west of Snake Cay

See Important Note Regarding Charts Page 1

© Copyright White Sound Press 2011

Page 137

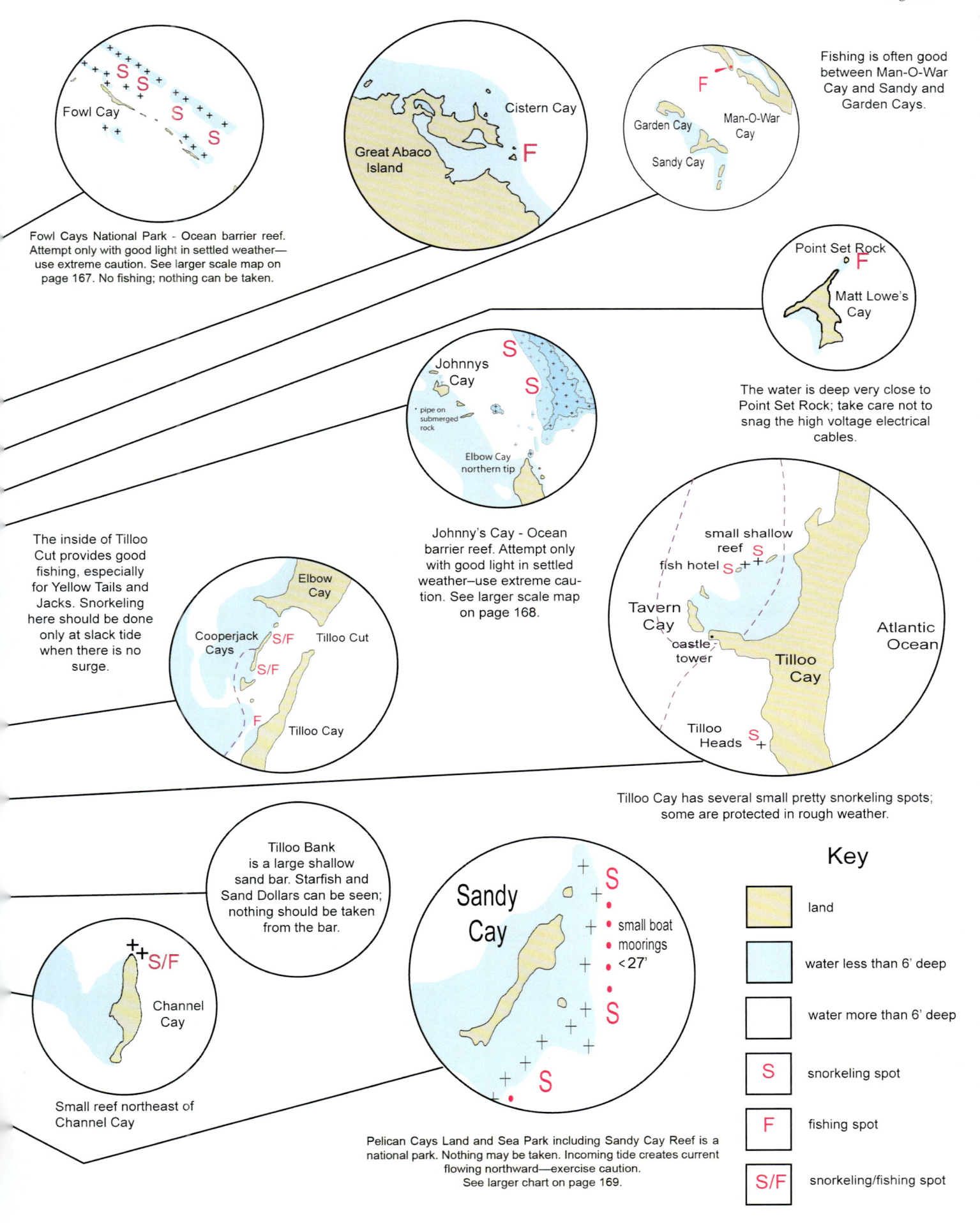

Fowl Cays National Park - Ocean barrier reef. Attempt only with good light in settled weather—use extreme caution. See larger scale map on page 167. No fishing; nothing can be taken.

Fishing is often good between Man-O-War Cay and Sandy and Garden Cays.

The water is deep very close to Point Set Rock; take care not to snag the high voltage electrical cables.

The inside of Tilloo Cut provides good fishing, especially for Yellow Tails and Jacks. Snorkeling here should be done only at slack tide when there is no surge.

Johnny's Cay - Ocean barrier reef. Attempt only with good light in settled weather–use extreme caution. See larger scale map on page 168.

Tilloo Cay has several small pretty snorkeling spots; some are protected in rough weather.

Tilloo Bank is a large shallow sand bar. Starfish and Sand Dollars can be seen; nothing should be taken from the bar.

Small reef northeast of Channel Cay

Pelican Cays Land and Sea Park including Sandy Cay Reef is a national park. Nothing may be taken. Incoming tide creates current flowing northward—exercise caution. See larger chart on page 169.

Key

- land
- water less than 6' deep
- water more than 6' deep
- **S** snorkeling spot
- **F** fishing spot
- **S/F** snorkeling/fishing spot

Walker's Cay Dive Chart

This chart was developed from information and a sketch chart provided by Jon Longair of Treasure Island, Florida. He wrote:

"We watched and followed [the dive] boat in and out of the marina all week and they all went the same way as depicted on the map. The big mistake is trying to follow the dive boat out the middle of the reef. Do not even try. There is a week's worth of diving right inside what we called the horseshoe. All around "Pillars," "Utopia," and "Jon's Point." If you had a week there you would never need to leave that area. Most of the other dive locations were deeper but I did not think that they were that much better if at all. The reef is treacherous though. You can be in 50' of water and step out of the side of your boat on to a 3' deep mound. The steepness of the reef is also what makes it so beautiful. Go slow and watch the colors. The area in front of Walker's is now a preserve. There is no fishing, lobstering, or spearing, even with a pole spear or Hawaiian sling. Just enjoying the pristine beauty God created. I have not dived the world but I can say without hesitation that this is the most magnificent place I have ever been."

Coordinates for Walker's Cay Dive Sites

Name (Depth)	latitude	longitude
Near Kevin's Crack	27° 18.980'	78° 25.590'
Kevin's Crack (60/90')	27° 18.890'	78° 26.600'
Aquarium (85')	27° 18.980'	78° 25.540'
190' Blue Canyon (80/190')	27° 18.760'	78° 25.610'
80-130' Canyon (80/130')	27° 18.710'	78° 25.610'
Small Ledge - Lobsters (80')	27° 18.890'	78° 22.500'
Shark Canyon (90')	27° 18.180'	78° 22.580'
Walker's Cay Dive Buoy (80')	27° 17.880'	78° 22.500'
Jon's Point	27° 17.271'	78° 22.958'
Pillars (48')	27° 17.266'	78° 22.551'
Utopia (48')	27° 17.218'	78° 22.572'
Larry's Sharks (60')	27° 17.910'	78° 21.980'

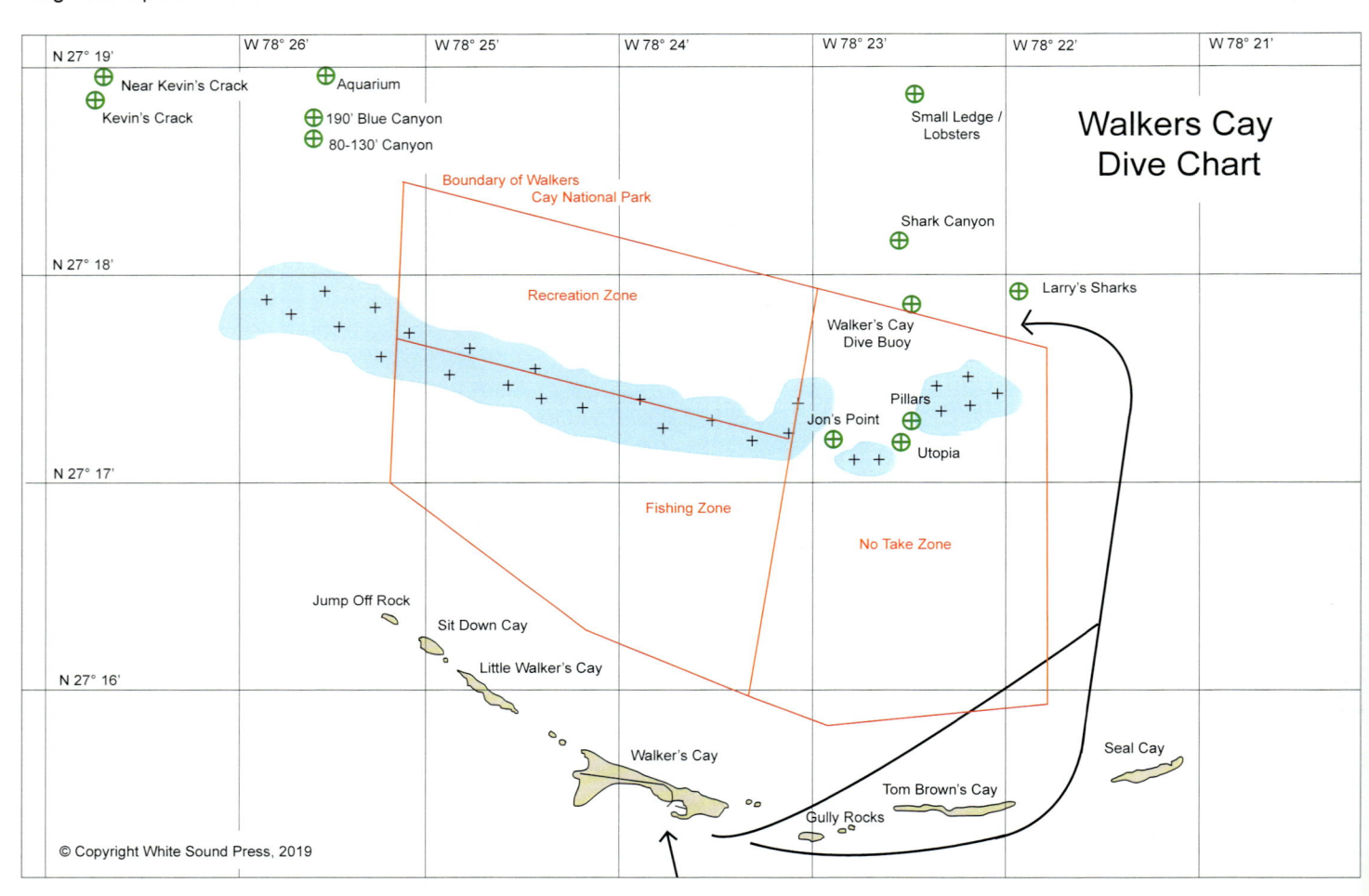

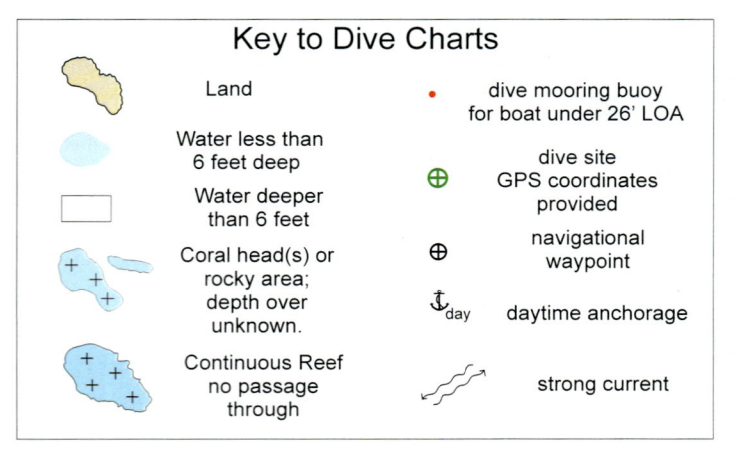

Turtle at Sandy Cay Reef, July 2010. Photo by Katie Dodge.

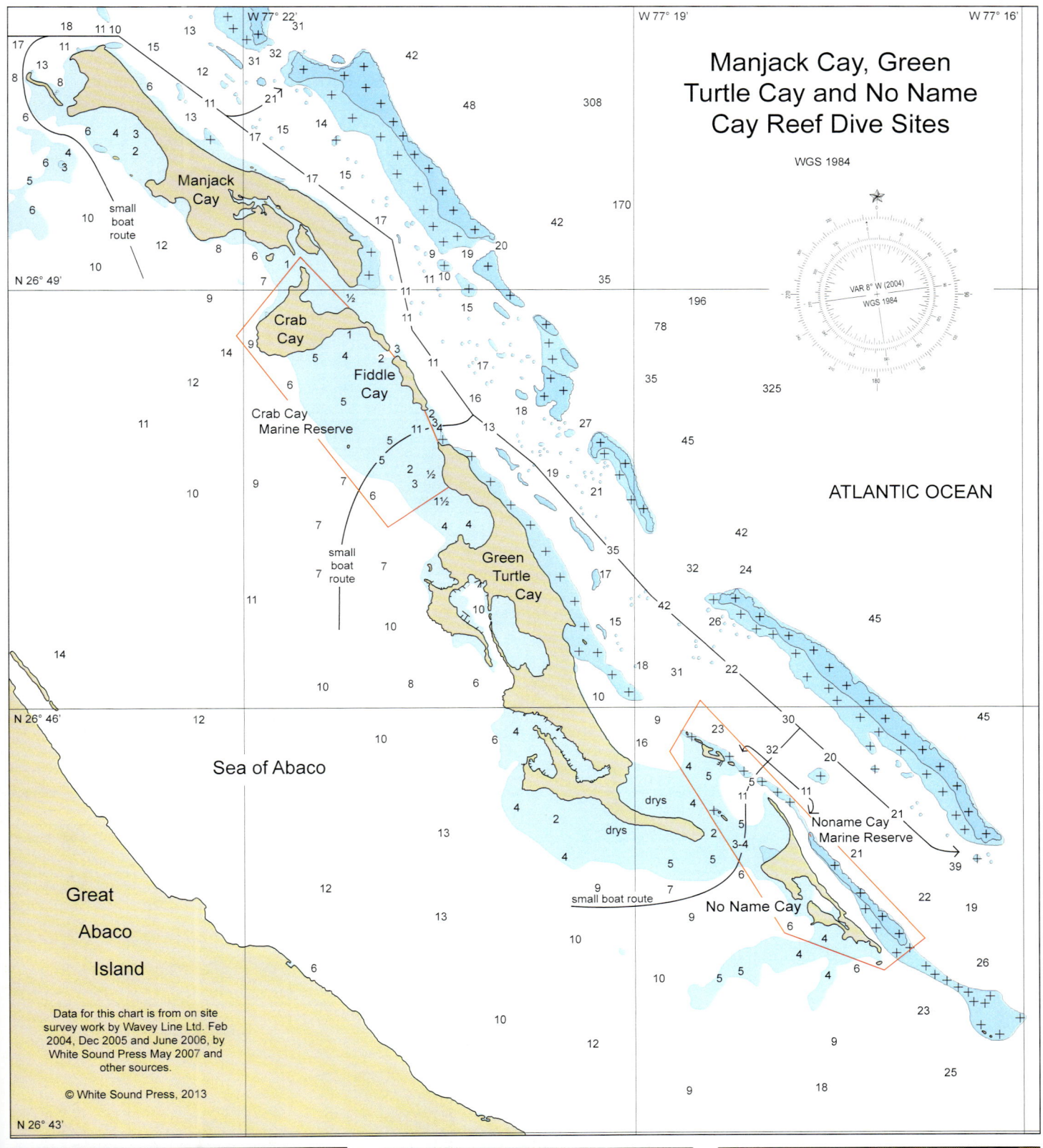

Manjack Cay, Green Turtle Cay and No Name Cay Reef Dive Sites

WGS 1984

VAR 8° W (2004)
WGS 1984

ATLANTIC OCEAN

Manjack Cay

small boat route

Crab Cay

Fiddle Cay

Crab Cay Marine Reserve

small boat route

Green Turtle Cay

Sea of Abaco

Great Abaco Island

Noname Cay Marine Reserve

No Name Cay

small boat route

Data for this chart is from on site survey work by Wavey Line Ltd. Feb 2004, Dec 2005 and June 2006, by White Sound Press May 2007 and other sources.

© White Sound Press, 2013

Juvenile Queen Angelfish.

Nassau Grouper

Flamefish.

photos © Mike Adair, Sports Photography. 2001

Great Guana Cay Reef North West End Dive Sites

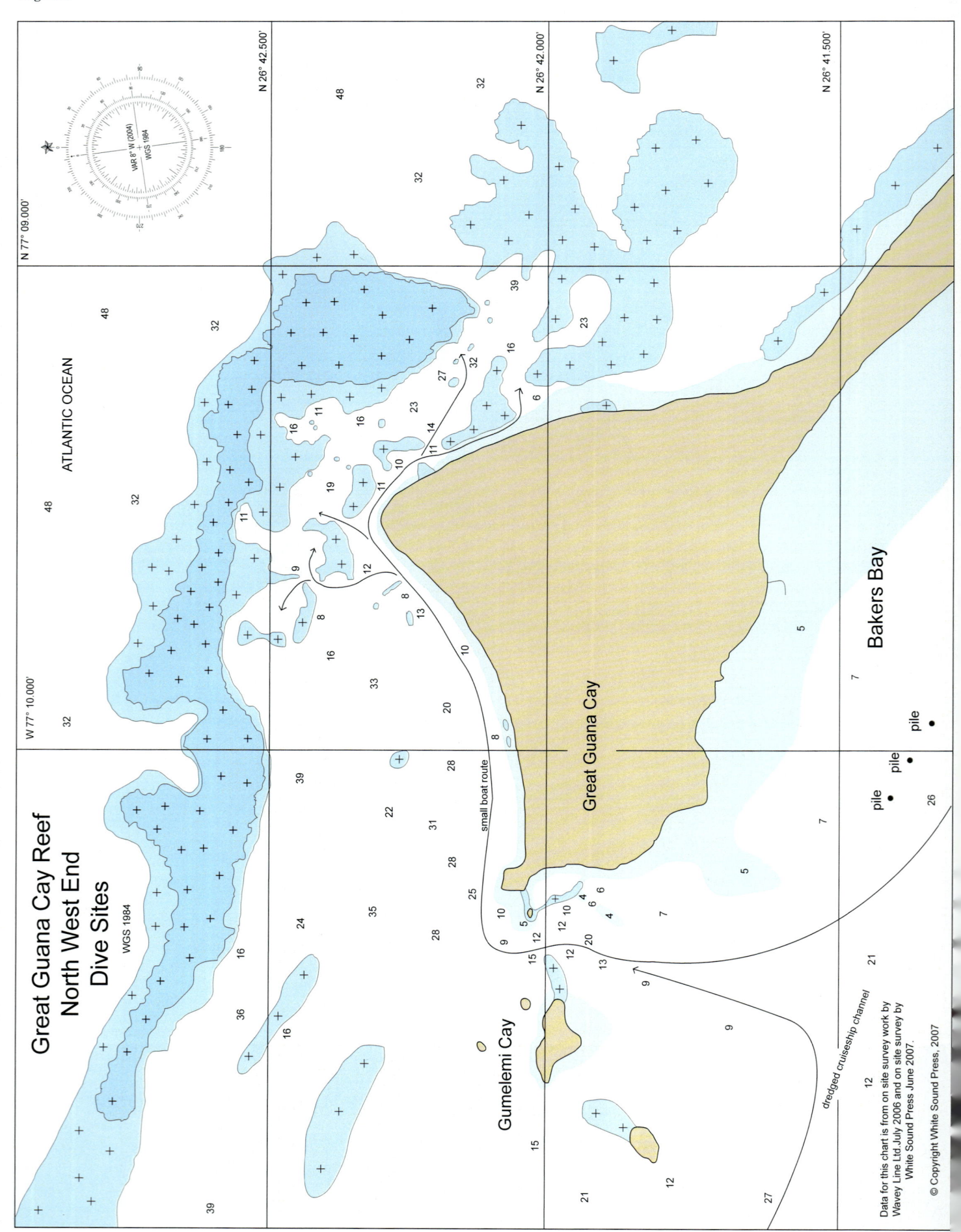

ATLANTIC OCEAN

Great Guana Cay

Bakers Bay

Gumelemi Cay

small boat route

dredged cruiseship channel

pile • pile • pile •

VAR 8° W (2004)
WGS 1984

WGS 1984

N 26° 42.500'
N 26° 42.000'
N 26° 41.500'
W 77° 10.000'
N 77° 09.000'

Data for this chart is from on site survey work by Wavey Line Ltd July 2006 and on site survey by White Sound Press June 2007.

© Copyright White Sound Press, 2007

Fowl Cays National Park
WGS 1984

Fowl Cay National Park includes all small cays and all reefs shown on this chart

Absolutely no fishing or Spearfishing is permitted in Fowl Cay National Park. Nothing may be taken.

park boundary (approx.)

ATLANTIC OCEAN

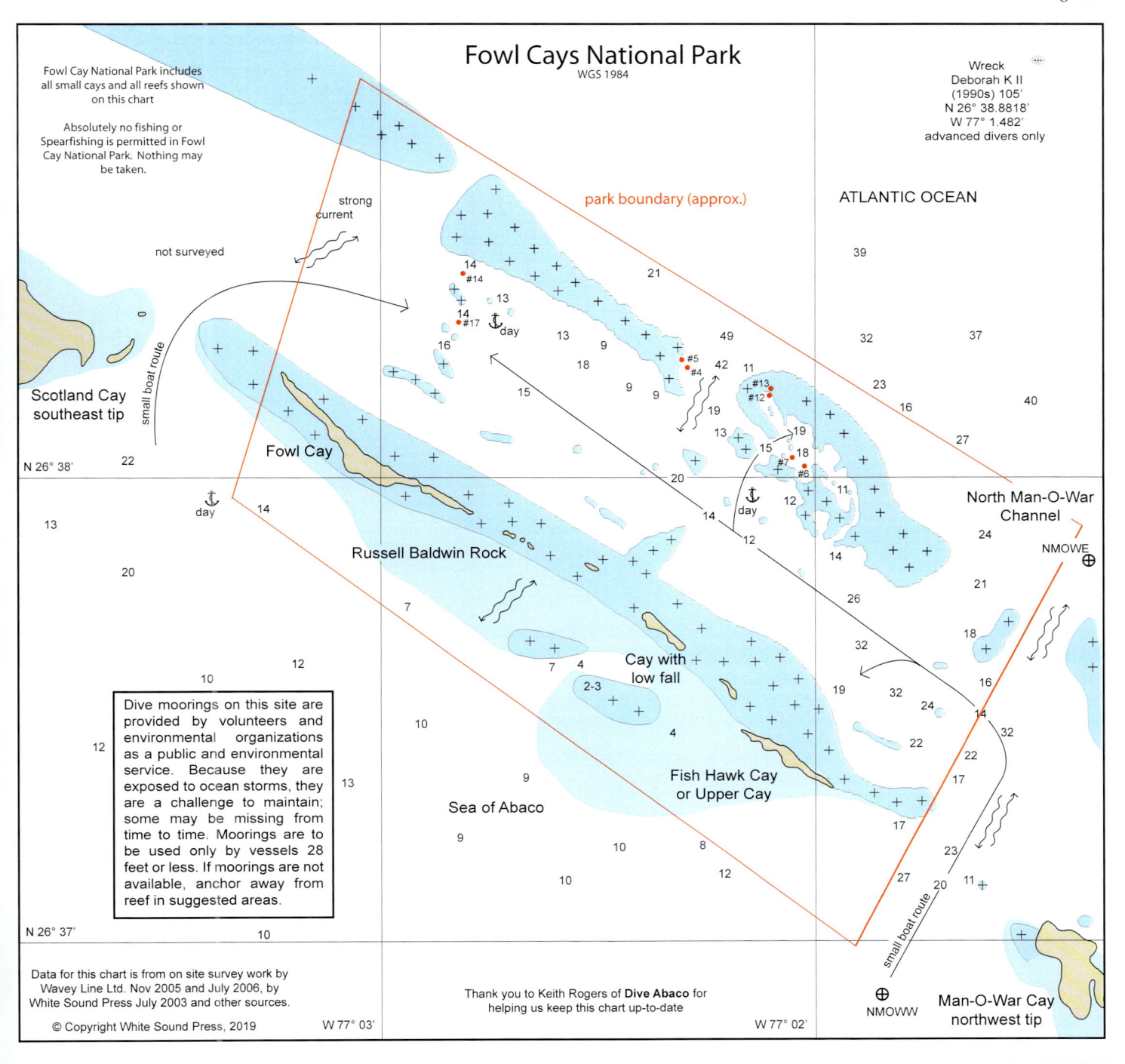

Wreck
Deborah K II
(1990s) 105'
N 26° 38.8818'
W 77° 1.482'
advanced divers only

strong current

not surveyed

Scotland Cay southeast tip

Fowl Cay

Russell Baldwin Rock

Cay with low fall

Fish Hawk Cay or Upper Cay

Sea of Abaco

North Man-O-War Channel

NMOWE

Man-O-War Cay northwest tip

NMOWW

Dive moorings on this site are provided by volunteers and environmental organizations as a public and environmental service. Because they are exposed to ocean storms, they are a challenge to maintain; some may be missing from time to time. Moorings are to be used only by vessels 28 feet or less. If moorings are not available, anchor away from reef in suggested areas.

Data for this chart is from on site survey work by Wavey Line Ltd. Nov 2005 and July 2006, by White Sound Press July 2003 and other sources.

© Copyright White Sound Press, 2019

Thank you to Keith Rogers of **Dive Abaco** for helping us keep this chart up-to-date

School of Doctor Fish. Photo by Katie Dodge, July 2014.

Mooring Numbers, Names, and GPS Coordinates

#	Name	Coordinates
#1	French Grunt Alley A	missing
#2	French Grunt Alley B	missing
#3	French Grunt Alley C	missing
#4	The Wall A	N 26° 38.233' W 77° 02.300'
#5	The Wall B	N 26° 38.248' W 77° 02.310'
#6	Frog Us	N 26° 38.016' W 77° 02.031'
#7	Frog Troy	N 26° 38.043' W 77° 02.053'
#8	Frog Big Boat	missing
#9	Big Boat	missing
#10	Flywheel Bay A	N 26° 38.131' W 77° 02.037'
#11	Flywheel Bay B	N 26° 38.144' W 77° 02.044'
#12	Grouper Alley	N 26° 38.174' W 77° 02.113'
#13	Shoots & Ladders	N 26° 38.191' W 77° 02.106'
#14	Tombstone A	N 26° 38.438' W 77° 02.082'
#15	Tombstone B	missing
#16	Tombstone C	missing
#17	Twin Reef A	N 26° 38.343' W 77° 02.838'
#18	Twin Reef B	missing
#19	Boy Scout	missing

The Abaco barrier reef stretches from Elbow Cay in the southeast to Walker's Cay in the northwest—a distance of about 105 miles (about 92 nautical miles); it is one of the largest barrier reefs in the world. The reef marks the northeast edge of Little Bahama Bank, provides some protection for the cays behind it, makes navigation and piloting challenging, consists of various kinds of corals, and provides habitat for fish, crawfish, turtles and anemonies. Depending on what you are doing and the weather, it can threaten your life or delight your senses with serenity and beauty. This photo taken from the northwest shows a corner of the reef at a small opening north of Allans-Pensacola and northeast of Umbrella Cay. Photo by Steve Dodge, 3 June 2013.

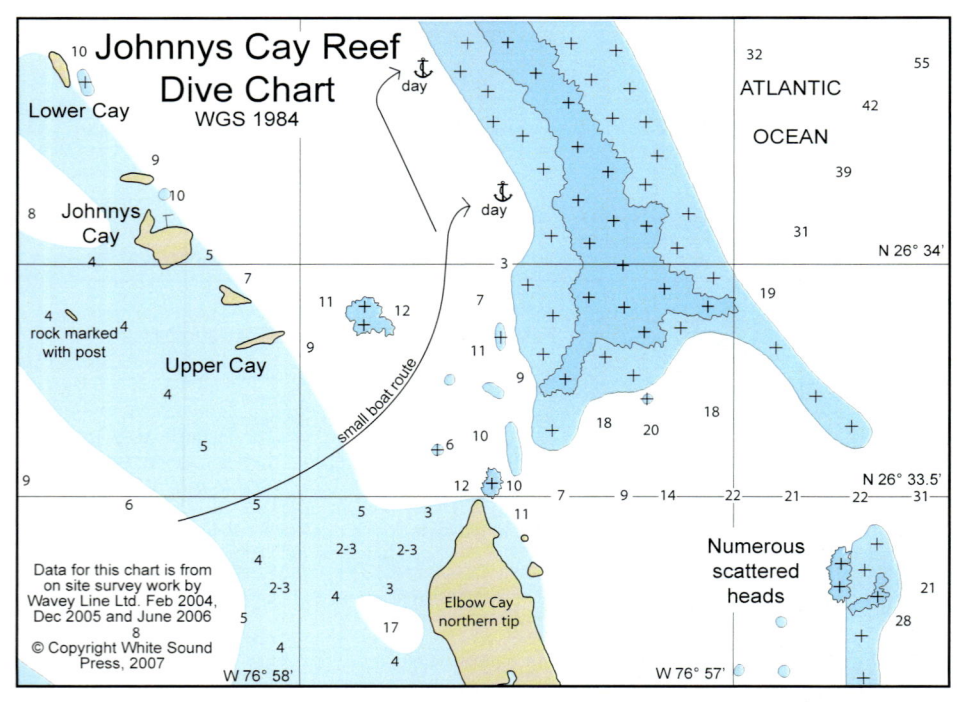

Johnnys Cay Reef is located just north of the northern tip of Elbow Cay and is a short boat trip from Hope Town. The day anchorages shown on the chart above are good in prevailing easterly winds.

Yellowtail Snappers at Sandy Cay Reef, July 2010. Photo by Katie Dodge.

Spotted Eagle Ray at Sandy Cay Reef, July 2011. Photo by Katie Dodge.

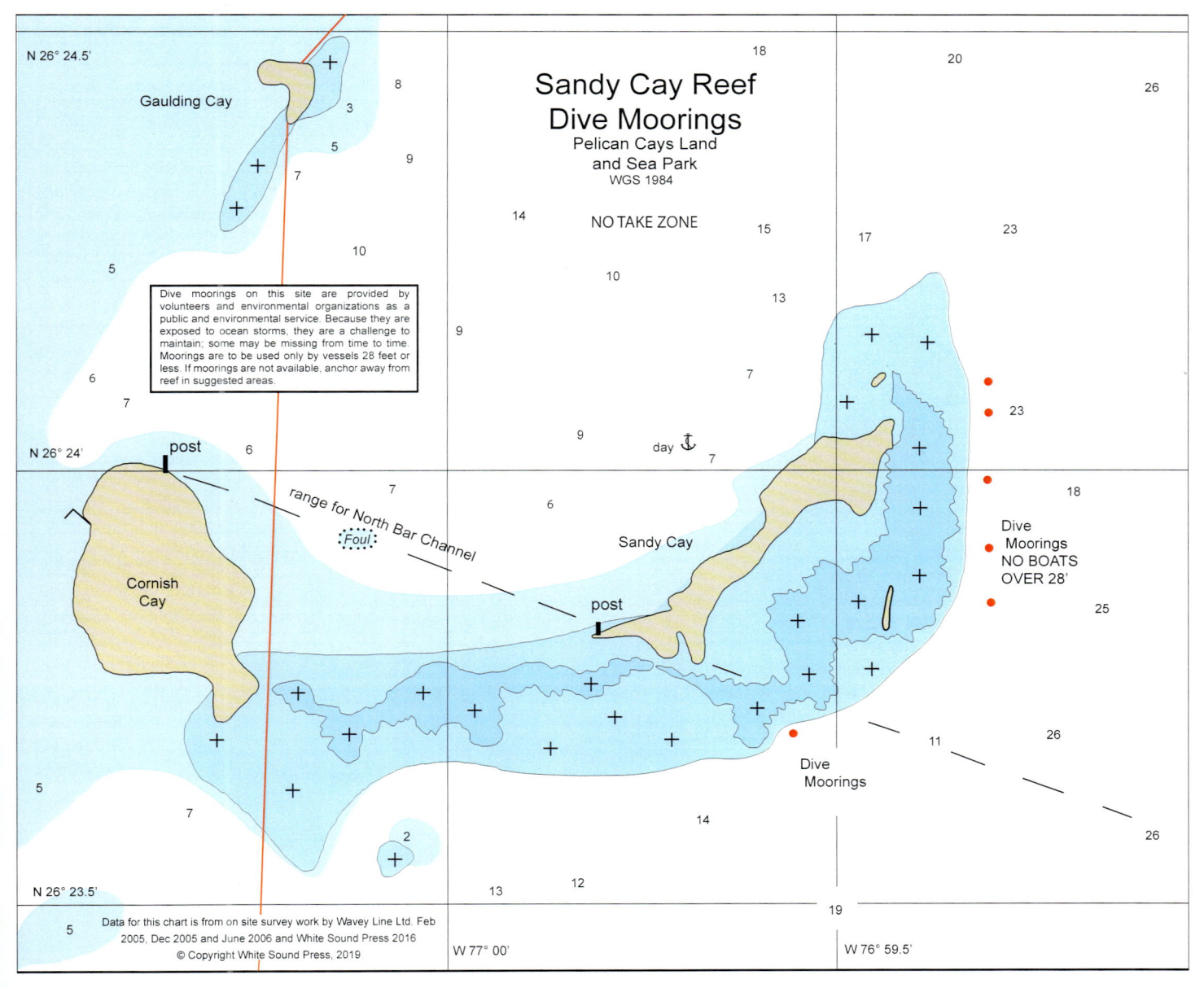

Sandy Cay Reef
Dive Moorings
Pelican Cays Land and Sea Park
WGS 1984

NO TAKE ZONE

N 26° 24.5'
N 26° 24'
N 26° 23.5'
W 77° 00'
W 76° 59.5'

Gaulding Cay

Dive moorings on this site are provided by volunteers and environmental organizations as a public and environmental service. Because they are exposed to ocean storms, they are a challenge to maintain; some may be missing from time to time. Moorings are to be used only by vessels 28 feet or less. If moorings are not available, anchor away from reef in suggested areas.

post

range for North Bar Channel

Foul

Cornish Cay

post

Sandy Cay

day

Dive Moorings NO BOATS OVER 28'

Dive Moorings

Data for this chart is from on site survey work by Wavey Line Ltd. Feb 2005, Dec 2005 and June 2006 and White Sound Press 2016
© Copyright White Sound Press, 2019

Sandy Cay and Sandy Cay Reef from the southwest., with the Pelican Cays and Atlantic Ocean in the background. The reef can be identified by the strip of darker water running north and south just east of the rock and the breaking waves near its southern end. Also, note the reef (dark patches of water) extending off to the west where some new moorings have been placed. Photo by Steve Dodge. Another aerial photo of Sandy Cay Reef can be found on page 4.

A small piece of Sargassum seaweed floating free at Sandy Cay Reef in June, 2010. Sargassum is often found in clumps floating at the surface and it usually supports a variety of sea life which lives just beneath it. It is very thick in the Sargasso Sea, a part of the Atlantic Ocean located several hundred miles east of Abaco characterized by slow moving ocean currents surrounded by fast moving ocean currents and large masses of floating Sargassum. Early mariners believed the weed would entrap their ships and that sea monsters living beneath the Sargassum would attack them. Photo by Katie Dodge.

Deep Draft (9') Cruising in Abaco

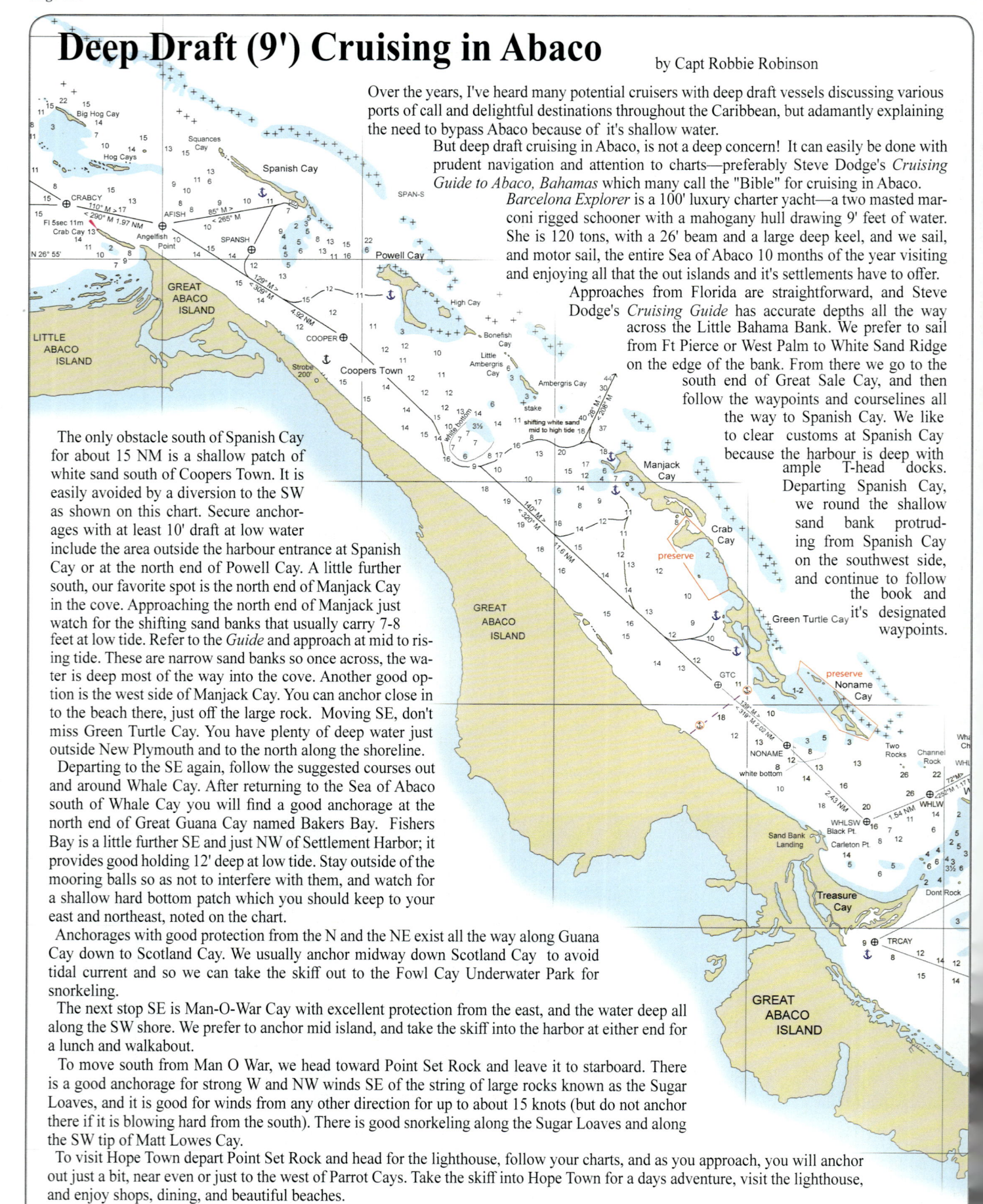

by Capt Robbie Robinson

Over the years, I've heard many potential cruisers with deep draft vessels discussing various ports of call and delightful destinations throughout the Caribbean, but adamantly explaining the need to bypass Abaco because of it's shallow water.

But deep draft cruising in Abaco, is not a deep concern! It can easily be done with prudent navigation and attention to charts—preferably Steve Dodge's *Cruising Guide to Abaco, Bahamas* which many call the "Bible" for cruising in Abaco.

Barcelona Explorer is a 100' luxury charter yacht—a two masted marconi rigged schooner with a mahogany hull drawing 9' feet of water. She is 120 tons, with a 26' beam and a large deep keel, and we sail, and motor sail, the entire Sea of Abaco 10 months of the year visiting and enjoying all that the out islands and it's settlements have to offer.

Approaches from Florida are straightforward, and Steve Dodge's *Cruising Guide* has accurate depths all the way across the Little Bahama Bank. We prefer to sail from Ft Pierce or West Palm to White Sand Ridge on the edge of the bank. From there we go to the south end of Great Sale Cay, and then follow the waypoints and courselines all the way to Spanish Cay. We like to clear customs at Spanish Cay because the harbour is deep with ample T-head docks. Departing Spanish Cay, we round the shallow sand bank protruding from Spanish Cay on the southwest side, and continue to follow the book and it's designated waypoints.

The only obstacle south of Spanish Cay for about 15 NM is a shallow patch of white sand south of Coopers Town. It is easily avoided by a diversion to the SW as shown on this chart. Secure anchorages with at least 10' draft at low water include the area outside the harbour entrance at Spanish Cay or at the north end of Powell Cay. A little further south, our favorite spot is the north end of Manjack Cay in the cove. Approaching the north end of Manjack just watch for the shifting sand banks that usually carry 7-8 feet at low tide. Refer to the *Guide* and approach at mid to rising tide. These are narrow sand banks so once across, the water is deep most of the way into the cove. Another good option is the west side of Manjack Cay. You can anchor close in to the beach there, just off the large rock. Moving SE, don't miss Green Turtle Cay. You have plenty of deep water just outside New Plymouth and to the north along the shoreline.

Departing to the SE again, follow the suggested courses out and around Whale Cay. After returning to the Sea of Abaco south of Whale Cay you will find a good anchorage at the north end of Great Guana Cay named Bakers Bay. Fishers Bay is a little further SE and just NW of Settlement Harbor; it provides good holding 12' deep at low tide. Stay outside of the mooring balls so as not to interfere with them, and watch for a shallow hard bottom patch which you should keep to your east and northeast, noted on the chart.

Anchorages with good protection from the N and the NE exist all the way along Guana Cay down to Scotland Cay. We usually anchor midway down Scotland Cay to avoid tidal current and so we can take the skiff out to the Fowl Cay Underwater Park for snorkeling.

The next stop SE is Man-O-War Cay with excellent protection from the east, and the water deep all along the SW shore. We prefer to anchor mid island, and take the skiff into the harbor at either end for a lunch and walkabout.

To move south from Man O War, we head toward Point Set Rock and leave it to starboard. There is a good anchorage for strong W and NW winds SE of the string of large rocks known as the Sugar Loaves, and it is good for winds from any other direction for up to about 15 knots (but do not anchor there if it is blowing hard from the south). There is good snorkeling along the Sugar Loaves and along the SW tip of Matt Lowes Cay.

To visit Hope Town depart Point Set Rock and head for the lighthouse, follow your charts, and as you approach, you will anchor out just a bit, near even or just to the west of Parrot Cays. Take the skiff into Hope Town for a days adventure, visit the lighthouse, and enjoy shops, dining, and beautiful beaches.

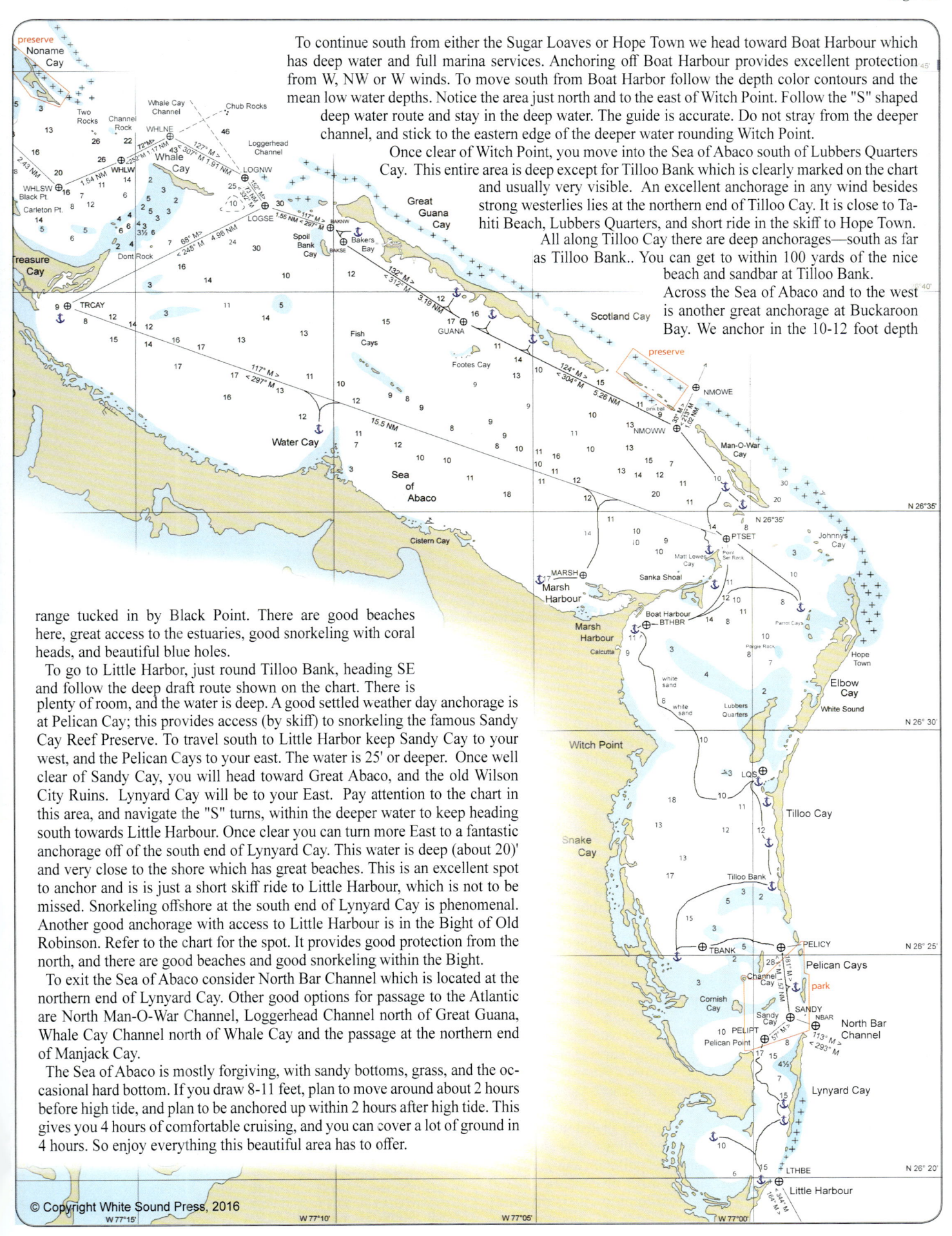

To continue south from either the Sugar Loaves or Hope Town we head toward Boat Harbour which has deep water and full marina services. Anchoring off Boat Harbour provides excellent protection from W, NW or W winds. To move south from Boat Harbor follow the depth color contours and the mean low water depths. Notice the area just north and to the east of Witch Point. Follow the "S" shaped deep water route and stay in the deep water. The guide is accurate. Do not stray from the deeper channel, and stick to the eastern edge of the deeper water rounding Witch Point.

Once clear of Witch Point, you move into the Sea of Abaco south of Lubbers Quarters Cay. This entire area is deep except for Tilloo Bank which is clearly marked on the chart and usually very visible. An excellent anchorage in any wind besides strong westerlies lies at the northern end of Tilloo Cay. It is close to Tahiti Beach, Lubbers Quarters, and short ride in the skiff to Hope Town.

All along Tilloo Cay there are deep anchorages—south as far as Tilloo Bank.. You can get to within 100 yards of the nice beach and sandbar at Tilloo Bank.

Across the Sea of Abaco and to the west is another great anchorage at Buckaroon Bay. We anchor in the 10-12 foot depth range tucked in by Black Point. There are good beaches here, great access to the estuaries, good snorkeling with coral heads, and beautiful blue holes.

To go to Little Harbor, just round Tilloo Bank, heading SE and follow the deep draft route shown on the chart. There is plenty of room, and the water is deep. A good settled weather day anchorage is at Pelican Cay; this provides access (by skiff) to snorkeling the famous Sandy Cay Reef Preserve. To travel south to Little Harbor keep Sandy Cay to your west, and the Pelican Cays to your east. The water is 25' or deeper. Once well clear of Sandy Cay, you will head toward Great Abaco, and the old Wilson City Ruins. Lynyard Cay will be to your East. Pay attention to the chart in this area, and navigate the "S" turns, within the deeper water to keep heading south towards Little Harbour. Once clear you can turn more East to a fantastic anchorage off of the south end of Lynyard Cay. This water is deep (about 20)' and very close to the shore which has great beaches. This is an excellent spot to anchor and is is just a short skiff ride to Little Harbour, which is not to be missed. Snorkeling offshore at the south end of Lynyard Cay is phenomenal. Another good anchorage with access to Little Harbour is in the Bight of Old Robinson. Refer to the chart for the spot. It provides good protection from the north, and there are good beaches and good snorkeling within the Bight.

To exit the Sea of Abaco consider North Bar Channel which is located at the northern end of Lynyard Cay. Other good options for passage to the Atlantic are North Man-O-War Channel, Loggerhead Channel north of Great Guana, Whale Cay Channel north of Whale Cay and the passage at the northern end of Manjack Cay.

The Sea of Abaco is mostly forgiving, with sandy bottoms, grass, and the occasional hard bottom. If you draw 8-11 feet, plan to move around about 2 hours before high tide, and plan to be anchored up within 2 hours after high tide. This gives you 4 hours of comfortable cruising, and you can cover a lot of ground in 4 hours. So enjoy everything this beautiful area has to offer.

© Copyright White Sound Press, 2016

Guide to the Most Common Marine Mammals of Abaco

By Diane Claridge, PhD

Bahamas Marine Mammal Research Organisation

An adult male Cuvier's beaked whale lunges out of the water, preparing for a deep foraging dive.

The Bahamas is an archipelago that boasts many natural attributes, none more spectacular than its marine life. The shallow carbonate banks and deep-water channels and basins of The Bahamas provide important habitat for marine mammals and an ideal study site for the Bahamas Marine Mammal Research Organisation (BMMRO). BMMRO is a Bahamian non-profit organisation whose mission is to promote the conservation of marine mammals in The Bahamas through scientific research and educational outreach.

Long-term study of marine mammals in Abaco

Since 1991, BMMRO has been conducting small vessel surveys primarily around Abaco Island to document the occurrence, distribution and abundance of marine mammals in The Bahamas. The majority of species found here are deep diving toothed whales that inhabit the pelagic waters surrounding the shallow Bahama banks. Many migrate through The Bahamas, but some species are year-round residents, including some of the world's least known whales. By photographing the pattern of natural nicks and scars on each animal's dorsal fin or tail flukes, a technique known as photo-identification, we are able to keep track of individuals—gaining an understanding of their population demographics, reproductive success, and social structure. BMMRO's field work has expanded over the past ten years to include larger vessel surveys in the Great Bahama Canyon, including at the US Navy's Atlantic Test and Evaluation Center in Tongue of the Ocean, where use of tactical sonars potentially pose a risk for some species. This work has provided a wider picture of marine mammal distribution in the northern Bahamas and have aided in identifying important areas for deep-diving whales. Genetic studies and pollutant analyses have helped to identify stocks and will allow further investigation of the health of local populations. Through on-going partnerships with universities and oceanographic institutes, BMMRO has many new projects underway including the use of time-depth recording tags to investigate beaked whale foraging behavior and hexacopters to photograph whales to assess their health.

Conservation of marine mammals in The Bahamas

Marine mammals in The Bahamas face many of the same threats from human activities as they do elsewhere in the world. These include ocean pollution including anthropogenic noise and marine debris, habitat alteration and coastal development, impacts of overfishing and entanglement in fishing gear, and vessel collisions. Over the past two decades, the number of bottlenose dolphins using the Sea of Abaco has declined which is likely the result of cumulative effects of many of these impacts. Like bottlenose dolphins, many

A sperm whale in the Great Abaco Canyon prepares to dive and BMMRO Researchers stand by to capture a photo of its tail flukes for photo-identification. Photo by Lindsey D. McCoy.

of our oceanic species consist of small, distinct subpopulations that are resident to the Abacos. Although most are not endangered species, conservation plans will need to be based on a population-level approach rather than species-level to be effective. All marine mammals are protected species in The Bahamas which provides the basis for developing conservation directives for local populations, and the recent establishment of 15 new marine protected areas will vastly increase protection of marine mammal habitats in The Bahamas. BMMRO's scientists will continue to work closely with the Government of The Bahamas and local environmental groups as well as our regional counterparts to ensure that marine mammal conservation needs, both current and future, are addressed.

Whale Camp

The Bahamas Marine Mammal Research Organisation is based in Sandy Point, Abaco, and runs Whale Camp each summer for Bahamian students (16 and older) to provide a first-hand experience in marine mammal research. The primary goals of Whale Camp are to engage and train young Bahamians in field research methods, to generate a passion for marine mammals, and to encourage a new generation of Bahamian scientists. The program is offered specifically to high school and university students with an interest in marine biology. Whale Camp exposes these students to the challenges of research and provides an eye-opening look at the diversity of marine mammals that can be found in The Bahamas, while investigating relevant conservation issues.

Cruisers – please report your sightings!

Our research efforts have been greatly enhanced by sighting reports which boaters have contributed over the years. As cruisers, you have a unique opportunity to observe rarely seen marine mammal species and it is important to keep an accurate log, take photographs and/or video, while respecting the animals' needs for space; and, please never try to touch or feed them as this may cause harm to you or the animal. While The Bahama Islands are home to at least twenty-five species of marine mammals, the following is a guide to the most commonly seen whales, dolphins and manatees in the Abacos and is intended to aid and encourage boaters to continue to report sightings. The species shown represent four groups of whales and dolphins, separated into their taxonomic families: oceanic dolphins, dwarf and pygmy sperm whales, sperm whales and beaked whales, as well as the West Indian manatee. All photographs were taken in The Bahamas.

Please report your marine mammal sightings to: info@bahamaswhales.org or call us at (242) 366-4155

To report stranded, injured, or dead marine mammals call The Bahamas Stranding Hotline: (242) 423-8427

Family Delphinidae – Oceanic Dolphins

The family Delphinidae is a large diverse group of species that may not appear all that similar externally, but they share features of their internal anatomy. For example, some dolphins have a pronounced beak or rostrum while others lack a beak entirely, but internally they all have sharp, conical teeth. These highly social animals can be found in groups ranging in size from a few individuals to several thousand; and, some species are known to live in complex societies consisting of related individuals. Twelve oceanic dolphin species have been recorded in The Bahamas.

Bottlenose dolphins (Tursiops truncatus), formerly called Atlantic or common bottlenose dolphins, are the most common marine

The shallow carbonate banks of Abaco provide important habitat for bottlenose dolphins.

Individual bottlenose dolphins have a unique pattern of nicks in its dorsal fin. Photographs of these natural markings allow researchers in The Bahamas to track individuals throughout their life. For example, these two dolphins are maturing males that have been known by BMMRO scientists since they were born in 2001 and 2003.

Oceanic bottlenose dolphins inhabit the pelagic waters surrounding the shallow Bahama Banks.

mammals seen in Abaco. It should be noted, however, that there are at least two distinct "breeding populations" or "ecotypes" of this species: coastal bottlenose dolphins that inhabit the shallow waters of Little Bahama Bank; and, oceanic bottlenose dolphins found in the deep waters surrounding Abaco. These populations diverged genetically several hundred thousand years ago and have since developed different physiological adaptations to their respective marine environments. The coastal ecotype is smaller in length reaching just over 8 feet and has relatively larger pectoral fins and dorsal fin which helps them to maneuver more readily around rocks and reefs to catch fish, and to regulate their internal body temperature (the temperature of the shallow Bank waters fluctuates much more than the deeper Atlantic Ocean). The coastal dolphins do not travel much beyond the barrier reefs of Abaco; and, while most individuals remain resident to the same area such as the Sea of Abaco for their lifetime, others are known to range across Little Bahama Bank. The deeper diving oceanic ecotype can reach 10 feet or more in length and can remain at depth for longer than their coastal cousins due to their ability to store more oxygen in their blood. They are usually seen in larger groups and appear to have a more extensive range. Photographs of individual oceanic bottlenose dolphins have shown movements between Abaco, Bimini and Exuma Sound.

Atlantic spotted dolphins (Stenella frontalis), are the more frequently seen of two different species of spotted dolphins found in the Abacos; the other species is the pan-tropical spotted dolphin (Stenella attenuata). Spotted dolphins are not born with spots, but actually accumulate them as they mature, becoming quite mottled-looking as adults. Hence, young spotted dolphins are often confused with bottlenose dolphins, and sometimes the two species will interact, which adds to the confusion. Spotted dolphins have a more slender snout, and although they can almost reach the same length as bottlenose dolphins, they have a smaller girth and thus body weight. Atlantic spotted dolphins are a year-round resident species in the Abacos. Individuals photo-identified 20 years ago can still be seen ranging along the eastern and southwestern coasts of Abaco. They are commonly seen in groups of 20-50 dolphins in the oceanic waters where they feed on flying fish and squid, and rarely venture on to the bank. However, in the northwestern part of Little Bahama Bank this species can regularly be found along the western edge of the banks during the daytime where they come to rest and socialize.

A bottlenose dolphin jumps out of the water showing the large pectoral fins characteristic of this coastal ecotype. Note that the tip of its right fin is missing; it was probably bitten off by a shark, their only predator.

Young Atlantic spotted dolphins are actually not spotted at all, but as they mature they become more and more spotted.

Risso's dolphins (Grampus griseus) are large light grey dolphins that can reach over 13 feet in length, and have a relatively tall, dark dorsal fin. Adults are typically covered with overlapping white scars caused by the teeth of their con-specifics making them look quite battered. They have a rounded head, lacking a beak, but have a deep vertical crease down the center of the forehead. As they mature, their forehead becomes prominently white, making them one of the easiest species to recognize at sea. Risso's dolphins are commonly seen in the Abacos each winter and spring, primarily on the Atlantic side of the islands. It is unknown where these groups range the rest of the year, but some individuals have been seen off Abaco repeatedly over the years.

The dorsal fins of adult male pilot whales (foreground) are much broader and taller than adult females or immature animals (background).

The prominent white forehead of the Risso's dolphins makes it a relatively easy species to recognize at sea.

Short-finned pilot whales (Globicephala macrorhynchus) can grow to 18 feet long and weigh over 5,000 pounds, with males being significantly larger than females. They have a bulbous forehead with no perceptible beak, a faint grey diagonal stripe behind each eye and a faint grey "saddle" behind and below the dorsal fin. The rest of their body dorsally is jet black, which prompted whalers to name them "blackfish", a term that also includes three other species known from The Bahamas (melon-headed whales, pygmy killer whales and false killer whales). Pilot whales can readily be distinguished from the other blackfish species by the position of their large, broad-based dorsal fin, which is set quite far forward on their body. They live in matrilineal pods consisting of up to three generations of related females and their offspring. On calm days, they can be seen in tight groups lying abreast, resting at the surface for hours. Pilot whales are seen in Abaco year-round but are more common during the spring and summer months, and are not a resident species. Pilot whales found in The Bahamas appear to have large ranging patterns; tagged whales have travelled from The Bahamas to The Carolinas suggesting they are part of the US southeast population.

Killer whales (Orcinus orca), or orcas, are probably the easiest cetacean species to recognize at sea due to their striking black and white pigmentation patterns. Orcas are the largest member of the oceanic dolphin family, with males reaching 30 feet in length and

The orca is one of the easiest species to identify at sea.

An orca lunges out of the water with a dwarf sperm whale in its mouth.

weighing 8 tons, while females reach only 23 feet and weigh 4 tons. The most conspicuous feature of these whales is the dorsal fin, which can grow over 6 feet tall in adult males. These top predators are found in all the world's oceans but are more abundant in higher latitudes where prey resources are more plentiful. Orca pods are seen almost every year in Abaco usually in the late spring and summer, including one group that has returned repeatedly over 15 years. While they have been observed feeding on dolphins and dwarf sperm whales around Abaco, they are most likely in the area in response to prey migrations such as tuna, and remain in the area for 1-2 days only.

Family Kogiidae – Dwarf and Pygmy Sperm Whales
Dwarf and pygmy sperm whales are small whales which share similar characteristics with sperm whales. All possess an underslung toothed lower jaw, and a toothless upper jaw. The head shape ranges from triangular to square, becoming blunter with age, and all have a single blowhole found on the left side of the head.

Dwarf sperm whales (Kogia sima) are the most common marine mammal seen in the oceanic waters around Abaco. Adults reach only 8-9 feet in length, and the dorsal fin is set mid-way down the body and is falcate or triangular in shape, so they can easily be

Dwarf sperm whales are most often found in small groups resting, or "logging", at the surface.

confused with dolphins at a distance. Pygmy sperm whales (Kogia breviceps) are slightly larger reaching up to 10 feet in length, but the dorsal fin is smaller and set further back on the body, making it easy to confuse this species with beaked whales. These small whales are often found solitary or in small groups in extremely deep water environments, and have adapted numerous ways to avoid predators such as killer whales. Both species have counter shading, being dark grey dorsally and white on the underside making it more difficult to see them from the surface or from below. They also have a white line of pigmentation on each side behind the head, known as a false gill, making them look like a shark. When threatened, they are able to expel ink which they have ingested from squid, their primary prey, creating a dark cloud in which they can escape. Their behavior while at the surface is very cryptic, and they are most typically seen logging, or lying motionless. When a vessel approaches them, they dive and swim away, making them very difficult study subjects!

Family Physeteridae – Sperm Whales
The sperm whale is the only species in the family Physeteridae. Sperm whales are the largest toothed whales in the world and are the only common great whale that can be seen year-round in The Bahamas.

Sperm whales (Physeter macrocephalus) have dark brown, wrinkled-looking skin and an enormous square-shaped head that comprises one third of their total body length. Males can attain a body length of 60 feet while females are considerably smaller,

Adult female sperm whales live in matrilineal groups called units in which females remain throughout their lives.

As a sperm whales begin a deep foraging dive, its raises its massive tail allowing scientists to photograph the unique pattern of nicks in the trailing edge. This adult female was first seen in Abaco in 1997.

reaching 35-40 feet in length when mature. Their single blowhole on the left side of the head at the front causes a distinctive "blow" which angles to the left and forward. When a sperm whale prepares to dive, it raises its massive tail, allowing us to photograph the distinctive pattern of notches in the trailing edge of the tail flukes. Sperm whales dive to great depths (>3,000 feet) for more than an hour at a time where they feed on large squid, their primary prey. Adult females form nursery groups which are long-term social units made up of related females that can be found in the Abacos year-round. Some of these females have been repeatedly seen in Abaco over the past 20 years. Mature males frequent the islands only during the winter breeding season and spend the rest of the year feeding in more productive Arctic waters.

Family Ziphiidae – Beaked Whales
The beaked whale family is characterized by having reduced dentition, with typically only two teeth located in the lower jaw which only ever erupt above the gum line in males when they become sexually mature. These teeth are more appropriately described as "tusks" because they are actually used for combat with other males and not for feeding purposes. Beaked whales can be shy whales generally found in small groups that inhabit extremely deep water, making field studies difficult. As a consequence, beaked whales represent the least known large mammals that exist today. in fact, some species have never been seen at sea, and are known only from old weathered skull fragments. Of the 22 recognized species of beaked whales found worldwide, three are known from The Bahamas.

Surface profiles of three beaked whale species known to The Bahamas (top to bottom): Blainville's beaked whale (Mesoplodon densirostris), Gervais' beaked whale (Mesoplodon europaeus), Cuvier's beaked whale (Ziphius cavirostris)

Blainville's beaked whales (Mesoplodon densirostris) are found in all the world's tropical and temperate waters and are one of the most common species seen around Abaco. These medium-sized whales reach 14-16 feet in length, with males being slightly larger, are brownish-grey in color and have a spindle-shaped body that tapers at both ends. They have a small dorsal fin found almost two thirds of the way back along their body and a well-defined beak or snout, which usually breaks the water first as the whale surfaces to breathe. Older whales have numerous white oval scars caused by cookie cutter sharks and multiple paired linear scars caused by the "tusks" of their con-specifics. Adult males look quite bizarre as they often have clusters of stalked barnacles growing on their protruding "tusks". There are small, resident subpopulations of Blainville's beaked whales inhabiting the deep submarine canyons around Abaco which BMMRO has been tracking over three generations. This unprecedented long-term study of a deep-diving, cryptic whale is recognized globally for its importance in informing our knowledge of the natural life history of this species.

Family Trichechidae
The West Indian Manatee (Trichechus manatus) consists of two subspecies: Florida manatee and Antillean manatee, both of which

Adult male Blainville's beaked whales look quite bizarre with stalked barnacles growing on the tip of their two teeth, or "tusks". Blainville's beaked whales live in a harem-like society and their tusks are used in interspecific fighting with other males for dominance

Blainville's beaked whales have a spindle-shaped body and their small dorsal fin is almost two-thirds of the way back.

"Gina" is a Florida manatee originally from Homosassa Springs but has been residing in The Bahamas since 1998. She has had at least four calves since arriving in The Bahamas.

A subadult male Blainville's beaked whale breaches, exposing a unique pattern of scarring on its side. The oval scars are caused by bites from the parasitic cookie cutter shark, while the linear scars are a result of interactions with adult male Blainville's beaked whales.

"Randy" is one of Gina's calves, and is a young male. Although born in the Berry Islands, Randy moved across to Little Bahama Bank in 2014 and has been photographed by boaters all around Abaco and Grand Bahama ever since.

can be found in The Bahamas, although only the Florida subspecies has been documented here recently.

Florida manatees (Trichechus manatus latirostris) are found in the southeastern United States, and mostly in Florida but as the population has increased in parts of their range, individuals are dispersing and venturing across the Florida Straits to The Bahamas and Cuba. Although the number of manatees in The Bahamas has increased in recent years and they are even breeding locally, they still remain quite rare here, with only about 20 manatees currently in the entire Bahamian archipelago. That said, three of these are often seen in Abaco. Florida manatees inhabit salt, fresh or brackish waters and feed on marine, estuarine, and freshwater vegetation. Although food is plentiful for manatees in The Bahamas, fresh water may be a limiting resource. Despite this, manatees do not need our help to survive here (or anywhere). BMMRO has been working with the Bahamas Department of Marine Resources to increase awareness about how people should behave around manatees to increase their chances of survival in The Bahamas. Appropriate "Manatee Manners" are (1) Do not feed them; lettuce lacks the nutrition that that they need and is readily available in our abundant sea grass beds. (2) Do not give them water to drink; they are incredibly resourceful and are capable of finding even the smallest fresh water source. By providing them food and water, we are encouraging them to spend time in marinas and harbors where they will eventually be hit by a boat. (3) Please respect their space and do not touch, chase or follow them. Despite their gentle demeanour, they are large animals (adults reach about 10 feet in length and weigh between 800 and 1,200 pounds) that can move very quickly when disturbed and you can get hurt. So please mind you manatee manners and let's keep wild animals wild! If you find a manatee that looks unhealthy and is in need of human intervention, please call The Bahamas Stranding Hotline: (242) 423-8427.

For more information contact us at:

Bahamas Marine Mammal Research Organisation
P.O. Box AB-20714
Marsh Harbour, Abaco, Bahamas
www.bahamaswhales.org
(242) 366-4155
Email: info@bahamaswhales.org

Follow us on Facebook: www.facebook.com/bmmro
And join our manatee club to keep track of what Bahamian manatees are up to:
www.facebook.com/groups/BahManateeClub

Fishing in Abaco

by Harry Weldon and Jon Dodge

The Abaco islands offer a beautiful and productive area for exciting fishing. The string of cays east of Great Abaco Island provide a protected to semi-protected area named the Sea of Abaco or Abaco Sound. Beyond most of the cays are rocks and reef formations up to about two miles offshore. While not continuous, a reef stretches from Walkers Cay in the north to just east of Hope Town, a distance of about 90 miles. About two to three miles offshore the bottom drops off to depths of 600 feet to over 1000 feet. The visiting fisherman to Abaco has three basic choices. Fish inside on the sound and flats, outside on the reef, or outside beyond the reef.

Fishing Inside

Almost any dock will have its resident gray snapper. Some of these will top out at three or four pounds. Trying to catch them, while entertaining, can be an exercise in frustration. The larger they are, the less likely you are to catch them. They didn't get to that size by incautious dining. The large ones have excellent eye sight and are very cautious feeders. Try using very small line (6lb or under) tied directly to the hook. With the hook fully hidden in a

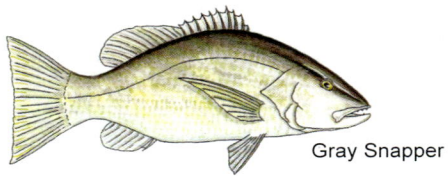

Gray Snapper

suitable bait, toss several pieces of cut bait in the water along with the hook and line. Allow the line to sink with the other pieces of bait. This might get you hooked up. More than likely though, the smaller snapper will take it before the larger one. Once you manage to tie into a good sized fish, the light line will snap after a quick wrap around a piling or mangrove root. This type of fishing can be lots of fun but please release all the small fry that are not going to make it to the kitchen.

Yellowtail snapper, grunt, bar jack, and many others will be found on small patches of reef or rock along any of the keys of the Abacos. Just look for any type of hard bottom structure. On a completely flat day, the surface of the Sea of Abaco may appear as flat as glass. This does not happen often, but when it does the

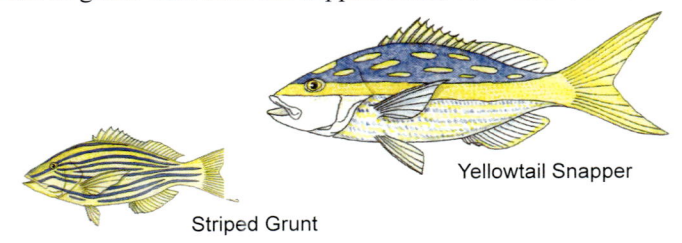

Yellowtail Snapper

Striped Grunt

bottom may be viewed as if looking into an aquarium. This is a great experience in itself and it also provides an opportunity to easily see any structure on the bottom. When the wind is up it is more difficult to identify hard structure, but it is still possible to do so.

Bait fishing with spinning gear should provide food for the table and a whole lot of fun. Frozen shrimp, conch, hermit crab, and cut ballyhoo will all work with this type of fishing. Eventually the barracuda will show up and, depending on your philosophy will either ruin the day or make it. A small live snapper with a suitable hook lightly through the back will put a barracuda on the end of your line and with six or twelve pound line give a good account of himself. Barracuda is not normally eaten by locals and unless going to the table, release him for someone else to catch.

If you prefer to troll, just drag a small white or yellow feather along the rocky edges of most cays. Yellowtail, bar jack, needle fish, and barracuda will be your most likely catch, but when you're

Barracuda

near an opening to the ocean the surprise factor goes way up. If you're going to be fishing inside, take a good look at the fish at the dock before you leave. If they're active and excited over a bit of bait tossed in the water and if the snappers darken around the eyes, then they're in a feeding mood and hopefully the fish elsewhere are also ready to feed. If the snapper that were active this morning show little interest, you might want to read a book. Midday seems to be a slow time for this type of fishing but the time of year is not much of a factor, though obviously winds and tide will make a difference to you, if not to the fish.

If you're not looking for food for the table, you might want to try your hand at bonefishing. Bonefishing is done on the flats during the last of the ebb tide and the first few hours of the incoming tide. It takes a skilled eye to spot bonefish swimming in the shallow water in search of food. Look for their tails and dorsal fins which break the surface and give them away. Once the fish have been found, it is up to the angler to present the bait to the fish. The most common bait used is natural conch, crab, or shrimp. Artificial bait like the wiggle jig, which is flat and does not dig into the bottom,

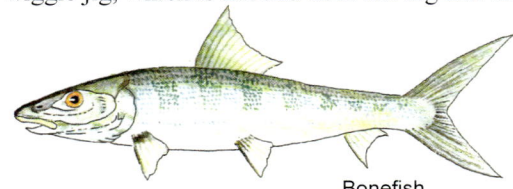

Bonefish

works well on sand or grass. Years of experience indicate that pink, which resembles shrimp, is the best color for artificial bait, but brown and yellow also seem to work well. Most bonefish are caught on spinning or fly tackle and six to twelve pound line. On the initial run, a four to six pound fish can run for a hundred yards or more- a memorable experience. Bonefish are a sport fish only and should always be released. Bonefishing is a year round sport in Abaco, but the winter months seem to provide more fish.

Fishing On the Reef

Reef fishing usually assures fish for the table. Fishing the reef is pretty much the same as fishing on the inside, it's just deeper and the fish are larger. The reefs around Abaco have a good supply of grouper, snapper, mackerel, yellowtail, and many other species that are usually easily caught. Large mutton snapper (8–15 pounds) concentrate for spawning the last of May and into June. Local fisherman have traditionally used heavy hand lines in 20-50 feet of water. You'll need some local knowledge, however, to find out just where they are. They're here all the time, but when they're spawning they can be found in large numbers if you know just where to fish the reef.

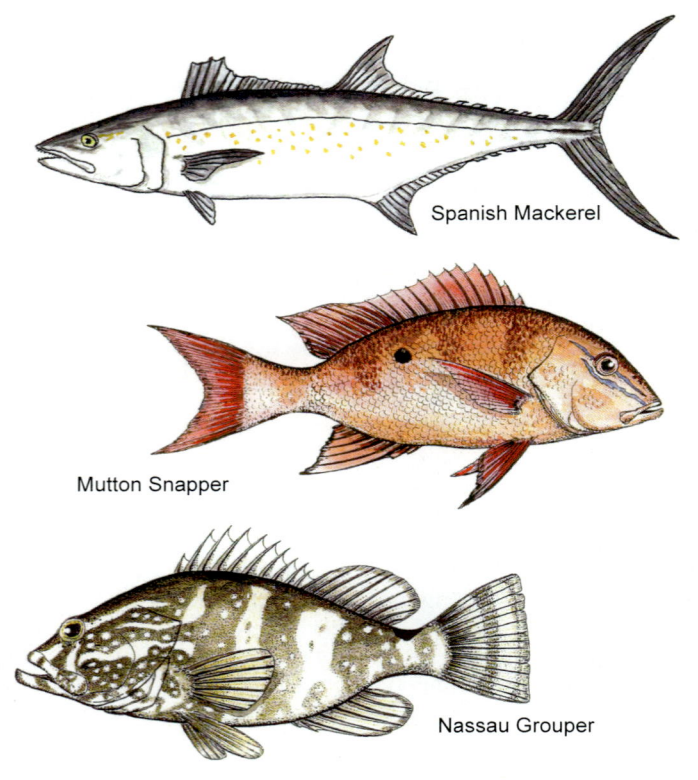

Spanish Mackerel

Wahoo

Mutton Snapper

Nassau Grouper

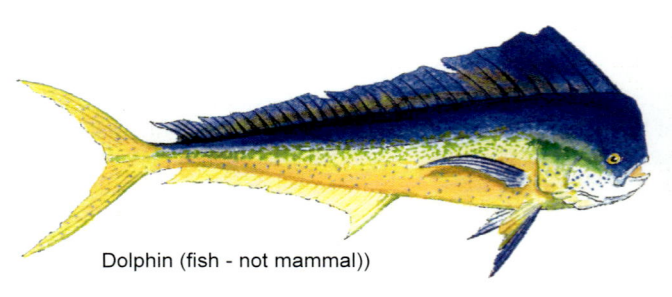

Dolphin (fish - not mammal)

Reef fishing can be done two ways: trolling or bottom fishing. Cut bait, such as ballyhoo or conch, is most commonly used. When trolling or casting with artificial bait, a small yellow lure or silver spoon is a good choice. A light wire leader is also suggested because of the possibility of spanish mackerel and barracuda. Barracuda and amberjack are found on the reef and put up a great fight, but local specimens have been found to have ciguatera, or fish poisoning, and should never be eaten.

Fishing Deep

Deep-sea fishing is for those who want to venture beyond the barrier reef and try for the "Big One." Marlin, sailfish, tuna, dolphin and wahoo can be found at the drop-off, which, in the Elbow Cay area, is approximately two to three miles east of the cay beyond the reef. The water off Hope Town goes out from the reef in steps of sixty, ninety, two hundred forty, and six hundred feet. The two hundred forty to six hundred foot break is what is referred to as the

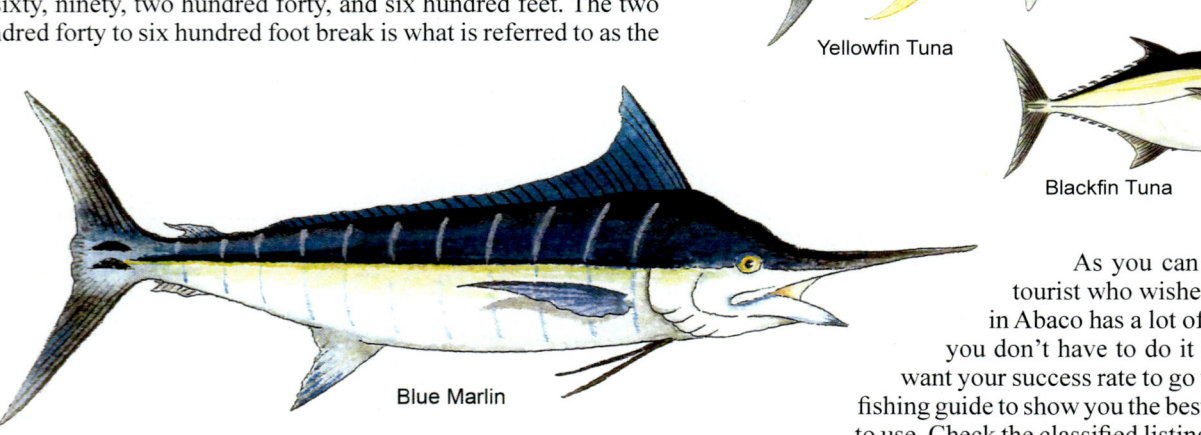

warm water a downrigger, wire or plainer to get the bait deep will increase your success, with wahoo being a common catch. July, August, and September are only fair but catches of blackfin tuna and an occasional dolphin are always possible. Fishing picks up in October and by Christmas is normally pretty good and continues to improve through February and March. Large schools of skipjack and cero mackerel are sometimes encountered but getting them to bite can be a challenge. For the small schooling tuna, especially the blackfin, a small white feather trolled way, way back can secure a hit. The trick then is landing the fish before a shark takes the better part. Sometimes deep jigging around the schooling tuna can result in hooking up with a nice fish. Another method is to chunk bait and drift lines deep for yellowfin and blackfin tuna. There's no question that successful ocean fishing during the quiet months requires a lot more work than at other times. If you feel like a little exercise and the weather is calm, stop the boat just at the two hundred foot mark before the drop off and deep jig for grouper, red snapper or amberjack.

Yellowfin Tuna

Blackfin Tuna

Blue Marlin

"drop off." Other than perhaps marlin, the best ocean fishing can be found at this line. Most boats troll skirted ballyhoo.

Weather permitting, mid-March through mid-April is normally the peak ocean fishing season, with large numbers of dolphin and tuna. By the end of June things have quieted down and with the

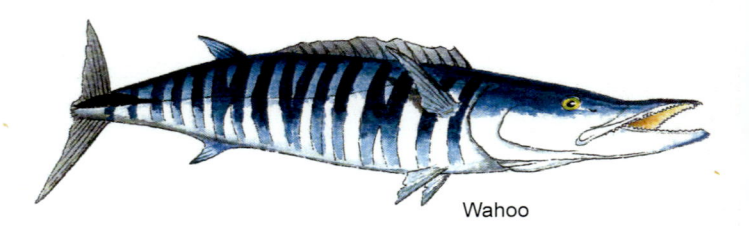

As you can see, the cruiser or tourist who wishes to try fishing here in Abaco has a lot of options. Of course you don't have to do it all yourself. If you want your success rate to go way up, hire a local fishing guide to show you the best spots and methods to use. Check the classified listings in the back of the book for a fishing guide in your area.

Anyone who fishes in the area should learn about local fishing rules and limits before going out. See page 15 for fishing regulations and pp 144 and 165 for the boundaries of the parks where no fishing is permitted. Remember to release any fish you cannot consume. If you're not going to eat it, please don't kill it.

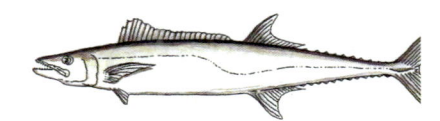

King Mackerel or Kingfish

Harry Weldon is the fishing editor for *The Cruising guide to Abaco, Bahamas*. Jon Dodge also contributed to this article.

Kim Neilson of West Palm Beach, Florida, created the paintings of fish used in this article. He has lived in Florida for over fifty years, and first went to the Bahamas in 1971 to fish and dive. He started drawing and painting Bahama charts and scenes in 1972, and started Gulfstream Trading Company in 1987. He works full time producing custom T-shirt designs for sport fishing boats, and custom charts of the Bahamas, the Florida Keys, or the Caribbean. Gulfstream Trading Company, 4300 N. Flagler Drive #15, West Palm Beach, FL 33407 (studio- 561-863-7133; cell- 561-758-8536).

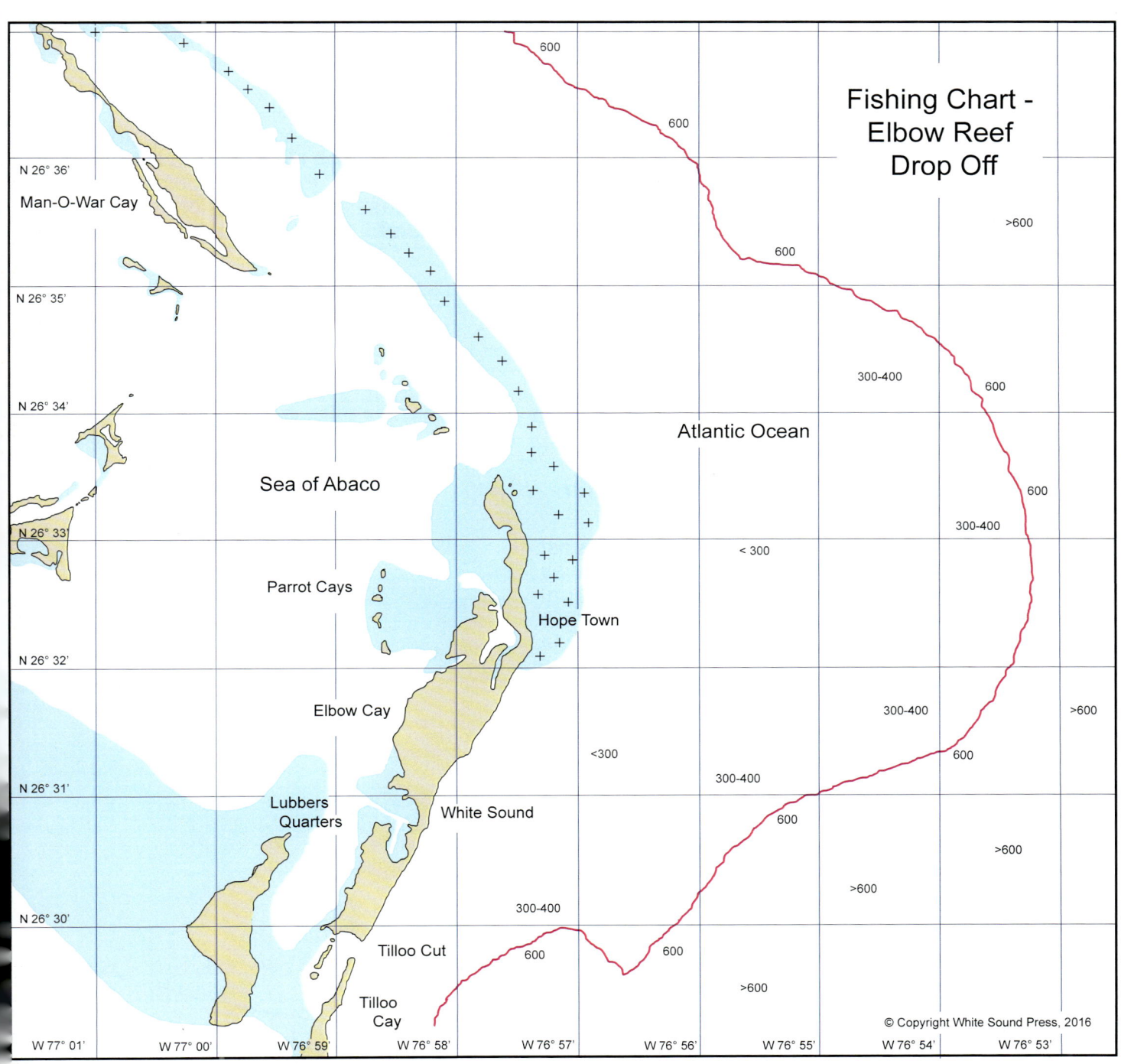

Fishing Chart - Elbow Reef Drop Off

© Copyright White Sound Press, 2016

One of the most productive areas to fish off of Hope Town is along the edge of the drop off. The line represents the steep drop off the edge of Little Bahama Bank from about 300' to 600'. In some places the lateral distance of this drop is no more than ten to twenty yards. At almost any time of year you can see boats working this line for Dolphin, Wahoo and the occasional bill fish. If you like to deep jig for bottom fish, on a calm day try holding in the 300 to 400 ft. range and fish for Red snapper and Grouper. Use the current to move you into deep water as you jig, otherwise you risk catching the bottom. This chart developed by Harry Weldon; revised 2016.

Small Boat and Dinghy Seamanship

Open Water Anchoring

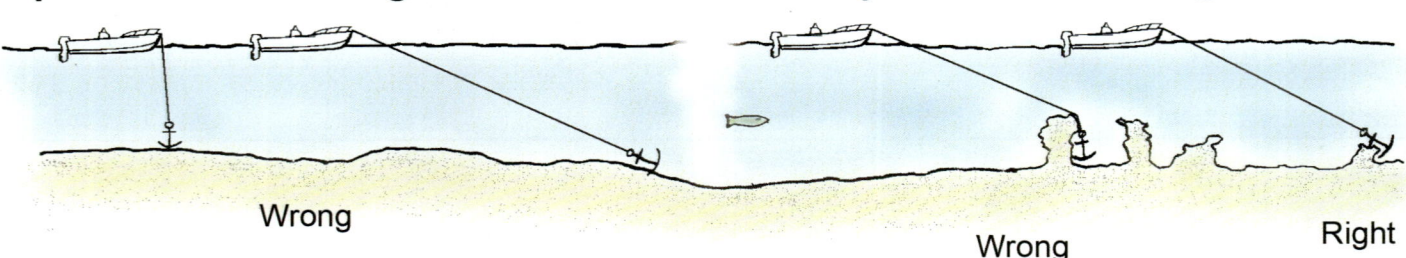

Wrong / **Right**

Anchors are designed to dig into the bottom at an angle--they do not work well unless enough line is let out--at least five times the water depth.

Rocky Bottom Anchoring

Wrong / **Right**

The anchor line should not rub and chafe against coral or rocks--if it does, the line may part and the boat could drift away. Also, please do not anchor in stands of living coral.

Tying to a Dock

Wrong Plan for Low Tide / **Wrong Plan for High Tide** / **Right Safe at any Tide**

A boat should never be allowed to rub against a dock, and should never be tied in such a way as to allow it to hang at low tide or be caught under the dock at high tide. Drop anchor while approaching dock--be careful not to get line caught in propeller--fend off dock--secure anchor line so bow is close enough to get off boat. Pull boat off to one side to get it further from dock, and secure it. Allow slack for tide.

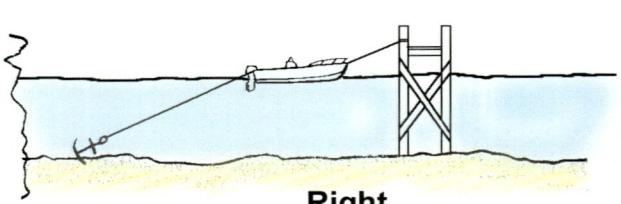

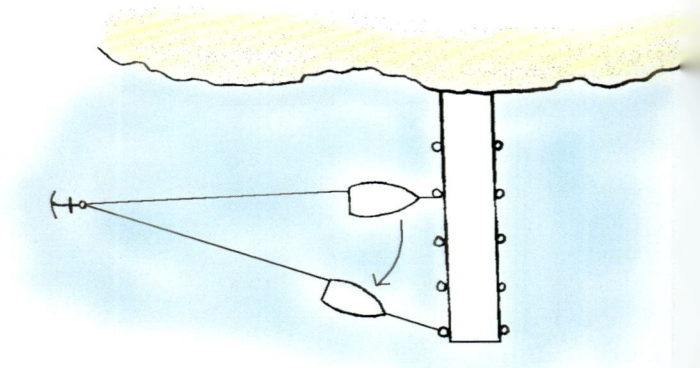

Securing a Boat near a Beach

Wrong — Outgoing tide has left boat stranded

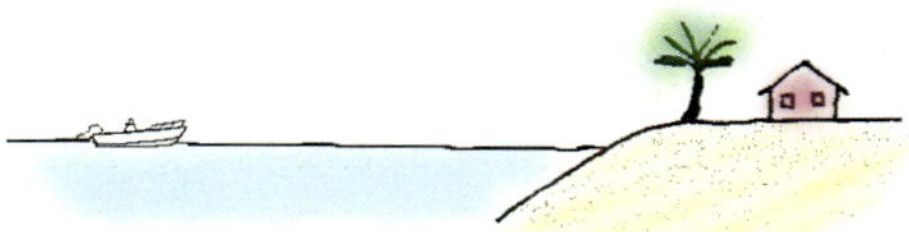

Wrong — Incoming tide has floated boat off beach; it has drifted away.

Right — After unloading on beach, walk boat out and anchor it in shallow water just off shore--it cannot be stranded; it cannot drift away.

Page 157

When you cruise Abaco

use the best, the most accurate, the only annually updated charts available, the ...

The Dodge Digital Charts of Abaco

For use with any Android device
—tablet or phone —

with Marine Navigator Lite (free) or Marine Navigator (less than $10.00 on the Google Play Store)

ONLY $29.95 online download
Available direct from White Sound Press,
www.wspress.com,   386 423-7880

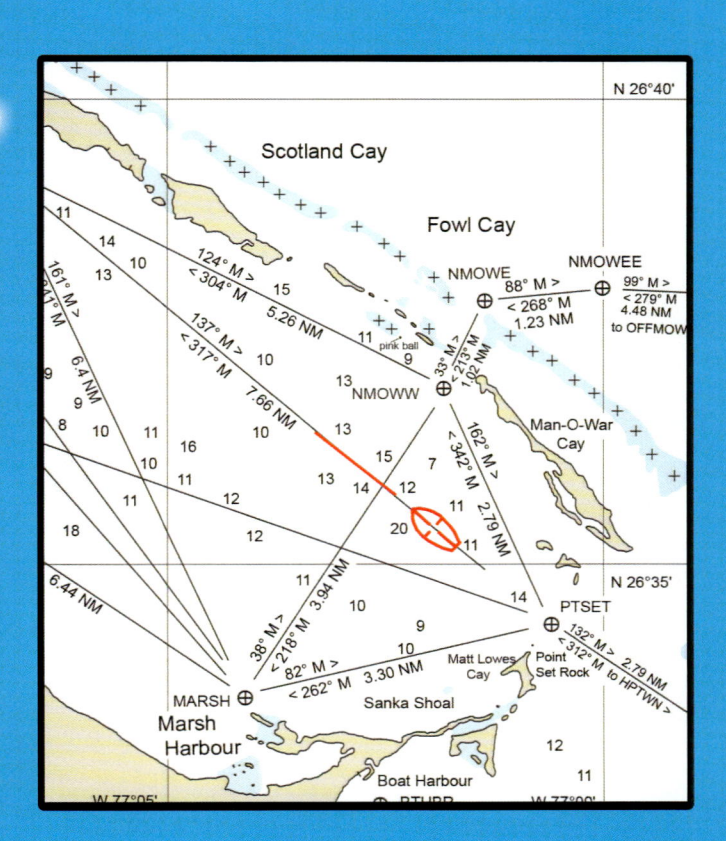

Enjoy cruising the Abacos more with Glendinning!

GLENDINNING

Cruising is more fun when it isn't work! Let Glendinning do the work so you can enjoy the ride!

- **ProPilot Joystick** – simple and intuitive control for easy docking anywhere!
- **Electronic Engine Controls** – for electronically & mechanically controlled engines!
- **Cablemaster** – automatically extend, retract and store your shore power cable!
- **Hosemaster** – powered retrieval and storage of your boat's water hose!
- **Pro-X Control Cables** – quality construction, dependable results!

740 Century Circle
Conway, SC 29526

Phone: (843) 399 - 6146
Fax: (843) 399 - 5005

www.GlendinningProds.com

Abaco Road Map

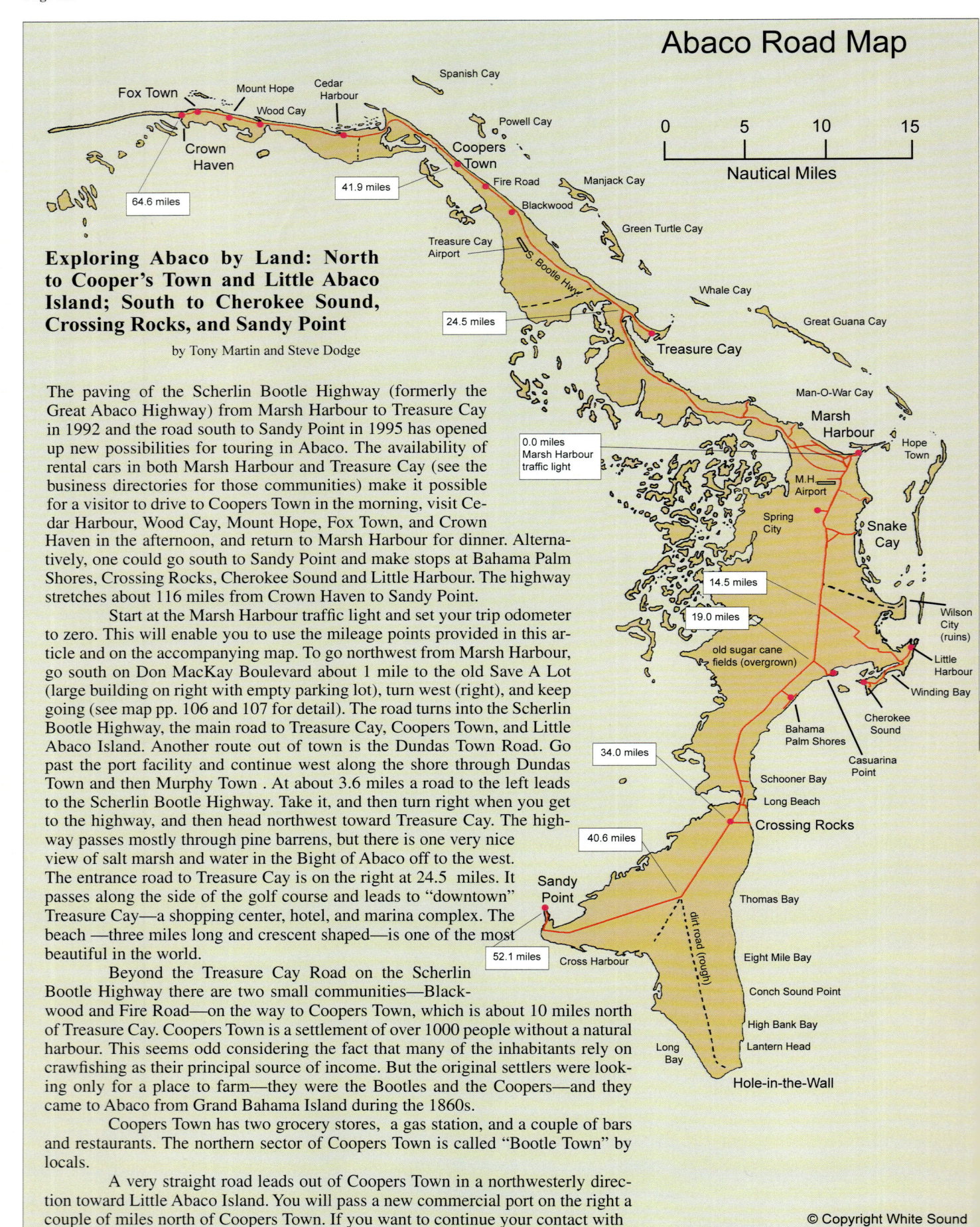

Exploring Abaco by Land: North to Cooper's Town and Little Abaco Island; South to Cherokee Sound, Crossing Rocks, and Sandy Point

by Tony Martin and Steve Dodge

The paving of the Scherlin Bootle Highway (formerly the Great Abaco Highway) from Marsh Harbour to Treasure Cay in 1992 and the road south to Sandy Point in 1995 has opened up new possibilities for touring in Abaco. The availability of rental cars in both Marsh Harbour and Treasure Cay (see the business directories for those communities) make it possible for a visitor to drive to Coopers Town in the morning, visit Cedar Harbour, Wood Cay, Mount Hope, Fox Town, and Crown Haven in the afternoon, and return to Marsh Harbour for dinner. Alternatively, one could go south to Sandy Point and make stops at Bahama Palm Shores, Crossing Rocks, Cherokee Sound and Little Harbour. The highway stretches about 116 miles from Crown Haven to Sandy Point.

Start at the Marsh Harbour traffic light and set your trip odometer to zero. This will enable you to use the mileage points provided in this article and on the accompanying map. To go northwest from Marsh Harbour, go south on Don MacKay Boulevard about 1 mile to the old Save A Lot (large building on right with empty parking lot), turn west (right), and keep going (see map pp. 106 and 107 for detail). The road turns into the Scherlin Bootle Highway, the main road to Treasure Cay, Coopers Town, and Little Abaco Island. Another route out of town is the Dundas Town Road. Go past the port facility and continue west along the shore through Dundas Town and then Murphy Town. At about 3.6 miles a road to the left leads to the Scherlin Bootle Highway. Take it, and then turn right when you get to the highway, and then head northwest toward Treasure Cay. The highway passes mostly through pine barrens, but there is one very nice view of salt marsh and water in the Bight of Abaco off to the west. The entrance road to Treasure Cay is on the right at 24.5 miles. It passes along the side of the golf course and leads to "downtown" Treasure Cay—a shopping center, hotel, and marina complex. The beach—three miles long and crescent shaped—is one of the most beautiful in the world.

Beyond the Treasure Cay Road on the Scherlin Bootle Highway there are two small communities—Blackwood and Fire Road—on the way to Coopers Town, which is about 10 miles north of Treasure Cay. Coopers Town is a settlement of over 1000 people without a natural harbour. This seems odd considering the fact that many of the inhabitants rely on crawfishing as their principal source of income. But the original settlers were looking only for a place to farm—they were the Bootles and the Coopers—and they came to Abaco from Grand Bahama Island during the 1860s.

Coopers Town has two grocery stores, a gas station, and a couple of bars and restaurants. The northern sector of Coopers Town is called "Bootle Town" by locals.

A very straight road leads out of Coopers Town in a northwesterly direction toward Little Abaco Island. You will pass a new commercial port on the right a couple of miles north of Coopers Town. If you want to continue your contact with

© Copyright White Sound International Limited, 2018

the real Bahamas, drive on. You will be rewarded with quizzical but friendly faces and the experiences that being "off the beaten track" often provide.

The landscape provides no pine at this point, just coppice. Five miles from Coopers Town you cross a causeway (locally known as "The Bridge"). This signals the beginning of Little Abaco, formerly a separate island. It has its own distinct character and life style.

Looking north from the causeway connecting Great and Little Abaco Islands. The Government reportedly has plans to replace the causeway with a bridge in order to resotre natural tidal flow to the Bight of Abaco.

Now you are heading generally west instead of northwest and pine begins to replace the coppice. There is a Lucayan Indian site and the ruins of an old sisal mill in this area. Both are off the paved road and should only be attempted with local knowledge and a truck with good road clearance.

Further along the road is a water tower which marks the edge of Cedar Harbour. The piles of conch shells, the fishing boats,

A dredged channel, breakwater and dock at Cedar Harbour, Little Abaco Island. Photo taken July 2002.

and the mangroves afford good photo opportunities. Four and a half miles further on (59.2 miles from Marsh Harbour) lies Wood Cay, settled by a family from Fire Road at the beginning of the century who were trying to get away from the wild hogs that kept eating their crops. The Tangelo Hotel is located here; it has twelve moderate sized, though comfortable and reasonably priced rooms, and a restaurant and bar. One of the most reliable local mechanics, Charley Mills, has his gas station and garage a little further along at Chuck's Auto Service. Again, the pine gives way to smaller trees and less than two miles further west we approach the smallest of Little Abaco's five settlements—Mount Hope. This is the only settlement not directly accessible by boat and appears on few maps. It is worth stopping to sample the food at B. J.'s Restaurant.

A typical scene of the Scherlin Bootle Highway passing through a pine forest. This photo was taken north of the Treasure Cay Airport.

Just a mile further along the highway is Fox Town, the largest and most scenic of Little Abaco's villages. Numerous small cays and rocks dot the harbour, and the Hawksbill Cays lie about a mile offshore. Fox Town has about 500 inhabitants, and its main winding street contains a wide variety of residences, some ultra modern with satellite dishes, others with wooden siding and little changed since the ancestors of the present inhabitants chose this site for its potential as a fishing community. Groceries and fuel are available at Fox Town Shell.

A mere half mile further on, we reach the end of the line—Crown Haven. It is 64.6 miles north of Marsh Harbour. Older members of this community once lived on Cave Cay, an isolated islet to the southwest, until a hurricane in the late thirties destroyed their homes. The authorities of the day provided land on the main island for them to start anew and Crown Haven was born. From here it is a short trip to get to Grand Bahama by boat, and local people often have closer connections with that island than the rest of Abaco. There is a passenger ferry service between Crown Haven and McLean's Town on Grand Bahama Island (see page 174).

To go south from Marsh Harbour to Sandy Point, begin by heading south on Don MacKay Boulevard from the traffic light. At the airport roundabout (about 3 miles) go straight. The road passes through pine forests. There are turnoffs to the left for Snake Cay (at about 6 miles), Cherokee Sound and Little Harbour (at 14.5 miles), Casuarina Point (19.0 miles), and Bahama Palm Shores, as well as other minor roads. Snake Cay is the old port for Owens-Illinois' lumber operation which was active during the 1960s; it is

The turnoff for Casuarina Point, 19 miles south of the Marsh Harbour traffic light.

Snake Cay: view of the inlet on the south side.

no longer in use. The road to Cherokee Sound was recently paved, but the side road from that to Little Harbour is still dirt, and it is rough. The Abaco Club on Winding Bay, operated by Southworth is on the road to Cherokee Sound about 9 miles from the Great Abaco Highway. There is an 18-hole "links" golf course, a club house, guest rooms private homes and a beautiful beach. Entry is generally

The beach at Winding Bay before development, July 2003.

limited to members and their guests. The Abaco Club at Winding Bay is the only major development in Abaco which was built with no facilities for boating (other than beachable small boats). This may well limit its long term viability. There is an aerial photograph of Winding Bay on page 151. Cherokee Sound, a picturesque and charming old fishing and boat building village, is 11.5 miles from

Cherokee Sound is an old fishing and boat building village. The long dock is visible above the town in this photo, March 2010.

the highway turnoff. Cherokee Sound's famous long dock is located to the southeast of the settlement. The Cherokee Food Fair is well stocked with groceries, and also offers apartments for transients at very reasonable rates. Pete's Pub and Gallery at Little Harbour offers food, drinks, bronze sculptures and other original art—all in a very casual, very friendly atmosphere. Casuarina Point is a small residential community comprised of the old executive housing built by Owens-Illinois and some new construction.

Some of Abaco's most beautiful beaches are located along the eastern coast of the island between Cherokee Sound and Hole-in-the-Wall, which is the southern tip of the island. These are difficult to access by boat because there are no harbours along this coast, but several of the beaches can now be easily accessed by land. A turnoff located about 22 miles south of Marsh Harbour (3 miles south of the Casuarina Point turnoff) leads to Bahama Palm Shores, a residential development with palm-lined streets, about 20-25 homes, and a beautiful ocean beach.

A few miles further south, at 29.7 miles from the traffic light, there is a turnoff to Serenity Point, a development by Anco Lands, which owns substantial acreage in southern Abaco. Serenity Point was planned to be a hillside residential development on a high ridge overlooking the wide gently curving ocean beach which forms Schooner Bay with the Atlantic Ocean beyond. The hillside was bulldozed and streets were laid out in rectangles and few if any lots were sold. The development, which has a beautiful and pristine beach (but no provision for boats) is now closed.

A mile or so further south there is a turnoff to Schooner Bay Village, a unique development in that the goal was to create a new Bahamian village to serve as a business, residential and commercial center for south Abaco. The central feature is a small (14 acre) harbour with deep water access from the Atlantic Ocean. The harbour was opened to the sea in June 2011 and is the only secure harbour of refuge between Hole-in-the-Wall and Little Harbour / Cherokee Sound. It has an island in the middle which has about 20 waterfront Bahamian style cottage residences. A wide promenade circles the harbour and was planned to feature two-storey owner-occupied Mom and Pop businesses—shops, offices, restaurants and inns. All buildings were to be traditional Bahamian style, and lot owners were to commit to building within one or two years to guarantee that the community will reach critical mass within a reasonable period of time. Plans called for a regional shopping center with a post office, bank and grocery store further up the ridge. The Sandpiper Inn with a restaurant and bar opened in December 2014, but little else has happened. An area reserved for farmland was operated for awhile by Lightbourne Farms and had distribution throughout the Marsh Harbour area, but operation ceased a year or so ago. The town is not developing as planned. A separate enterprise, The Blackfly Fishing Lodge opened north of Schooner Bay a few years ago, and seems to be doing well. See the chart and more detailed description on page 126-.

Long Beach is an older development with several homes another mile or so south. The beach here is beautiful as well. The turnoff is about 33 miles south of the Marsh Harbour traffic light.

About 1 mile further south (34.0 miles from Marsh Harbour) is the road to Crossing Rocks, a small town located just off the Atlantic Ocean Beach. During 2000 the town was moved a little inland after the devastation of hurricane Floyd. There is a bar and restaurant—Trevor's Midway Motel— at the entrance road. The town is a short drive east on the road. It has a pretty beach with some off-lying rocks.

At 6.6 miles beyond the Crossing Rocks road (and 40.6 miles south of Marsh Harbour) the highway forks. The road to Hole-in-the-Wall goes southeast. It is 15 miles to the lighthouse and very rough; it should be attempted only in a truck with good road clearance. It passes through the Sandy Point Forest Preserve, which is administered by the Bahamas National Trust and is home to the endangered Abaco parrot. Eco-tours of this area are sometimes available.

The paved road to the southwest goes to Sandy Point, the only settlement on the west side of Great Abaco Island. It is 11.5 miles from the fork, and the road parallels a beautiful beach which is often used for community cookouts. Sandy Point is a small fishing village which has grocery stores, restaurants, and rooms for rent. Nancy's Sea Side Inn, located on the waterfront a block north of the public dock, is a good lunch stop. Oeisha's Resort caters mostly to bonefishermen; rooms are moderately priced (phone 242 366-4139). Five miles northwest of Sandy Point (by water only) is Gorda Cay, developed by the Disney Corporation as a cruise ship stop they named Castaway Cay. The *Disney Magic* began regular visits to the island in July, 1998. A ferry service operated by Bahamas Ferries connects Sandy Point to Nassau for automobiles as well as passengers. See page 174 for more detail.

There are several beautiful beaches on the southeastern coast of Great Abaco Island. This photo is of the beach at Bahama Palm Shores with Cherokee Sound in the distance. Photo by Steve Dodge.

The aerial below was taken in 2010 while Schooner Bay was under construction and shows the southern half of the Schooner Bay beach. The photo at the right was taken from the southern end of the beach and shows the northern end two miles away. Photos by Steve Dodge.

A Brief History of Abaco

by Steve Dodge
Professor Emeritus
Millikin University

The Spaniards called it Habacoa,* and they were not impressed. Although they were the first Europeans to explore Abaco and the Bahamas, they settled on larger islands further to the south such as Hispaniola and Cuba, then moved on to conquer large and wealthy Indian civilizations in Mexico and Peru. When the enslaved Indians of Cuba and Hispaniola died of smallpox and overwork, the Spaniards sailed to Habacoa and other Bahamian islands to recruit new Indian slaves. Thus, the Lucayan Indians, whom Columbus had described as gentle and kind, were victims of genocide and were gone before 1550. The sites of their numerous settlements have been discovered and various artifacts have been found, but none of the sites in Abaco have been fully excavated by archaeologists. The British eventually colonized Eleuthera Island and New Providence Island (Nassau) in the Bahamas, and claimed the entire archipelago as their colony, but no permanent settlements were made in Abaco for over 200 years after the departure of the Lucayans. The French made an attempt to establish a colony in Abaco in 1625. They called it Lucaya or Lucayonique, but it was not successful and no trace of the settlement has been found. The early French maps of Abaco are generally more accurate than others which have survived, but pirates undoubtedly knew the waters better than anyone else.

Abaco was well situated for piracy. The small cays offered excellent anchorages as well as good lookout points, and the combination of the shallow banks and the off-shore barrier reef discouraged pursuers. Few records exist concerning the haunts of pirates, but we do know that Vain the Great Pirate based himself at Green Turtle Cay in Abaco after fleeing Nassau when the first royal governor, Woodes Rogers, arrived in 1717. He was discovered by Benjamin Hornygold, a recently-converted pirate sent by Rogers, but Vain managed to escape from Green Turtle Cay and from the Bahamas. Other pirates, a few wreckers, and some transient fishermen may have made their residence at Abaco from time to time, but there were no permanent settlements by the 1770s when the British North American colonies declared their independence from Britain.

Not all the colonists supported the patriot cause during the American Revolution; from 10 to 20 percent of the population favored Great Britain. Their reasons were various. Some genuinely liked George III, some disliked the patriots, and some feared that democracy and republicanism would imperil their security or their property. These loyalists were treated badly by the patriots—their property was often confiscated and they were expelled from the villages in which they lived. Many moved to areas such as New York and Florida which were controlled by Britain during the war. When Britain conceded independence to the United States, many of the loyalists chose to move again rather than become citizens of the United States. Encouraged by exaggerated claims for the agricultural and commercial potential of Abaco, some of them became convinced that it would be a good place to build a new British Empire.

Over 600 persons left New York for Abaco in August, 1783. They settled at Carleton, named after Sir Guy Carleton, the British commanding officer in New York. The location of Carleton was unknown for many years and many wild guesses were made. While working in the Bahamas Archives and at Lands and Surveys in 1979, I found two original land grant deeds for parcels which were adjacent to Carleton, and determined that the town had been located near the north end of the Treasure Cay Beach. This was subsequently confirmed by an archaeological dig by Bob Carr and the discovery of a map of Carleton drawn in 1784 found at the Public Records Office in London by Gail Saunders. Before the loyalists had been at Carleton for three months, a minor dispute regarding each man's responsibility to work in the cooperative provisions store had escalated into a revolution. Many of the town's residents supported a Committee of Safety which overthrew the authority of Captain John Stephens and placed him under arrest. When they received word that reinforcements were on the way from the British garrison at St. Augustine, they feared these troops would support Stephens, so two-thirds of the residents left Carleton, moved six leagues (18 miles) to the southeast, and founded Marsh's Harbour. Within the next five years some of the remaining settlers at Carleton moved on to other locations, and Carleton ceased to exist.

The dissident group at Marsh's Harbour was joined by additional refugees from New York, some of whom founded Maxwell, which was named for the Governor of the Bahamas and was adjacent to Marsh's Harbour. It was probably located on the southeastern shore, perhaps at Boat Harbour, which is now the site of the Great Abaco Beach Hotel and Boat Harbour Marina. Refugees from Florida came to Abaco also. A group settled in southern Abaco at Spencer's Bight (about 10 miles south of Marsh's Harbour) and a former member of the Carolina Rangers, Lt. Col. Brown, was granted a large parcel of land at Eight Mile Bay, about eight miles south of Spencer's Bight, where he intended to establish a plantation. Within a year or two he moved his slaves from Abaco to Caicos, where he had acquired another grant of crown land. As far as can be determined this was the only attempt by a loyalist to cultivate cotton on a large scale in Abaco.

Many of the loyalists were displeased with Abaco. They had come to Abaco to farm, but they found only small pockets of soil on the limestone island. Rainfall was plentiful, but there were long, dry periods when crops dried and burned up. Life was not as easy as the promotional literature said it would be. When the free provisions provided by the Crown were exhausted, many of the new migrants decided to leave the island. About 2000 had come to Abaco during the middle 1780s, but only 400 (200 whites and 200 blacks) were left in 1790. Those who had money or influence probably left Abaco. Those who stayed probably had no alternative.

The few hundred loyalists who remained in Abaco were joined by migrants from Harbour Island, Eleuthera, an old Bahamian settlement. Young men from Harbour Island were reportedly impressed with the beauty of the Abaco girls, and also with the large and unexploited fishing grounds of Abaco. They knew that survival in the Bahamas meant that one had to fish as well as farm, and new communities were established on the outer cays which were close to the reef and the best fishing. New Plymouth was founded on Green Turtle Cay. It was the most important settlement in Abaco during most of the nineteenth century. Its men relied on farming, fishing, and wrecking–no one became wealthy, but they made a living. According to tradition, Wyannie Malone, a widow from South Carolina, was the founder of Hope Town on Elbow Cay. During the 1820s a single young couple settled on Man-O-War Cay; in 1977 230 of Man-0-War's population of 235 could trace their ancestry to Pappy Ben and Mammy Nellie. A small settlement was also established on Great Guana Cay.

The settlers who survived in Abaco learned to be self-sufficient. They had no choice in the matter; they lacked government mail service until 1867 when the House of Assembly provided a subsidy for a privately-owned vessel to make one round trip per month between Nassau and Abaco. Nassau, capital of the Bahamas, was no great metropolis–its population was only 10,000 in 1864–bu

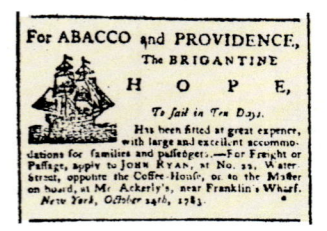

The first group of loyalists to leave New York for Abaco did so in September, 1783. This advertisement for the sailing of the *Hope*, which carried a second or third group of immigrants to Abaco, appeared in the *Royal Gazette* (New York) on October 24, 1783.

it was Abaco's only link with the outside world. The Abaconians attempted to become involved in various export operations during the late nineteenth and the early twentieth centuries–pineapples, sisal, lumber, sponge–all provided a living for a large number of Abaconians for a period of time, but failed to move the economy much beyond the subsistence level. The problem was not that the people did not work hard; the problem was that they lacked knowledge of foreign markets. They always seemed to be doing the right thing at the wrong time or in the wrong way. They shipped pineapples to the United States in bulk, and frequently lost a large portion of the crop to spoilage in the ships' holds. They shifted into sisal production just as the market for sisal was deteriorating.

One of the most reliable sources of income for Abaconians during the mid-nineteenth century was wrecking, but it declined in importance long before 1900. Wrecking did not necessarily mean luring a ship to its destruction. It meant salvaging the cargo and usable parts of ships that wandered onto the reef or the banks. Wreckers saved many sailors' lives. Because Abaco is situated adjacent to one of the busiest north-south shipping lanes in the Atlantic, a seemingly inexhaustible supply of ships were wrecked in Abaco during the 19th century. One of the best-known wrecks was that of the *U.S.S. Adirondack*, a brand new steam sloop which was the pride of the Union Navy in 1862. En route to Nassau to

The *U.S.S. Ossipee*, shown here, was a sister ship to the *U.S.S. Adirondack*, the remains of which can still be seen on the reef near Man-O-War Cay. This photograph was provided courtesy of the Naval Historical Foundation, Collection of W. Beverly Mason, Jr.

inform Union ships there to search for the infamous Confederate raider, the Alabama, the *Adirondack* struck the reef at Man-O-War Cay, where her remains can still be seen. Shortly after this wreck, the British Imperial Lighthouse Service contributed to the decline of wrecking by building lighthouses throughout the Bahamas. The lighthouse at Hope Town on Elbow Cay was completed in 1863, despite attempts by local residents to protect their livelihoods by sabotaging the construction project.

By 1900 Hope Town was the largest and most prosperous settlement in Abaco. It was the seat for a commissioner, and its population of almost 1200 lived by fishing, sponging, shipping and boat building. Abaco boats were admired for their design as well as their fine construction, and were known as the best in the Bahamas. Abaco dinghies, small open boats with a single sail, were sought by most Bahamian fishermen, and Abaco-built smacks (sloops with bowsprits) and schooners brought a premium in the marketplace. During World War I and the early 1920s, large lumber-carrying schooners of more than 200 tons were built at Hope Town and at Man-O-War Cay. There is only one boat carpenter left in Hope Town today -- Winer Malone builds Abaco dinghies in his shed near the harbour using only hand tools and providing the visitor with an accurate view of how boats were built in Abaco a century ago. Man-O-War Cay is the most active boat building center in

Abaco today. Albury Brothers Boats builds outboard powerboats. Beginning in 1979 fiberglass as well as wood hulls were made. These Bahamian-built boats are typically heavier and stronger than their US-built counterparts; they are built to withstand many years of hard use in high seas. They are sought after by fishermen and others throughout the islands, so contemporary Abaco continues to export boats as it has done since the early nineteenth century.

The first glimpse of twentieth-century life style in Abaco was Wilson City, a company town located about 10 miles south of Marsh's Harbour. Founded in 1906, it was the marvel of its

The mill at Wilson City. Photo from Gray Russell, former resident of Wilson City. Copied by Steve Dodge with assistance of Leo Savola.

age, boasting modern conveniences such as electricity and an ice plant, both rarities in the Out Islands. It was built by the Bahamas Timber Company, which operated a saw mill and dock facilities at the site. Many residents of Hope Town and Marsh's Harbour moved to Wilson City where they found steady employment, but this operation was short-lived; the company closed the mill at Wilson City in 1916. Several years later, during the early 1920s, two developments provided Abaco with improved communication with the outside world. The installation of a radio-telephone station at Hope Town made instant communication with Nassau possible, and the diesel-powered Priscilla replaced the Albertine Adoue schooner which had been serving as the mail boat.

The improved transportation and communication had only a limited impact on the Abaconians. The depression of the early 1930s inhibited economic development, and the lives of most Abaconians were still very similar to those of their ancestors some 100 years before. Boat building and fishing, supplemented by small farming, were the principle economic activities, and most Abaconians lived at or near the subsistence level. Real change did not occur until after World War II, when the lumber industry was revived by Owens-Illinois Corporation and tourists from the United States, Canada, and Britain discovered Abaco.

Owens-Illinois had acquired the 100 year lease originally granted to the Bahamas Timber Company. In 1959 the company built the first roads which connected the several communities on Great Abaco, and the first motor vehicles were introduced. An airport was built at Marsh Harbour and port facilities were constructed at Snake Cay. The company cut the Caribbean Pine forest of Abaco and exported it for use as pulpwood. Marsh Harbour boomed–several banks and a small shopping center with a supermarket were constructed. When Owens-Illinois completed its pulpwood operation in Abaco during the late 1960s, the company decided to utilize its investments and labor force in Abaco by building a huge sugar plantation. Sugar was exported from Abaco in 1968, 1969 and 1970, but the company lost money and the operation, which is the largest farm in the Bahama Islands, was closed. The land was sold to the government of the Bahamas, and the government, after considering various schemes, including converting it into a ranch for raising cattle, then leased it to B. J. Harmon, a Florida company which grew and exported citrus. A neem farm has been started and is successfully growing and producing neem products. Tourism developed slowly after World War II when cruising yachtsmen and others discovered the islands. Some bought land at very reasonable prices and built vacation or retirement homes. Many of these people have become a permanent part of Abaconian society. Dr. George Gallup's family still maintains a vacation house he built in Hope Town during the 1950s, and Randolph Johnston, an artist from New England, settled at Little Harbour, Abaco, at about the same time. He built a beachside home and studio where he produced lost wax castings in bronze for gallery shows in New York and Paris. Small resorts and hotels were established to service tourists who preferred the quiet and measured pace of a vacation in Abaco to the more active life-style of Nassau and Freeport, which became major tourist destinations during the 1950s and 1960s. Abaco is still off the beaten tourist track and offers the visitor an opportunity to enjoy unspoiled waters, reefs, and cays, good swimming, snorkeling, sailing and beachcombing -- all in an atmosphere of clean air and friendly, honest people. Though an increasing number of tourists visit Abaco each year, the charm and warmth of its environment and its people have not changed.

In 1967 the Progressive Liberal Party (PLP), led by Lynden Pindling, gained a majority in the House of Assembly and formed a government. The party represented the black majority (85% of the population of the Bahamas is black), and Abaco, which is about 50% white, voted for the opposition. When the PLP decided to seek independence for the Bahamas in 1972, many of the residents of Abaco resisted it. They petitioned Queen Elizabeth II, and asked to be separated from the Bahamas so they could remain a British Crown Colony. Citing the loyalty of their ancestors to the Crown, they begged the Queen to reciprocate. Their petition was not granted, and though a small group contemplated the possibility of a revolution to separate Abaco from the Bahamas and make it independent, those plans received little support. Although many Abaconians eventually shifted their support to the PLP government of Lynden Pindling, Abaco remained a centre of opposition activity. Its representatives in the House of Assembly were usually members of the official opposition party, the Free National Movement, and were frequently involved in debates and disputes with government representatives. The Pindling government was defeated in the general election held on 19 August 1992, and Hubert Ingraham, FNM representative for Coopers Town, Abaco, became the new Prime Minister. The change of government was achieved democratically and peacefully. Ingraham brought a new burst of economic activity and long overdue reforms such as the implementation of local government. He was re-elected in 1997 for a second five-year term. In May 2002 the FNM lost a general election and Perry Christie, leader of the PLP, became Prime Minister. Five five years later, in May 2007, the FNM which was again led by Hubert Ingraham, won control of the government, and five years after that, in 2012, the PLP won control of the House of Assembly and Perry Christie returned to power as Prime Minister. The Bahamians celebrated the 40th anniversary of their independence on 10 July 2013, and during that time only three different men served as Prime Minister. The nation has been successful in achieving significant economic growth and has developed a viable democratic political system. Bahamians are rightfully proud of their achievement.

*The name Habacoa is of Taino (Indian) origin. It meant Large Upper Outlier and was originally used to refer to the island now called Andros. The name first appeared on a Spanish map in 1500 when Juan de la Cosa used it to designate a large island in the northern Bahamas. The Taino name for Abaco was Lucayoneque, which means Peoples' Distant Waters Land. See Julian Granberry, "Lucayan Toponyms," *Journal of the Bahamas Historical Society* 13 1 (October, 1991), 3-12.

Steve Dodge, who is also the author of this *Cruising Guide to Abaco, Bahamas*, is Professor Emeritus of History at Millikin University in Decatur, Illinois. He has also written *Abaco: The History of an Out Island and its Cays* (1983, 1995, 2005).

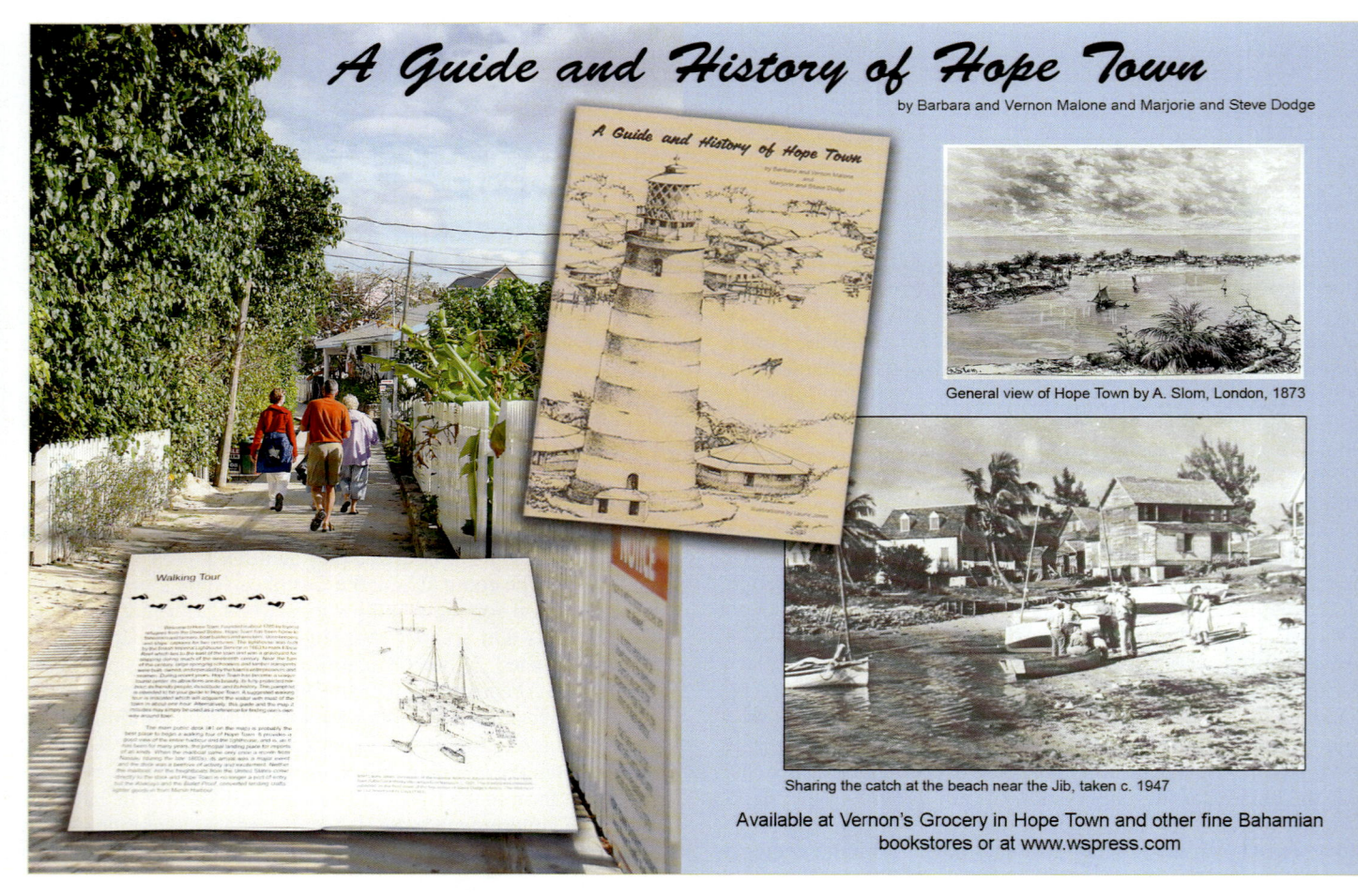

A Guide and History of Hope Town
by Barbara and Vernon Malone and Marjorie and Steve Dodge

General view of Hope Town by A. Slom, London, 1873

Sharing the catch at the beach near the Jib, taken c. 1947

Available at Vernon's Grocery in Hope Town and other fine Bahamian bookstores or at www.wspress.com

Medical Tips
for Tropical Waters

Raymond Heimbecker
Jane Garfield
Justin Noice

It is fortunate that in the Abacos we have few serious health hazards. Our visitors should be aware of special problems that can be easily avoided, which would otherwise spoil a wonderful vacation. Do take simple precautions to prevent or at least mitigate what could become serious problems.

The problems we see most frequently in the Abacos are:

1. Ear infections, both acute and chronic, usually only in the ear canal, but can be SCUBA diving injury
2. Ciguatera fish poisoning, and, rarely, fish spoilage
3. Serious sunburn due to excessive U. V. exposure
4. Skin reactions due to poison wood, jelly fish, sea lice, and, rarely, from Portuguese Man-O'War
5. Trauma, mostly face and hand lacerations, often fish hooks, but also fish fillet knives! Also, we see sprains and fractions which occur while boating.

Before travelling each year you should have your ear canals checked and cleared of all wax. Tetanus Toxoid is the only immunization often required before you travel (every ten years).

Only rarely do we see patients with acute heart or abdominal problems, strokes, major fractures or life threatening accidents. But when these emergencies occur there are physicians available in Marsh Harbour to provide immediate care and arrange for transfer to a hospital if need be. A number of air ambulance services will come to the Bahamas to pick up patients. The local physicians can call these when needed. The patient or the family must be able to provide a credit card which has the funds available to cover the six to ten thousand dollar bill which will be incurred. If the medical situation is urgent but not life threatening, arrangements can often be made for one of the charter airlines to fly the patient out. In all but the most severe weather a patient can be in a hospital within two hours.

Sun Protection ... whenever possible!

EAR PROBLEMS

Ear problems occur all too frequently. In most cases these involve the ear canal and are caused by a fungus. We advise those swimmers who are prone to these itchy, painful, sometimes discharging ear infections to treat them preventively by placing a few drops of white vinegar and clean water, half and half, in the ear canal. This solution should be used before and after each and every snorkeling trip or dive. This will go a long way toward preventing serious ear canal infections. Scuba divers can and do develop middle ear problems due to poor equalization. Even though diving in the Abacos is usually quite shallow, the routine SCUBA precautions are important. If the diver has any mild nasal congestion, the use of a decongestant before each dive would be helpful. No one with a cold should dive, and no one should continue a dive if equalization is difficult. Most important of all, a dive must be immediately aborted if the diver experiences pain, bleeding, or dizziness. Each year there are three to four perforated ear drums as a result of ignoring these basic precautions. Finally, in regard to diving, all should be aware that blue holes can be extremely dangerous for even experienced divers.

FISH POISONING

The second medical problem, and one that is not uncommon, is tropical fish poisoning or ciguatera. It is caused by a photosynthetic dinoflagellate (a microscopic free swimming organism). The flagellates live among the algae on coral reefs. Especially (but not only) when the reefs are stirred up, these organisms are eaten by small fish and enter the food chain. Larger reef fish eventually harbour the toxin which accumulates in the flesh of the fish. The unwary person who eats the ciguateric fish may become ill. The reef fish most commonly involved are the larger grouper, barracuda, and snappers. The free swimmers, that is, fish that do not feed on the reef, are not involved. The smaller reef feeders are usually less dangerous because both by weight and age they accumulate less poison.

There is no way to detect or neutralize the toxin in an affected fish, and no amount of cooking or freezing will detoxify an affected fish. All of the old wives tales of how to test fish meat for ciguatera are just myths and do not work. Obviously the best way to deal with ciguatera is to avoid it. The best way to do that is to ask local Abaconians what kind of fish to avoid before eating fish, and do not eat fish if you do not know what kind it is.

Occasionally someone may eat a "mystery" fish and toxic fish poisoning may follow. The first symptom is often numbness and tingling, especially around the mouth, lips, and tongue. This may be followed by nausea, vomiting, diarrhea, severe aches and pains, and generalized weakness. The poison is neurotoxic. A unique symptom is heat/cold reversal. Hot water or warm weather may feel cold and vice versa. Each person seems to react differently. Some will recover in a few weeks; some will be debilitated for many months. Although we haven't seen this in the Abacos, the person may become comatose and die. The most serious chronic effects are prolonged muscle weakness and temperature inversion. Once a person has developed ciguatera, that person will remain hypersensitive for the rest of their lives.

There have been two recent breakthroughs in our knowledge of ciguatera. First, an easily used colorimetric test to determine whether or not a fish is ciguateric is now available. Second, we now have a treatment for the severely ill comatose patients. This is Mannitol, a solution that must be given intravenously. Unfortunately, it is of no use for the other symptoms of the poisoning. .

The other common fish poisoning is simply spoilage caused by inadequate refrigeration. The well known symptoms of nausea, vomiting and diarrhea are usually short lasting. The only treatment is oral fluid replacement. All the members of the mackerel family are extremely susceptible to this type of spoilage. It is extremely important especially in the summer to put fish on ice as soon as they are caught, and to cook them immediately after they come off the ice.

SKIN PROBLEMS

The most common problems doctors encounter in the Abacos involve the skin. Severe sun burn, poison wood, and stings from Portuguese Men O'War, other jelly fish, or sea lice can all cause skin inflammations that can make a person miserable.

Sunburn: Visitors from northern climates are often unaware that even in the winter the Abaco sun is strong and can produce severe burns. Proper clothing and modern barrier creams that cut down on both ultraviolet A and B exposure are vital. For swimmers and divers water resistant sunblock creams are a must. Severe burns will require fluid replacement and a trip to the clinic. Local aloe plants, when sliced length wise and applied directly to the burned area, may provide some relief.

Poison wood is a bush or a tree that has clusters of five, seven or nine dark green shiny green leaves (see illustration). The bark is gray, but is mottled with black stains caused by sap, which seeps through the bark and then turns black. Walking through the thick bush, or clearing land, are the usual ways for the susceptible person to get a poisonwood rash. The oily sap, transferred to the skin by

Poison Wood (Metopium Toxiferum) is a tree which has clusters of five, seven or nine shiny leaves and mottled gray, tan and black bark. It is more volatile than Poison Ivy and is common throughout Abaco.

contact with the leaves or bark, causes the rash. It is similar to, but far more intense than, poison ivy. Within three days extreme itching and burning occur, and redness and blisters appear. Some persons report success in removing the sap from the skin shortly after contact with WD-40, which is apparently much more effective than soap and water. Local resident Dave Gale reports that Abaco Neem body lotion, salve, or oil stops poison wood itch immediately, and that it is much more effective than cortisone cream. If the rash is severe, widespread, or around the eyes, a trip to the clinic is indicated. If the juice gets into the eyes it may cause loss of vision and even blindness. The **Manchineel** tree (rare) is even more dangerous than poisonwood.

The **Portuguese Man O'War** can cause a severe stinging burning rash that may be painful for several days. Be sure to warn your children who otherwise would be attracted by the bright and iridescent blue colours of the balloon shaped Man O'War as it drifts up on the beaches. These "balloons" are difficult to see while swimming and may cause severe burning if one swims through the long tentacles. They may appear on ocean beaches after strong onshore winds; they are rare in sheltered waters. If stung, leave the water and carefully remove any tentacles remaining on your skin with tweezers or a gloved hand to minimize the bursting of additional stinging capsules. There is no magic potion to cure these stings. Scrubbing and rubbing the area could well make things worse; rubbing alcohol, once thought to be a "cure" does not really help, but some say vinegar brings relief. Usually the sharp stinging pain subsides within a few hours, and is completely gone after a few days. If the stung person develops shortness of breath, backache or muscle pain

The Portuguese Man O'War looks like a clear bluish or purple balloon floating on the surface. Its tentacles can be over ten feet long. Photo used with the permission of key-biscayne.com.

he/she should be brought to the nearest clinic.

Fire coral and fire sponges may be encountered on the reefs. They can cause a painful rash. The most important rule is to wear gloves at all times and DON'T touch or pick up anything.

An itchy skin rash has become a problem for some summer visitors during recent years. It is popularly attributed to "**sea lice,**" but no such animal actually exists. The rash is most likely caused by the larvae of the Thimble Jellyfish (Linuche Unguiculata). These almost invisible larvae are produced in large clusters called "blooms" by the adult jellyfish during the summer months. They may be carried by wind and currents into shore. When the larvae contact with people the larvae discharge stinging nematocysts which may persist for several days (for further information see *The Journal of the American Medical Association*, vol. 269, no. 13, April 7, 1993, p. 1669). Usually nothing is felt at the time; the rash develops several hours after contact. It is always most pronounced in the areas covered by swimwear, and small children are particularly vulnerable, often developing a severe rash accompanied by a fever, nausea, and vomiting. And this can happen even if the child has just been playing at the edge of the sea rather than actually swimming in the water. These severe cases should be seen by a phsysician. In general the rash subsides in 96 hours.

Avoid sea lice if possible; rely on local knowledge. Recently a number of Abaconians have applied meat tenderizer to susceptible areas before swimming and have avoided trouble altogether. Others have found that the use of a product named Safe Sea, applied before swimming, has kept them free of the rash. A fresh water and soap shower after removing the bathing suit or trunks taken as soon as possible after swimming may wash away enough larvae so that a rash will not occur. If a rash does develop, cortisone cream may help the itchiness. Some who have been stung by sea lice or jellyfish, have found that a product named Lands End Oil alleviates the itching and discomfort. A clinic visit is only necessary for severely affected patients. There is evidence that a previous bout with sea lice sensitizes the person, and that the next exposure may result in an instant stinging sensation while in the water.

SPINES AND BARBS, CUTS AND LACERATIONS

Sea urchin spines and sting ray barbs cause discomfort and pain. The sea urchin that is most likely to cause problems in Abaco is the one with short white spines. The unwary wader or swimmer may step on or touch one of these--the spines penetrate the skin and break off to become very painful. There are usually many imbedded spines that require individual removal. The old remedy of immediately applying lemon juice or other more easily available acid softens the spines but doesn't help extract them. An infection often sets in around the spines. Obviously, prevention is best--wear flippers and gloves and water shoes--but also, beware that sea urchin spines can penetrate these, so watch where you walk and what you touch.

Sea Urchins are frequently found in crevices with their toxin-laden spines sticking out. Photo © Teresa Zubi; used with permission.

A much more painful problem is caused by sting ray barbs. Rays often bury themselves in the sand in shallow water. An unwary person walking quietly may surprise the ray by stepping on it. The ray then objects strenuously and struggles to free itself by flipping its barbed tail into the person's foot, ankle, or leg. The pain is immediate, intense and unless treated, long-lasting. Application of heat (hot water) may provide relief. A person who has not been stung should "test the waters" to avoid complicating the patient's problems by scalding. In the field, it may be possible to provide relief by utilizing the hot water exhausted from the outboard motor. Use a bucket to collect the water, and remember to check the temperature before applying it. Local physicians sometimes inject local anesthetic int the area to provide pain relief. Also, meticulous cleaning and removal of any barb fragments is important. Prevention is best--look before you walk, and shuffle and splash some water around--enough to awaken and frighten a buried ray into finding another spot for napping.

A new potential hazard for snorkelers and divers in Abaco is the lion fish. A recent migrant to the southeastern United States (2000) and to Abaco (2005), the fish is native to the Pacific and Indian Oceans. It is a strange-looking but beautiful fish with dark red stripes and various protruding tentacle-like body parts. Long spines comprise its dorsal fin (on top of its back)—these point forward as well as up, and carry a poisonous toxin. If contact occurs with humans, immediate intense pain results making movement of limbs difficult, and sometimes paralysis and nausea occurs as well. According to one website, treatment is immersing the affected area in hot water to increase blood flow, possibly local anesthesia to reduce pain, and an x-ray to determine if there are any broken spine fragments. If present, they should be removed to prevent infection. In general, lion fish are not aggresive. Do not touch.

The strange-looking but beautiful lion fish carries a toxin in its sprines. Photo © John White, used with permission.

Visitors often acquire coral cuts while swimming or exploring. The best treatment is immediate and frequent cleaning with soap and water. Antiseptic and antibiotic creams are useless and provide a wonderful culture medium for skin bacteria. Leave the cut open if possible, or bandage it loosely and change the bandage frequently.

More serious lacerations, especially those that are bleeding heavily, require immediate attention. STOP the bleeding by direct pressure. Don't bother with pressure points. Five minutes of uninterrupted pressure (time it) right over the bleeding area will stop 99% of all bleeding. Don't peek--just keep strong pressure on, and if possible elevate the bleeding area above the heart. Follow this with bulky dressing firmly applied with tape, but keep the pressure on as much as possible. Tournequets are considered obsolete and can be dangerous. If necessary the local doctors will close the wounds. If there is numbness or inability to move any injured part, go to the nearest physician as soon as possible.

For small lacerations there are excellent bandages available. They can be acquired from a doctor or pharmacy at home and should be in everyone's first aid kit. These bandages are called SteriStrips and are produced by 3M. The most useful ones are one-quarter inch in width. Use these to close small lacerations closely and accurately. They look like regular bandages with a narrow center section. If you do not have SteriStrips on hand, you can make your own from regular bandaids.

FINDING MEDICAL HELP

Finding medical help in Abaco is not difficult but serious medical problems often require emergency air evacuation to hospitals in Nassau or Florida.

The Ministry of Health operates clinics in Coopers Town, Green Turtle Cay, Man-O-War, and Hope Town which are staffed by nurses. These clinics are open at certain times and can also open when emergencies occur. A physician occasionally attends these clinics. The Government Clinic in Marsh Harbour is staffed by physicians and nurses and is the central clinic for South Abaco.

In Marsh Harbour and Treasure Cay there are also excellent private medical clinics staffed by experienced physicians and nurses. Hours vary but they are usually open Mon-Fri from 9-5. Walk-in patients during office hours are generally welcomed, subject to the clinic's existing appointment schedule. If you can, please call ahead. After hours emergency assistance **is not available** from some of the private clinics unless the individual has already established a patient relationship with the clinic; this is a result of insurance company rules. If a visitor wants to assure that emergency service will be available from a private clinic, he or she should establish a patient relationship prior to the emergency.

During the past few years several of the volunteer Fire & Rescue organizations have developed the capability to respond to medical emergencies, provide paramedical assistance if necessary and to transport patients to medical facilities. Such units exist in Hope Town, Guana Cay, Man-O-War and Green Turtle Cay. Hope Town Fire Rescue also provides waterborne medical response capability for Bahamas Air Sea Rescue (BASRA).

If you experience an emergency, broadcast your emergency on VHF 16 stating your location and the nature of the problem. The appropriate organization will then respond and you will be switched to their working channel. Although you will hear mention of the working channels used by various organizations on the Cruisers Net each morning, they are not monitored 24 hours a day and **VHF 16 is the ONLY channel on which to make an emergency call.** You should however avoid using the working channels reserved for emergency use for normal conversation because you might block important communications during an emergency response.

We hope you won't need this information and that with awareness of some of the avoidable hazards you will not encounter them. Please have a healthy, happy and safe time in this wonderful area.

Dr. Raymond Heimbecker did volunteer medical work in Abaco for over three decades and has been Honorary Out Island Surgeon in The Bahamas since 1996. Dr. Jane Garfield was the resident physician in Hope Town and Man-O-War Cay and is now retired in Blue Hill, Maine. Justin Noice is a member of Hope Town Fire and Rescue and lives on Elbow Cay.

EMERGENCY

List Arranged North to South

Green Turtle Govt. Clinic, (229) 798-0233
Green Turtle Fire & Rescue, 577-9068, 577-4109, VHF 16
Green Turtle Police, 525-8686
Guana Cay Police, 814-8506, VHF 16
Treasure Cay Fire, 826-9911
Treasure Cay Police, 367-2560, 367-3437
Marsh Harbour Government Mini Hospital, 827-5785
Marsh Harbour Fire Department, 577-2000, 808-2000
Marsh Harbour Medi Centre (Prvt. Clinic) - 577-9999
Marsh Harbour Police, 367-2580, 806-7016
Abaco Family Medicine, Marsh Harbour, (Private Clinic) - 458-1234
Auskell Clinic, Marsh Harbour, (private Clinic), 577-0113
Hope Town Government Clinic, 577-4257
Hope Town Fire and Rescue - **Call on VHF 16 first,** 577-0259, 801-5085
Hope Town Police, 824-3497, 441-5580
Sandy Point Police, 577-3568
US Embassy, 328-3496, 357-7004

Note: Within categories this directory is generally organized north to south. We attempted to source only known valid working numbers due to the continued unknown status of regular phone service restoration. We intend to expand the reference again at a time after services are restored.

General Abaco Business Contacts

AIRLINES AND CHARTERS

Abaco Freight (561) 502-2632, (561) 689-1010
SEE OUR AD page 14
Airgate Aviation (386) 478-0600
SEE OUR AD page 105
Air Unlimited (407) 585-4300
SEE OUR AD page. 3
American Airlines (800) 433-7300
Aztec Airways (954) 601-3742
Bahamas Air (242)702-4140, (800)222-4262
Cherokee Air (242)807-7900, toll free (866) 920-997,(561)277-1124
Island Wings (954) 617-8804, (954) 274-6214
Island Tyme Cargo (561) 267-8810
Silver Airways (801) 401-9100
Western Airways (242) 367-2222, (242) 377-2222

AUTOMOBILE PARTS AND REPAIRS

Auto Marine Professionals, (MH) 801-2886
Parts City, (MH) 699-0400, 805-7410
(SEE OUR AD Back Cover)
Clear Skys Auto Marine (MH) 357-6710, 805-6913

AUTO RENTALS

A&P Car Rental (MH) 367-2655, 577-0745, 577-0748
SEE OUR AD page 87
Barefoot Car Rentals (MH) 699-3223, 577-7373
SG Car Rentals (MH) 577-8589

BAKERY

The Sweet Spot (Fox Town) 806-1204
McIntosh's Bakery (GTC) 699-0381
Nick's Cafe and Bakery (GTC) 826-1085
Scrumdillyumptious Sweets (Central Pines) 458-8141
T's Bakery Delights (Central Pines) 812-7239
Aunt Dell's Sugarloaf Bakery & Eats (MH) 458-3708, 475-3106
Sea Biscuit Bakery & Company (HT) 804-1517
Tiffany's Treats (HT) 554-9830.
Vernon's Bakery (HT) 824-7739
Kent LeBoutillier (HT) 577-0512
Lubber's Bakery (LQ) 556-4750

BANKS

Sun Cash (Central Pines) 393-4778, 300-4786
Commonwealth Bank (MH) 502-6900
First Caribbean International Bank (MH) 699-1703
Royal Bank of Canada (MH) 357-0176, 322-2045
Scotiabank (MH) 356 1697, 356 1698, 356 1699

BEAUTY SALONS AND BARBERS

Chopping Block (HT) 375-9329

BICYCLE RENTALS

D&P Carts (GTC) 359-6605

BOAT ENGINE REPAIR

Robert's Marine (GTC) (242) 375-8758
Guana Cay Marine Services (GC) 777-5071
Edwin's Boatyard (MOW) 365-6006
SEE OUR AD page 77
Marsh Harbour Boatyard (MH) 367-5205, 826-6429
SEE OUR AD page 85
The Outboard Shop (MH) 475-9952
Classic Marine (HT) 457-2296
Lighthouse Marina (HT) 577-0283, 366-0154, (305)735-8550

BOAT RENTAL

Donny's Boat Rental (GTC) 365-4119, (407) 610-7000
Sunset Marine (GTC) 365-4634, (772) 539-9514
Dive Guana (GC) 577-0661
Conch Pearl (MOW) 577-5277
Abaco Yacht and Charter Services (MH) 577-0826
Cruise Abaco (MH) 577-0148, (351) 473-4223
SEE OUR AD page 94
Blue Wave Boat Rental (MH) 367 3910
The Moorings (MH) (888) 350-3575
Cat's Paw (HT) 577-0517
Island Marine (HT) 808-4615

CELL PHONE & INTERNET SERVICES

Aliv (MH) 807-0548
BTC (MH) 225-5282
Wimax (MH) 577-0462, 376-8057
Cable Bahamas (MH) 300-2200

CONSTRUCTION SERVICES

FR & Sons (GTC) 359-6667
Sands Construction (GC) 577-0332
Abaco Aggregate and Cement (MH) 813-7981
Abaco Spray Foam (MH) 826-0455
Abaco Tug and Transport (MH) 807-6055
Adrian Reid Construction (MH) 456-6469
All Trax Heavy Equipment (MH) 577-7876
CBS Bahamas 475-5728
C -Jay's Building Contractors (MH) 677-1817
CMM Construction (MH) 812-6248
Coastal Services (MH) 826-0455
Curry's Cabinetry (MH) 577-0121
Custom Atlantic Construction (MH) 376-8404
Douglas Palacious Const (MH) 467-6700
Drill Rig Marine Construction (MH) 577-3625
G Seven Construction (MH) 373-9638
Green Capital Construction (MH) 456-1182
Gusto Debris Removal (MH) 826-0262
Howard Construction (MH) 801-7865
Lion's Construction (MH) 805-0778, 646-2983
KD Construction (MH), 577-6188
Millers Builders & Construction (MH) 577-4679
Ojay's Construction (MH) 375-9774, 817-0123
Lucayan Surveying Company (MH) 477 5953
S.C.M. Construction (MH) 458-1529
S&K Heavy Equipment (MH) 810-3289
SL's General Construction & Repair 809-2504
Simms Construction (MH) 806-1183
Talcove Construction (MH) 225-4372
Terry's Heavy Lift (MH) 375-8840
WM Construction Company (MH) 827-1010
Your Dream Maintenance and Construction (MH) 429-2007
ZAKK's Construction & Maintenance Company (MH) 808-0156, 458-3820, 458-5007
Abaco Construction (HT) 825-7966
Gates Construction (HT) 475-4221
The Thompson Group (HT) 813-0045

CUSTOMS BROKERS

Arawak (242) 577-0060
SEE OUR AD page 83
CMM Professional Services 458-6320
Fine Living Customs Brokerage 458-6074
Fredrick's Agency 818-1011, 458-0445,
JCI Customs Brokers 367-3382 or 458-3382

DIVING & SNORKELING

Brendals Dive Center and Adventure Tours (GTC) 365-4411, 458-7868
SEE OUR AD page 55
Dive Guana, 577-0661
Bahamas Underground (MH) 359-6128
Percy's Diving Equipment (MH) 475-5989

ELECTRICAL AND GENERATORS

FR & Sons (GTC) 359-6667
Dale's Electric Company (MH) 357-6642
Island Boy Supply Company (MH) 818-0008
Parks & Parks Electrical (MH) 425-8357
VPI Services & Diesel Specialist (MH) 825-9223
Engineered Electrical Services (MH) 577-0511

FISHING AND/OR TOUR GUIDES

Reel Serious (GTC) 365-4019, 577-8195
Sea Vibes (GTC) 577-4394
Brendals Dive Center and Adventure Tours (GTC) 365-4411, 458-7868
Jason McIntosh (GTC) 458-6276
Reel Serious Charters (GTC) 577-8195
Abaco Flyfish Connection & Charters (GTC) 365-4261
Ronnie Sawyer (GTC) 357-6667
Capt. Buddy Pinder (MH) 242-577-7612.
Capt. Justin Sands(MH) 359-6890
Samuel McIntosh (MH) 475-2357
Capt. Plug's Adventures (HT) 801-5085
Hope Town Boat Charters- Fishing and Tour Guide Services (HT) 577-7309
IslandBoy Excursions (HT) 808-1789
Local Boy (HT) (242) 458-1685

FISHING TACKLE

Island Boy (MH) 357-6670
SEE OUR AD page 87

FREIGHT SERVICES

Abacays Carib Freight 367-6247, 577-6248
Abaco A & D Trucking 824-1373, 577-1221
Abaco Freight, 805-6932, (561) 502-2632
All Bahamas Courier & Shipping 458-7817
Bahamas Ferries 376-7289 or (561) 845-5047
Bimini Shipping 826-1085
Blue Window Logistics 347-7129
Centauri Transport 727-4129
CSC 577-0332
Dean's Shipping 394-0245
FedEx 554-9739
Seacor Island Lines 646-0007, (954) 920-9292
United Abaco Shipping (The Duke) (561)840-9393.

FUEL

Walkers Cay (833) 869-2553
Rosie's Place (Grand) 727-6051
Spanish Cay Resort and Marina (SC) (954) 213-6195, 807-0317
The Other Shore Club (GTC) 365-4226
Green Turtle Club and Marina (GTC) (443) 912-5839
Sunset Marine (GTC) 365-4634, 772-539-9514
Treasure Cay Marina (TC) 954-525-7711
Orchid Bay Marina(GC) 365-5175, 365-5182
Quality Star Auto Service (MH) 367-2979
Abaco Beach Resort and Marina (MH) (877) 533-4799, 367-2158
Lighthouse Marina (HT) 577-0283

GIFT SHOPS

Spanish Cay Resort and Marina (SC) (954) 213-6195, 807-0317
Low Tide Gift Shop (GTC) (954) 284-7341
Pineapples Boutique (GTC) 821-8892
Big O's (No Name Cay) 577-9008
SEE OUR AD page 59
Albury's Sail Shop (MOW) (863) 610-2416
SEE OUR AD page 79
Abaco Ceramics (MH) 375-8774
SEE OUR AD page 88
Driftwood News & Gifts, SEE AD page 79
Abaco Inn (HT) 816-1114
Bahama Handprints (HT) 816-1114
Da Crazy Crab (HT) 819-8630
Ebb Tide (HT) 577 3148
Firefly Resort (HT) 255-8635
Hope Town Canvas, SEE AD page 102
Lighthouse Marina (HT) 366-0154, 577-0283, (305) 735-8550
Sun Dried T's SEE AD page 102
Pete's Pub and Gallery (Little Harbour) 577-5487, 357-6648
Abaco Neem (South Abaco) 367-4117

GOLF CART RENTALS

D&P Cart Rentals (GTC) 359-6605
Harbour View Cart Rentals (GTC) 365-4411, 458-7868
Kool Karts (GTC) 477-5920
Sea Side Cart Rentals (GTC) 577-5497
Cash's Carts (TC) 359-6610
T&A Cart Rentals(GTC) (561) 594-2433, 375-8055
Dive Guana (GC) 577-0661
Elbow Cay Carts (HT) 366-0530
Getaway Cart Rentals (HT) 357-6672, 477-5201
Hope Town Cart Rentals(HT) 458-0442
Island Cart Rentals (HT) 577-0316, 577-0317, (561) 208-8160
Lighthouse Cart Rentals (HT) 475-2625, 475-0218

GROCERY STORES

Curry's Food Store (GTC) 699-1073
Man-O-War Grocery (MOW) 577-6449
Sam's Eggs (MOW) 818-4920
Abaco Grocery (MH) 577-2014
SEE OUR AD page 85
Quality Meat and Spices (MH) 816-4551
Vernon's Grocery (HT) 824-7739
SEE OUR AD page 102
Abaco Big Bird (South Abaco) 828-0215
Driftwood Farms (South Abaco) 557-1015

HARDWARE AND LUMBER

Robert's Hardware (GTC) 699-1258, 475-3843
Freeport's Hardware Center (TC) 824-4636
Guana Hardware (GC) 477-5765
Man-O-War Hardware (MOW) 826-6513
SEE OUR AD page 78
Bahamas Electric Motor & Generator Tool & Equipment Rentals (MH) 424-0700
Island Boy Supply Company (MH) 818-0008
The Paint Place (MH) 367-2271, 829-1141
Premier Imports (MH) 824-4044
SEE OUR AD page 87
Imports Unlimited (HT) 824-8310

HOTELS, RESORTS

Rosie's Place (Grand Cay) 533-7709
Spanish Cay Resort and Marina (SC) (954) 213-6195
SEE OUR AD page 47
Bahamas Beach Club (TC) (800) 284-0382
R&S Property Management (TC) 825-7934
Bluff House (GTC) (954) 284-7341
The Green Turtle Club (GTC) (443) 912-5839
Island Property Management(GTC) 357-6566
James Inn (Cooper's Town) 828-3011
Abaco Beach Resort & Boat Harbour Marina (MH) (877) 533-4799, 367-2158
SEE OUR AD page 93
Abaco Hillside Hotel (MH) 367-0112
Abaco Suites (MH) 816-2007
Bay Street Suites (MH) 577-0016
Island Breezes Hotel (MH) 577-0427
Tranquility Hideway Villas (MH) 533-6117
Abaco Inn (HT) 816-1114, (242) 802-5856.
SEE OUR AD page 109
Elbow Cay Properties (HT) (561) 270-0606
Firefly (HT) 255-8635
Hope Town Inn and Marina (HT) (242)366-0003, (850) 588-4855
SEE OUR AD page 100
Tanny Key Vacation Rentals (HT) (561) 267-6922
Pete's Pub (Little Harbour) 577-5487
Abaco Club (South Abaco) 367-0077
Blackfly Lodge (South Abaco) 577-5577
Sandpiper Inn (South Abaco) 699-2056
The Delphi Club (South Abaco) 577-1698

LAUNDRY SERVICE

Hudson's Laundromat (TC) 577-5303,
Orchid Bay Marina (GC) 365-5175
Jay's-One Shop Stop (MH) 367-4235
Lighthouse Marina (HT) 366-0154

LIQUOR STORES

Best Selections (TC) 817-0790.
Simpson's Liquor Store (TC) 825-5422
A.G. Wines & Spirits (MH) 577-2015
Jimmy's Wine and Spirits (MH) 603-2629
Lighthouse Liquors (HT) 475 8028.
Captain Jack's Wholesale (HT) 814-4757
Hope Town Wine and Spirits (HT) 366-0154, (242) 577-0283
SEE OUR AD page 99
On the Rocks Liquor (S. Abaco) 828-0215

MARINAS / DOCKAGE

Walker's Cay (North Abaco) (833) 869-2553
SEE OUR AD page 29
Rosie's Place (Grand Cay) 533-7709
SEE OUR AD page 31
Spanish Cay Marina (SC) (954) 213-6195 or 807-0317
SEE OUR AD page 47
Donny's Boat Rentals & Moorings (GTC) 365-4119, (407) 610-7000
Green Turtle Club Marina (GTC) (443) 912-5839
The Other Shore Club (GTC) 365-4226
Orchid Bay Marina (GC) 365-5175
Boat Harbour Marina (MH) (877) 533-4799, 367-2158
SEE OUR AD page 93
Hope Town Inn and Marina, 366-0003
SEE OUR AD page 100
Lighthouse Marina (HT) 366-0154, 577-0283, (305)735-8550
SEE OUR AD page 99
Sunset Marina (HT), 485-9255
SEE OUR AD page 107
Pete's Pub Moorings (Little Harbour) 577-5487
Abaco Yacht Club at Winding Bay (South Abaco) 367-0077

PARTY RENTALS

HIM Party Rentals (MH) 533-6117
Happy Feet Party Rentals (MH) 806-1403

PHARMACY

Abaco Island Pharmacy (MH) 802-2544
The Chemist Shoppe (MH) 817-3106
SEE OUR AD page 89

RESTAURANTS

Spanish Cay Resort and Marina (SC) (954) 213-6195, (242) 807-0317
Calypso Coffee House (GTC) 817-8136
Green Turtle Club (GTC) (443) 912-5839
McIntosh's Restaurant (GTC) 699-0381
Pineapple's Bar and Grill (GTC) 821-8892
Tranquil Turtle Beach Bar and Restaurant (GTC) 365-4200, 826-0654
The Wrecking Tree (GTC) 824-6378
Big O's (No Name Cay) 577-9008
SEE OUR AD page 59
Cafe La Florence (TC) 824-9393
Grabbers Bed Bar & Grill (GC) 365-5133
Sailor's Sweets (MOW) 818-4920
The Bistro at Abaco Beach Resort (MH) (877) 533-4799, 367-2158
Cat 5 Restaurant (MH) 816-3595
Colours by the Sea (MH) 699-3294
Abaco Inn (HT) 816-1114, (242) 802-5856
SEE OUR AD page 109
Firefly Resort (HT) 225-8635
Hope Town Inn and Marina (HT) 366-0003
Mackey's Take Out (HT) 810-0767
Nathalee's Kitchen (HT) 458-6717
On da Beach Bar and Grill (HT) 824-4223
Willie's Kitchen and Bar (HT) 802-5754, (242) 813-7490
Pete's Pub (Little Harbour) 577-5487
SEE OUR AD page 120
Hungry Again (Cherokee Sound) 458-2191
Sandpiper Inn (South Abaco) 699-2056
The Delphi Club (South Abaco) 577-1698

Tide Tables - 2022
Sea of Abaco • Abaco • Bahamas
NOAA Tide Station at Pelican Harbour (Sandy Cay at Pelican Cays Land and Sea Park)

Times are given for the Sea of Abaco at Pelican Harbour, but tides throughout Abaco vary by only a few minutes. Heights are in reference to Mean Lower Low Water (MLLW). Times are in Eastern Standard Time (EST) and Eastern Daylight Time (EDT) when appropriate.

January

Day	Time	Ht (ft)	Day	Time	Ht (ft)
1 Sa	12:07 AM / 06:33 AM / 01:10 PM / 06:51 PM	-0.7 / 3.3 / -0.4 / 2.4	16 Su	12:46 AM / 07:09 AM / 01:45 PM / 07:21 PM	-0.1 / 2.7 / 0.0 / 2.0
2 Su ●	01:03 AM / 07:28 AM / 02:05 PM / 07:47 PM	-0.8 / 3.4 / -0.5 / 2.5	17 M ○	01:27 AM / 07:48 AM / 02:23 PM / 08:02 PM	-0.1 / 2.7 / 0.0 / 2.0
3 M	01:58 AM / 08:21 AM / 02:58 PM / 08:42 PM	-0.8 / 3.5 / -0.6 / 2.5	18 Tu	02:07 AM / 08:26 AM / 03:01 PM / 08:41 PM	-0.2 / 2.8 / 0.0 / 2.1
4 Tu	02:53 AM / 09:14 AM / 03:50 PM / 09:37 PM	-0.7 / 3.4 / -0.5 / 2.5	19 W	02:46 AM / 09:03 AM / 03:37 PM / 09:20 PM	-0.2 / 2.8 / -0.1 / 2.2
5 W	03:48 AM / 10:05 AM / 04:41 PM / 10:32 PM	-0.6 / 3.3 / -0.5 / 2.5	20 Th	03:26 AM / 09:40 AM / 04:13 PM / 10:00 PM	-0.1 / 2.8 / -0.1 / 2.2
6 Th	04:43 AM / 10:57 AM / 05:31 PM / 11:28 PM	-0.4 / 3.1 / -0.4 / 2.5	21 F	04:07 AM / 10:18 AM / 04:49 PM / 10:42 PM	-0.1 / 2.7 / -0.1 / 2.3
7 F	05:40 AM / 11:48 AM / 06:22 PM	-0.2 / 2.8 / -0.3	22 Sa	04:51 AM / 10:57 AM / 05:28 PM / 11:27 PM	0.0 / 2.6 / -0.1 / 2.4
8 Sa	12:24 AM / 06:38 AM / 12:40 PM / 07:12 PM	2.5 / 0.0 / 2.6 / -0.2	23 Su	05:39 AM / 11:40 AM / 06:09 PM	0.1 / 2.5 / -0.1
9 Su ◐	01:22 AM / 07:39 AM / 01:33 PM / 08:03 PM	2.4 / 0.2 / 2.3 / -0.1	24 M	12:16 AM / 06:34 AM / 12:28 PM / 06:55 PM	2.4 / 0.1 / 2.3 / -0.2
10 M	02:19 AM / 08:42 AM / 02:28 PM / 08:53 PM	2.4 / 0.3 / 2.1 / 0.0	25 Tu ◑	01:11 AM / 07:35 AM / 01:22 PM / 07:48 PM	2.5 / 0.2 / 2.2 / -0.2
11 Tu	03:16 AM / 09:43 AM / 03:23 PM / 09:43 PM	2.4 / 0.4 / 1.9 / 0.0	26 W	02:12 AM / 08:42 AM / 02:24 PM / 08:46 PM	2.6 / 0.4 / 2.1 / -0.3
12 W	04:09 AM / 10:41 AM / 04:17 PM / 10:32 PM	2.4 / 0.3 / 1.8 / 0.0	27 Th	03:15 AM / 09:51 AM / 03:30 PM / 09:48 PM	2.7 / 0.1 / 2.1 / -0.3
13 Th	04:59 AM / 11:34 AM / 05:08 PM / 11:18 PM	2.4 / 0.3 / 1.8 / 0.0	28 F	04:20 AM / 10:58 AM / 04:37 PM / 10:52 PM	2.9 / 0.0 / 2.1 / -0.5
14 F	05:45 AM / 12:21 PM / 05:55 PM	2.5 / 0.2 / 1.8	29 Sa	05:22 AM / 12:00 PM / 05:40 PM / 11:54 PM	3.0 / -0.2 / 2.2 / -0.6
15 Sa	12:03 AM / 06:28 AM / 01:04 PM / 06:40 PM	-0.1 / 2.6 / 0.1 / 1.9	30 Su	06:21 AM / 12:57 PM / 06:40 PM	3.2 / -0.3 / 2.4
			31 M	12:52 AM / 07:15 AM / 01:50 PM / 07:36 PM	-0.7 / 3.3 / -0.5 / 2.5

February

Day	Time	Ht (ft)	Day	Time	Ht (ft)
1 Tu ●	01:48 AM / 08:07 AM / 02:40 PM / 08:29 PM	-0.7 / 3.3 / -0.5 / 2.6	16 W ○	01:46 AM / 08:00 AM / 02:30 PM / 08:17 PM	-0.2 / 2.8 / -0.1 / 2.3
2 W	02:42 AM / 08:57 AM / 03:28 PM / 09:20 PM	-0.7 / 3.3 / -0.6 / 2.7	17 Th	02:27 AM / 08:37 AM / 03:05 PM / 08:56 PM	-0.2 / 2.9 / -0.2 / 2.5
3 Th	03:34 AM / 09:44 AM / 04:14 PM / 10:10 PM	-0.6 / 3.1 / -0.5 / 2.7	18 F	03:08 AM / 09:14 AM / 03:40 PM / 09:36 PM	-0.2 / 2.8 / -0.2 / 2.6
4 F	04:25 AM / 10:30 AM / 04:59 PM / 10:59 PM	-0.4 / 2.9 / -0.4 / 2.6	19 Sa	03:50 AM / 09:52 AM / 04:17 PM / 10:17 PM	-0.2 / 2.8 / -0.3 / 2.6
5 Sa	05:15 AM / 11:16 AM / 05:43 PM / 11:49 PM	-0.2 / 2.7 / -0.3 / 2.5	20 Su	04:35 AM / 10:33 AM / 04:55 PM / 11:02 PM	-0.2 / 2.6 / -0.3 / 2.7
6 Su	06:07 AM / 12:02 PM / 06:27 PM	0.0 / 2.4 / -0.2	21 M	05:24 AM / 11:16 AM / 05:38 PM / 11:52 PM	-0.1 / 2.5 / -0.3 / 2.7
7 M	12:39 AM / 07:01 AM / 12:50 PM / 07:13 PM	2.4 / 0.2 / 2.1 / 0.0	22 Tu	06:17 AM / 12:05 PM / 06:26 PM	0.0 / 2.3 / -0.2
8 Tu ◐	01:32 AM / 07:59 AM / 01:41 PM / 08:02 PM	2.4 / 0.3 / 1.9 / 0.1	23 W ◑	12:47 AM / 07:18 AM / 01:02 PM / 07:22 PM	2.7 / 0.1 / 2.1 / -0.2
9 W	02:27 AM / 08:59 AM / 02:37 PM / 08:54 PM	2.3 / 0.4 / 1.8 / 0.2	24 Th	01:50 AM / 08:26 AM / 02:06 PM / 08:25 PM	2.7 / 0.2 / 2.0 / -0.2
10 Th	03:24 AM / 10:01 AM / 03:35 PM / 09:49 PM	2.3 / 0.5 / 1.7 / 0.2	25 F	02:57 AM / 09:37 AM / 03:17 PM / 09:34 PM	2.7 / 0.2 / 2.0 / -0.2
11 F	04:20 AM / 10:58 AM / 04:32 PM / 10:43 PM	2.3 / 0.4 / 1.7 / 0.1	26 Sa	04:06 AM / 10:46 AM / 04:28 PM / 10:42 PM	2.8 / 0.1 / 2.1 / -0.2
12 Sa	05:12 AM / 11:49 AM / 05:25 PM / 11:33 PM	2.4 / 0.3 / 1.8 / 0.1	27 Su	05:10 AM / 11:48 AM / 05:32 PM / 11:46 PM	2.9 / -0.1 / 2.3 / -0.3
13 Su	05:59 AM / 12:35 PM / 06:12 PM	2.5 / 0.2 / 1.9	28 M	06:09 AM / 12:43 PM / 06:31 PM	3.1 / -0.2 / 2.5
14 M	12:20 AM / 06:42 AM / 01:16 PM / 06:56 PM	0.0 / 2.6 / 0.1 / 2.1			
15 Tu	01:04 AM / 07:22 AM / 01:54 PM / 07:37 PM	-0.1 / 2.8 / 0.0 / 2.2			

March

Day	Time	Ht (ft)	Day	Time	Ht (ft)
1 Tu	12:45 AM / 07:01 AM / 01:32 PM / 07:24 PM	-0.4 / 3.1 / -0.4 / 2.6	16 W	01:38 AM / 07:49 AM / 02:16 PM / 08:07 PM	0.0 / 2.8 / 0.0 / 2.5
2 W ●	01:39 AM / 07:50 AM / 02:18 PM / 08:13 PM	-0.5 / 3.1 / -0.4 / 2.8	17 Th	02:22 AM / 08:28 AM / 02:53 PM / 08:48 PM	-0.1 / 2.8 / -0.2 / 2.7
3 Th	02:29 AM / 08:36 AM / 03:01 PM / 08:59 PM	-0.5 / 3.1 / -0.5 / 2.8	18 F ○	03:05 AM / 09:07 AM / 03:29 PM / 09:29 PM	-0.2 / 2.9 / -0.3 / 2.8
4 F	03:17 AM / 09:19 AM / 03:42 PM / 09:43 PM	-0.4 / 2.9 / -0.4 / 2.8	19 Sa	03:49 AM / 09:47 AM / 04:06 PM / 10:10 PM	-0.3 / 2.8 / -0.4 / 3.0
5 Sa	04:03 AM / 10:01 AM / 04:22 PM / 10:27 PM	-0.3 / 2.7 / -0.3 / 2.8	20 Su	04:33 AM / 10:28 AM / 04:45 PM / 10:54 PM	-0.3 / 2.7 / -0.4 / 3.0
6 Su	04:49 AM / 10:42 AM / 05:01 PM / 11:10 PM	-0.2 / 2.5 / -0.2 / 2.7	21 M	05:20 AM / 11:11 AM / 05:27 PM / 11:41 PM	-0.3 / 2.6 / -0.4 / 3.0
7 M	05:35 AM / 11:24 AM / 05:41 PM / 11:55 PM	0.0 / 2.3 / -0.1 / 2.6	22 Tu	06:11 AM / 11:58 AM / 06:13 PM	-0.2 / 2.4 / -0.3
8 Tu	06:23 AM / 12:08 PM / 06:24 PM	0.2 / 2.0 / 0.1	23 W	12:33 AM / 07:06 AM / 12:51 PM / 07:06 PM	3.0 / 0.0 / 2.3 / -0.2
9 W	12:43 AM / 07:16 AM / 12:57 PM / 07:11 PM	2.4 / 0.4 / 1.9 / 0.2	24 Th	01:30 AM / 08:08 AM / 01:51 PM / 08:06 PM	2.9 / 0.1 / 2.1 / -0.1
10 Th ◐	01:37 AM / 08:14 AM / 01:52 PM / 08:05 PM	2.3 / 0.5 / 1.7 / 0.3	25 F ◑	02:35 AM / 09:16 AM / 03:00 PM / 09:14 PM	2.8 / 0.2 / 2.1 / 0.0
11 F	02:36 AM / 09:16 AM / 02:53 PM / 09:05 PM	2.3 / 0.6 / 1.7 / 0.4	26 Sa	03:44 AM / 10:26 AM / 04:13 PM / 10:27 PM	2.8 / 0.2 / 2.1 / 0.1
12 Sa	03:36 AM / 10:16 AM / 03:55 PM / 10:05 PM	2.3 / 0.5 / 1.8 / 0.3	27 Su	04:53 AM / 11:33 AM / 05:23 PM / 11:37 PM	2.8 / 0.1 / 2.2 / 0.0
13 Su	05:33 AM / 12:10 PM / 05:51 PM	2.4 / 0.4 / 1.9	28 M	05:57 AM / 12:31 PM / 06:25 PM	2.9 / 0.0 / 2.4
14 M	12:01 AM / 06:23 AM / 12:57 PM / 06:41 PM	0.3 / 2.5 / 0.3 / 2.1	29 Tu	12:40 AM / 06:53 AM / 01:23 PM / 07:19 PM	-0.1 / 2.9 / -0.2 / 2.6
15 Tu	12:51 AM / 07:08 AM / 01:38 PM / 07:26 PM	0.1 / 2.6 / 0.2 / 2.3	30 W	01:36 AM / 07:43 AM / 02:08 PM / 08:08 PM	-0.2 / 2.9 / -0.3 / 2.8
			31 Th	02:27 AM / 08:28 AM / 02:50 PM / 08:53 PM	-0.3 / 2.9 / -0.3 / 2.9

April

Day	Time	Ht (ft)	Day	Time	Ht (ft)
1 F	03:14 AM / 09:11 AM / 03:30 PM / 09:35 PM	-0.3 / 2.8 / -0.4 / 3.0	16 Sa ○	02:42 AM / 08:36 AM / 02:52 PM / 09:01 PM	-0.3 / 2.8 / -0.4 / 3.2
2 Sa	03:58 AM / 09:52 AM / 04:08 PM / 10:15 PM	-0.3 / 2.7 / -0.3 / 2.9	17 Su	03:29 AM / 09:20 AM / 03:34 PM / 09:46 PM	-0.4 / 2.7 / -0.5 / 3.3
3 Su	04:41 AM / 10:31 AM / 04:44 PM / 10:54 PM	-0.2 / 2.5 / -0.2 / 2.9	18 M	04:17 AM / 10:05 AM / 04:17 PM / 10:34 PM	-0.4 / 2.6 / -0.5 / 3.3
4 M	05:23 AM / 11:10 AM / 05:21 PM / 11:34 PM	-0.1 / 2.3 / -0.1 / 2.7	19 Tu	05:07 AM / 10:53 AM / 05:03 PM / 11:24 PM	-0.4 / 2.5 / -0.5 / 3.3
5 Tu	06:05 AM / 11:50 AM / 05:59 PM	0.1 / 2.1 / 0.0	20 W	05:59 AM / 11:44 AM / 05:56 PM	-0.3 / 2.4 / -0.4
6 W	12:16 AM / 06:50 AM / 12:32 PM / 06:40 PM	2.6 / 0.2 / 2.0 / 0.2	21 Th	12:18 AM / 06:57 AM / 12:42 PM / 06:53 PM	3.2 / -0.1 / 2.3 / -0.2
7 Th	01:01 AM / 07:38 AM / 01:19 PM / 07:27 PM	2.5 / 0.4 / 1.9 / 0.3	22 F	01:18 AM / 07:59 AM / 01:46 PM / 07:57 PM	3.0 / 0.0 / 2.2 / 0.0
8 F	01:52 AM / 08:32 AM / 02:13 PM / 08:20 PM	2.4 / 0.5 / 1.8 / 0.5	23 Sa ◑	02:23 AM / 09:05 AM / 02:56 PM / 09:08 PM	2.9 / 0.1 / 2.2 / 0.1
9 Sa	02:48 AM / 09:31 AM / 03:14 PM / 09:21 PM	2.4 / 0.6 / 1.8 / 0.5	24 Su	03:30 AM / 10:12 AM / 04:07 PM / 10:21 PM	2.8 / 0.1 / 2.3 / 0.2
10 Su	03:48 AM / 10:30 AM / 04:16 PM / 10:24 PM	2.3 / 0.6 / 1.9 / 0.5	25 M	04:36 AM / 11:13 AM / 05:13 PM / 11:29 PM	2.7 / 0.1 / 2.4 / 0.1
11 M	04:46 AM / 11:23 AM / 05:13 PM / 11:24 PM	2.4 / 0.5 / 2.0 / 0.4	26 Tu	05:37 AM / 12:08 PM / 06:11 PM	2.7 / 0.0 / 2.6
12 Tu	05:38 AM / 12:10 PM / 06:04 PM	2.5 / 0.3 / 2.2	27 W	12:30 AM / 06:31 AM / 12:56 PM / 07:02 PM	0.1 / 2.7 / -0.1 / 2.8
13 W	12:18 AM / 06:25 AM / 12:52 PM / 06:50 PM	0.2 / 2.6 / 0.1 / 2.5	28 Th	01:24 AM / 07:19 AM / 01:39 PM / 07:48 PM	0.0 / 2.6 / -0.2 / 2.9
14 Th	01:08 AM / 07:10 AM / 01:32 PM / 07:34 PM	0.1 / 2.7 / -0.1 / 2.7	29 F	02:12 AM / 08:03 AM / 02:19 PM / 08:29 PM	-0.1 / 2.6 / -0.2 / 3.0
15 F	01:55 AM / 07:53 AM / 02:12 PM / 08:18 PM	-0.1 / 2.7 / -0.3 / 3.0	30 Sa ●	02:56 AM / 08:44 AM / 02:57 PM / 09:09 PM	-0.1 / 2.5 / -0.2 / 3.0

Tide Table for December 2021 can be found on page 172

© Copyright White Sound Press, 2022
White Sound Press
379 Wild Orange Drive
New Smyrna Beach, FL 32168

Tide Tables - 2022
Sea of Abaco • Abaco • Bahamas
NOAA Tide Station at Pelican Harbour (Sandy Cay at Pelican Cays Land and Sea Park)

Times are given for the Sea of Abaco at Pelican Harbour, but tides throughout Abaco vary by only a few minutes. Heights are in reference to Mean Lower Low Water (MLLW). Times are in Eastern Standard Time (EST) and Eastern Daylight Time (EDT) when appropriate.

May				June				July				August			
Time	Ht	Time	Ht	Time	Ht	Time	Ht	Time	Ht	Time	Ht	Time	Ht	Time	Ht
1 Su 03:38 AM −0.1 09:24 AM 2.4 03:33 PM −0.2 09:47 PM 2.9		**16** M ○ 03:10 AM −0.4 08:55 AM 2.6 03:06 PM −0.6 09:25 PM 3.5		**1** W 04:36 AM 0.1 10:15 AM 2.1 04:18 PM 0.1 10:38 PM 2.8		**16** Th 04:39 AM −0.4 10:24 AM 2.6 04:34 PM −0.5 10:56 PM 3.5		**1** F 04:52 AM 0.3 10:32 AM 2.2 04:34 PM 0.3 10:53 PM 2.9		**16** Sa 05:13 AM −0.2 11:05 AM 2.9 05:18 PM −0.2 11:31 PM 3.5		**1** M 05:32 AM 0.4 11:25 AM 2.7 05:34 PM 0.5 11:39 PM 3.0		**16** Tu 06:19 AM 0.1 12:26 PM 3.2 06:48 PM 0.4	
2 M 04:18 AM −0.1 10:02 AM 2.3 04:09 PM −0.1 10:24 PM 2.9		**17** Tu 04:01 AM −0.5 09:45 AM 2.6 03:55 PM −0.6 10:16 PM 3.5		**2** Th 05:16 AM 0.2 10:55 AM 2.0 04:57 PM 0.2 11:17 PM 2.7		**17** F 05:34 AM −0.3 11:21 AM 2.6 05:31 PM −0.3 11:51 PM 3.4		**2** Sa 05:30 AM 0.3 11:12 AM 2.2 05:14 PM 0.3 11:31 PM 2.9		**17** Su 06:04 AM −0.2 12:01 PM 2.9 06:15 PM 0.0		**2** Tu 06:08 AM 0.4 12:07 PM 2.7 06:19 PM 0.6		**17** W 12:43 AM 3.0 07:06 AM 0.3 01:18 PM 3.1 07:43 PM 0.6	
3 Tu 04:58 AM 0.0 10:41 AM 2.2 04:46 PM 0.0 11:03 PM 2.8		**18** W 04:53 AM −0.4 10:37 AM 2.5 04:47 PM −0.5 11:10 PM 3.4		**3** F 05:56 AM 0.3 11:37 AM 2.0 05:37 PM 0.3 11:58 PM 2.7		**18** Sa 06:29 AM −0.2 12:21 PM 2.6 06:31 PM −0.1		**3** Su 06:07 AM 0.4 11:54 AM 2.3 05:57 PM 0.4		**18** M 12:23 AM 3.3 06:55 AM −0.1 12:58 PM 2.9 07:14 PM 0.2		**3** W 12:18 AM 2.9 06:46 AM 0.4 12:52 PM 2.8 07:09 PM 0.6		**18** Th 01:33 AM 2.7 07:54 AM 0.5 02:13 PM 3.0 08:42 PM 0.8	
4 W 05:39 AM 0.1 11:20 AM 2.0 05:24 PM 0.1 11:44 PM 2.7		**19** Th 05:48 AM −0.3 11:33 AM 2.4 05:43 PM −0.4		**4** Sa 06:38 AM 0.3 12:21 PM 2.0 06:21 PM 0.4		**19** Su 12:47 AM 3.2 07:25 AM −0.1 01:22 PM 2.6 07:34 PM 0.1		**4** M 12:09 AM 2.8 06:46 AM 0.4 12:38 PM 2.3 06:43 PM 0.5		**19** Tu 01:16 AM 3.0 07:46 AM 0.1 01:55 PM 2.9 08:14 PM 0.4		**4** Th 01:02 AM 2.7 07:28 AM 0.4 01:43 PM 2.9 08:05 PM 0.7		**19** F ◐ 02:26 AM 2.5 08:45 AM 0.6 03:09 PM 2.9 09:43 PM 0.9	
5 Th 06:21 AM 0.2 12:02 PM 1.9 06:05 PM 0.2		**20** F 12:06 AM 3.3 06:46 AM −0.2 12:33 PM 2.4 06:43 PM −0.2		**5** Su 12:41 AM 2.6 07:22 AM 0.4 01:09 PM 2.0 07:10 PM 0.5		**20** M 01:44 AM 3.0 08:21 AM −0.1 02:25 PM 2.6 08:40 PM 0.3		**5** Tu 12:50 AM 2.7 07:25 AM 0.4 01:25 PM 2.4 07:34 PM 0.6		**20** W ◐ 02:09 AM 2.7 08:37 AM 0.2 02:54 PM 2.8 09:17 PM 0.6		**5** F ◐ 01:53 AM 2.6 08:17 AM 0.4 02:39 PM 3.0 09:08 PM 0.7		**20** Sa 03:23 AM 2.3 09:39 AM 0.7 04:08 PM 2.8 10:45 PM 1.0	
6 F 12:27 AM 2.6 07:07 AM 0.4 12:48 PM 1.9 06:50 PM 0.4		**21** Sa 01:05 AM 3.1 07:46 AM −0.1 01:38 PM 2.4 07:48 PM 0.0		**6** M 01:26 AM 2.5 08:07 AM 0.4 02:00 PM 2.1 08:04 PM 0.6		**21** Tu ◐ 02:43 AM 2.7 09:16 AM 0.0 03:28 PM 2.6 09:46 PM 0.4		**6** W 01:35 AM 2.6 08:08 AM 0.3 02:16 PM 2.5 08:31 PM 0.6		**21** Th 03:05 AM 2.5 09:29 AM 0.3 03:51 PM 2.8 10:20 PM 0.7		**6** Sa 02:50 AM 2.5 09:12 AM 0.3 03:41 PM 3.1 10:15 PM 0.7		**21** Su 04:23 AM 2.2 10:35 AM 0.7 05:05 PM 2.8 11:43 PM 1.0	
7 Sa 01:14 AM 2.5 07:56 AM 0.5 01:39 PM 1.8 07:42 PM 0.5		**22** Su ◐ 02:07 AM 2.9 08:46 AM 0.0 02:46 PM 2.4 08:58 PM 0.2		**7** Tu ◐ 02:15 AM 2.5 08:53 AM 0.4 02:54 PM 2.2 09:04 PM 0.6		**22** W 03:41 AM 2.5 10:10 AM 0.1 04:27 PM 2.7 10:51 PM 0.4		**7** Th ◐ 02:25 AM 2.5 08:55 AM 0.3 03:11 PM 2.7 09:33 PM 0.6		**22** F 04:02 AM 2.3 10:21 AM 0.4 04:47 PM 2.8 11:21 PM 0.7		**7** Su 03:54 AM 2.5 10:13 AM 0.2 04:45 PM 3.2 11:22 PM 0.6		**22** M 05:20 AM 2.3 11:30 AM 0.7 05:58 PM 2.9	
8 Su 02:05 AM 2.4 08:49 AM 0.5 02:36 PM 1.9 08:40 PM 0.6		**23** M 03:10 AM 2.8 09:48 AM 0.0 03:53 PM 2.5 10:08 PM 0.2		**8** W 03:07 AM 2.4 09:40 AM 0.3 03:50 PM 2.4 10:06 PM 0.5		**23** Th 04:38 AM 2.4 11:01 AM 0.1 05:22 PM 2.7 11:50 PM 0.4		**8** F 03:20 AM 2.4 09:46 AM 0.1 04:09 PM 2.9 10:38 PM 0.5		**23** Sa 04:58 AM 2.2 11:13 AM 0.4 05:40 PM 2.8		**8** M 05:01 AM 2.5 11:17 AM 0.1 05:48 PM 3.4		**23** Tu 12:35 AM 0.9 06:13 AM 2.3 12:21 PM 0.7 06:45 PM 3.0	
9 M ◐ 03:00 AM 2.4 09:41 AM 0.5 03:35 PM 2.0 09:43 PM 0.5		**24** Tu 04:12 AM 2.6 10:45 AM 0.0 04:55 PM 2.6 11:14 PM 0.3		**9** Th 04:01 AM 2.4 10:29 AM 0.1 04:44 PM 2.6 11:07 PM 0.3		**24** F 05:32 AM 2.3 11:49 AM 0.1 06:12 PM 2.8		**9** Sa 04:20 AM 2.4 10:41 AM 0.0 05:08 PM 3.1 11:41 PM 0.3		**24** Su 12:16 AM 0.7 05:51 AM 2.2 12:02 PM 0.4 06:29 PM 2.9		**9** Tu 12:26 AM 0.4 06:06 AM 2.6 12:20 PM 0.0 06:48 PM 3.6		**24** W 01:20 AM 0.8 07:00 AM 2.5 01:08 PM 0.6 07:28 PM 3.1	
10 Tu 03:55 AM 2.4 10:31 AM 0.4 04:31 PM 2.2 10:44 PM 0.5		**25** W 05:10 AM 2.5 11:37 AM 0.0 05:50 PM 2.7		**10** F 04:56 AM 2.4 11:18 AM −0.1 05:38 PM 2.9		**25** Sa 12:44 AM 0.4 06:22 AM 2.2 12:34 PM 0.1 06:57 PM 2.8		**10** Su 05:20 AM 2.4 11:37 AM −0.1 06:06 PM 3.3		**25** M 01:05 AM 0.6 06:41 AM 2.2 12:48 PM 0.4 07:14 PM 2.9		**10** W 01:25 AM 0.3 07:07 AM 2.8 01:21 PM −0.1 07:45 PM 3.7		**25** Th 02:00 AM 0.7 07:43 AM 2.6 01:51 PM 0.5 08:08 PM 3.2	
11 W 04:48 AM 2.4 11:19 AM 0.2 05:24 PM 2.4 11:42 PM 0.3		**26** Th 12:13 AM 0.2 06:03 AM 2.4 12:24 PM −0.1 06:39 PM 2.8		**11** Sa 12:06 AM 0.2 05:51 AM 2.4 12:09 PM −0.2 06:30 PM 3.1		**26** Su 01:31 AM 0.3 07:08 AM 2.2 01:16 PM 0.1 07:39 PM 2.9		**11** M 12:42 AM 0.2 06:21 AM 2.5 12:35 PM −0.3 07:03 PM 3.5		**26** Tu 01:50 AM 0.6 07:26 AM 2.2 01:32 PM 0.4 07:56 PM 3.0		**11** Th 02:19 AM 0.1 08:05 AM 3.0 02:19 PM −0.2 08:38 PM 3.8		**26** F 02:38 AM 0.6 08:23 AM 2.7 02:32 PM 0.5 08:45 PM 3.3	
12 Th 05:39 AM 2.5 12:04 PM 0.0 06:13 PM 2.7		**27** F 01:06 AM 0.1 06:51 AM 2.4 01:07 PM −0.1 07:24 PM 2.9		**12** Su 01:03 AM 0.0 06:45 AM 2.5 01:00 PM −0.4 07:23 PM 3.3		**27** M 02:15 AM 0.3 07:51 AM 2.1 01:57 PM 0.1 08:20 PM 2.9		**12** Tu 01:40 AM 0.0 07:20 AM 2.6 01:33 PM −0.4 07:59 PM 3.6		**27** W 02:31 AM 0.5 08:09 AM 2.3 02:14 PM 0.3 08:36 PM 3.1		**12** F 03:11 AM 0.0 09:00 AM 3.1 03:14 PM −0.2 09:29 PM 3.8		**27** Sa ● 03:13 AM 0.5 09:01 AM 2.9 03:12 PM 0.5 09:21 PM 3.3	
13 F 12:36 AM 0.1 06:29 AM 2.5 12:48 PM −0.2 07:01 PM 3.0		**28** Sa 01:53 AM 0.1 07:36 AM 2.3 01:47 PM −0.1 08:04 PM 2.9		**13** M 01:58 AM −0.2 07:39 AM 2.5 01:52 PM −0.5 08:15 PM 3.5		**28** Tu 02:56 AM 0.2 08:32 AM 2.2 02:37 PM 0.1 08:59 PM 2.9		**13** W 02:36 AM −0.1 08:17 AM 2.7 02:29 PM −0.5 08:53 PM 3.7		**28** Th 03:10 AM 0.5 08:49 AM 2.4 02:55 PM 0.3 09:14 PM 3.1		**13** Sa 04:00 AM −0.1 09:53 AM 3.2 04:08 PM −0.1 10:18 PM 3.7		**28** Su 03:47 AM 0.5 09:39 AM 3.0 03:52 PM 0.4 09:57 PM 3.3	
14 Sa 01:28 AM −0.1 07:17 AM 2.6 01:33 PM −0.4 07:48 PM 3.2		**29** Su 02:36 AM 0.0 08:17 AM 2.2 02:25 PM 0.0 08:43 PM 2.9		**14** Tu ○ 02:52 AM −0.3 08:34 AM 2.6 02:44 PM −0.6 09:08 PM 3.6		**29** W ● 03:35 AM 0.2 09:13 AM 2.2 03:16 PM 0.1 09:37 PM 3.0		**14** Th 03:29 AM −0.2 09:14 AM 2.8 03:26 PM −0.4 09:47 PM 3.7		**29** F 03:47 AM 0.4 09:29 AM 2.5 03:34 PM 0.3 09:50 PM 3.1		**14** Su 04:47 AM −0.1 10:44 AM 3.3 05:01 PM 0.0 11:07 PM 3.5		**29** M 04:21 AM 0.4 10:17 AM 3.1 04:32 PM 0.5 10:33 PM 3.2	
15 Su 02:19 AM −0.3 08:06 AM 2.6 02:19 PM −0.5 08:36 PM 3.4		**30** M ● 03:17 AM 0.0 08:57 AM 2.2 03:03 PM −0.1 09:21 PM 2.9		**15** W 03:46 AM −0.4 09:28 AM 2.6 03:38 PM −0.6 10:02 PM 3.6		**30** Th 04:14 AM 0.2 09:52 AM 2.2 03:55 PM 0.2 10:15 PM 2.9		**15** F 04:22 AM −0.2 10:09 AM 2.9 04:22 PM −0.4 10:39 PM 3.6		**30** Sa 04:23 AM 0.4 10:07 AM 2.6 04:13 PM 0.4 10:26 PM 3.1		**15** M 05:33 AM 0.0 11:35 AM 3.3 05:54 PM 0.2 11:54 PM 3.2		**30** Tu 04:55 AM 0.4 10:56 AM 3.1 05:14 PM 0.5 11:10 PM 3.1	
		31 Tu 03:57 AM 0.0 09:36 AM 2.1 03:40 PM 0.0 09:59 PM 2.9						**31** Su 04:58 AM 0.4 10:46 AM 2.6 04:53 PM 0.4 11:02 PM 3.1						**31** W 05:31 AM 0.4 11:38 AM 3.2 06:00 PM 0.6 11:51 PM 2.9	

Tide Table for December 2021 can be found on page 172

© Copyright White Sound Press, 2022
White Sound Press
379 Wild Orange Drive
New Smyrna Beach, FL 32168

Tide Tables - 2022
Sea of Abaco • Abaco • Bahamas
NOAA Tide Station at Pelican Harbour (Sandy Cay at Pelican Cays Land and Sea Park)

Times are given for the Sea of Abaco at Pelican Harbour, but tides throughout Abaco vary by only a few minutes. Heights are in reference to Mean Lower Low Water (MLLW). Times are in Eastern Standard Time (EST) and Eastern Daylight Time (EDT) when appropriate.

September

Day	Time	Ht (ft)	Day	Time	Ht (ft)
1 Th	06:11 AM / 12:24 PM / 06:50 PM	0.4 / 3.2 / 0.7	16 F	12:55 AM / 07:09 AM / 01:29 PM / 08:04 PM	2.6 / 0.7 / 3.0 / 0.9
2 F	12:37 AM / 06:56 AM / 01:16 PM / 07:47 PM	2.8 / 0.4 / 3.2 / 0.8	17 Sa ◐	01:47 AM / 07:59 AM / 02:24 PM / 09:03 PM	2.4 / 0.8 / 2.9 / 1.0
3 Sa ◑	01:30 AM / 07:48 AM / 02:15 PM / 08:51 PM	2.7 / 0.5 / 3.2 / 0.8	18 Su	02:44 AM / 08:55 AM / 03:24 PM / 10:05 PM	2.3 / 0.9 / 2.8 / 1.1
4 Su	02:32 AM / 08:49 AM / 03:21 PM / 10:00 PM	2.6 / 0.5 / 3.2 / 0.8	19 M	03:46 AM / 09:56 AM / 04:24 PM / 11:05 PM	2.3 / 1.0 / 2.8 / 1.1
5 M	03:41 AM / 09:57 AM / 04:29 PM / 11:09 PM	2.5 / 0.5 / 3.3 / 0.7	20 Tu	04:47 AM / 10:56 AM / 05:20 PM / 11:57 PM	2.3 / 1.0 / 2.9 / 1.0
6 Tu	04:51 AM / 11:07 AM / 05:35 PM	2.6 / 0.4 / 3.4	21 W	05:41 AM / 11:51 AM / 06:09 PM	2.4 / 0.9 / 3.0
7 W	12:13 AM / 05:58 AM / 12:13 PM / 06:35 PM	0.6 / 2.8 / 0.3 / 3.6	22 Th	12:42 AM / 06:29 AM / 12:40 PM / 06:53 PM	0.9 / 2.6 / 0.8 / 3.1
8 Th	01:09 AM / 06:58 AM / 01:14 PM / 07:30 PM	0.4 / 3.0 / 0.2 / 3.7	23 F	01:22 AM / 07:12 AM / 01:25 PM / 07:33 PM	0.8 / 2.8 / 0.6 / 3.2
9 F	02:00 AM / 07:53 AM / 02:10 PM / 08:21 PM	0.3 / 3.2 / 0.1 / 3.7	24 Sa	01:59 AM / 07:52 AM / 02:07 PM / 08:11 PM	0.6 / 3.0 / 0.5 / 3.2
10 Sa ○	02:48 AM / 08:44 AM / 03:02 PM / 09:08 PM	0.1 / 3.4 / 0.0 / 3.7	25 Su ●	02:34 AM / 08:31 AM / 02:48 PM / 08:48 PM	0.5 / 3.2 / 0.4 / 3.3
11 Su	03:33 AM / 09:33 AM / 03:53 PM / 09:54 PM	0.1 / 3.5 / 0.1 / 3.5	26 M	03:08 AM / 09:09 AM / 03:30 PM / 09:26 PM	0.4 / 3.3 / 0.4 / 3.2
12 M	04:16 AM / 10:19 AM / 04:42 PM / 10:39 PM	0.1 / 3.5 / 0.2 / 3.3	27 Tu	03:43 AM / 09:48 AM / 04:12 PM / 10:04 PM	0.3 / 3.4 / 0.3 / 3.1
13 Tu	04:59 AM / 11:05 AM / 05:30 PM / 11:23 PM	0.2 / 3.5 / 0.3 / 3.1	28 W	04:20 AM / 10:29 AM / 04:56 PM / 10:45 PM	0.3 / 3.5 / 0.4 / 3.0
14 W	05:41 AM / 11:51 AM / 06:19 PM	0.3 / 3.3 / 0.5	29 Th	04:59 AM / 11:13 AM / 05:43 PM / 11:30 PM	0.3 / 3.5 / 0.4 / 2.9
15 Th	12:08 AM / 06:24 AM / 12:39 PM / 07:10 PM	2.8 / 0.5 / 3.2 / 0.7	30 F	05:43 AM / 12:02 PM / 06:36 PM	0.3 / 3.4 / 0.6

October

Day	Time	Ht (ft)	Day	Time	Ht (ft)
1 Sa	12:20 AM / 06:33 AM / 12:57 PM / 07:35 PM	2.7 / 0.4 / 3.4 / 0.7	16 Su	01:10 AM / 07:15 AM / 01:40 PM / 08:23 PM	2.3 / 0.8 / 2.8 / 1.0
2 Su	01:17 AM / 07:31 AM / 01:59 PM / 08:40 PM	2.6 / 0.5 / 3.3 / 0.8	17 M ◐	02:06 AM / 08:11 AM / 02:37 PM / 09:22 PM	2.2 / 0.9 / 2.7 / 1.0
3 M	02:24 AM / 08:37 AM / 03:07 PM / 09:50 PM	2.5 / 0.6 / 3.3 / 0.8	18 Tu	03:07 AM / 09:13 AM / 03:37 PM / 10:19 PM	2.2 / 1.0 / 2.7 / 1.0
4 Tu	03:36 AM / 09:50 AM / 04:17 PM / 10:57 PM	2.6 / 0.6 / 3.3 / 0.7	19 W	04:09 AM / 10:16 AM / 04:33 PM / 11:11 PM	2.3 / 1.0 / 2.7 / 0.9
5 W	04:47 AM / 11:02 AM / 05:21 PM / 11:57 PM	2.7 / 0.5 / 3.3 / 0.5	20 Th	05:04 AM / 11:14 AM / 05:24 PM / 11:56 PM	2.4 / 0.9 / 2.8 / 0.8
6 Th	05:51 AM / 12:08 PM / 06:20 PM	2.9 / 0.4 / 3.4	21 F	05:53 AM / 12:06 PM / 06:10 PM	2.6 / 0.8 / 2.9
7 F	12:50 AM / 06:48 AM / 01:06 PM / 07:12 PM	0.4 / 3.2 / 0.3 / 3.4	22 Sa	12:36 AM / 06:36 AM / 12:54 PM / 06:52 PM	0.6 / 2.9 / 0.6 / 3.0
8 Sa	01:38 AM / 07:39 AM / 02:00 PM / 08:00 PM	0.2 / 3.4 / 0.2 / 3.4	23 Su	01:14 AM / 07:18 AM / 01:39 PM / 07:33 PM	0.4 / 3.1 / 0.4 / 3.0
9 Su	02:22 AM / 08:26 AM / 02:49 PM / 08:45 PM	0.1 / 3.5 / 0.1 / 3.3	24 M	01:51 AM / 07:58 AM / 02:23 PM / 08:14 PM	0.2 / 3.3 / 0.3 / 3.0
10 M	03:04 AM / 09:10 AM / 03:36 PM / 09:29 PM	0.1 / 3.5 / 0.2 / 3.2	25 Tu ●	02:29 AM / 08:39 AM / 03:07 PM / 08:56 PM	0.1 / 3.4 / 0.1 / 3.0
11 Tu	03:44 AM / 09:53 AM / 04:21 PM / 10:11 PM	0.1 / 3.5 / 0.2 / 3.0	26 W	03:09 AM / 09:22 AM / 03:53 PM / 09:39 PM	0.0 / 3.6 / 0.1 / 2.9
12 W	04:23 AM / 10:35 AM / 05:06 PM / 10:53 PM	0.2 / 3.4 / 0.3 / 2.8	27 Th	03:50 AM / 10:07 AM / 04:40 PM / 10:24 PM	-0.1 / 3.6 / 0.1 / 2.8
13 Th	05:03 AM / 11:17 AM / 05:50 PM / 11:35 PM	0.3 / 3.3 / 0.5 / 2.6	28 F	04:35 AM / 10:55 AM / 05:30 PM / 11:14 PM	0.0 / 3.6 / 0.2 / 2.7
14 F	05:43 AM / 12:01 PM / 06:37 PM	0.5 / 3.1 / 0.7	29 Sa	05:24 AM / 11:47 AM / 06:25 PM	0.1 / 3.5 / 0.3
15 Sa	12:20 AM / 06:27 AM / 12:48 PM / 07:28 PM	2.4 / 0.7 / 2.9 / 0.8	30 Su	12:08 AM / 06:19 AM / 12:44 PM / 07:25 PM	2.6 / 0.2 / 3.4 / 0.4
			31 M	01:10 AM / 07:21 AM / 01:47 PM / 08:30 PM	2.5 / 0.3 / 3.2 / 0.5

November

Day	Time	Ht (ft)	Day	Time	Ht (ft)
1 Tu ◐	02:19 AM / 08:31 AM / 02:53 PM / 09:36 PM	2.5 / 0.5 / 3.1 / 0.5	16 W ◐	01:26 AM / 07:29 AM / 01:45 PM / 08:28 PM	2.1 / 0.8 / 2.5 / 0.7
2 W	03:31 AM / 09:44 AM / 04:00 PM / 10:38 PM	2.6 / 0.5 / 3.1 / 0.4	17 Th	02:24 AM / 08:30 AM / 02:39 PM / 09:17 PM	2.2 / 0.8 / 2.5 / 0.6
3 Th	04:39 AM / 10:55 AM / 05:03 PM / 11:35 PM	2.7 / 0.5 / 3.0 / 0.3	18 F	03:19 AM / 09:31 AM / 03:32 PM / 10:02 PM	2.3 / 0.7 / 2.5 / 0.5
4 F	05:40 AM / 11:59 AM / 06:00 PM	2.9 / 0.4 / 3.0	19 Sa	04:10 AM / 10:27 AM / 04:21 PM / 10:46 PM	2.5 / 0.6 / 2.5 / 0.3
5 Sa	12:26 AM / 06:34 AM / 12:56 PM / 06:51 PM	0.1 / 3.1 / 0.3 / 3.0	20 Su	04:57 AM / 11:20 AM / 05:09 PM / 11:28 PM	2.8 / 0.4 / 2.6 / 0.1
6 Su	01:11 AM / 06:34 AM / 12:48 PM / 06:38 PM	0.0 / 3.3 / 0.2 / 2.9	21 M	05:42 AM / 12:09 PM / 05:56 PM	3.0 / 0.2 / 2.6
7 M	12:54 AM / 07:06 AM / 01:35 PM / 07:22 PM	0.0 / 3.3 / 0.1 / 2.8	22 Tu	12:11 AM / 06:27 AM / 12:58 PM / 06:42 PM	-0.1 / 3.2 / 0.0 / 2.6
8 Tu ○	01:34 AM / 07:48 AM / 02:19 PM / 08:04 PM	0.1 / 3.3 / 0.1 / 2.7	23 W ●	12:54 AM / 07:13 AM / 01:46 PM / 07:29 PM	-0.3 / 3.4 / -0.1 / 2.6
9 W	02:13 AM / 08:28 AM / 03:01 PM / 08:44 PM	0.0 / 3.3 / 0.1 / 2.6	24 Th	01:40 AM / 08:00 AM / 02:35 PM / 08:17 PM	-0.4 / 3.5 / -0.2 / 2.6
10 Th	02:52 AM / 09:08 AM / 03:43 PM / 09:25 PM	0.1 / 3.2 / 0.2 / 2.4	25 F	02:27 AM / 08:49 AM / 03:26 PM / 09:08 PM	-0.4 / 3.6 / -0.2 / 2.6
11 F	03:30 AM / 09:48 AM / 04:25 PM / 10:06 PM	0.2 / 3.1 / 0.3 / 2.3	26 Sa	03:17 AM / 09:40 AM / 04:18 PM / 10:02 PM	-0.4 / 3.5 / -0.2 / 2.6
12 Sa	04:10 AM / 10:30 AM / 05:08 PM / 10:49 PM	0.3 / 2.9 / 0.5 / 2.2	27 Su	04:11 AM / 10:34 AM / 05:14 PM / 11:00 PM	-0.3 / 3.4 / -0.1 / 2.5
13 Su	04:52 AM / 11:15 AM / 05:55 PM / 11:36 PM	0.5 / 2.8 / 0.6 / 2.1	28 M	05:09 AM / 11:31 AM / 06:12 PM	-0.1 / 3.3 / 0.0
14 M	05:38 AM / 12:01 PM / 06:44 PM	0.6 / 2.7 / 0.7	29 Tu	12:02 AM / 06:13 AM / 12:32 PM / 07:12 PM	2.5 / 0.1 / 3.1 / 0.1
15 Tu	12:29 AM / 06:30 AM / 12:52 PM / 07:36 PM	2.1 / 0.8 / 2.6 / 0.7	30 W ◐	01:09 AM / 07:21 AM / 01:34 PM / 08:13 PM	2.5 / 0.2 / 2.9 / 0.1

December

Day	Time	Ht (ft)	Day	Time	Ht (ft)
1 Th	02:17 AM / 08:33 AM / 02:37 PM / 09:12 PM	2.6 / 0.3 / 2.8 / 0.0	16 F ◐	01:36 AM / 07:45 AM / 01:46 PM / 08:20 PM	2.1 / 0.6 / 2.3 / 0.3
2 F	03:22 AM / 09:42 AM / 03:38 PM / 10:07 PM	2.7 / 0.3 / 2.6 / 0.0	17 Sa	02:30 AM / 08:46 AM / 02:38 PM / 09:07 PM	2.3 / 0.5 / 2.2 / 0.2
3 Sa	04:22 AM / 10:46 AM / 04:35 PM / 10:57 PM	2.8 / 0.3 / 2.5 / -0.1	18 Su	03:24 AM / 09:46 AM / 03:32 PM / 09:56 PM	2.4 / 0.4 / 2.2 / 0.0
4 Su	05:14 AM / 11:43 AM / 05:27 PM / 11:43 PM	2.9 / 0.2 / 2.4 / -0.1	19 M	04:16 AM / 10:45 AM / 04:27 PM / 10:45 PM	2.7 / 0.2 / 2.2 / -0.2
5 M	06:02 AM / 12:33 PM / 06:15 PM	3.0 / 0.1 / 2.4	20 Tu	05:08 AM / 11:41 AM / 05:21 PM / 11:35 PM	2.9 / 0.0 / 2.3 / -0.4
6 Tu	12:27 AM / 06:46 AM / 01:19 PM / 06:59 PM	-0.1 / 3.0 / 0.0 / 2.3	21 W	06:00 AM / 12:34 PM / 06:14 PM	3.1 / -0.2 / 2.3
7 W	01:08 AM / 07:27 AM / 02:02 PM / 07:41 PM	-0.1 / 3.0 / 0.0 / 2.2	22 Th	12:26 AM / 06:51 AM / 01:27 PM / 07:07 PM	-0.5 / 3.3 / -0.3 / 2.4
8 Th ○	01:47 AM / 08:06 AM / 02:42 PM / 08:22 PM	-0.1 / 3.0 / 0.0 / 2.2	23 F ●	01:18 AM / 07:42 AM / 02:19 PM / 08:00 PM	-0.7 / 3.4 / -0.4 / 2.5
9 F	02:26 AM / 08:45 AM / 03:22 PM / 09:01 PM	-0.1 / 2.9 / 0.1 / 2.1	24 Sa	02:11 AM / 08:34 AM / 03:11 PM / 08:54 PM	-0.7 / 3.5 / -0.5 / 2.5
10 Sa	03:04 AM / 09:24 AM / 04:02 PM / 09:42 PM	0.0 / 2.9 / 0.1 / 2.1	25 Su	03:05 AM / 09:27 AM / 04:04 PM / 09:50 PM	-0.7 / 3.5 / -0.5 / 2.6
11 Su	03:44 AM / 10:04 AM / 04:42 PM / 10:23 PM	0.1 / 2.8 / 0.2 / 2.0	26 M	04:01 AM / 10:20 AM / 04:57 PM / 10:48 PM	-0.6 / 3.3 / -0.4 / 2.6
12 M	04:24 AM / 10:44 AM / 05:24 PM / 11:07 PM	0.2 / 2.7 / 0.3 / 2.0	27 Tu	04:59 AM / 11:15 AM / 05:51 PM / 11:48 PM	-0.4 / 3.2 / -0.4 / 2.6
13 Tu	05:08 AM / 11:26 AM / 06:06 PM / 11:54 PM	0.4 / 2.6 / 0.3 / 2.0	28 W	06:01 AM / 12:11 PM / 06:47 PM	-0.2 / 2.9 / -0.3
14 W	05:55 AM / 12:09 PM / 06:50 PM	0.5 / 2.5 / 0.4	29 Th	12:50 AM / 07:06 AM / 01:09 PM / 07:42 PM	2.6 / 0.0 / 2.7 / -0.2
15 Th	12:44 AM / 06:48 AM / 12:56 PM / 07:34 PM	2.0 / 0.6 / 2.4 / 0.3	30 F	01:54 AM / 08:13 AM / 02:08 PM / 08:38 PM	2.6 / 0.1 / 2.4 / -0.2
			31 Sa	02:56 AM / 09:21 AM / 03:08 PM / 09:29 PM	2.6 / 0.2 / 2.2 / -0.2

Tide Table for December 2021 can be found on page 172

© Copyright White Sound Press, 2022
White Sound Press
379 Wild Orange Drive
New Smyrna Beach, FL 32168

Tides: Highs, Lows, Neaps, Springs, Etc.

Tides are caused by the gravitational pull of the sun and the moon on the earth's oceans, and also the centrifugal force which results from the earth's annual circular trek around the sun.

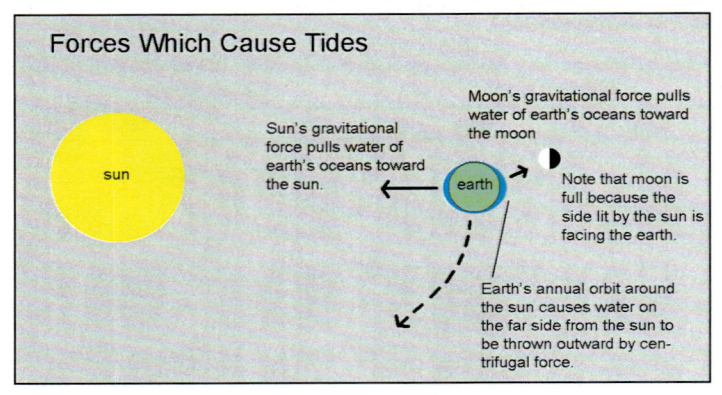

Forces Which Cause Tides

Sun's gravitational force pulls water of earth's oceans toward the sun.

Moon's gravitational force pulls water of earth's oceans toward the moon

Note that moon is full because the side lit by the sun is facing the earth.

Earth's annual orbit around the sun causes water on the far side from the sun to be thrown outward by centrifugal force.

Although the moon is much smaller than the sun, it is much closer to the earth, and its effect on tides is about twice as great as that of the sun.

In Abaco there are generally two high tides and two low tides each day. The difference between them generally varies from about 2.5' to 3.5' (vertically).

This variation is the result of the differing alignment of the sun, the moon, and the earth. When the moon is new (no visible moon) the bodies are lined up and the gravitational force of the sun and moon pull together in a line. Therefore the high tides are higher and the low tides are lower.

New Moon

When the moon is half, the gravitational forces are at right angles and tend to cancel each other, and tidal fluctuation is not as great. These tides are called **neap tides**.

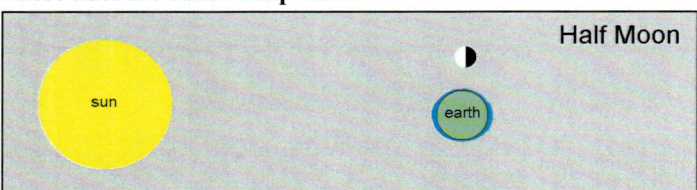

Half Moon

When the moon is full the moon's gravitation pull supplements the centrifugal force (result of the earth's annual orbit around the sun) and high tides are again higher and low tides are lower than during neap tides.

Full Moon

When the moon is new or full the tides are described as **spring tides**. Note that this has nothing to do with the season of the year, even though the term is the same. Some persons call these tides moon tides. This is an incorrect and rather confusing way to refer to them because all tides—neaps as well as springs—are caused, in great part, by the moon.

Tide Table - December 2021

Times given are for the Sea of Abaco at Pelican Harbour, but tides throughout Abaco vary by only a few minutes. Heights are in reference to Mean Lower Low Water (MLLW). Times are in Eastern Standard Time for December 2021.

Day	Time	Ht	Day	Time	Ht	Day	Time	Ht	Day	Time	Ht
1 W	05:07 AM / 11:35 AM / 05:22 PM / 11:40 PM	3.1 / 0.0 / 2.7 / -0.4	9 Th	05:59 AM / 12:16 PM / 06:55 PM	-0.1 / 3.0 / -0.1	17 F	12:35 AM / 06:55 AM / 01:29 PM / 07:07 PM	0.0 / 2.8 / 0.1 / 2.1	25 Sa	06:01 AM / 12:11 PM / 06:48 PM	0.? / 2.? / 0.?
2 Th	05:59 AM / 12:30 PM / 06:16 PM	3.3 / -0.2 / 2.7	10 F	12:53 AM / 07:04 AM / 01:15 PM / 07:53 PM	2.4 / 0.2 / 2.8 / 0.0	18 Sa	01:14 AM / 07:33 AM / 02:08 PM / 07:47 PM	-0.1 / 2.8 / 0.1 / 2.1	26 Su	12:48 AM / 06:58 AM / 01:01 PM / 07:36 PM	2.? / 0.? / 2.? / 0.?
3 F	12:30 AM / 06:51 AM / 01:24 PM / 07:08 PM	-0.6 / 3.5 / -0.4 / 2.7	11 Sa	01:57 AM / 08:11 AM / 02:15 PM / 08:49 PM	2.4 / 0.3 / 2.6 / 0.1	19 Su	01:51 AM / 08:11 AM / 02:47 PM / 08:26 PM	-0.1 / 2.8 / 0.0 / 2.1	27 M	01:44 AM / 08:00 AM / 01:56 PM / 08:27 PM	2.? / 0.? / 2.? / -0.?
4 Sa	01:21 AM / 07:42 AM / 02:18 PM / 08:01 PM	-0.7 / 3.7 / -0.5 / 2.7	12 Su	03:00 AM / 09:18 AM / 03:13 PM / 09:42 PM	2.5 / 0.4 / 2.4 / 0.1	20 M	02:29 AM / 08:49 AM / 03:25 PM / 09:04 PM	-0.1 / 2.8 / 0.0 / 2.1	28 Tu	02:43 AM / 09:06 AM / 02:55 PM / 09:21 PM	2.? / 0.? / 2.? / -0.?
5 Su	02:13 AM / 08:35 AM / 03:11 PM / 08:55 PM	-0.7 / 3.7 / -0.5 / 2.7	13 M	03:57 AM / 10:20 AM / 04:08 PM / 10:31 PM	2.5 / 0.4 / 2.3 / 0.1	21 Tu	03:07 AM / 09:26 AM / 04:04 PM / 09:44 PM	0.0 / 2.8 / 0.1 / 2.0	29 W	03:43 AM / 10:11 AM / 03:55 PM / 10:16 PM	2.? / 0.? / 2.? / -0.?
6 M	03:06 AM / 09:28 AM / 04:05 PM / 09:51 PM	-0.6 / 3.6 / -0.4 / 2.6	14 Tu	04:48 AM / 11:15 AM / 04:58 PM / 11:15 PM	2.6 / 0.3 / 2.2 / 0.0	22 W	03:46 AM / 10:05 AM / 04:43 PM / 10:25 PM	0.1 / 2.8 / 0.1 / 2.0	30 Th	04:41 AM / 11:14 AM / 04:56 PM / 11:12 PM	3.? / -0.? / 2.? / -0.?
7 Tu	04:01 AM / 10:22 AM / 05:00 PM / 10:48 PM	-0.5 / 3.5 / -0.3 / 2.5	15 W	05:34 AM / 12:04 PM / 05:44 PM / 11:56 PM	2.7 / 0.3 / 2.1 / 0.0	23 Th	04:27 AM / 10:44 AM / 05:22 PM / 11:08 PM	0.2 / 2.7 / 0.2 / 2.1	31 F	05:38 AM / 12:13 PM / 05:54 PM	3.? / -0.? / 2.?
8 W	04:58 AM / 11:18 AM / 05:57 PM / 11:49 PM	-0.3 / 3.2 / -0.2 / 2.5	16 Th	06:16 AM / 12:48 PM / 06:27 PM	2.7 / 0.2 / 2.1	24 F	05:11 AM / 11:26 AM / 06:04 PM / 11:56 PM	0.2 / 2.6 / 0.2 / 2.1			

Determining water depth at times between low and high tides

It should be clear that at half way between low and high tides the water level will be half way between its low and high levels. At other times, if some degree of precision is sought, it is not desirable to use a simple linear progression because water movement is not uniform. Instead, water levels tend to hover at both low tide and high tide, and change in level occurs most rapidly at half tide. The following rule of twelfths can be used to determine water levels fairly accurately.

Time	To Determine Depth	Example*
low tide	from tide table	4'
1 hr. after low	add 1/12 ** (+3")	4' 3"
2 hrs. after low	add 3/12 (+9")	4' 9"
3 hrs. after low	add 6/12 (+18")	5' 6"
4 hrs. after low	add 9/12 (+27")	6' 3"
5 hrs. after low	add 11/12 (+33")	6' 9"
6 hrs. after low	add 12/12 (+36")	7'

* Example assumes 4' depth at MLW with low water at datum and high water at 3' above datum. Difference in levels is therefore 3' (or 36").

** Add 1/12 of the difference between low tide and high tide (compute this from the tide table).